Christian Perspectives on Politics

Christian Perspectives on Politics

Revised and Expanded

J. Philip Wogaman

Westminster John Knox Press
Louisville, Kentucky

Book design by Sharon Adams
Cover design by Night & Day Design

First published in 1988 by
FORTRESS PRESS

This edition published by
WESTMINSTER JOHN KNOX PRESS
Louisville, Kentucky

This book is printed on acid-free paper that meets the American National Standards Institute Z39.48 standard. ∞

PRINTED IN THE UNITED STATES OF AMERICA

00 01 02 03 04 05 06 07 08 09 — 10 9 8 7 6 5 4 3 2 1

Library of Congress Cataloging-in-Publication Data is on file at the Library of Congress, Washington, D.C.

ISBN 0-664-22201-3

To
Thomas D. Wogaman

CONTENTS

PREFACE

I welcomed the publisher's invitation to present a revised edition of this book for two reasons. In the first place, my own interest in politics as a subject for Christian reflection continues unabated. People are incurably religious; they are also unavoidably political. The intersection between the religious and the political is endlessly fascinating. It is also indescribably important. The one reflects the deepest meanings of our existence. The other is the arena in which our life is played out in human history. Life is more than political, but politics permeates and affects virtually everything. In the dozen years since the first edition appeared, I have become even more convinced of that.

The other reason for issuing a new edition is that there have been so many important changes in the political landscape these past twelve years. By far the most important has been the collapse of the Soviet Union and the virtual ending of the Cold War. No longer is the world bipolar, with two great superpowers confronting each other, threatening mutual destruction with thermonuclear war. Nuclear arsenals remain, but they are smaller and not so pointedly aimed. The nations of the world are less required to choose up sides as client states and more challenged to forge together a new global order. Economic changes of similar import have taken wing, some prompted by the changed political situation, and others a natural consequence of technological changes. As Thomas Friedman has lately remarked, the world has gone from the haves and have nots to the swift and the slow. The "slow" are also the "have nots," of course. But the economic interdependency of the world is now inescapable, and the opportunities to draw the less prosperous regions of the world into the benefits of a new economic order beckon in fresh ways—and with new urgency.

The cultural situation is also changing. Most obvious is the fact that Marxism, a vigorous system of belief and practice for most of the twentieth century, is now in total disarray. I think it likely that aspects of Marxist thought will continue to challenge and enlighten us. But taken as a whole, this secular religion appears to have had its day. Given the immensity of its power and influence a few short years ago, this transition is quite astonishing. As a religious system, Marxism has failed to answer the deeper questions and profound longing of the human spirit. Its analysis of human nature has proved superficial. Its politics and economics have not delivered on the big promises its thinkers have offered. Insofar as Marxism has exerted an influence on Christian political thinking—either positively or negatively—there have been substantial changes. That is particularly evident in some of the theologies of liberation and in some versions of Christian neoconservatism.

Meanwhile, within the United States, these past dozen years have seen the continued rise of right-wing Christianity as a political force. Paralleling to some extent the political power of fundamentalism in a number of other countries and in other religions, this has challenged both the self-consciousness of more moderate religious groups and the practical instincts of political leaders. Such forces are extremely volatile. They defy enduring definition or classification. But any summary of Christian political thought at this point in history must surely take them into account.

Quite apart from these political, economic, and cultural factors, life changes have affected my own perspectives on politics. The first edition of this book was published while I was still immersed in academic life as a full-time professor of Christian social ethics. The book flowed easily out of life-long scholarly interests. Since 1992, however, I have served as pastor to a Washington, D. C. congregation that has been about as close to the heart of American public life as a church could be. The congregation includes persons of both political parties—including, for a time at least, the top leadership of both parties. Major issues, including the impeachment crisis of 1998–99, were inescapable here. I have been challenged to think ever more seriously about the actual problems of public life in light of the faith. And the routines of preaching and pastoral ministry have greatly enriched my thinking about the meaning of the faith itself.

Notwithstanding such personal and public changes, the essential features of the first edition remain in place. The book was not offered then as the last word, nor is it now. Every author should have constantly before him or her the words of the apostle Paul, "now we see in a mirror dimly . . . "! Nevertheless, such books will continue to be needed so long as humanity remains political and so long as we are driven to think of politics from the heart of our faith. And I am excited that its appearance coincides with the beginning of a whole new millennium of world and Christian history.

The new edition has profited from the comments and reviews evoked by its predecessor. I am especially grateful for the encouraging and critical comments of Charles E. Curran, Max Stackhouse, Franklin Gamwell, Roger L. Shinn, the late John C. Bennett, and my Westminster John Knox editor, Stephanie Egnotovich. My wife, Carolyn, remains my most dependable source of encouragement and helpful criticism.

PART 1

Thinking about Politics

Introduction

How shall we think about politics? The premise of this volume is that it is possible for Christians to think, as Christians, about politics and that when they do so they make a contribution to the civil society of which they are a part. I would even go further to say that when Christians seek to exclude politics from their thinking they are bound to distort their theologies—for politics is an inescapable aspect of human existence, with direct relevance to the divine/human encounter.

Christians may have very important contributions to make to contemporary political debate. I believe they do. But Christians did not invent politics, nor can they do their thinking about it in isolation from others. In the first two chapters, before taking up the Christian interpretation of politics, we must consider, in more general terms, what politics means and why it is so important to the life of human community. Chapter 3, new to this edition, will then briefly summarize high points in the long history of Christian political thought. Whatever the differences among Christians and at different points in history, it is clear that there has scarcely ever been a time when politics was not an important item on the Christian agenda.

1

The Perennial
Novelty of Politics

> The search to reveal the political world goes on and will
> never be finished, just as the work of discovering the
> physical world continues from generation to generation
> of scholars.
> —*William T. Bluhm (1978)*[1]

It is difficult to say anything really new about politics. And yet, the
subject is inexhaustible. When one picks up one of the ancient classics about politics—such as Plato's *Republic,* or Aristotle's *Politics,*
or the Hebrew books of Judges or Jeremiah—one is struck by how
relevant it is to current political life and thought. It is almost as if
the ancient writers were dealing with situations very familiar to us
today, often with greater profundity than present-day writers. But
those who have sought to reduce politics to some once-and-for-all
science have discovered, to their chagrin, that each political situation is also unique and that political history presents us with novelty at every turn.

Political leaders sometimes make the mistake of continuing the
same formula for success after circumstances have altered, only to
discover that their formula now guarantees failure. So it was, for example, when Democratic members of the U.S. Congress faced the
elections of 1994, confident that the usual approach to mainly economic issues would suffice to maintain the power they had enjoyed
for many years. Little did they realize how deep the popular dis-
content with Congress had grown to be and, in particular, how powerful the religious right had become. Usual methods and issues

---

[1]William T. Bluhm, *Theories of the Political System: Classics of Political Thought and
Modern Political Analysis,* 3d ed. (Englewood Cliffs, N.J.: Prentice-Hall, 1978), 500.

could not save them from a sweeping reversal of fortune. By 1998 the tide had begun to turn again, and those who had relied upon religious extremism to gain power discovered that the formula had lost much of its charm. So it was earlier when President Ferdinand Marcos employed the, for him, standard formula of corrupt electoral politics in the Philippine elections of 1986 on the assumption that the majority of Filipinos would remain politically passive one more time—but a massive reversal was in store. So it must have been when Marie Antoinette wondered aloud why the peasants, if hungry, did not eat cake.

Political leaders of consequence have often been noted for their grasp of opportunity in changing circumstances. Sometimes schooled in the history of political thought (though perhaps more often not), they have had an intuitive grasp of new possibilities and the personal capacity to take advantage of them. Sometimes they have created the necessary following; sometimes they have themselves been created by a great human movement. One of the fascinating aspects of the history of politics is how often leaders have emerged from the total obscurity of humble backgrounds to lead nations and empires. That is obviously true of many of the leaders of Western democracies in the twentieth century, for such men and women have often had the advantages of universal educational opportunity and access to essentially open political institutions. But it is also true of more authoritarian or closed political societies. Who could have predicted the rise of the shepherd-king, David, to power in ancient Israel, or the stunning political role of Joan of Arc, or the emergence of Stalin or Hitler? It is always easier to analyze after the fact how a particular leader or movement has been able to seize power and change the course of history than it is to predict any such thing for the future.

Some theories may be helpful in predicting political developments, such as the expectation that the political mood may shift, pendulum style, from periods of innovation to periods of conservation or consolidation, or the expectation that a population that is deeply frustrated culturally or economically may be ripe for extremism or reaction. But even here, the course of history may prove unpredictable. The United States, in the throes of frustration over the Vietnam War, economic recession (combined with high inflation), and outrage over the Watergate scandal, may have seemed ripe for a truly extremist political reaction during the 1970s. One might at least have expected a strong movement of the pendulum from the left to the right. The presidencies of Gerald Ford and

Jimmy Carter hardly conformed to what one might have expected. And while the leadership of Ronald Reagan was a sharp turn to the right, one wonders why the conservative reaction was so late in coming and why, when it did come, it had to be camouflaged so much in the actual Reagan campaigns of the 1980s. Looking backward half a century, one similarly notes that Franklin D. Roosevelt found it so expedient to campaign not as a radical innovator but as one who could be trusted to keep faith with the inherited economic verities that had gotten the United States into a terrible depression. In retrospect, it is always possible to say why things have happened as they did. It is not so easy to say what will happen in the future!

We should not be surprised by this. Politics has to do with people, and people are both predictable and unpredictable. If there is such a thing as freedom of the will, then we must expect to be surprised, now and again, by human behavior. An exact science of human behavior is not a possibility so long as the object of study is not fully predictable. At the same time, the predictable element in human life is substantial enough to make the discussion of politics interesting and productive.

But politics is also terribly important. For good or ill, its effect upon human life and conduct and well-being can scarcely be exaggerated. Politics is important in determining whether a people will be at war or in peace. It is fundamental in the distribution of economic goods, including the definition of property rights. Politics is basic to the definition of crime and the determination of how it will be punished. It affects the degree to which people will be free to speak, to write, to worship. It defines who will be accepted as members of the community, and who will be placed at the margins. It seriously influences the rearing of children by determining the circumstances of family life and establishing much of the subject matter of their education. It enters into the self-awareness of a people, their self-identity, and it projects in large measure their sense of historic destiny and accomplishment.

The interface between religion and politics is also obviously important. In every culture, religion has been important to people who were most concerned about politics, and politics has been important to people who were most concerned about religion; and, not infrequently, these have been the same people. Attitudes of religious people toward politics have varied enormously, and vice versa. But the importance of the relationship between the two is crucial to each. Those who are serious about politics must take religion seriously.

Those who are most deeply committed religiously must pay attention to politics.

There are, of course, many different ways in which religious people can pay attention to politics. The struggle for political power can be portrayed as the essence of the religious life and, at the other extreme, politics can be conceived, religiously, as the summary of all the evil against which the righteousness of God is ultimately arrayed. Both attitudes take politics seriously. Later, we shall explore some of the attitudes toward politics which are most important in the contemporary theological scene. These attitudes differ sharply, but neither regards politics as unimportant.

Similarly, for reasons we shall also explore more fully later, political practitioners and theorists cannot afford to take religion lightly. Whether they define their own life purposes in self-consciously religious ways or regard religion as trivial or dangerous, they must attend to its political effects. I do not think there has ever been a time when this has not been so; but the political effects of religion have been especially visible in the late-twentieth-century world. Religiopolitical movements of great consequence have emerged in settings as diverse as Iran, Sri Lanka, and Ireland, and some of the world's most perilous trouble spots are made all the more troublesome by the rigidities and passions of religious fanaticism. In North America, both right-wing fundamentalism and mainline religious convictions have affected political outcomes substantially.

Many seasoned political leaders in the contemporary world would doubtless like to see this religious influence simply go away, particularly when it is arrayed against their own political purposes. But both religion and politics are here to stay, and their profound mutual interaction will also continue. Whether or not this is "good"— or to what extent it is "good"—is itself inherently a religious question. For religion may be understood, at bottom, as the essence of what we believe to be true and good. The values and truths by which we live, and for which we may even be prepared to die, are constitutive of our religious faith. It is these values and truths which are most important to us in the forming of culture and society. There is, to be sure, also a sense in which religion is derived from society, to the point that Emile Durkheim and others have thought of religion only as the projection of social needs.

But religion is also the basis on which anybody can judge the adequacy of the beliefs and values by which any particular society lives. Religion can be "used" by politicians. But if the political order is to be subjected to review or criticism on the basis of value questions, the source of review and criticism is ultimately a religious one. Thus, the medieval drama of popes and princes seeking to use and to limit one another is a perennial one in every political society.

This volume seeks to interpret the meaning of politics from a moral/theological frame of reference and, in light of this, to suggest how certain political problems ought to be approached by those who share that frame of reference. My theological frame of reference is a Christian one, although it will be immediately apparent in part 2 that there are many mutually inconsistent interpretations of what Christian faith entails. It may also be apparent that Christian theological interpretations often overlap or parallel non-Christian views. One should not be surprised by that. The great religious systems are, after all, dealing with an objective world shared in common. In their moral teachings they often confront the same problems and arrive at similar conclusions. This does not mean that these problems can simply be approached in a pragmatic way, by-passing the ultimate theological issues, for the value frame of reference by which we define satisfactory solutions to problems is profoundly theological. But one must expect commonalities in value orientation among religious systems seeking to deal with the same world. Hence, there are serious differences among Christians and there are important similarities between Christians and non-Christians. And sometimes Christians find themselves making common cause with non-Christians in political struggles against still other Christians and non-Christians!

The deeper implication of this is not that Christians should forget their faith when approaching political questions but that they can make important contributions to the public dialogue precisely as they seek to clarify the ultimate grounds of their faith and action. In approaching people with whom I am in some disagreement about such matters, I would far rather get their religious views straight in order to see as clearly as possible how those views affect their political perspectives. We might learn something from each other, where we likely would not if the ultimate grounds for our views were always withheld from view.

To be sure, the combination of religion and politics has often resulted in explosive, intractable conflict—not least in the contemporary world. During and after the European religious struggles of the sixteenth and seventeenth centuries, sensible politicians and religious leaders alike concluded that greater mutual tolerance was urgently needed if civilization was not to tear itself apart. Similar conclusions were drawn in the 1990s by visionary leaders alarmed by the ethnic and religious struggles in the Balkans, Middle East, Northern Ireland, and parts of Africa.

The practical value of tolerance is an important political conclusion to draw, but it is also loaded with religious implications. The personal and political virtue of tolerance can, indeed, best be understood and expressed in theological terms, a point to which we must attend below. First, however, more needs to be said about politics itself. We have spoken of it as a perennial subject and alluded to its importance and its relationship to religion, but we have not yet said what it is. We do well, even before exploring the subject theologically, to ask what politics is and what the key terms of reference are.

2

What Is Politics?

> Every political theory is formed within the framework
> of a broader system of philosophy, from which it derives
> basic axioms and assumptions. . . . The answers a
> writer gives to the questions "What is ultimately real?",
> "What is ultimately good?", and "What can I know
> about the good and the real, and how can I know it?"
> are crucial."
>
> —*William T. Bluhm (1978)*[1]

> Thus, we cannot attain a "real" definition of politics
> which can be used independently of the ideological
> preferences of political agents.
>
> —*Raymond Plant (1986)*[2]

These two writers probably do not agree about philosophy or ideology, but both clearly doubt whether an objective definition of politics is possible. Both have made the point, and it is a good point, that our basic understanding of politics is bound to be influenced by our ultimate views. After all, when Karl Marx utters the word "politics" does he mean the same by it as Aristotle? When Martin Luther speaks of "the state," does the word mean the same thing to him as to Mahatma Gandhi or to John Locke or to Jacques Maritain?

---

[1]Bluhm, *Theories of the Political System,* 8.

[2]Raymond Plant, "Politics," in *The Westminster Dictionary of Christian Ethics,* ed. James F. Childress and John Macquarrie (Philadelphia: Westminster Press, 1986), 485.

Probably not. And yet we cannot begin to explore our differences if we do not begin with some common understandings. Marx and Aristotle do indeed mean different things when they speak of politics, but it is not as if one were speaking of music and the other of chemistry. Both have certain commonly experienced realities of social power in mind. But each interprets the character of those realities from a drastically different view of human societies. These differences reflect, in turn, serious differences of ultimate philosophical viewpoint. It is possible to compare and contrast their various views partly because each is so clear in the development of his unique perspective and partly because each offers us an interpretation of what is, after all, the same world (though experienced in different periods of history). But the question remains, to what extent can people use the same basic terms in the same basic way while still disagreeing profoundly in their political views? Is it possible to use basic terms, like "politics" and "the state," in a book of this kind, without ideological bias?

Ideological bias may creep in without our knowing it, of course; but still we must be as clear as we can about what we mean by key terms.

THE STATE AND POLITICS

In popular speech "state" is often treated as synonymous with "government," and "politics" is the maneuvering of politicians to gain and retain power. That will do for many purposes. But government is a visible set of institutions, and there are realities about the state that run deeper and involve even those who do not make up the government. In some respects every citizen is a part of the state, at least in countries where citizenship is possible. But most citizens are not a part of the government. Many countries distinguish between the head of state (e.g., the king or queen or president) and the head of government (the prime minister). The two functions are rolled into one in the presidency of the United States, but the division of powers in the U.S. means that the president is not even wholly the head of the government. So the state is more than the government, although the two are closely related.

Politics also means more than common usage suggests. Originally it meant the interactions of citizens in the polis, the Greek city-state. When Aristotle speaks of the human being as by nature a "political animal," he is not at all suggesting that we are simply extroverted power-grabbers. His point is that our essential humanity is marked by our rational interactions with others in the community. Politics is the polis, or civil community, ordering its life together on the basis of the public good. And to be human is to be a participant in that kind of community. While modern connotations of the term "politics" tend to emphasize the struggle over power, that is largely a struggle over what the community is to do. Politics can also refer to such struggles in other kinds of groups—as in church politics, or corporate politics, or union politics, or school politics. Sometimes the struggle is primarily an intellectual or emotional one, with some people attempting to persuade others. Sometimes the struggle is violent.

In this book, politics will be referred to primarily as it relates to the state. But what is the state?

In his classic sociological essay on "Politics as a Vocation," Max Weber remarked that the state cannot be defined in terms of its objectives since these may be shared by other kinds of groups. Rather, he insisted, the state is defined by the means it can employ to secure its ends—specifically its use of physical force. Quoting with approval Leon Trotsky's remark that "every state is founded on force," Weber remarked that "if no social institutions existed which knew the use of violence, then the concept of 'state' would be eliminated." Weber does not argue that the state uses only violence to achieve its ends, but that its ultimate power to do so is what defines it as the state. By this he does not mean that other groups and private individuals may not use violence, too, but that only the state "claims the *monopoly of the legitimate use of physical force* within a given territory."[3] Nor does Weber's point rest on a facile equating of the term "force" with the term "violence"—or a neglect of the distinctions to be made between different kinds of "force" and different kinds of "violence." He, in common with Trotsky and others, has in mind that application of "force" that violates the will by requiring people to do what they do not want to do or by removing them from the sphere of political action altogether. (We shall say more about this below.) Weber's definition enjoys much historical support, and not just from Trotsky either. Luther, reflecting in some measure the earlier understanding of Saint Augustine and possibly Saint Paul as well, speaks of the state in essentially coercive terms.[4] It is the realm of

---

[3]Max Weber, "The Vocation of Politics," in *From Max Weber: Essays in Sociology,* ed. and trans. H. H. Gerth and C. Wright Mills (New York: Oxford University Press, 1958 [1921]), 78.

[4]See especially Luther's essay, "Secular Authority: To What Extent It Should Be Obeyed," in *Works of Martin Luther* (Philadelphia: A. J. Holman, 1930), 3:228–73.

force made necessary by the sinfulness of humanity, existing along-side and protecting the constructive realm of love made possible by the gospel. And the contemporary theologian John C. Bennett uses language reminiscent of Weber in writing that "the state is the in-stitution in which the ultimate social authority and power are lo-cated, authority and power which are necessary to maintain order and to give conscious direction to the life of a society."[5] Like Weber, but unlike Luther, Bennett puts the negative functions of the state in the service of positive ends, and, by speaking of "social authority" alongside "power," implies that something more than naked force is involved.

Perhaps most of us could agree with Weber, Bennett, and others that the ultimate use of force has historically been a very important aspect, if not the definitive characteristic, of the state—whether the state has been a tribe, a city-state, an empire, or a contemporary nation-state, and whether the state has been democratic, fascist, Marxist, monarchical, or theocratic.

But since no state has ever, at least to my knowledge, had a com-plete monopoly on the use of force (even within its own territory), the *way* in which the state gathers in and uses the power available to it may be important in understanding what the state finally is. Weber wrote of the "legitimate" use of force, Bennett of "authority." Both of these closely related terms imply a special kind of accept-ability for some uses of force in human society over against other uses. This will need to be looked at below. But for now, in defining the state, I am impressed by the simple fact that somehow the state exists as an embodiment of the will of the people.

Two American sociologists have contributed helpful understand-ings of the state and political power. One of these is Talcott Parsons, who refers to political power as the "capacity to control the rela-tional system as a system."[6] The other is Robert M. MacIver, who notes similarly that political power "alone is the organ of the whole community."[7] Both writers thus emphasize that the state represents in some way the integration of the power of a whole community so that, in effect, the whole community can be mobilized to accomplish something together. That is not to say that there are not other cen-

---

[5]John C. Bennett, "State," in *Westminster Dictionary of Christian Ethics,* 602. See also idem, *Christians and the State* (New York: Charles Scribner's Sons, 1958).

[6]Talcott Parsons, *The Social System* (Chicago: Free Press, 1951), 126.

[7]Robert M. MacIver, *The Web of Government* (New York: Macmillan Co., 1947), 94.

ters of power in the community—MacIver is especially careful to emphasize that point. But it is to say that all of these centers can be mobilized to act together, and that when this occurs it is the state.

How does this relate to coercion? MacIver, like Weber and Bennett, also stresses the state's monopoly on the "final power of coercion." That does not mean that only the state *uses* coercion—violent criminals do that, and so, on occasion, do loving parents! The point is that the power of the state cannot be set aside by some other body within society—while the power of every other person or group within society can be set aside by the state. One of the reasons why imperial powers and (in the modern world) superpowers are so resented by weaker nations is that the enormously superior power of the former can be used in such a way as to make it impossible for smaller countries to be states—that is, to control their own ultimate decision making and action. To be a state, a society must have the capacity to decide and act as a whole, on its own, for its own ends.

The state, in short, is *society acting as a whole, with the ultimate power to compel compliance within its own jurisdiction.*[8] Does such an understanding of the state help bring the realities of politics into focus?

It certainly does not mean that when the state acts everybody within the given society *agrees* with what is being done. If that were a requirement of the definition, then there could be no state anywhere, for no society (at least that I know of) has ever been absolutely unanimous in its judgment about anything. I doubt that even the Vatican state or the traditional theocratic Tibetan state was ever devoid of *some* dissent, and most modern states are seething cauldrons of political conflict much of the time. But still they act, still they exist as the state.

In even the most complex, conflict-ridden modern state, there is still a sense in which it is everybody acting together. When the state acts it is with resources generated by the whole society. Even private actions prompted by grave dissent from the actions of the state can have the ironic effect of contributing support to those actions.

---

[8]I have used "jurisdiction" here rather than "geographical territory" because the reach or jurisdiction of the state is not strictly a geographical matter. The jurisdiction of the state can reach beyond its own borders to affect the behavior and interests of its own citizens traveling abroad or on the high seas, while at the same time certain alien residents within a country may be partly immune from that country's laws.

To cite a personal illustration: In 1967 an article of mine in *The Christian Century* examined the moral basis for U.S. military involvements in Vietnam and concluded that the war could not be supported morally. The article, in other words, voiced my opposition to the war on Christian moral grounds. For writing this article, I was paid some $40 or $50 by the magazine, which was declared as a part of my net income for that year. On that basis, something like $8 or $10 of this was paid to the federal government in income taxes. Of that $8 or $10 perhaps $2 was used to help conduct the war in Vietnam. Thus, by writing an article critical of the war I was engaged in an economic activity helping to wage it!

Such is the daily irony of actions of state. The state is always doing things I disapprove of, while also doing other things I consciously support and still further things of which I am unaware or unconcerned one way or another. But, as a member of the community, as a part of what Parsons calls the "social system," I am contributing in a variety of ways to the success of whatever the state may be doing.

Can we avoid this involvement by refusing to pay our taxes or otherwise refusing to do what the state requires of us as it seeks to implement its objectives? Various movements in different countries have made use of tax avoidance as a way of refusing to participate in what the state is doing. But it turns out to be more difficult than such movements generally suppose, partly because most modern states have ingenious ways of collecting the money anyway (such as legally attaching one's bank account or confiscating one's physical possessions) and partly because when one functions as a part of the system of economic production and exchange one is helping generate the wealth needed by the state, whether or not one is specifically paying taxes. Of course, one can become an outlaw, or one can leave the state altogether. But that hardly affects this understanding of the state since we have defined the state as society (made up of those who are regularly functioning members of society) acting as a whole.

TESTING THIS
UNDERSTANDING OF THE STATE

Does this way of viewing the state make sense in light of the variety of conflicting ideological conceptions of the state one has to choose from?

The purest case of wholehearted agreement I can think of (and I record it with some embarrassment) is that of the fascist dictator,

Benito Mussolini. Mussolini went much further in identifying state and society, almost as though there could be no aspect of society, no actions by individuals or by smaller groups, that were not caught up in the state. I disagree with this because society is not always, or even usually, "acting as a whole." People have private lives, and there are meaningful small-group and family activities in even the most totalitarian societies. But Mussolini saw these only as expressed through the state. And he saw the state functioning essentially through its leader; in the case of Italy, of course, Mussolini himself. The fascist doctrine is frankly, explicitly totalitarian. As Mussolini wrote: "Anti-individualistic, the fascist conception of life stresses the importance of the State and accepts the individual only in so far as his interests coincide with those of the State, which stands for the conscience and the universal will of man as a historic entity."[9] And, he continued, "The fascist conception of the State is all-embracing; outside of it no human or spiritual values can exist, much less have value. Thus understood, fascism is totalitarian, and the fascist State—a synthesis and a unit inclusive of all values—interprets, develops and potentiates the whole life of a people."[10] Having little respect for individual persons as persons, Mussolini clearly would be quite comfortable with the definition of the state as "society acting as a whole"!

What about the contract theories of political life, such as those of Thomas Hobbes, John Locke, and Jean Jacques Rousseau? In the case of Rousseau, depending on how one interprets the ambiguous references to the "general will," the state does emerge as a social whole, focusing the intentions and actions of a whole people and expressing the meaning of their lives together. Hobbes and Locke are more explicitly individualistic—the former on the basis of a highly pessimistic account of human self-centeredness, the latter on the basis of a more constructive portrayal of human interests. But in both cases, the very essence of the state lies in the agreement of all members of society to surrender their individual right of self-protection into the corporate power of the whole community so that the latter will be powerful enough to defend the rights of all. Each person retains important individual rights (to Locke these are

---

[9]Benito Mussolini, "The Doctrine of Fascism," in *Social and Political Philosophy,* ed. J. Somerville and R. E. Santoni (Garden City, N.Y.: Doubleday Anchor Books, 1963 [1933]), 426.
[10]Ibid.

17

summarized as the rights to life, liberty, and the pursuit of property) but, through the state as social contract, we all act together to ensure those rights for each and all. By joining the contract (in most cases through our birth), we consent in advance to the actions of the state that are in accordance with the contract—even our own punishment, should we ourselves infringe upon the provisions of the contract by injuring our fellow citizens.

The contract theory is not totalitarian. There are clear limits upon what the state may or may not do in accordance with the social contract. But when the state acts properly in accordance with the terms of that contract, it truly is all of us acting together. The Marxian view of the state appears to be *very* different. Marx and his followers have always insisted that the state is nothing but the ruling class, taking different forms corresponding to the different epochs of economic history. As *The Communist Manifesto* puts it, concerning the present period of capitalism, "the executive of the modern state is but a committee for managing the common affairs of the whole bourgeoisie."[11] How can there be a society acting as a whole if society is not a "whole" but rather the arena of conflict between fundamentally antagonistic economic classes, one which is dominant and exploiting the other? As if to emphasize the point, classical Marxism even developed the notion of the disappearance of the state, foreseeing a time when the final abolition of class conflict in the classless society would make the state no longer necessary.[12] This view, which also implies an almost wholly coercive understanding of the state, makes the state the representative not of the wholeness or unity of society but of its fragmentation.

Still, for our purposes, there could be little Marxian disagreement with the view that the exploited class, while not participating in the directing of the state, must act as directed *by* the state. The very essence of the Marxian understanding of the state is that it exists

---

[11]Karl Marx and Friedrich Engels, *The Communist Manifesto,* in *Basic Writings on Politics and Philosophy,* ed. Lewis S. Feuer (New York: Doubleday Anchor Books, 1959 [1848]), 9.

[12]See, e.g., Friedrich Engels, "The Origin of the Family, Private Property and the State," in *Basic Writings on Politics and Philosophy,* 394: "We are now rapidly approaching a stage in the development of production at which the existence of these classes not only will have ceased to be a necessity, but will become a positive hindrance to production. They will fall as inevitably as they arose at an earlier stage. Along with them the state will inevitably fall."

to compel the members of the exploited class to fall into line, to respect the exploitative property rights and relations of production and exchange, to provide the resources whereby the dominant class—which really does run the state—can pursue its interests. Not everything is the state in this theory. Different classes and individual persons also act individually in nonpolitical ways. Quarrels occur within the bourgeoisie, for instance, which are not settled by the state as such. Private voluntary groups, such as churches, are not political as such, although they, too, act so as to confirm the existing interests of the dominant class. But insofar as the state exists, it focuses power derived from all segments of society, whether they like it or not. The act of revolution, in Marxian theory, is first of all the act of seizing power so that the state now is directed by and reflective of the interests of the previously exploited class. That class, in the era of capitalism, is the proletariat. And the interests of the proletariat are alone to be equated with those of society as a whole. When the future classless society has been achieved, the state will no longer be needed. But, as long as it does exist, it mobilizes the whole social system. It thus seems clear to me that even the Marxian understanding of the state is consistent with the definition we have advanced here.

A very different, almost organic view of the state is offered by medieval Thomism (largely following Aristotle). That political vision depicts human society in hierarchical form. In the well-ordered society, our station in life is fitted by birth and/or by our innate abilities. Governance is by those who are best fitted to rule. The suppression of conflict, the punishment of iniquity, the protection of the community from aggression—all of the negative state functions—are well displayed here. But the larger social vision is one in which the relationships between those who rule and those who obey are fixed, natural, and not inherently negative or exploitative. Much of the overall fabric of life is nonpolitical. Indeed, even the relationships of rule to obedience are present in all the orders of society, such as the family and the church. The state, depicted by Thomism as one of the two "perfect" institutions (the other being the church), is charged with rule over the temporal affairs of the whole society. It is "perfect" in that it possesses all of the powers and resources within itself that are necessary to the proper fulfillment of its appointed ends. It thus represents society as a whole insofar as it properly acts in accordance with its role. The peasant or artisan may aspire to no share in the functions of governmental rule, but it is her or his economic production that ultimately sustains the political aristocracy and enables them to give effect to their decisions, just as the levies of troops are made broadly throughout the population. All, needless to say, are expected to act in accordance with the edicts of princes.

No doubt the supreme test of any definition of the state is whether it can be used by the anarchists, who do not approve of the state in any form. Leo Tolstoy, for instance, regarded the essential coerciveness of the state as the cause, not the cure, of humanity's wickedness[13] and, in our own time, Robert Nozick sees the state as a profoundly unjust intrusion upon the natural property rights of free persons.[14] Both understand the state to be, essentially, a coercive institution. Whether in the form of Tolstoy's Christian anarchism or modern libertarianism, this approach to the state appears seriously opposed to all efforts to make people act together. Tolstoy certainly believed in mutual love and cooperation within the community, but not in a coerced love or a coerced cooperation. Nozick and the libertarians are certainly not opposed to mutual assistance and acts of charity. But they are utterly opposed to efforts to require uniformity of action or cooperation by the whole society toward common ends.

In a way, then, our definition of the state, describing as it does the state the anarchists are eager to abolish, is exactly suited to their theoretical understanding. They are unalterably opposed to the state, to society acting as a whole; but they implicitly define it in almost exactly this way, particularly when we include the provision that the state has ultimate power to compel compliance within its own jurisdiction. That is exactly what the anarchists are against when they speak against the state.

And so we have come full circle, from Mussolini's glorification of the state as everything to the anarchists' interest in abolishing it altogether. And within this circle we have found no important perspective on politics that is fundamentally incomprehensible when examined in light of this definition. That does not necessarily mean that this way of viewing the state has no ideological tendencies of its own. But it does mean that it can serve the ongoing discussion of different political perspectives unusually well.

---

[13]See Leo Tolstoy, *My Religion* (New York: T. Y. Crowell, 1885), and idem, *The Kingdom of God Is within You* (New York: Farrar, Straus & Co., 1961 [1905]).

[14]See Robert Nozick, *Anarchy, State and Utopia* (New York: Basic Books, 1974).

THE CONCEPT OF SOVEREIGNTY

The state is, by definition, the location of the supreme power within a society. In our discussion we have noted that some states are so dominated by others that they can scarcely be said to have ultimate power over their own destiny. When that is so, their sovereignty itself is in question. And it is noteworthy that when small countries (such as some of those in Central America) complain bitterly to larger ones (such as the United States) about this external domination, it is to voice the protest that their sovereignty is being infringed upon. Without sovereignty, a society scarcely exists as a state at all. Many societies have existed historically only as part of great empires, in which case it is the empire that is the state, not the small society.

The concept of sovereignty is a partly mythical one, of course, in a world where power and independence have been limited even for the most powerful states. No state *totally* controls its own destiny, no power exists *altogether* unchecked by other external powers. Important aspects of social existence spill across national boundaries, rendering the concepts of both state and sovereignty relative.

Nevertheless, the term "sovereignty" is useful because it helps us focus on the ultimate sources of power. Historically, the term has sometimes been attached to the person of the chief of state, for the reigning monarch has been, in a sense, the embodiment of the collective will of the whole community. Sometimes that has been taken quite literally, as in the Jamesian doctrine of divine right of kings and Louis XIV's announcement that "the state is me" (*l'état c'est moi*). But even the political theorists of imperial Rome had a more sophisticated understanding of sovereignty than that. The emperor's power, absolute as it often was, still existed by the implied consent of the citizenry.[15] They, not he, were ultimately sovereign. Certainly that is so if the state is society acting as a whole. Society itself is the sovereign source of political power.

But is it even legitimate to speak of *human* sovereignty in light of the ultimate limitations upon political power? Jacques Maritain

---

[15]This Stoic conception was voiced by the Roman legal theorist Ulpian as follows: "The will of the Emperor has the force of law, because by the passage of the *lex regia* the people transfers to him and vests in him all its own power and authority" (*Digest of Justinian,* cited in George H. Sabine, *A History of Political Theory,* 3d ed. [New York: Holt, Rinehart & Winston, 1961]), 171.

21

has been noteworthy among those insisting that no human being or group is ultimately sovereign since God alone is finally the source of all power and since legitimate exercises of human power are in accordance with the moral law intrinsic to our human nature. Deeply concerned by totalitarian absolutism, which he considers to be founded upon the ideas of sovereignty in Hobbes, Rousseau, and Jean Bodin, Maritain argues that human political power is accountable to a transcendent source of power. In his own words,

> In the political sphere, and with respect to the men or agencies in charge of guiding peoples toward their earthly destinies, there is no valid use of the concept of Sovereignty. Because, in the last analysis, no earthly power is the image of God and deputy for God. God is the very source of the authority with which the people invest those men or agencies, but they are not the vicars of God. They are vicars of the people; then they cannot be divided from the people by any superior essential property.[16]

Maritain, it seems to me, makes two points that are useful to our understanding of the limitations on the term "sovereignty": first, that there are factual limitations on any human political power, for no power is total in a world of competing wills and natural limits; and second, that the term "sovereign" must not be allowed to convey an ethical and theological implication that any identifiable human power is not subject to higher moral criticism. The first point is simply factual. It is especially interesting to observe the limits to even the most absolute of states, to see the little cracks of humanity and inefficiency that appear in even the most awesome of totalitarian states. In some respects (which I do not wish to overstate), totalitarian states may be even more inefficient than other kinds. But to identify the sources and focal points of political power and to identify this as the sovereignty of the state is not to argue that sovereignty is unlimited. At that point, it seems to me that Maritain's objections to the term are at the level of definition.

His other point, however, is normative. The ultimate accountability of the state is, finally, an ethical and theological question and different kinds of ethical and theological answers will be given to it.

---

[16]Jacques Maritain, *Man and the State* (Chicago: University of Chicago Press, 1951), 50.

That question lies beyond the scope of this chapter, but it is at the heart of the theological discussions that will follow.

POLITICAL POWER

I have used the term "political power" so far as though everybody means the same thing by it. At some levels of popular usage, political power conjures up images of violence and coercion, with shadowy Machiavellian figures lurking in the background manipulating people and events. Political power is taken to mean the power to *make* people do things, like it or not. And there is enough truth in the characterization to suffice for many practical purposes. The American phrase, "you can't beat city hall," states the point for everybody who has ever been frustrated by the (usually minor) political and legal injustices that simply cannot be overcome. A certain aura of invincibility built up around such demonic political figures as Adolf Hitler and Joseph Stalin, contributing to the myth that such dictators literally "forced" their respective countries to obey them.

But the popular connotation obscures a very important truth about political power. Force and violence (and manipulation) are indeed often a part of the picture. But political power preeminently arises from the human will. And where the human will is involved, *influence* over decision is more important than the mechanical application of force.

Franz Neumann makes the point in his distinction between two different forms of power: "control of nature" and "control of man."[17] The former is "mere intellectual power." It is based on our understanding of nature and the current state of our technology. Our power to "make" the lights go on by flipping a light switch depends on vast previous scientific discoveries, inventions, and technologies and the fact that the switch is connected to a wiring system, bulbs, fixtures, and a functioning source of electrical energy. Given all of this, our definite act of flipping the switch can be expected to have a definite effect. That is a form of control of nature. Similarly, placing a dam across a river is a kind of control over nature. Killing an animal (or a person) is control over nature. Sending people to the moon is control over nature. All the political power in the world

---

[17]Franz Neumann, *The Democratic and the Authoritarian State* (New York: Free Press, 1957), 3.

cannot do some things if the state of existing technology will not permit it. For instance, with all of his immense political power, the Caesar Augustus could not have lighted his imperial palace with electricity or watched a television program there (although no doubt he had compensating forms of lighting and entertainment).

Control of nature is relevant to political power, but political power involves an additional dimension. Political power involves more than simply "making" things happen. Political leaders can sometimes order the death of opponents or disobedient subjects—and that entails control of nature. But controlling the *behavior* of human beings means influencing them to do what we want them to do. We cannot literally *make* them act as we want them to. Of course, we have visions of tortured victims of an oppressive state, writhing in pain on the rack, breaking down finally and agreeing to do whatever may be necessary to stop the pain. Torture can be very *persuasive* with most of us! But our will must still be motivated before we will act as others want us to act. Some people have been able to withstand incredible amounts of torture, finally released only by death. Some have willingly died rather than do or say what an oppressive ruler wants them to do or say. Most of us lack the courage displayed by the story of the Roman messenger (was it to the Carthagians?) who voluntarily thrust his hand into the fire to demonstrate Roman steadfastness. Most of us are not heroes. But surely there is a threshold for most people below which they will ignore danger or pain in order to do what they really want to do. Threats and physical abuse are effective beyond doubt; but not at all in the clear, calculable sense of control of nature.

Political power, according to Neumann, "is social power focused on the state. It involves control of other men for the purpose of influencing the behavior of the state, its legislative, administrative and judicial activities."[18] Consequently, he continues, "those who wield political power are compelled to create emotional and rational responses in those whom they rule, inducing them to accept, implicitly or explicitly, the commands of the rulers."[19] Politics, he concludes, is therefore "the struggle of ideas as well as of force."[20] This is a very basic point, easily overlooked in our preoccupation with the importance of raw force, violence, coercion.

---

[18]Ibid.
[19]Ibid., 4.
[20]Ibid., 5.

The point can be applied all over the political terrain. It is very important for us to grasp its fundamental implication: *Every human interest or value having any influence over the will of any person is potentially a form of political power.* Anything that can affect human attitudes and decisions may potentially be politicized.

Most politicians are well aware of the importance of economics, and some doubtless believe that economic interest is the *only* influence in the final analysis. Clearly it is important. People have bodily needs which must be met for the sake of survival and comfort, and much human culture is built around the relative value of prosperity over against destitution.

But economics is not everything in politics. National pride can, at certain moments of history, sweep aside all considerations of personal gain in the determination of political purpose. Admired folk heroes or celebrities can influence their admirers politically (why else would U.S. presidential candidates assemble support committees made up of Hollywood stars whose celebrity status is essentially irrelevant to the political agenda at hand?). In 1964 President Lyndon B. Johnson gained a good deal of support from the endorsement of Dr. Benjamin Spock, the best-selling pediatrician-author, presumably because of his influence among the millions of readers of his books. Such people may or may not also be real authorities on the issues of the day. More often than not, they know comparatively little. But that is beside the point so far as their political power is concerned. The fact that they can influence people, for *whatever reason,* can, under the right circumstances, translate into political power. A presidential campaign committee (and often campaigns for lesser offices) will carefully target specific interest groups (farmers, teachers, business, labor, etc.) with appeals tailored to the perceived interests and values of the particular group.

And then there is religion. In our own time we are learning anew the almost awesome power of religion to affect the political will of vast numbers of people of all sorts of religious persuasions. Buddhists, Muslims, Jews, Hindus, Christians—be they fundamentalist or liberal or whatever else—may be touched politically through their religious values. That is an explosive political reality in our time in many countries. The rise of the so-called religious right in America, the Shiite Muslims in Iran, Buddhists in Burma, and conservative rabbis in Israel all illustrate the influence—potential and actual—of intense religious fervor in public life. One can observe a corresponding decline in political influence of more moderate religious forces in some parts of the world. Increases and decreases in political influence tend to be ephemeral. At the beginning of the twenty-first century, mainline Protestant denominations—such as the Presbyterians, Methodists, and Episcopalians—have relatively less influence than they enjoyed a few decades earlier. But such groups may have greater influence today than they did at the founding of the republic, when fewer than 10 percent of the American people belonged to any church.

The power of religion in politics was understood shrewdly by Niccolo Machiavelli. His advice to the prince on the subject of religion remains a classic. In respect to virtuous character, Machiavelli observes that "it is not essential . . . that a Prince should have all the good qualities." "But," he continues, "it is most essential that he should seem to have them." It can in fact be risky for a ruler to be too moral, but it is at the same time a serious mistake not to *appear* to be moral and religious. "Thus," he writes, "it is well to seem merciful, faithful, humane, religious, and upright, and also to be so; but the mind should remain so balanced that were it needful not to be so, you should be able and know how to change to the contrary."[21] Machiavelli summarizes the point in what appears to be a thoroughly cynical passage:

> A Prince should therefore be very careful that nothing ever escapes his lips which is not replete with the five qualities above named, so that to see and hear him, one would think him the embodiment of mercy, good faith, integrity, humanity, and religion. And there is no virtue which it is more necessary for him to seem to possess than this last; because men in general judge rather by the eye than by the hand, for every one can see but few can touch. Every one sees what you seem, but few know what you are, and these few dare not oppose themselves to the opinion of the many who have the majesty of the State to back them up.[22]

As a final piece of political shrewdness, Machiavelli observes that "if a Prince succeeds in establishing and maintaining his authority, the means will always be judged honorable and be approved by every one. For the vulgar are always taken by appearances and by results, and the world is made up of the vulgar, the few only finding room when the many have no longer ground to stand on."[23]

---

[21]Niccolo Machiavelli, *The Prince*, ed. Charles W. Eliot (New York: P. F. Collier, 1938 [1513]), 36:58.
[22]Ibid.
[23]Ibid., 59.

Machiavelli's work has been condemned as cynical by generations of moralists from his time to the present, and his name has even passed into the language to symbolize cynical and ruthless political behavior. But our purpose now is not to assess the morality of the man or his writings, but rather to note the shrewdness of his analysis of power. Machiavelli was very far from regarding real political power as purely a matter of coercive force (though he certainly understood the importance of coercion and fear as political motivators). He was clear in understanding that anything that affects the consciousness of the people and that touches upon their values is relevant to political power.

Anything capable of influencing human behavior is potentially a form of political power. Machiavelli, if anything, is broader in his understanding of this fact than the realpolitik or hardheaded political realism with which his name is so often associated, for Machiavelli understood that brute force is not the only component of political power. To call attention to Machiavelli's perceptiveness about this is not, of course, to endorse the cynicism and duplicity he advises the prince to use for political ends. But it does help to understand why political leaders have found it necessary to appeal to such a wide range of human values, hopes, and fears in order to gain their ends.

LEGITIMATE AUTHORITY

We have considered the state as society acting as a whole, sovereignty as the ultimate repository of political power, and political power as, above all, the power to influence the will and political behavior of people. Drawing these points together now, we may ask why people are prompted to obey rulers and laws even against their own inclinations. Why are people willing to act together, through the state, even when the state is violating values or interests that are very important to them?

In every civil society people are conditioned to obey political authority whether or not they agree with its policies. Those who hold political authority command more than police forces and armies, and the secret of their power also extends beyond their capacity to persuade. They can count, more or less, on the disposition of people to obey their authority because people believe it is right or prudent to do so. If political authority is accepted as *legitimate* by a community, it will generally be obeyed.

The legitimacy of political authority is largely a moral concept, expressing the deeply rooted belief of a people that that authority manifests those values by which the people live. But it can also express the belief that it is in the best *interest* of the people to obey the agreed-upon authority. The moral or even religious character of legitimacy is obvious in some cases, such as the Shinto myths undergirding Japanese imperial authority a generation ago and Saint Paul's admonition, "Let every person be subject to the governing authorities. For there is no authority except from God, and those that exist have been instituted by God" (Rom. 13:1). The medieval mind, governed in part by this kind of view, regarded constituted authority as a direct expression of God's will. Under extreme circumstances, when a ruler was seen by the church to have deviated from the divine law at important points, the church might, through interdiction, require the people to withdraw their support from that ruler as a condition of receiving the sacrament. Under such pressure, Emperor Henry IV was forced to humiliate himself before Pope Gregory VII at the castle of Canossa in 1077 before the pope would restore the emperor's authority. At stake was whether the nobility, and below them the people, were to regard the emperor's authority as legitimate.

A different kind of drama was enacted when the English king Henry VIII was excommunicated for divorcing his first wife, Catherine of Aragon. To maintain the legitimacy of his authority as king, Henry had to sever relations with the Catholic Church—which he did in 1534—and establish himself as supreme head of the Church of England. Political considerations were doubtless uppermost in the minds of the main participants in this drama, the pope included. But the religious element was of primary importance to the people in general. Hence, Henry had to secure sufficient support from the nobility and church hierarchy in England to retain the legitimacy of his rule.

The medieval conception of political legitimacy has largely broken down in the modern world. But legitimacy is still very important. The contract tradition in political thought—associated primarily with Hobbes, Locke, and Rousseau—developed the notion that political authority is legitimate insofar as it represents a prior commitment by citizens to obey the law in exchange for the benefits of the state. Hobbes, who understood the natural state of society to be one of ruinous conflict, saw the state as the power freely given up by the people so that a single strong ruler would be able to maintain the peace for all. Locke, whose view of human nature was not quite as pessimistic, nevertheless also understood political authority as existing by virtue of our covenant with one another to preserve property and peace against danger. In such thinkers' terms, we have even consented to our own punishment if we should violate the law; we would be bound to regard even those who are appointed to punish us as having that authority legitimately. We are morally bound in the sense that we have bound ourselves in our commitment to our fellow citizens that we will all obey the rulers. But we also obey because we recognize that it is ultimately in our own best interest.

While we think of the contract tradition as an Enlightenment and modern phenomenon, it is worth noting that it also has quite ancient roots—not only in the Stoic Roman lawyers, to whom we have already referred, but even in ancient Greece (where Socrates is reported, in Plato's *Crito,* to have had something of the contract understanding of political legitimacy in his explanation of why he could not flee Athens to avoid the sentence of death).

Sometimes legitimacy is conferred upon a state that is widely considered to be evil and oppressive. The term "legitimacy" then takes on the minimal sense of acceptance of the best of the available alternatives. Under those circumstances, obedience to the government may seem preferable to anarchy or to an even more intense tyranny. Even tyrants, insofar as they are able to govern at all, can often count on that minimal degree of legitimacy in their rule. When actual revolution does occur, it comes as an announcement that many people no longer accept the existing rule as legitimate and that they are prepared to replace it with a rule that they do consider to be legitimate. (In the case of principled anarchists, of course, *no* rule is regarded as legitimate.)

It is often rightly pointed out that most political orders would break down quickly were it not for the voluntary obedience of most people most of the time. The direct enforcement powers of the state may be considerable, but they are rarely adequate to compel everybody to act in accordance with law on all occasions. But where the state is considered to be legitimate, people are generally willing to act in accordance with its command regardless of their preferences.

GOVERNMENT

The state usually acts through government. As perceived by most people most of the time, government is the legitimate expression of the state's authority. The relationship between state and government is so intimate that it is not surprising that the two terms are often used interchangeably, although doing so obscures the deeper reality of the state.

Some of the earliest works in political philosophy distinguish forms of government (e.g., monarchy, aristocracy, and democracy) and, following Montesquieu and others, contemporary discussion makes much of the three powers or functions of government (legislative, executive, judicial). These typologies are helpful in analyzing different forms and functions of government, although government, in reality, is much more complex. In respect to the functions of government, even with the separation of powers characteristic of Britain or America, a casual observer can note that each of the three exercises, to some extent, the powers of the other two. Each, in particular, makes policy that is binding upon the society—that is, each makes law, even where the legislative branch is kept separate and respected as ultimate lawmaker. The executive, within the framework set by legislature and judiciary, establishes policy and guidelines—in effect, a more detailed form of law. The courts, by interpreting the law and Constitution (that deeper form of law not immediately accessible to change by the legislature), also "make" law—and it is difficult to see how it could be otherwise without abandoning the principle of judicial review. As a matter of fact, though, every aspect of government participates in one way or another, at some level or another, in the making and interpretation of laws which will, in some way or another, be binding upon all who are bound by the legitimate authority of the government.

Public policy represents the directions taken by government on behalf of the state. It is what we are all doing together, through the government, when we act as a whole.

THE STRUGGLE
FOR POLITICAL POWER

The struggle for control over government is therefore indescribably important. Control over government comes down to control over what the whole society will do or not do. Given the fact that most people will obey what they consider to be legitimate authority, the control of the direction actually given to the exercise of that authority is, in effect, control of the actions of most people when and as they act as a whole community.

The struggle takes many forms. In an absolute state, where it has been established quite clearly who the one absolute ruler will be, the struggle for power is the struggle to influence the thinking of that one ruler. Thus, the court politics of Louis XIV was not simply a matter of proper etiquette at Versailles. Real power hinged on whether one was favorably regarded by the monarch and whether one could use one's access to the king to influence his thinking on issues of concern. (Thus, it really *mattered* who got to tuck him into bed at night, with the elaborate rituals devised for that function!) Access to Hitler or Stalin similarly represented real power in Germany or the USSR. There was no prospect in those countries of changing rulers; power meant affecting what the ruler would do. So one would do well to know what kinds of beliefs, interests, or values needed to be played upon to influence the rulers. Just as Machiavelli's prince must be careful not to offend the values or prejudices of the people he would rule, those who seek to influence the prince must take care not to offend the latter's values or prejudices. But those who do succeed in influencing the ruler have a hold on actual political power.

A similar struggle for power also occurs in democratic states through various forms of lobbying. Whether the effort is being made to influence legislators, executives, or judges, it remains true that whoever or whatever can affect their judgment holds a form of political power. The struggle of opposed lobbying groups attempting to influence passage or defeat of a bill can be almost awesome, particularly since such groups often represent large constituencies and important interests. Lobbying also occurs with the executive branch. Special access to a president of the United States or a prime minister of Britain can affect actual outcomes. Any public leader is going to have some people who, through friendship or respect, are trusted more than others. In a situation where electoral campaigns are largely financed by private donations, those who give the most are likely to have the greatest influence. Senator Paul Simon put this succinctly in his memoirs:

> Anyone in a major elected public office who tells you that he or she is not influenced by campaign contributions is either living in a dream world or is lying. . . . I have never promised anyone a thing for a campaign contribution. When I still served in the Senate and got to my hotel room at midnight, there might be twenty phone calls waiting for me, nineteen from people whose names I did not recognize, the twentieth from someone who gave me a $1,000 campaign contribution or raised money for me. At midnight I'm not going to make twenty phone calls. I might make one. Which one do you think I will make? So will every other incumbent Senator. That means that the financially articulate have inordinate access to policymakers. Access spells influence. The

problem permeates our government and too often dictates what we do.[24]

It is even possible to influence public policy by the right kind of access to civil servants in the bureaucracy, who also exercise political power (sometimes more substantively than elected officials). Even the judiciary can be "lobbied," although the forms in which this can be done are more tightly constrained by law and custom. Ideally—and sometimes actually—public servants are influenced only by conceptions of the public good. But the ability to communicate with a public official about the public good can represent political power. And, of course, many public servants are also prompted by values other than the public good.

The most visible aspect of the struggle for political power is when clear control of government is at stake, as in elections in democratic states or as in revolutions. Here the issue is who will control the apparatus as a whole. Whoever wins will thereby inherit whatever support society gives to legitimate rule. Though not unlimited, this power can be very great. It confers upon the holder the right to make decisions on behalf of others and to implement them with resources drawn even from one's political opponents.

The struggle for power, in its various forms, is a wondrously complex phenomenon. Some of it is conducted openly, with great drama. Much of it occurs behind the scenes, sometimes with great subtlety. Part of it addresses the question, "Who will govern?"; part of it, "What will be done?" In most societies there are cultural constraints affecting this struggle, and those who disregard such constraints tamper with the fundamental values determining legitimacy. I suspect that this, more than anything else, is what determined the outcome in the impeachment and attempted removal of President Clinton from office in 1998–99. The president's actions, giving rise to the impeachment, were widely viewed as scandalous. But throughout the year of the nation's exposure to the scandal, his support in public opinion polls remained constant and high. More was at stake here than an expression of moral disapproval. The removal of a president from office is a power move of great importance. Large numbers of people clearly did not regard the offense as having sufficient weight to warrant that outcome, thereby setting a historical

---

[24]Paul Simon, *PS: The Autobiography of Paul Simon* (Chicago: Bonus Books, 1999), 306.

precedent making the impeachment mechanism more readily available as a weapon in the political struggle.[25]

Notwithstanding the constraints, however, the underlying reality is that those who prevail in the struggle for power determine, in large measure, what other people will do when they all act together as a political society. In some form or other, that struggle will always be a reality in politics.

---

[25]My discussion of this, written at the time of the impeachment process, is in J. Philip Wogaman, *From the Eye of the Storm: A Pastor to the President Speaks Out* (Louisville, Ky.: Westminster John Knox Press, 1998). I remarked there that future historians may be especially puzzled by the curious gulf between the thinking of media pundits, a majority of whom seemed to favor the president's removal from office, and public opinion, which rallied to his support. Other factors were at work, including widespread perceptions that the Clinton presidency had been very effective at many points. This last point could not help but highlight the attempt to remove this president from office as a part of the ongoing struggle for political power.

3

Historical Legacies
of Christian Political Thought

> For Christians cannot be distinguished from the rest of
> the human race by country or language or customs.
> They do not live in cities of their own; they do not use a
> peculiar form of speech; they do not follow an eccentric
> manner of life. . . . At the same time they give proof of
> the remarkable and admittedly extraordinary consti-
> tution of their own commonwealth. They live in their
> own countries, but only as aliens. They have a share in
> everything as citizens, and endure everything as for-
> eigners. Every foreign land is their fatherland, and yet
> for them every fatherland is a foreign land. . . . To put
> it simply: What the soul is in the body, that Christians
> are in the world.
> —*Epistle to Diognetus (second or third century A.D.)*[1]

Christians have had to deal with politics from the very beginning.
One could not characterize the New Testament as a political document, and yet its deep relevance to political thought has affected all
subsequent generations. At certain points, such as the thirteenth
chapter of Paul's letter to the Romans, political thoughts are voiced
explicitly ("Let every person be subject to the governing authorities;
for there is no authority except from God, and those authorities that
exist have been instituted by God" and "the authority does not bear
the sword in vain! It is the servant of God to execute wrath on the

---

[1] *Epistle to Diognetus,* in Cyril C. Richardson, ed., *Early Christian Fathers* (Philadelphia: Westminster Press, 1953), 216–19.

wrongdoer.") Often Christian political thinking has been characterized by the kind of paradox—or ambivalence—that the passage
from the *Epistle to Diognetus* illustrates. Christians are *in* the
world, but they are not altogether *of* the world. Their citizenship
transcends the earthly political order even though their responsibility before God is (somehow) to participate in that order.

Christian perspectives on how to balance the scales have varied
greatly through the centuries. They have ranged from near-absolute
withdrawal from the fallen, sinful world to uncritical endorsement
of the civil communities in which Christians have found themselves.
Some earlier Christian thought seems to us now to be hopelessly
simple, even naive. Much, on the other hand, is highly sophisticated, even profound. The story of Christian political thought is long
and complicated. It is much too long, really, to explore in a volume
whose purposes are not primarily historical.[2] Nevertheless, a few
observations about the historical legacy can help make the point
that present-day generating centers of Christian political thought
did not spring out of whole cloth.

THE EARLY CHURCH

The ambivalence of early Christian views of the state is understandable. Often persecuted during the first centuries, Christians
could not but regard much political authority as evil. (Revelation 13,
with thinly disguised symbolism, refers to it as "the beast.") On
the other hand—and possibly for that very reason—they felt it
important to impress the governing authorities with their law-
abidingness. Why persecute *us?* Are we not, of all people, the ones
whom the state has least to fear? The second-century pagan writer
Celsus had accused the Christians of being irresponsible in their political views. If all behaved like the Christians, Celsus had charged,
the ever-threatening barbarians would overrun the empire and the
emperor would be bereft of all support. In reply, one of the earliest
of the great Christian theologians, Origen (ca. 182–ca. 251), argued

---

[2]I have explored this historical terrain more fully in J. Philip Wogaman, *Christian
Ethics: A Historical Introduction* (Louisville, Ky.: Westminster John Knox Press, 1993).
Even that book, or any other history of two thousand years of Christian thought, must be
highly selective. See also J. Philip Wogaman and Douglas M. Strong, eds., *Readings in
Christian Ethics: A Historical Sourcebook* (Louisville, Ky.: Westminster John Knox Press,
1996).

that if all should do as the Christians, all would be law-abiding and the emperor would have nothing to fear:

> For if, in the words of Celsus, "they do as I do," then it is evident that even the barbarians, when they yield obedience to the word of God, will become most obedient to the law, and most humane; and (the religion of Christ) will one day triumph, as its principles take possession of the minds of men more and more every day.... [I]f all the Romans ... embrace the Christian faith, they will, when they pray, overcome their enemies; or rather, they will not war at all, being guarded by that divine power which promised to save five entire cities for the sake of fifty just persons.[3]

The pacifist assumptions behind this writing (Celsus had explicitly criticized the Christians for refusing to bear arms) were even more evident in some of the earlier Christian writings. Thus, Justin writes in the second century that "we who once killed each other not only do not make war on each other, but in order not to lie or deceive our inquisitors we gladly die for the confession of Christ"[4] and "we who were filled with war, and mutual slaughter, and every wickedness, have each through the whole earth changed our warlike weapons—our swords into ploughshares, and our spears into implements of tillage."[5] Still, the paradox remained. While eschewing war and violence, at least for the most part, early Christians did not generally question the legitimacy of the state as an expression of God's purposes on earth. While having no political role to play, these Christians often supported those who did with their prayers and their obedience. The little prayer of *1 Clement* voiced that around A.D. 96.

> You, Master, gave them imperial power through your majestic and indescribable might, so that we, recognizing it was you who gave them the glory and honor, might submit to them, and in no way oppose your will. Grant them, Lord, health, peace, harmony, and stability, so that they may give no offense in administering the government you have given

---

[3]Origen, *Against Celsus,* in Alexander Roberts and James Donaldson, eds., *The Ante-Nicene Fathers: Translations of the Writings of the Fathers down to A.D. 325,* vol. 4 (New York: Charles Scribner's Sons, 1926 [1885]), book 8, chapters 68 and 70.

[4]Justin, First Apology, in Richardson, *Early Christian Fathers,* 39.

[5]Justin, *Dialogue with Trypho* CX, in *The Ante-Nicene Fathers,* vol. 1, p. 254.

them. For it is you, Master, the heavenly "King of eternity," who give the sons of men glory and honor and authority over the earth's people.[6]

In view of the persecutions suffered by Christians during that period, that is a surprisingly positive statement about the legitimacy of the state. But we also notice here the implication that judgments can be made about how political power is exercised. The prayer is "that they may give no offense in administering the government."

The great watershed, so far as Christian relationship to the state is concerned, occurred with the rise to power of Constantine in A.D. 313. The first Christian emperor absolutely reversed the political status of Christians. Previously they had been at best tolerated and at worst persecuted. Now they were favored. That shows in most subsequent Christian thought about the state. Theologians such as Lactantius, Ambrose of Milan, Augustine, and the Cappadocians represented "establishment" thinking. It may not have been as much a shift in the acceptance of the legitimacy of the state, even in its exercise of police powers, as is sometimes asserted. After all, even the earliest writers spoke of those in power as being ordained by God. But the accountability of power to God could be asserted and examined more directly.

The greatest of the early theologians was certainly Augustine (A.D. 354–430). His most important political writing, *The City of God,* was prompted by the Gothic invasion of Rome in 410 and the charge that Rome had become vulnerable because it had become Christian. Augustine asserted that the seeds of Rome's weakness had always been present in its self-centeredness. The city of earth, exemplified by Rome, is made up of those who love themselves first—even to the point of being contemptuous of God. The city of God, on the other hand, is made up of those who love God—even to the point of being contemptuous of themselves. The two cities are forever intertwined, but also forever at odds. The state can hold within it people who are really citizens of the city of God, but the reverse is also true. The church, as the best exemplification on earth of the city of God, also has elements within it of the city of earth. Implicitly, the task of the state is to hold the disintegrative tendencies of the city of earth in check so the gracious work of God among humankind can proceed.

The earthly city, expressed in political terms, can even be seen as

---

[6] *1 Clement,* in Richardson, *Early Christian Fathers,* 72.

a positive good when it is not simply a vehicle for selfishness. Augustine puts it this way:

> For the things which this city desires cannot justly be said to be evil, for it is itself, in its own kind, better than all other human good. For it desires earthly peace for the sake of enjoying earthly goods, and it makes war in order to attain this peace; since, if it has conquered, and there remains no one to resist it, it enjoys a peace which it had not while there were opposing parties. . . . These things, then, are good things, and without doubt the gifts of God. But if they neglect the better things of the heavenly city, which are secured by eternal victory and peace never-ending, and so inordinately covet these present good things that they believe them to be the only desirable things, or love them better that those things which are believed to be better—if this be so, then it is necessary that misery follow and ever increase.[7]

Augustine's high conception of the church laid the foundation for a thousand years of Christian thinking about its central role as channel of God's grace to humanity. His realism concerning the state marked a clear departure from earlier pacifist tendencies. His was the first articulation of a doctrine of "just war," a conception of war that accepted its legitimacy as a sometime necessary evil while circumscribing its actual exercise with the conditions under which a Christian could approve it. He also helped set the stage for the ongoing struggle over questions of church-state relations.

CHRISTIAN POLITICAL THOUGHT
IN THE MIDDLE CENTURIES

People today pay scant attention to what happened between the breakup of the ancient Roman Empire and the beginnings of modernity. More than a thousand years elapsed between the time of Augustine and the vast transformations associated with the Renaissance, the Reformation, the era of exploration and discovery, the Enlightenment, and the Industrial Revolution. That millennium of time witnessed important developments in Christian political

---

[7]Augustine, *The City of God,* in Philip Schaff, ed., *A Select Library of the Nicene and Post-Nicene Fathers of the Christian Church,* vol. 2 (Buffalo, N.Y.: Christian Literature Co., 1887), 405.

thought.[8] Part of it was in the easy accommodation of Christian ethics to the feudalistic patterns that emerged after the disintegration of the empire. Western Europe had broken into a large number of territorial states—if they could be called that—each governed hierarchically. The parallel authority structures of church and state gave rise, in time, to tensions and the need to articulate the relationship between sacred and secular in public life.

Neither political institutions nor political thought could in any sense have been described as democratic. And yet it is interesting that the theory of popular sovereignty retained some force as a holdover of Roman law (which had made something of the notion that even the emperors governed by the implied consent of the people).

The high water mark of medieval political thought was in the work of the thirteenth-century theologian and philosopher, Thomas Aquinas. Thomas's achievement was made possible by the emergence of universities and, especially, by the recovery of the writings of Aristotle. Much of Aristotle's political thought was appropriated directly by Thomas, though Thomas put a theological stamp on all of it. Like Aristotle, Thomas analyzed the state (and all other human institutions) in terms of its fundamental purpose or end. The state, like the church, is a "perfect society" in that it possesses within itself the means necessary to the achievement of its ends. The ends of the state are temporal. They include the maintenance of peace and justice, through the restraint of evil-doing:

> Since some are found to be dissolute and prone to vice and not easily amenable to words, it was necessary for such to be restrained from evil by force and fear, in order that, at least, they might desist from evil-doing, and leave others in peace, and that they themselves, by being habituated in this way, might be brought to do willingly what hitherto they did from fear, and thus become virtuous.[9]

Thomas's view of the state is not, however, restricted to its negative purposes in the restraint of evil. It also includes actions for the

---

[8]Among the classic studies of political thought during this long period see R. W. and A. J. Carlyle, *A History of Mediaeval Political Theory in the West,* 6 vols. (Edinburgh and London: W. Blackwood and Sons, 1903–36), Ernst Troeltsch, *The Social Teaching of the Christian Churches,* 2 vols. (Louisville, Ky.: Westminster John Knox Press, 1992), and George H. Sabine, *A History of Political Theory,* 3d ed. (New York: Holt, Rinehart & Winston, 1961).

[9]Thomas Aquinas, *Summa Theologica,* ed. Anton C. Pegis, vol. 1 (New York: Random House, 1945), Q. 95. Art. 1.

sake of the common good of the people. His conception of law holds the state accountable for its special enactments to the natural law that ultimately reflects the mind of God. Natural law may be discerned by the human mind (even such a totally non-Christian mind as that of Aristotle), but since the mind is often clouded by sin, we can better understand natural law through the revelation of divine law. The latter leads toward eternal salvation. While the end of the state is not salvation, *per se,* the civil laws adopted and enforced by the state are taken to support the mission of the church, which is salvation.

Thomas refined the earlier Augustinian formulation of the just war. Especially noteworthy is his principle of double effect. Actions that are intrinsically evil (such as the killing of innocent people in war) may be permissible if they are the unintended but necessary consequence of actions that are morally justified (such as the defense of the city against aggression). Under such circumstances, the action must be judged by a rule of proportion: the evil tolerated must be proportionate to the good intended.

Thomistic thought was destined to dominate Roman Catholic political thought down to and well into the twentieth century. Meanwhile, the authoritarian aspects of Thomas's thought were beginning to be questioned. The conciliar movement of the late fourteenth and early fifteenth centuries represented an effort to democratize the church. The movement collapsed after a few decades, but seeds had been planted with implications that extended beyond the church into the political realm. The conciliar movement's emphasis upon the whole body of the church as the location of the church's authority—and the accountability of pope and hierarchy to the whole church—was anticipated by the political and ecclesial thought of Marsilius of Padua (ca. 1280–1343). Marsilius understood state sovereignty to be the possession of the whole people (and church sovereignty in the whole body of the faithful). He wrote that the legislator "is the people or the whole body of citizens, or the weightier part thereof, through its election or will expressed by words in the general assembly of the citizens."[10] While Marsilius did not have a decisive influence on his own times, his writing is a useful reminder of two things. First, the old Stoic-Roman conception of popular sovereignty was still lurking under the surface of Western thinking about the state, never totally eclipsed. Second, the flowering of

---

[10]Marsilius of Padua, *The Defender of Peace,* ed. and trans. Alan Gewirth, vol. 2 (New York: Columbia University Press, 1956), Discourse 1, chapter 13, part 3.

democratic thought in the Enlightenment and in the modern world did not spring out of whole cloth.

Christian political thought through the middle centuries was certainly not dominated by pacifism. Amidst the violence of warring principalities, crusades against the infidels, and the repression of heretics, even the disciplines of just war doctrine must have appeared unduly restraining to some. And yet the pacifist motif in much early Christian thought was not entirely eclipsed either. One thinks especially of the saintly Francis of Assisi, who renounced worldly possessions for himself and the order he founded and went about doing good and reconciling people in conflict. Among the many stories about him, we are especially impressed by his efforts to reconcile crusading Christians and Muslims during his lifetime. While the Franciscans and other charitable monastic orders did not contribute greatly to the stream of political thought, they are a reminder that all such thought, for Christians, must be set somehow in a context of loving service.

A further stream of experience and thought is worth noting. There emerged, during the middle centuries, a body of moral thinking based upon the confessional. This was not without political consequences. The church, as custodian of the sacraments, was understood to have the formal power of extending or withholding the means of grace that are necessary to salvation. Among believers, this was a source of immense power. If salvation of one's soul is everything, then loss of access to the necessary sacraments is to be avoided at all cost. If, as we noted in chapter 2, anything that influences the will is potentially political, then the church's ability to give or withhold the sacraments could be—and sometimes was—politicized. A whole nation could be—and on a handful of occasions was—interdicted, with all of its subjects formally denied the sacraments. That was, to say the least, persuasive to rulers whose subjects suddenly had the strongest possible motive to remove them from power! During the middle centuries confessional manuals of discipline were developed, with instructions to the priest hearing confessions. Such and such a sin warranted such and such a penance. Mostly this had to do with highly personal sins. But the same principle could be, and sometimes was, invoked on a very large political stage. Here, for example, was the Holy Roman Emperor, King Henry IV, excommunicated by Pope Gregory VII in 1076 and forced to stand barefoot in the snow before the Castle of Canossa where the pope had taken refuge in order to receive the pope's absolution. Similarly, in the thirteenth century, Pope Innocent III forced the notorious King

John of England to submit in a dispute over control of key ecclesial posts and church property.

TOWARD MODERNITY

Five or six centuries ago, vast social and cultural changes began to sweep across the Western world with great consequences for Christian political thought. Exploration and discovery turned an insular Europe into but a part of a global environment. Cultural renaissance produced explosive new developments in art and literature. Scientific stirrings, based partly on late medieval philosophical developments, were to change settled views of the natural world. The Protestant Reformation broke apart the medieval synthesis of church and society.

The Reformation impacted Christian political thought in a variety of ways. Martin Luther (1483–1546) did not challenge accepted hierarchical conceptions of political authority—at least not much. But his view of the dignity of secular callings had implications for public service and, even more important, his doctrine of the two realms gave new emphasis to the old Augustinian idea of the two cities. To Luther, the secular realm, while it can be a proper "calling" for a Christian ruler, cannot be based simply upon the gospel of love. We live in a sinful world, from which sin will never be entirely eradicated. Therefore it will always be necessary for the state to use the power of the sword to restrain evil. "First take heed and fill the world with real Christians before ruling it in a Christian and evangelical manner," he wrote. "This you will never accomplish; for the world and the masses are and always will be un-Christian, although they are all baptized and are nominally Christian."[11] Thus, he writes, "these two kingdoms must be sharply distinguished and both be permitted to remain; the one to produce piety, the other to bring about external peace and prevent evil deeds; neither is sufficient in the world without the other."[12]

John Calvin (1509–1564) likewise emphasized the distinction between the secular realm of power and the spiritual realm of grace, although his conception of the glory and sovereignty of God was to have more radical implications for the social order. To Calvin, the

---

[11]Martin Luther, "Secular Authority: To What Extent It Should Be Obeyed," in *Works of Martin Luther,* vol. 3 (Philadelphia: A. J. Holman Co. and Castle Press, 1930), 237.
[12]Ibid.

task of Christians is to seek out and perform the will of God, and that can push us beyond our inherited place in the social order. Calvin did not invent democracy or capitalism (mistaken interpretations of Max Weber's thesis in *The Protestant Ethic and the Spirit of Capitalism* to the contrary notwithstanding). But the implication of God's sovereignty is that no human sovereignty is above criticism and that anyone is at least potentially able to discern God's will, regardless of their formal station in life. Calvin did not speak in such terms, but his thought contained the possibilities. Not surprisingly, modern democracy flourished first in countries most influenced by Calvinism: Switzerland, Scotland, England, North America.

Calvin was quite explicit in his insistence that government is a positive good. He disputed those who "consider the whole nature of government a thing polluted, which has nothing to do with Christian men."

> That is what, indeed, certain fanatics who delight in unbridled license shout and boast: after we have died through Christ to the elements of this world, are transported to God's Kingdom, and sit among heavenly beings, it is a thing unworthy of us and set far beneath our excellence to be occupied with those vile and worldly cares which have to do with business foreign to a Christian man. . . . But as we have just now pointed out that this kind of government is distinct from that spiritual and inward Kingdom of Christ, so we must know that they are not at variance.[13]

Civil government, he argued, "has as its appointed end, so long as we live among men, to cherish and protect the outward worship of God, to defend sound doctrine of piety and the position of the church, to adjust our life to the society of men, to form our social behavior to civil righteousness, to reconcile us with one another, and to promote general peace and tranquillity."[14]

Luther and Calvin both took actions that are an embarrassment to contemporary Christians: Luther with his diatribe against the peasants, Calvin with his complicity in the burning of Michael Servetus as a heretic. Each, however, helped open the floodgates of

---

[13]John Calvin, *Institutes of the Christian Religion,* ed. John J. McNeill, The Library of Christian Classics, vol. 20 (Philadelphia: Westminster Press, 1960), Book 4, chapter 20, p. 2.

[14]Ibid.

reform that were destined, in time, to transform Christian thinking about the state.

Democratic thought began to reassert itself during the Enlightenment in the "contract" writings of Thomas Hobbes, John Locke, Jean Jacques Rousseau, and the many thinkers and movements inspired by their views. Each was influenced to some extent by Christian ideas, Locke probably more than the others. Hobbes's pessimistic account of human nature may owe something to the Christian doctrine of original sin as well as his own observations. Locke's thought has grounding in the ancient Stoic tradition, preserved, as we have noted, even in the Middle Ages. It is worth noting that Locke's *First Treatise of Civil Government* was almost entirely a biblically based refutation, festooned throughout with scriptural "proof-texts," of the then-current notion of the divine right of kings.

The gathering impetus toward respect for human rights, including even the challenging of long-accepted institutions of slavery and subordination of women, was furthered by the "left wing" of the Reformation, which included the English "Diggers" and "Levellers" as well as the Quakers.[15] Such Christian movements emphasized the radical equality of all persons, often grounding their thinking in a direct reappropriation of the teachings of Jesus. The religious revivals associated with the Wesleyans in eighteenth-century England and evangelicals such as Charles Grandison Finney in nineteenth-century America had a profoundly democratizing effect even when not dealing explicitly with political questions. John Wesley himself, ironically, supported the British cause in the American Revolution. But the true implications of Wesleyanism may have been expressed more authentically by the American Methodists who distanced themselves from British Methodism during that period in order not to be understood as opposing American independence. Both British and American Methodists of that era declared themselves against slavery, the British by challenging the slave trade, the Americans by insisting that members of the newly created Methodist Episcopal Church could not be slaveholders.

The Quakers probably offered the most consistent opposition to slavery, and Finney, the famous evangelist, the most articulate witness. As early as 1835, Finney asserted that "one of the reasons for the low state of religion at the present time is that many Churches

---

[15]I have discussed these movements in *Christian Ethics: A Historical Introduction*, especially in chapters 12 and 15.

have taken the wrong side on the subject of slavery, have suffered prejudice to prevail over principle, and have feared to call this abomination by its true name."[16] It took the churches longer to recognize the full equality of women, but even at the beginning of the feminist movement in nineteenth-century America, the principal leaders often explored the issues biblically and theologically.

TWENTIETH-CENTURY
CHRISTIAN POLITICAL THOUGHT

The twentieth century witnessed the rise of very specific theological analysis of political life, paralleling statements and actions taken by church bodies of all sorts. In subsequent chapters of this book, I will make reference to much of this, but we can conclude the present chapter by mentioning some of the highlights.

As the century began, Roman Catholic teaching had begun to explore modern political and economic developments more directly with a series of papal encyclicals beginning with *Rerum Novarum* of Pope Leo XIII (1891) and including *Quadragisimo Anno* of Pope Pius XI (1931), *Mater et Magistra* (1961) and *Pacem in Terris* (1963) of Pope John XXIII, and the many encyclicals of Pope Paul VI and Pope John Paul II toward the century's end. Along the way, the Second Vatican Council (1962–1965) expressed a sea change in Catholic thinking about church-state relations, religious liberty, and issues of political participation in the modern world. The effect of this century of Catholic teaching was to move the church from a more reactive fear of democracy toward deep affirmations of human rights.

Among Protestants, the beginning of the century had seen the social gospel movement shift from the periphery to the center of Christian thinking. Figures such as Washington Gladden and Walter Rauschenbusch applied the gospel in fresh ways to the economic consequences of the Industrial Revolution, emphasizing the rights of workers and the responsibility of society to care for the poor. Eclipsed for a time by World War I, that movement reasserted itself in different forms during the 1930s and 1960s. Meanwhile the churches, both as individual denominations and through the expanding ecumenical movement, issued declarations on the major

---

[16]Charles Grandison Finney, *Lectures on Revivals of Religion* (New York: Fleming H. Revell Co., 1868 [1835]), 273.

issues of the day. For instance, the Oxford Conference on Life and Work (1937) provided a clear-headed analysis of the political and economic dangers of the rising fascism and communism, along with the weaknesses and dangers of *laissez-faire* capitalism. The World Council of Churches, officially founded in 1948, provided an ongoing arena for debate and informed witness on a whole range of socio-political developments during the last half of the twentieth century.

Every era has seen its creative minds, but twentieth-century Christianity has been unusually blessed in that respect. Such thinkers as Karl Barth, Paul Tillich, Reinhold and Richard Niebuhr, Georgia Harkness, John Howard Yoder, Gustavo Gutierrez, Martin Luther King Jr., Rosemary Radford Ruether, and Bernard Haring—to name but a few and to neglect very many—have stimulated and shaped the church in the modern world. The influence of these and other Christian thinkers will be more evident in the chapters to follow.

CONCLUSION

Even so cursory a summary of the long story of Christian political thought may be sufficient to illustrate the point that this really is an enduring legacy. New problems arise and must be dealt with in fresh ways. Yet the rich spiritual and intellectual legacies of past Christian thought cannot but help us as we attempt to sort out the challenges we face at the beginning of another new millennium.

PART 2

Generating Centers
of Christian Political Thought

Introduction

Reflecting the turbulence of this era and the intrinsic importance of politics, it is not surprising that many Christian thinkers of our time in all parts of the world have written on politics. The writings are many and varied, and we cannot explore all of them here. It will be helpful, nevertheless, to introduce several of the major viewpoints as a way of sharpening the important issues. We can call the principal viewpoints "generating centers" of Christian political thought as a way of reminding ourselves that we are dealing with tendencies of thought and that each of these tendencies is currently in dynamic development. I will make no strong case for classifying particular thinkers in any of these categories, nor even for the categories themselves, since the purpose of this part of the book is not so much to classify thinkers as it is to explore issues.

Before proceeding to discuss five generating centers of contemporary Christian political thought in the following chapters, I pause to note that two such tendencies which were very important a generation or two ago have now virtually collapsed. The first of these is the traditional Roman Catholic viewpoint that the church should use the state for its own institutional enhancement and to secure cultural victories over competing religious bodies. That tendency has disintegrated in the aftermath of the Second Vatican Council and the work of such Catholic thinkers as John Courtney Murray, S.J. The traditional position, sometimes referred to as "Thesis-Hypothesis," held that the church should seek religious liberty when in minority status but that it should insist upon special privilege as the true religion when dominant. Vatican II's Declaration on Religious Liberty changed all this by grounding religious liberty, not in political opportunism, but in universal principles derived from analysis of human nature and Christian love. The point was underscored, perhaps even more deeply, by the Declaration on Non-Christian

Religions, which referred to positive values in such religions, suggesting that, one way or another, the non-Christian religions also reflect the activity of God. The theoretical work of Vatican II opened the way to widespread ecumenical contact in terms of mutual respect between Catholicism and other religious bodies all over the world, with an understanding that religious differences ought not to be resolved by invoking the power of the state. It is noteworthy that every one of the lively current viewpoints involves Catholic as well as Protestant Christian thinkers. Small shadings of difference remain to remind us of the old lines between Catholic and Protestant political thought, but they have become faint. Any Catholic thinker today, regardless of viewpoint, will find some Protestant thinkers with whom he or she is in closer agreement than with many Catholics—and vice versa. A Rip Van Winkle who were to wake up today after thirty-five years' sleep would find the contemporary scene unrecognizably different so far as the line between Catholic and Protestant political thought is concerned.

The other viewpoint that has virtually collapsed, the one more often associated with Protestant fundamentalism, holds that the church should have nothing to do with politics since the church's only proper business is the saving of individual souls. The breakdown of that position is strikingly illustrated by the emergence of such North American televangelists as Jerry Falwell and Pat Robertson and the subsequent emergence of such political movements as the Christian Coalition. Robertson's and Falwell's own positions on the political responsibility of Christians are almost indistinguishable from those of the mainline church liberals with whom they are in sharp disagreement on nearly every substantive issue. Many other evangelical Christians are, if anything, more liberal in their conception of the church's social responsibility. Evangelical Christianity is torn asunder over the issues themselves. But there are no longer many leaders urging the church to remain aloof from significant encounter with public policy questions.

Meanwhile, the political-religious scene has changed substantially even in the dozen years since the first edition of this book appeared. The virtual collapse of Marxism as a major intellectual force has occasioned shifts in the thinking of liberation theologians, a number of whom had been influenced considerably by that system of thought—although liberation theology remains an important generating center. The collapse of Marxism has had an equally important but opposite effect on neoconservatism, for that movement came into being very largely as a reaction against the influence of

Marxism. Still, neoconservatism continues to thrive on the basis of other concerns. I have found it desirable to add yet another generating center in this edition of the book—the evangelicals. While their presence was felt a dozen years ago, the evangelicals have developed into a major force in American religious and political life.

So the scene continues to shift. In part 2, I characterize five generating centers of thought on how Christians and churches ought to relate to political problems and institutions. A review of these intellectual tendencies reveals distinctive emphases, but it also demonstrates the mutual influence of widely divergent views upon one another. This part of the book, again, should not be regarded as airtight classification. There are points of overlap, there are major omissions, and not a few of the figures treated in one section could also be dealt with in one or more of the other chapters. Nevertheless, this can remind us that there really are differences of perspective and that these differences have consequences.

4

Christian Pacifist
and Anarchist Perspectives

> Every modern state is totalitarian. It recognizes no
> limit either factual or legal. This is why I maintain that
> no state in the modern world is legitimate. No present-
> day authority can claim to be instituted by God, for all
> authority is set in the framework of a totalitarian state.
> This is why I decide for anarchy.
> —*Jacques Ellul (1976)*[1]

On the face of it, there are some rather obvious conflicts between the
political order and Christian faith. One wonders, at first glance,
whether a Christian can affirm politics in any form. Jacques Ellul,
in the quotation above, questions whether there are any legitimate
states in the modern world. We may ask the broader question of
whether there is something about the state that precludes Christians from accepting it as legitimate in any era. Based on the
understanding of the state as outlined in chapter 2, some serious
problems arise.

If the state represents, in a real sense, society acting as a whole,
what are we to do when the "whole" is inconsistent with the Christian part? All acting together can mean disloyalty to God as revealed
in Jesus Christ. For what state ever conducted itself in a Christian
manner? Inevitably, in the conflicts of power with power, interest
with interest, ego with ego, compromises must be struck. The pure

---

[1]Jacques Ellul, *The Ethics of Freedom* (Grand Rapids: Wm. B. Eerdmans, 1976), 396.

ethic of the gospel is bound to be watered down as it is compromised with secular interests of the most blatantly selfish sort. This is bound to be true even if saintly Christians have control of the state. For one thing, it is difficult to maintain one's saintliness while continuing to govern; for another, the process of governing requires compromise (even parents of small children must respect that principle!).

The nub of the problem historically has been the fact that violence and coercion have been, so typically, involved in state action. We will reserve until later the question whether violence and coercion *must* be used by the state, but in any case it is difficult to think of a state which has not had recourse to such negative means of implementing its will. States go to war (self-righteous innocence being duly declared on both sides), and injury, death, and destruction are freely inflicted. States maintain police forces, and the police are authorized to use physical, sometimes even lethal, force to ensure compliance with the law. Social deviancy is punished by forcibly caging people in jails and, in extreme cases in some societies, even by putting people to death.

How can such things be reconciled with fundamental respect for the personhood of others, much less with the deeper sensitivities of Christian love? Historically, indeed, there has been a very strong current of Christian opposition to violence. In his classic study of Christian attitudes toward war, Roland Bainton records pacifism as one of the persisting views among Christian thinkers; and he, along with other students of the question, notes that early Christian social thought and practice was *typically* pacifist.[2]

The issue is joined most obviously in respect to violence and coercion. But even lesser incentives utilized by the state can also be seen as efforts to get people to do what they do not really *want* to do.[3] It is difficult to see how a state could exist without violating, in some way, the soul and body of people.

At issue here is whether the state can be legitimized by Christians. As we have seen, legitimation means the moral approval

---

[2]Roland H. Bainton, *Christian Attitudes toward War and Peace* (Nashville: Abingdon Press, 1960). See also C. J. Cadoux, *The Early Church and the World* (Naperville, Ill.: Alec R. Allenson, 1925) and Ernst Troeltsch, *The Social Teaching of the Christian Churches* (New York: Macmillan Co., 1931).

[3]The moral ambiguity of social incentives is discussed as a "dilemma of Christian civilization" in J. Philip Wogaman, *A Christian Method of Moral Judgment* (Philadelphia: Westminster Press, 1976), 189–90.

given to a political order and to the power it exercises. If that power is typically and necessarily and by definition exercised in ways that are contrary to fundamental principles of Christian ethics, then how could Christians provide it with legitimation?

The question was posed forcefully a hundred years ago by the Christian anarchist Leo Tolstoy.[4] Tolstoy understood the principle of nonresistance to evildoers (Matt. 5:39) to be the heart of the gospel of Jesus. His own moment of revelation came with the sudden conviction that Jesus really meant it—that this utter renunciation of violence and force was what Christian faith and Christian love finally mean. Tolstoy believed that the source of evil in the world is, in fact, the whole structure of violence and coercion itself. Human beings are basically good. They behave in inhuman ways when they are treated in a dehumanizing manner. If we could abolish armies and police forces and prisons, we would set the stage for a flowering of the essential goodness of humanity. Tolstoy thus thoroughly delegitimized existing state structures, and he may therefore be classified as a thoroughgoing Christian anarchist.

I know of no major Christian thinker today who could as readily be classified in that way, although we shall have to explore the extent to which the logic of positions taken by some contemporary thinkers may or may not have anarchist implications. In any case, however, there are three contemporary Christian theologians whose substantially pacifist views seem to call the basic legitimacy of the state into question. By examining the work of these thinkers we may help clarify whether a kind of pacifist-anarchist orientation may not best represent Christian teaching. (Using the terms "pacifist" and "anarchist" together we must remember two things: [1] many pacifists explicitly affirm the legitimacy and importance of the state, and [2] anarchism *can* be combined with pacifism, in which case it is not at all the violent anarchism known to popular stereotypes.)

POLITICS AS THE NEGATION
OF CHRISTIAN FREEDOM

No contemporary Christian thinker of any note can match the antipolitical rhetoric of the French lay theologian-sociologist Jacques Ellul. Taking his words simply at face value, this can be confusing,

---

[4]Leo Tolstoy, *My Religion* (New York: T. Y. Crowell, 1885), and idem, *The Kingdom of God Is within You* (New York: Farrar, Straus & Co., 1961 [1905]).

since Ellul can also be quoted in acknowledgment of the necessity of politics and (though more rarely) the contributions of politics. But with Ellul it is particularly important to probe beneath the surface.

The deeper theological current in his work is the affirmation that God, the Wholly Other, confronts us at the core of our being with the gift of freedom.[5] This gift, offered to us in Jesus Christ, is the only possibility of our liberation from the realm of necessity in which humanity is otherwise enmeshed. Most of the actual contents of contemporary culture—our cities,[6] our technology,[7] our uses of propaganda,[8] but above all our politics[9]—illustrate our bondage to the orders of necessity. Thus bound, we are not fully human. Our freedom is not a kind of ideal to be sought, still less a human attribute to be cultivated. It is a gift to our whole self to be affirmed, in faith, by our whole self. People instinctively seek freedom out of their sense of alienation and bondage, but their efforts to make their own freedom are frustrated because they do not touch the root. Indeed, human efforts to make our own freedom are much more likely to deepen the morass of bondage. It is only when our freedom has its origin in God, the Wholly Other who absolutely transcends the plane of our worldly culture, that it truly exists as freedom and not as a disguised form of necessity.

In writing of the "false presence of the kingdom," Ellul takes sharp issue with the tendency in much twentieth-century theology to treat secular history as the sphere of God's redemptive activity.[10] This false identification of the Lordship of Christ fails to see that Christ's presence in history has its own location, over against secular history. History, indeed, "has no privileged significance. It is nothing but a sort of appendage to man. Man is the important thing, not history. The latter exists because man lives, and history adds no value whatsoever to man."[11] All of the historical accomplishments of

---

[5]See especially Ellul, *Ethics of Freedom*. Ellul is obviously indebted to Karl Barth in his theological views. But Barth was never as antipolitical (nor as pacifist) as Ellul.

[6]Jacques Ellul, *The Meaning of the City* (Grand Rapids: Wm. B. Eerdmans, 1970).

[7]Jacques Ellul, *The Technological Society* (New York: Alfred A. Knopf, 1964).

[8]Jacques Ellul, *Propaganda* (New York: Alfred A. Knopf, 1965).

[9]Jacques Ellul, *The Politics of God and the Politics of Man* (Grand Rapids: Wm. B. Eerdmans, 1972); *The Political Illusion* (New York: Alfred A. Knopf, 1967); *The False Presence of the Kingdom* (New York: Seabury Press, 1972); and *Violence: Reflections from a Christian Perspective* (New York: Seabury Press, 1972).

[10]Ellul, *False Presence of the Kingdom*, 19–22.

[11]Ibid., 21.

human beings—their technology, arts, politics, and so on—ultimately add up to nothing. The real kingdom, expressed in the Lordship of Christ, is shared in by those who openly and freely acknowledge that Lordship. And it is the "receiving of the Kingdom of Heaven in faith" which "signifies the Lordship of Christ."[12] That is not at all to be confused with the historical accomplishments that Christians sometimes falsely take to be the work of the kingdom.

With this background, we are not surprised to find a volume issuing from Ellul's pen with the title, *The Political Illusion*. Above everything, contemporary politics is based on the illusion that our problems can actually be solved through politics. The tendency to politicize problems misunderstands both the problems and the real character of politics. Politics deals essentially in the accommodations of persons and groups that can be characterized as more or less equitable. When people attempt to use politics to realize values and find ultimate solutions to their problems, they rather erode the values and deepen the problems. Thus, the Marxists characteristically have failed to see that history has "developed differently from the way they had projected," and they "remain immobilized in an absolute idealism."[13] But even democrats, who believe in the possibility and reality of democratic participation in political process, are locked into illusions. For the political order is governed by the assumptions and systems of mass technological society, and even those who are elected to high office have very little effect on outcomes that matter.[14]

Despite this, Ellul holds that Christians have a considerable responsibility to participate in politics—but not as that is usually conceived. Their participation is not to use the political order to achieve Christian values or ends. It is rather to constitute a point of tension between the political order and the real life of humanity as seen and given through Jesus Christ. That is, in fact, an immensely important service to the political order—but not on its own terms. It is to constitute a perpetual, inescapable challenge to the illusions and oppressions of the political order. It is to help gain a certain space or breathing room from the suffocation of politics. In an eloquent

---

[12]Ibid., 22.
[13]Ellul, *Political Illusion,* 85.
[14]Ibid., 163–84.

passage on the reconciling presence of Christians in political life, Ellul writes that

> if Christians are to be in political life to bear witness, if this is in truth their only motive, then Christians are needed in all parties and movements. . . . Others will then look with astonishment at these odd people who instead of doing like others, i.e., hating one another for political reasons, are full of love for one another beyond these secondary barriers.[15]

This "only motive" for Christians being involved in political life may be a theologically convincing one. But it is one that bears scarcely at all upon the actual substance of politics. Instead, it is hardly distinguishable from other forms of witnessing to the faith. It is a way of demonstrating through one's life and one's relationships that one is "free in Christ," that one is free to love others without ulterior motive, that one is free of illusions, that one is free from the need to prove something to oneself about the significance of one's life. That kind of witnessing is a proclamation of the gospel.

But where does this leave politics *as such?*

Ellul is not altogether negative about politics as such. He does acknowledge certain values of a practical, rational sort to be realized through the state: "We have to work hard to get it admitted, by ourselves first of all, that politics is an honest concrete exercise in administration or management but that it has no spiritual, ideological, or doctrinal content. . . . Realism, by helping us to see politics in its actuality, demystifies it."[16] Presumably there is a certain need in human affairs for such an "honest concrete exercise." Moreover, Ellul has acknowledged that freedom—in many ways his central ethical category—cannot remain disembodied. It "cannot remain inward and spiritual." It must "find incarnation as it affirms itself in a political, economic, or social setting."[17] So the question whether freedom is to "find incarnation" also has a political dimension; whether people are to experience freedom is also, to some extent, at stake in the political process—even though that is best *gained* in the political process through the over againstness of Christians whose assertions of freedom place limits upon the overreaching tendencies of the state.

And further, Ellul acknowledges that even "the opponent of an

---

[15]Ellul, *Ethics of Freedom,* 379–80.
[16]Ibid., 382.
[17]Ibid., 399.

existing government is himself in a sense part of the system."[18] To some extent, Ellul may here be recognizing the point raised in chapter 2 about all of us having to act as the state acts, whether we like it or not. But his larger point is, I think, a reiteration of his general theme that when we act in accordance with the structures of necessity—even to oppose them—we are committed to that level of living. Which is to say that we, too, are enmeshed in the structures of necessity. By bearing our witness over against the state we may rather be asserting our freedom—and that is not the same thing as doing what the state is doing.

I do not believe we should make much of these small caveats. In the main, Ellul has mounted a powerful theological critique of the state as such. His affirmation of anarchism, voiced in the quotation at the head of this chapter, is quite explicit. In part, it is a prudential judgment based upon his reading of the totalitarian realities of the state in this era. And yet, as he characterizes politics in our era it is hard to escape the conclusion that his indictment could apply to the state in almost any era. For even though the state has peculiar new instruments of oppression at its disposal in our time, and even though modern ideologies are better suited to totalitarianism than the political thought of some previous eras, it is still true that the state has characteristically represented something other than the realm of freedom. When has the state not been the summary of the power interests of society? When have those interests not reflected fallen humanity rather than redeemed humanity?

That point is perhaps clearest in Ellul's strong theological rejection of violence.[19] While "realistic appraisal shows that violence is inevitable in all societies, whatever their form,"[20] this inevitability is because violence belongs to the order of necessity. It has no part in Christian freedom. The freedom we have in Christ is also freedom from the necessity of violence, and when we engage in violence we cannot do so as an expression of that freedom we have in Christ. Ellul acknowledges that in this, as in other aspects of life, our freedom is imperfect and Christians do engage in violence. But when we do so we must realize that we have "fallen back into the realm of necessity," and that we are no longer the free beings whom "God wills

---

[18]Ibid., 386.
[19]See especially Ellul, Violence.
[20]Ibid., 93.

and redeemed at great cost."[21] Indeed, the mark of our essential humanity—that which differentiates us radically "from all other animals"—is our being under the commandment "Thou shalt not kill."[22] When we abandon this (as often we do), we are abandoning our true freedom and our authentic humanity.

Nor can we, by engaging in violence, ever hope to be more "effective." Indeed, when Christians are "effective," as the world understands the word, "this only implies that society has absorbed our action and is using it to its own ends and for its own profit."[23] Our actions only confirm the structures of necessity by which the world is bound.

We must note carefully that Ellul is not asking the world, or even Christians, to abandon violence because he considers violence to be immoral. Violence is not something we can, in any simple way, *choose* to avoid. It is something, rather, from which we have to be *liberated*. It is a state of being, the typical human state of being apart from liberation in Jesus Christ. Indeed, apart from Christian freedom and the whole faith perspective that implies, it makes no sense to speak of nonviolence. Nor does Ellul, therefore, speak of tactical advantages of nonviolent action (in, say, the Gandhian mode). For this, too, apart from Christian freedom would also belong to the order of necessity and would not ultimately alter the violence of the world.

Still, on the purely prudential level, Ellul does speak of the utter *futility* of violence. In a series of five laws of violence, Ellul argues that violence cannot, finally, accomplish any good thing: First, "once you start using violence, you cannot get away from it"; second, "violence creates, begets and procreates violence"; third, "it is impossible to distinguish between justified and unjustified violence, between violence that liberates and violence that enslaves. . . . Every violence is identical with every other violence"; fourth, "violence begets violence—*nothing else*"; and fifth, "the man who uses violence always tries to justify both it and himself."[24] These laws of violence, which Ellul offers essentially without qualification, mean that even though violence is inevitable (as a part of the realm of necessity), it cannot under any circumstances accomplish any good or represent the will of God.

Again, Ellul does not wish to moralize about violence, still less to

---

[21]Ibid., 137.
[22]Ibid., 146.
[23]Ellul, *Politics of God and the Politics of Man,* 140.
[24]Ellul, *Violence,* 93–108.

condemn people, even Christians, who engage in it. He compares the "order of violence" in the world to laws of gravitation, remarking that "there is no sense in asking whether gravitation is a good thing or a bad one."[25] But seen from the perspective of Christian freedom, and in the light of cold realism as well, violence is stripped of every possible justification.

But is it possible to have a politics without violence? We shall have to return to this question in relation to other Christian thinkers, for it is crucial to know whether the total repudiation of violence necessarily implies the total renunciation of politics as well. There may be enough ambiguities and paradoxes in Ellul's thought to render a clear answer to the question difficult. But he does not himself shrink from the conclusion that his overall view is anarchist. In his book on violence he declares flatly, "It is impossible to be a Christian and at the same time to conduct a successful politics, which necessarily requires the use of some kind of violence."[26] That does not mean, necessarily, that a Christian could not engage in politics for other kinds of reasons (other than "to conduct a successful politics")—such as to be a witness over against the oppressive pretensions of the state or to manifest the life of love among those who are engaged in politics.

But still, Ellul has called the state into serious question. Paradoxically, he has recognized its necessity but not its legitimacy. Christians must relate to it in some sense, of course—just as they must relate to other aspects of the fallen world, the realms of necessity by which unredeemed humanity is bound. But that is far from providing theological legitimation for the political enterprise as such, still less for seeking to reform the state for purposes derived from Christian insight. The struggle to determine what the state will do (which is what we all will do, acting together by necessity if not by choice) is not, cannot be, a struggle for Christians acting as Christians. I think Ellul might accept the definition of the state outlined in chapter 2 (society acting as a whole), but that very understanding of the state would reinforce his contention that the political order belongs to the realm of necessity, not of freedom. To be Christian is to witness against the pretensions of society "acting as a whole," not to confirm the legitimacy of such actions by helping to define their ends.

---

[25]Ibid., 91.
[26]Ibid., 160.

Is Ellul's perspective the right one for Christians? His understanding of the importance of Christian freedom has deep theological roots; he has elaborated this with greater richness and nuance than we have had space to recognize here. His portrayal of the structures of necessity likewise strikes a responsive chord, as does his characterization of the totalitarian tendencies of the modern state. His grasp of the prima facie theological problem posed by violence is also compelling. I am, moreover, struck by his unwillingness to take shortcuts in finding ways to avoid all this. He has few illusions about the natural perfectibility of human beings, and he therefore does not encourage us to suppose that human goodness will blossom forth if we but remove the impediments of violence and politics. His brand of anarchism, if it be that, is thus far removed from that of a Tolstoy or that of the Marxist classless society (with its new socialist humanity). In that, Ellul is a Christian realist. He is also a realist in challenging illusions about the positive effects of violence. Violence is evil. And Ellul joins a host of Christian thinkers throughout history who have refused to treat it as a good thing.

But I remain troubled by two key points in his discussion. First, it does not seem to me that Christian freedom—important as it is—constitutes the one, all-inclusive reality by which Christian ethics is framed. When reduced to this, theology has sometimes had a tendency toward overspiritualization (which in theological terms entails a tendency toward docetism). But theology must also speak of the importance of the doctrine of creation and understand that it matters very much whether the purposes of God in the act of creation are realized or frustrated. Whether people are adequately fed, clothed, cared-for medically, given concrete opportunities to develop their natural capacities, and so on, is not a purely neutral or simply practical question. Granted, we do not live by bread alone and we cannot, by means of bread and clothing and shelter, usher in the kingdom of God. But the lack of such physical necessities of life can still frustrate the intentions of that kingdom. The point is that the question of the adequacy of material resources to sustain human life—and the related question of the suitability of institutional structures to the created purposes of human life—is indeed susceptible to political action. What is actually *done* politically bears upon the concrete possibilities of life in this world. It is a pretension—Ellul is right about this—to treat the political order as an order of salvation. But has he seen clearly enough how the political order can serve or frustrate the concrete realization of salvation in this physical, though fallen, world?

Having raised this question on the theological level, we must also ask whether Ellul is right in his categorical denial that any good thing can be accomplished through violence. To be sure, Christians must agree that violence, per se, is evil. But the issue often confronts Christians not as a question of good versus evil but of greater versus lesser forms of evil. The five "laws of violence" do, it seems to me, point to characteristic truths about violence. Violence does, usually, create vicious circles entailing use of more and more violence. Violence does beget more and more violence—usually. Violence usually does enslave; and when we use it we do invite our adversaries to use it too. These observations hold with sufficient frequency to give every Christian pause. But it is a question, still, whether violence always and of necessity has such results, or whether this is only usually the case. Is Ellul right in asserting that "violence begets violence—*nothing else?*"[27]

When this question is posed as a practical and not a dogmatic one, we are invited to think of instances when violence may, in balance, have done more good than harm—or when a refusal to resort to violence has done more harm than good. Clearly many wars have only contributed to further cycles of repression and violence. But would one argue, in balance, that the military struggle against Hitler did *nothing* more than beget more violence? Or that all of the revolutions of recorded history have yielded *only* further repression? Or that the uses of coercion by police forces have *always* contributed only to further repression or crime? Or that in situations such as Rwanda, Burundi, Sierra Leone, Liberia, and the Balkans (all in the 1990s), when the international community either did not intervene or were very tardy in doing so, less harm was caused by the inaction than would have been by more timely intervention?

History does not disclose its alternatives, and it is possible to answer such questions dogmatically only because we can never know for sure whether we were right or wrong. But before accepting Ellul's laws of violence as absolutes, we should think long thoughts about the possible effects of our being wrong. Countless lives may depend upon it.

THE POLITICS OF JESUS

Still, the theological problem of violence and its relationship to the state can be explored from other angles. One very important one in our time is certainly John Howard Yoder's "politics of Jesus."

---

[27]Ibid., 100.

Yoder's position, elaborated in his book by that name,[28] is based on his view that

1. Jesus utterly renounced the way of violence,
2. the *way* in which Jesus renounced violence was politically relevant,
3. Jesus' political relevance was in fact the reason for his crucifixion,
4. through the resurrection, God has affirmed the messianic status of Jesus, and that Jesus' way should be our way,
5. we must not temporize in our obedience to God's will, as shown in Jesus Christ, not even to be more "effective," because
6. it is not our responsibility as Christians to manage the course of history—that is God's place—and
7. if we are faithful to the will of God, as demonstrated in the life, death, and resurrection of Jesus, we will by that token be relevant politically, and
8. the triumph of God's justice and righteousness can be trusted to come in God's own time.

Specifically, therefore, we are not to use the methods of violence as shortcuts to guarantee the triumph of righteousness in human affairs. Violence has been shown, in the life of Jesus, confirmed by God through the resurrection, to be contrary to the kingdom—it cannot be the basis on which the kingdom is to be built.

Is this perspective sectarian or quietistic? Yoder strenuously maintains that it is not. It is, in fact, deeply and directly *engaged*. Yoder insists that Christians must be deeply involved in the struggle for justice and that his position is not to be mistaken for sectarianism.[29] Jesus did not attempt to manage history; but Jesus was deeply relevant to politics. The political and religious authorities would not have found it necessary to execute Jesus if he had not been a threat to their own political agendas. So, somehow Jesus' way, nonviolence and all, had profoundly political effects. So, also, subsequent Christians can be effective politically by following Jesus' way. But if, instead, Christians abandon that way by opting for violent shortcuts, they can hardly be said to be advancing the real purposes of God.

---

[28]John H. Yoder, *The Politics of Jesus* (Grand Rapids: Wm. B. Eerdmans, 1972).

[29]Thus Yoder rejects what he considers to be the false dichotomy between "church" and "sect" types developed by Ernst Troeltsch and many later Christian ethicists.

Yoder's development of Christian pacifism is an especially powerful one, in part because he (like Ellul) does not base it on illusions about the innate goodness of human nature or the inevitable effectiveness of nonviolent methods in the short run and in part because he (perhaps unlike Ellul) accepts the importance of being relevant to the political process.

Does Yoder ultimately question the legitimacy of the state, as Ellul seems to do? It does not seem to be his intention to do so.[30] In an earlier work, he writes appreciatively of the ordering function of the state on the basis of New Testament texts such as Romans 13 and 1 Peter 2.[31] And in that work he affirms a positive Christian responsibility to witness to the state. In a discussion of the concept of legitimacy, he notes the limitations of traditional views (for example, in that they overlook that we often must submit to more than one political authority at a time).[32] Nevertheless, he strongly affirms our responsibility to be subject to political authority: "It is the powers that *be* to which we ought to be subjected under God for the sake of conscience."[33] Clearly Yoder here affirms that political authority has a certain moral standing, binding upon the conscience of Christians. Moreover, the attempt to influence that authority to act in certain ways, and not in others, implies the legitimacy of the authority itself and the moral superiority of some political alternatives to others: "No tyrant can be so low on the scale of righteousness that the Christian could not appeal to him to do at least a little better; no 'Christianized' society can be so transformed as not to need constant criticism."[34]

But this remains a severely qualified concept of legitimacy. It is all somewhere below a truly Christian level of being and doing. The following quotation suggests that the legitimacy of the state exists only as a concession to the inevitability of evil:

> In the relevant alternatives which we hold before men of state to give body to our critique, none will be good in the Christian sense; they will only be less evil. The term

---

[30]In personal correspondence, for which I am especially grateful, he has disavowed such an interpretation of his position.

[31]John H. Yoder, *The Christian Witness to the State* (Newton, Kan.: Faith and Life Press, 1964), 36.

[32]Ibid., 43–44.

[33]Ibid., 43.

[34]Ibid., 59.

> *legitimate* expresses this kind of qualified acquiescence according to the less wrong. When, for instance, we say . . . that police activity is legitimate and war is illegitimate, even for nations *legitimate* does not mean right and good; it points rather to the minimal level of wrong (i.e., of disconformity to Christ, our only standard of right and good) which is the best we can expect under the circumstances.[35]

While a more positive conception of political legitimacy might accompany the more positive functions of state (such as "coordinating social cooperation"), Yoder is clear that the nub of the political question is what kind of sanctions are to be employed to assure cooperation.[36] If those sanctions entail the state's use of the "sword," then it is clear that something less than a Christian understanding of right and good is involved.

The point is that even the positive functions of state—its welfare role, its sponsorship of education, its creation of facilities for recreation and the arts, its construction of highways, its provisions of fire protection and agricultural services and support to economic and social ventures of all sorts—depend, almost inevitably, upon the ability of government to raise money through taxation. And taxation, finally, means that people are *compelled* to pay. The whole police power of the state stands behind the tax collector! Taxes are not to be understood as suggested guidelines for voluntary contributions to public causes! Since that is the case, Yoder has effectively qualified the moral legitimacy of even the positive features of government. "The Christian," he writes, "is called not to *obey* the state, which would imply actually receiving from the state his moral guidance, but to *be subject,* which means simply that he shall not rebel or seek to act as if the state were not there."[37] His or her submission to the state may be in the form of obedience (if he or she can approve what the state asks) or in a disobedience that accepts punishment (if the state's demand is in conflict with obedience to Christ).

Another way to ask the question of legitimacy is to ask whether a Christian could faithfully serve as an officer of the state. Yoder has no problems with Christians serving as schoolteachers, forestry workers, and so on—or even with Christians serving in the legislative branch of government. He does not finally exclude even the police-type activities, but in his discussion of this it is clear that he has severe reser-

---

[35]Ibid.
[36]Ibid.
[37]Ibid., 75.

vations about it. It is not, for him, a question whether such activity is morally legitimate (in a legalistic sense) but whether a Christian, as Christian, could possibly be *called* to exercise such a social role. "This writer," he notes, "has met no one testifying to such an exceptional call."[38] In light of this, one might wonder about the acceptability of the legislative function as well, since the decisions of legislators establish social purposes, levels of taxation, and means of enforcement (unless, of course, a Christian legislator would be called in every instance of decision to vote against enforcement and sanctions).

The question of the state's legitimacy may be clouded further by the analysis of Yoder's *Politics of Jesus,* which was summarized at the beginning of this section. That volume seems to exclude even more categorically the Christian's involvement in coercion and violence. To be sure, even there Yoder affirms the responsibility of Christians to be subject to the powers that be—again in that dual sense of obeying the powers when they can be obeyed in conscience and disobeying them and accepting the penalties when they are in conflict with Christian conscience. But the image conveyed by the book is constantly that of the Christian confronted by the state and confronting the state (even in subjection, even in obedience) as a fundamentally alien force. There is little there to suggest a role for the Christian *in* the state, as an active part of the state's functioning. The question may be more important than Yoder realizes. For if the state's functioning well has some kind of theological importance attached to it, then Christians have theological reasons for wanting to assure that it does function well—and they could only approve the "calling" of some of their number to participate in the enterprise. If the police role of the state represents a legitimate need, however qualified that may be, then by what theological rationale could one stand in judgment of a Christian's claim to be exercising a call to be a police officer?

Yoder can legitimately point to vocational differences and note that the general vocation of Christians is to act toward the transformation of society by the gospel. If all would be as Christians, then there would no longer be the need for the state to bear the sword. Christians, then, best serve the state by bearing their clearest witness to the power of love in human affairs. They best serve the state, paradoxically, by creating through their personal and social existence a new reality to which the state must respond—as Jesus did, and for which Jesus was condemned to die, but as a result of

---

[38]Ibid., 57.

which God's new reality was indeed enabled to break forth in human history. Yoder's articulation of that theme can be very persuasive among genuinely committed Christians, for it focuses the attention and the energy of the church upon the positive, creative, loving works in response to God's gracious gift in Jesus Christ. And it makes it possible for Christians to respond more directly to the way of life represented by Jesus himself.

Still, does not this positive reality remain dependent, to some degree, upon the order-maintaining (and justice-securing) functions of state? If not, then wherein is there even a qualified legitimacy for those functions, and why is the subjection of Christians to such powers to be invoked at all? If the positive reality is, to some extent, dependent upon those functions of state, then how can Christians legitimately claim a vocational exemption from participation in them?

Part of Yoder's response to this appears to be found in his insistence that Christians do not have an obligation to "manage the world."[39] God, ultimately, stands behind our faithful service, transforming the world through this faithfulness and not through misguided efforts to control the course of history. The resurrection, finally, is our theological warrant for confidence in the power of God to sustain us in the way of Jesus. The resurrection is God's seal of approval upon that way, and God's judgment upon all that is contrary to it. We, in fact, are released from our obsessions, our compulsions to manage things by use of violent shortcuts.

Yoder's politics accepts some of the negatives of coercion and violence as being worse than others. The police power of the state can be given a quite-conditional acceptance, where international war cannot. International war, if conducted in accordance with a "crusade" mentality, is clearly worse than war that is disciplined by people who take the just war doctrine seriously (though in acknowledging this Yoder remains firmly committed to pacifism).[40] Relative judgments can and must be made. But authentic Christian discipleship is still committed to the way of peace and love.

In the end, Yoder's theological case for pacifism—while one of the most serious and compelling to be offered by a twentieth-century theologian—remains somewhat ambiguous in its understanding of the state. The qualifications whereby it surrounds the legitimacy of the political realm appear to constitute, at the same time, inhibitions against vigorous Christian action in the state.

---

[39]Yoder, *Politics of Jesus,* 236, 248, and passim.

[40]Yoder, *When War Is Unjust* (Minneapolis: Augsburg, 1984).

I have elsewhere suggested that Yoder may not have taken seriously enough the objective stakes that people have in political outcomes.[41] As in the case of Ellul, we may wonder whether there is here a strong enough doctrine of creation. Has Yoder sufficiently grasped the degree to which God's purposes for people in this world can be *defeated* when material needs are neglected and when institutions and laws are oppressive? Is it enough to say that God will assure the final triumph of righteousness—later? How seriously are we to take the suffering of people in the meantime? Even later, will God not have to work through people to assure the triumph of righteousness, or are we to believe that God will intervene in human history through some nonhuman channel (such as a literal enactment of the scenario in the book of Revelation)? Clearly, Yoder does take human suffering seriously. Clearly, he does not wish simply to consign human political responsibility to God's hands, folding the hands, so to speak, and acquiescing to the world's evils. But the full implications of his categorical exclusion of violence from the range of permissible Christian action, combined with denigration of "effectiveness" as a primary goal for Christians, requires us to pose such questions. In face of the vast sea of human evil and injustice, can we so simply renounce an ultimate recourse to physical violence in the expectation that God will manage history for us in the end? Is there not here a more substantial delegitimation of the political process than even Yoder himself would finally be willing to settle for?

THE CHRISTIAN "STORY" AND THE NEW LIFE IN CHRIST

Before drawing that conclusion, we must consider the work of still another contemporary pacifist theologian. James Wm. McClendon Jr., a Baptist thinker, acknowledges substantial indebtedness to Yoder, although his own approach suggests both additional possibilities and further difficulties in that position.[42]

In common with Yoder, McClendon considers the use of violence to be inconsistent with Christian faith; if anything, he may be even more categorical in his pacifist witness, for I do not find in his work the same (however qualified) acceptance of a police role in human society. Moreover, like Yoder, he insists that the nonviolent commitment is

---

[41]Wogaman, *Christian Method of Moral Judgment,* 127.

[42]James Wm. McClendon Jr., *Ethics: Systematic Theology,* vol. 1 (Nashville: Abingdon Press, 1986).

not a strategy of withdrawal from society and from relevance. Christians are fully engaged, fully committed to the struggle for social justice. But they do not use the methods of violence in that struggle: "Military service may be no longer open to the followers of one who was crucified by soldiers, but peace-making service is."[43] Like Yoder, he emphasizes that this is not irresponsible, that it is not "sectarian" in the Troeltschian sense of that term.[44]

McClendon sets the problem in the context of a "theology of story,"[45] emphasizing that meaning comes from the connected narratives of our lives and our communities. Christian theology is the narrative of the Christian community, preeminently as this is recorded in scripture. The decision of faith is the identification of the self with the narrative and the decision that one's own life narrative will be a connected whole that is consistent with the faith narrative of the Christian community. To make that commitment and to develop one's life in harmony with it is to have a Christian character. Whether or not we have such a character is a more fundamental, more inclusive question than the immediate problem of making our decisions in a Christian way. McClendon is, in fact, critical of what he terms "decisionism" in Christian ethics—the tendency to reduce our ethics to the decisions we make.[46] The aspect of "decisionism" making connection

---

[43]Ibid., 274.

[44]Ernst Troeltsch distinguished between the "church-type" and the "sect-type" of social organization of Christianity. The former attempts to organize society on the basis of the fundamental Christian idea. The latter regards the world as "fallen" and has no hope of being able to encompass society as a whole in the church. The sect-type is made up of those who are totally committed. They seek to manifest God's perfect will within their own Christian community, but are essentially withdrawn from the world. This dichotomy has been refined by several generations of Christian ethicists and sociologists of religion. But neither they nor Troeltsch regarded these ideal types as more than tendencies that are more or less illustrated by actual religious bodies.

[45]In his development of narrative theology, McClendon is largely dependent upon the work of theologian Stanley Hauerwas.

[46]In this, McClendon is particularly critical of my own work as expressed in *A Christian Method of Moral Judgment*. See especially his *Ethics*, 48–59. McClendon's argument against "decisionism" is that it locates morality in the will rather than in the character of the moral agent. In effect, each new situation requires us to decide for or against the good, and morality consists in deciding for the good. But I am not sure how accurate his characterization of those whom he labels "decisionists" really is. For many of them, certainly myself included, would readily agree that the fundamental "decision" is not in the situation of moral choice but rather in the life-transforming acceptance of God's grace and in the identification of the self with the will and purposes of God. But having made that identification, are we not still left with the question of what to do in this often confusing world as we seek to be faithful? Can we rely simply upon Christian intuition to guide us?

with the problem of this book is its tendency to treat ethical problems as ones of doing what we must to secure ends or consequences which we, as Christians, can affirm. The more or less inevitable result of decisionism, therefore, is to lead us to accept any means that will gain the sought-for ends; the means are, in the traditional term, justified by the ends. But the more authentic Christian stance is one of identifying with the Christian tradition (the narrative, the "story") and living out a Christian character. Christians who thus act out what they are (their character) simply do not do some kinds of things that are utterly inconsistent with that character.

McClendon also emphasizes the Christian commitment to the church. The church is a *believers' church*. It is made up of people who have made a conscious decision to identify with it. (McClendon strongly affirms a believer's baptism, in opposition to infant baptism.)[47] A church made up of people who have not made the commitment is almost a contradiction in terms; it is at least a thoroughly cheapened community of faith. Within the community of faith we hold one another accountable to the Christian narrative which we share in common. But, again, he does not see this as sectarian in the Troeltschian sense of that term: "Withdrawal can be no general strategy for Christian existence—this Way is not a way for escape into isolated community, but a way of witness by an engaged community."[48] Christians of the contemporary world, as those who lived in biblical days, "live in interaction with the surrounding society of the 'principalities and powers,' engaging in many (though not all) of the practices of that society."[49]

A striking aspect of McClendon's discussion is his understanding that the social and political world is not "one smooth global unity."[50] And, "there is no single form of social whole to be designated 'society.'"[51] There are many narratives, many communities, many cultures. The world presents "an indefinite congeries of powerful practices, spread over time and space, so that any number of these practices may impinge upon believers in a variety of ways, while our witness to them will necessarily take a corresponding variety of forms." Thus "conscientious withdrawal from the practice of warfare may be

---

[47]McClendon, *Ethics,* 258–59. McClendon writes that "Christian ethics . . . must deplore the intrinsic failure of infant baptism."

[48]Ibid., 274.

[49]Ibid., 231.

[50]Ibid., 230.

[51]Ibid., 171.

coupled with conscientious engagement in practices of peacemaking or education, economics or the arts."[52] To be relevant, we do not have to conform to a monolithic culture, since culture is not monolithic.

In a word, our community of faith becomes one of many such communities, perhaps with their own narratives, contending for the world's allegiance—seeking, as it were, to define the world's meaning to the world's peoples. The Christian community, the church, "is to be an example and foretaste of what God in Christ intends for all human community," providing, thus, a "model for the world."[53] We are to exhibit to the world the meaning of the new life in Christ, with all of its new possibilities. To break faith with that new reality by adopting the world's means, such as violence, is to undercut the fundamental reality of the church at its very roots. It is also to display lack of confidence in the transforming power of that new reality in the world. In a criticism of Reinhold Niebuhr, McClendon calls him to task for holding "a strategy for (discriminately) sinful living in an (indiscriminately) sinful world, rather than a strategy for transformed life in a world become new in Christ Jesus (2 Cor. 5:17)."[54] This flows from Niebuhr's excessive emphasis upon the "ubiquity and power of original sin" and entails a "neglect of the resurrection in favor of an exclusive emphasis on the cross."[55]

The point has weight. An overemphasis upon sin can lead to a loss of confidence in the reality of God's redeeming power in human life. A strong doctrine of original sin stands at the threshold of cynicism. And a cynical attitude toward the concrete possibilities of God's gracious action within and at the end of history is inconsistent with biblical faith. Whether Niebuhr has gone that far is open to disagreement. In my own view, Niebuhr was carefully balanced in most of his writings. We shall have more to say about Niebuhr later, especially in chapter 11.

But, as to McClendon's own views, is there not also a danger in underemphasizing the reality and ubiquity of sin even, perhaps, within the life of the believers' church itself? If the doctrine of original sin points to an inescapable reality in human affairs, then must we not come to terms with it? Of course, McClendon believes he *is* coming to terms with sin in the way presented through the Christian

---

[52]Ibid., 231.

[53]Ibid.

[54]Ibid., 320.

[55]Ibid. While making these points, McClendon acknowledges Niebuhr's skill in interpreting the world "as world."

gospel—the transforming new reality of God's love in Jesus Christ. And no Christian can deny the centrality of that. The issue is whether that transforming reality can be counted upon to do *all* that must be done or may be done by Christians in their struggle against sin in this fallen world. McClendon is very clear in his rejection of "decisionism." He will have none of the notion that we must seek to control actual outcomes. In a criticism of my own views, he takes issue with the thought that Christians are responsible, "when and as they can," to "direct the course of history."[56] While this overstates my position somewhat, at least in the suggestion that it is possible or desirable for Christians to take control of all human events,[57] he is certainly right in citing me among those Christian ethicists who consider it a Christian responsibility to seek to influence history, to be concerned about actual consequences, to seek to be *effective* in human events. The question is whether he is right in his criticism of that position! That is a question fraught with significance for the political stance of Christians! For if we are to be concerned about actual consequences—about what actually happens in human events—then we really do have to weigh and measure our decisions and not categorically exclude actions that oppose power to power on its own terms in what Luther called the "strange work of love."[58]

McClendon's rejection of that option may have brought him to the threshold of irresponsibility—much as he wishes, on another level, to affirm the concrete transforming power of God's gracious love. The problem is that almost everywhere we look in this world people are suffering misery and oppression. And for vast numbers of them, the transforming power of God's gracious love has not, at least not yet, brought relief. Tolstoy can say that love will be directly effective, since Tolstoy regards antisocial behavior as a result of violent and oppressive institutions. As we have already seen, Yoder will not accept so facile a conception of sin. Consequently Yoder, in order to exclude some of the measures normally associated with being "effective" (such as use of violence), must appeal finally to faith in God to make it all come out in the end. That must finally be McClendon's position as well, for

---

[56]Ibid., 52.

[57]I have strongly emphasized Christian humility before the transcendence of God and applied this specifically to our political life in my *Protestant Faith and Religious Liberty* (Nashville: Abingdon Press, 1967) and *Faith and Fragmentation: Christianity for a New Age* (Philadelphia: Fortress Press, 1985).

[58]This aspect of Luther's thought is developed in an interesting way by Paul Tillich in *Love, Power, and Justice* (New York: Oxford University Press, 1954), 49.

McClendon also avoids the more facile Tolstoyan solution to the problem of dealing with social evil. This makes both Yoder and McClendon (as well as Ellul) more serious thinkers than Tolstoy. But it does not remove the question whether they are, in the end, irresponsible.

To illustrate: there are in the United States at this time of writing more than 30 million people officially defined as being below the poverty line. Despite the dismantling of a good deal of the welfare program in 1996, some governmental assistance continues to provide some relief to poor people (little enough, to be sure; but without such programs the plight of poor people would be demonstrably worse). The financing of such programs is through taxation—money not given voluntarily but required by law and enforced, if necessary, by physical sanctions. Yoder is at least somewhat receptive to this, by virtue of his qualified acceptance of the state's internal police power (although Yoder does not feel that a Christian can normally be called to the work of police protection). McClendon is simply negative about the use of violence. But we must ask *seriously* whether benefits for poor people and many other obvious benefits based, ultimately, on the taxing powers of government are to be abjured in the name of the new life in Christ.

Similarly, we may note that until the 1960s there was widespread discrimination against African Americans—especially, though not exclusively, in the southern states. An African American found it almost impossible to find hotel or restaurant accommodations, and, when found, they were usually made available in demeaning ways. African Americans were consigned to the lowest paid, most menial jobs— where jobs were available. Housing was not freely available on the open market, either for sale or for rental. These socially reinforced forms of discrimination were complemented by a whole fabric of "Jim Crow" laws by states and localities assuring separate and unequal treatment for black people wherever they might turn. But in the 1950s and 1960s, as a result of litigation and the civil rights movement, the full force of federal law in the United States was turned against racial discrimination. These laws were enforced by the FBI, police, National Guard units, and even the United States Army itself. There were some brutal confrontations, although the massive weight of the federal enforcement powers—combined with the nonviolent techniques of the civil rights movement—helped keep actual violence at a minimum.[59]

---

[59]In this connection it is important to remember that the nonviolent methods of the civil rights movement (which would be affirmed enthusiastically by most pacifists) had to be consolidated into law by the power of the state, with its police and armed forces ultimately securing the desired ends.

Again the question must be posed: Is such a use of coercion to assure a concrete result to be renounced in the name of the new life in Christ? Is it contrary to the spirit of the gospel to seek to use the powers of the state to assure justice for the poor and oppressed?

McClendon's analysis of society leads to a different kind of question. Does his pluralistic social model ("there is no single form of social whole to be designated 'society' ")[60] do justice to the systemic interrelationships of the social world? Granted, of course, that the world presents us with a bewildering diversity of cultures, subgroups, power centers, and narrative histories, is it not also the case that social wholes do exist and that our behavior is to a substantial and increasing extent tied to the behavior of others? Walter Rauschenbusch (another Baptist) understood perfectly well that evil social institutions can literally force good people to do bad things. But social institutions can also be structured in such a way that unjust people are restrained from implementing their desires to oppress and exploit other people.

The question for those tempted by McClendon's analysis is whether they think it is even *possible* to avoid doing what the state is doing. In chapter 2, I have suggested that whatever the state is doing at any time, we are all doing it together. McClendon's position would seem to depend upon denying that, or at least of asserting that it is our Christian responsibility to thrust the whole weight of our lives against what the state is doing when its actions are contrary to the new life in Christ. McClendon might be willing to affirm this latter statement. But then is it not the case that even the normal activities of social life—which do not involve us directly in violence or other sin—are ultimately supportive of those very things?

In the end, pacifism may inescapably be linked to anarchism, even though there are significant relative differences among the different forms of pacifism and of anarchism.[61] In the end, each of the thinkers we have considered in this chapter significantly weakens

---

[60]McClendon, *Ethics,* 171.

[61]The point obviously depends upon one's definitions of pacifism and anarchism. Such Christian pacifists as Walter G. Muelder and Paul Deats Jr. clearly accept the legitimacy of the state, including its internal police functions. Similarly, Martin Luther King Jr., while generally opposed to violence and while decrying the use of police as instruments of oppression, affirmed the use of police for the upholding of justice. In the context of the present volume, such thinkers belong more in the fourth "generating center" of mainstream political thought although they have strong affinities with Yoder and McClendon. In this chapter I have limited the term "pacifism" to thinkers who are categorically opposed to violence per se, and these thinkers are also anarchists to the degree the state ultimately depends upon some use of violence for its very existence as state.

the theological legitimation of the political order. In the end, this perspective falls short for those of us who wish to affirm that order and our responsibilities in and through it.

Nevertheless, one should not conclude this chapter without acknowledging the seriousness of the insights such thinkers contribute to the political ethic of Christians. They will not allow us to forget that violence is evil. While acknowledging the reality of sin, they will not allow us to neglect the transforming power of God's love in all human affairs. Their witness, even to those who disagree with their categorical way of expressing it, is an enduring reminder that Christians can never be casual about acting coercively or violently, that such actions are often counterproductive (doing more harm, ultimately, than good), and that it is all too easy for Christians and others to become corrupted by the exercises of power. I agree with Karl Barth that a Christian should *almost* be a pacifist![62] But I also agree with his judgment that that perspective on politics is ultimately an inadequate one.

We turn next to a perspective that is very different, though usually expressed with equal self-assurance.

---

[62]See Karl Barth, *Church Dogmatics,* III/4 (Edinburgh: T. & T. Clark, 1961 [1951]), 455.

5

Christian Liberationist Perspectives

The work of Christ is presented simultaneously as a liberation from sin and from all its consequences: despoliation, injustice, hatred. This liberation fulfills in an unexpected way the promises of the prophets and creates a new chosen people, which this time includes all humanity.

—Gustavo Gutierrez (1973)[1]

Liberation theology is a second generating center of Christian political thought in the late twentieth century. It burst on the scene with startling creativity in the late 1960s and early 1970s. It has included writings characterized as black theology,[2] political theology,[3]

---

[1] Gustavo Gutierrez, *A Theology of Liberation: History, Politics and Salvation,* trans. Caridad Inda and John Eagleson (Maryknoll, N.Y.: Orbis Books, 1973), 158.

[2] See, e.g., James H. Cone, *God of the Oppressed* (New York: Seabury Press, 1975); idem, *Black Theology and Black Power* (New York: Seabury Press, 1969); J. Deotis Roberts, *Liberation and Reconciliation: A Black Theology* (Philadelphia: Westminster Press, 1971); Major Jones, *Christian Ethics for Black Theology* (Nashville: Abingdon Press, 1974), and Cornel West, *Prophesy Deliverance! An Afro-American Revolutionary Christianity* (Philadelphia: Westminster Press, 1982).

[3] See, e.g., Dorothee Soelle, *Political Theology* (Philadelphia: Fortress Press, 1974); Joseph M. Petulla, *Christian Political Theology: A Marxian Guide* (Maryknoll, N.Y.: Orbis Books, 1972); William Coats, *God in Public: Political Theology beyond Niebuhr* (Grand Rapids: Wm. B. Eerdmans, 1974); and Jürgen Moltmann et al., *Religion and Political Society* (New York: Harper & Row, 1974).

feminist theology,[4] and others. Third World voices have been prominent, especially in Latin America.[5] By the end of the century, liberation theology had lost a certain amount of its initial force, particularly to the extent it had been allied with socialist or Marxist views. The collapse of the Soviet Union as the principal center of world communism greatly diminished the appeal of Marxism as a political-economic system, and liberation theologians had already rejected it as a religious perspective. Dynamic new developments in global economic life made socialism less attractive, although the terms of relationship between the free market and governmental participation in economic life are not settled and may never be. We will return to that theme later in the book. In any event, the generative force of liberation theology is not dependent upon an outworn ideology. Liberation theology, for all its uniqueness in the late twentieth century, represents the recurrence of the ancient Christian protest against oppression, exploitation, and poverty.

While the rich variety of liberationist writings defies easy characterization, most of the writers are united in one overpowering theme: the gospel of Jesus Christ is represented most authentically in the liberation of the world's oppressed peoples from their bondage. The gospel is not an otherworldly escape from the hard realities of this world. Rather, it addresses those realities directly, empowering the oppressed to seize control of their own destiny and to establish a new order of freedom and justice. Liberation theologians take oppression

---

[4]See, e.g., Rosemary Radford Ruether, *Liberation Theology: Human Hope Confronts Christian History and American Power* (New York: Paulist Press, 1972); idem, *New Woman/New Earth: Sexist Ideologies and Human Liberation* (New York: Seabury Press, 1975); idem, *To Change the World: Christology and Cultural Criticism* (New York: Crossroad, 1981); Mary Daly, *Beyond God the Father* (Boston: Beacon Press, 1973); and Clare Benedicks Fischer et al., eds., *Women in a Strange Land: Search for a New Image* (Philadelphia: Fortress Press, 1975).

[5]See, e.g., Juan Luis Segundo, *Liberation of Theology* (Maryknoll, N.Y.: Orbis Books, 1976); Gutierrez, *Theology of Liberation;* Jose Miguez Bonino, *Doing Theology in a Revolutionary Situation* (Philadelphia: Fortress Press, 1975); idem, *Christians and Marxists: The Mutual Challenge to Revolution* (Grand Rapids: Wm. B. Eerdmans, 1976); idem, *Toward a Christian Political Ethics* (Philadelphia: Fortress Press, 1983); Hugo Assmann, *Theology for a Nomad Church* (Maryknoll, N.Y.: Orbis Books, 1976); and Canaan S. Banana, *The Theology of Promise: The Dynamics of Self-Reliance* (Harare, Zimbabwe: College Press, 1982). For an interesting collection of theological testimonies by fifteen Christians in the Sandinista movement and the government of Nicaragua, see Teofilo Cabestrero, *Revolucionarios por el Evangelio* (Bilbao, Spain: Editorial Desclee de Brouwer, 1983).

very seriously. The central preoccupation of black theologians such as James Cone is with the long history of racial oppression, especially with the dominance of white people over black people in countries such as the United States and South Africa. The central preoccupation of feminist theologians such as Dorothee Soelle and Rosemary Radford Ruether is with the age-old dominance of men over women. The main emphasis of the Third World liberation theologians such as Gustavo Gutierrez and Jose Miguez Bonino has been with what they have taken to be the exploitation of the world's poor people by international capitalism. The nuances of difference between the various writers are very great, but all proclaim the direct identification of Jesus Christ with the cause of the oppressed. And all insist that Christians have as their primary agenda the liberation of the oppressed and the establishment of a new order of justice on earth. Above all, this is a *political* task. The main theme of liberation theology is expressed in several ways.

THE EXODUS METAPHOR

The story of the exodus in Hebrew scripture provides a central metaphor for the liberationist perspective. God acted in the history of Israel to liberate the Hebrew slaves from their captivity in Egypt, thereby also constituting them as a nation. That liberating action was central to the meaning of Hebrew scripture and ultimately the New Testament as well. "The Exodus," writes Gustavo Gutierrez, "is the long march towards the promised land in which Israel can establish a society free from misery and alienation." This is not a separate, specialized "religious" event. Rather, the exodus is the "deepest meaning" of the whole biblical narrative; "it is the root of the situation." And "it is in this event that the dislocation introduced by sin is resolved and justice and injustice, oppression and liberation, are determined."[6] Nor is the New Testament something basically different. "The work of Christ," Gutierrez writes, "forms a part of this movement and brings it to complete fulfillment." The work of Christ, therefore, brings a liberation that "fulfills in an unexpected way the promises of the prophets and creates a new chosen people, which this time includes all humanity."[7]

---

[6]Gutierrez, *Theology of Liberation,* 157.
[7]Ibid., 158.

Gutierrez voices the belief of most of the liberation theologians in asserting that "the Exodus experience is paradigmatic."[8] It models the situation humanity faces today, for the people who are in bondage today (economic, racial, sexist, etc.) can also count on God as the fundamental source of their liberation.

CONSCIENTIZATION AND ACTION

The oppressed are not, of course, invited to await their liberation passively. The empowering God is the God who enables the oppressed to seize control of their own lives and situations, to throw off their shackles, and to establish a new order. The empowering God enables such people to become political *actors* for the first time, no longer merely objects of the power of others.

They are first given new insight. The word "conscientization," employed by many liberation theologians, has a complex meaning. It includes the consciousness-raising whereby the oppressed come to understand the institutions and systems that have oppressed them. It also includes the new awareness of one's own equal worth as a person. One no longer is in bondage to the oppressor's view that one is inferior. And it also includes a new grasp of what must be done to secure actual liberation.

In *Pedagogy of the Oppressed,* Paulo Freire explores this process of gaining a new consciousness and insight into the requirements of liberation.[9] An important point made there is that education for liberation is not patterned on the paternalistic teacher/pupil basis but rather is an enabling of people to think critically as they interact with the sources of their oppression. Liberation theology has developed, in this spirit, a creative relationship with small groups of Christians—the "base communities"—who study scripture and pray together in a mutual exploration of the theological meaning of their concrete patterns of existence, their subjection, and who gain a mutual sense of empowerment. Politically speaking, these base communities constitute a new reality that must be taken into account by those who hold power. The base communities are, in a real sense, political power bases. The Latin American *comunidades de base* find

---

[8]Ibid., 159.

[9]Paulo Freire, *Pedagogy of the Oppressed,* trans. Myra Bergman Ramos (New York: Seabury Press, 1970).

their North American parallels in black and feminist caucuses and support groups and, for that matter, in many quite ordinary black local church congregations.

THE MARXIST INFLUENCE

How exactly is oppression understood by liberation theology? Where does the operative theory come from?

One has the impression, in reading accounts of the base communities (such as Ernesto Cardenal's *El Evangelio en Solentename*),[10] that theoretical insight into the social, economic, and political sources of oppression is the simple gift of scripture gained through group study. No doubt people who are invited to study scripture in a liberationist perspective will find very much there to enliven their understanding of the sources of human oppression by which they are victimized. But more secular forms of socioeconomic and political theory may have a role to play as well.

The question is often raised whether liberation theology has drawn its socioeconomic and political theory primarily from Marxism. Indeed, it is often suggested that liberation theology is little more than Marxism with a Christian face. Many of the liberation theologians, particularly the Latin Americans, did substantially and consciously rely upon Marxist forms of analysis. This occurred at several levels.

First, liberation theologians have always sought to be sure that Christian faith will not be used as ideological support for selfish interests and repressive institutions. In an interesting chapter on the Marxian theme of religion as the "opiate of the people," Miguez Bonino welcomes the criticism "as a valid warning against the self-deception and confusion which so easily creep into a political programme of any sort when it is clothed in religious language."[11] The chapter disputes whether it is necessary for religion to play such a role. But when religion is not consciously self-critical at this point, it is likely to drift into justifying and supporting the status quo. "We can easily see," he writes, "how religious faith can be used for reactionary purposes. It does not need to be a conscious use: it even functions

---

[10]Ernesto Cardenal, *El Evangelio en Solentename* (Managua: Editorial Nueva Nicaragua, 1978).

[11]Miguez Bonino, *Christians and Marxists,* 48–49.

better when it is practised unwittingly."[12] If we do not attend to politics directly and critically, he suggests elsewhere, we are likely to find Christianity used by default in support of the wrong things: "We urgently need a Christian ethics of politics precisely in order that we may avoid a wrong politicization of Christianity."[13] Clearly Miguez Bonino and all the other liberation theologians do not think it necessary for Christianity to lapse into a passive support for oppressive forces. To the extent that Marxism is irredeemably antireligious (a debatable issue), such theologians deviated from pure Marxism.

At the same time, and at the next level, these theologians accept the notion that real truth is revealed through praxis—a term that is itself derived from Marxist literature.[14] Knowledge about things that matter is not derived through exposure to abstract "truths"; rather it is in reflecting upon our actions to affect things that matter. A theology of liberation, writes Gutierrez, "offers us not so much a new theme for reflection as a *new way* to do theology." Such a theology "does not stop with reflecting on the world, but rather tries to be part of the process through which the world is transformed." This theology "is open—in the struggle against the plunder of the vast majority of people, in liberating love, and in the building of a new, just, and fraternal society—to the gift of the Kingdom of God."[15] Such words are reminiscent of Marx's own dictum that "the philosophers have only *interpreted* the world, in various ways; the point, however, is to *change* it."[16] Politics is therefore fundamental, for politics is where things are made to happen. One cannot be neutral about the question of power in human society. It is what is behind oppression; it is what has to be used to overcome oppression. Christians cannot do their theological work away from, apart from, the struggle for power. It is precisely in that struggle that they come to understand

---

[12]Ibid., 63.

[13]Miguez Bonino, *Toward a Christian Political Ethics,* 17.

[14]The term "praxis" as used in Latin American liberation theology and Marxism reflects especially the influence of the earlier Italian Marxism of Antonio Gramsci and Rodolfo Mondolfo. That tradition is substantially more open and pragmatic than the bolshevism of V. I. Lenin. "Praxis" refers to the reciprocal effects of action upon thought and thought upon action in the process of revolutionary transformation of society.

[15]Gutierrez, *Theology of Liberation,* 15.

[16]Karl Marx, "Theses of Feuerbach," in *Basic Writings on Politics and Philosophy* by Karl Marx and Friedrich Engels, ed. Lewis S. Feuer (New York: Doubleday Anchor Books, 1959 [1848]), 245.

both the manner of God's self-revelation in history and the systemic structures of human society against which they must contend.

At a third level, liberation theology wholeheartedly agrees with Marxist analysis in identifying with the oppressed in the struggle against the oppressor. Christians have a "preferential option for the poor"—an expression that, while somewhat clumsily translated from Spanish into English, still conveys the point that Christians choose to side with the poor in their struggle against the rich and powerful. Moreover, most of the Latin American liberation theologians largely accept a Marxian interpretation of class conflict and the causes of poverty. Black theologians, like James Cone, and feminist theologians, like Rosemary Radford Ruether, are not as classically Marxist at this point. For them, the categories of racial oppression and sexual oppression are not simply reducible to economic class exploitation—although both of these writers (and many other black and feminist theologians) are also sharply critical of capitalism as a primary source of human oppression. They would add that Christians have a kind of preferential option for blacks and for women in their struggles for liberation.

In the case of the Latin American liberation theologians the acceptance of Marxist tools of analysis often included variations on Lenin's theory of imperialism. Expressed simply, this is the notion that the poverty of the people of Third World countries is a function of the prosperity of the people in the First World. As expressed by Lenin, capitalism in North America and Europe was forced to expand its sources of supply and markets to the underdeveloped regions of the world to avoid the full effect of the contradictions inherent in capitalism. Lenin's theory of imperialism had two effects of great importance in the development of Marxism in the twentieth century: (1) It provided an explanation for the postponement of the (to Marx) inevitable collapse of capitalism. The export of capital (and thus, of exploitation) to Third World countries meant that the full effects of exploitation would (for yet a while longer) not be felt by industrial workers in the developed capitalist countries. Hence those workers would not yet make the still-inevitable revolution. (2) The export of capital to the Third World means that the workers of the underdeveloped, largely agrarian societies can now be understood as a part of the machinery of capitalism. They may appear to be peasants in a feudalistic economy; actually, they are a part of the worldwide proletariat. This second point means that Third World peasants can now be made to think of themselves in classical Marxist terms as a part of the proletariat in the struggle against the bourgeoisie.

Not all expressions of the doctrine of imperialism are derived from classical Marxism or Leninism, of course; and not all Marxists agree with the notion that Third World poverty is a function of First World (capitalist) prosperity.[17] But the close affinity at this point of typical liberation theology with typical Marxism has meant that the liberation theologians could easily make use of Marxian tools of analysis in characterizing the causes and structures of oppression faced by Third World poor people. Such tools are less usable in respect to racial and sexual forms of oppression, although many of the black theologians and feminist theologians clearly regard international capitalism as an important part of the overall structure of oppression faced by black people and women. Although both racism and sexism have involved substantial elements of economic exploitation—both historically and at the present time—few black or feminist theologians seem willing to reduce racism or sexism to capitalism alone. Their analysis of the sources of oppression is therefore less Marxist than the Latin Americans'.

THE CALL TO REVOLUTION

The influence of Marxism is also expressed, at least to some degree, in the open advocacy of revolution that is typical of many liberation theologians. *Revolution* is to be contrasted with *reformism*. Reformism implies that the social-economic-political system is fundamentally sound but only needs improvements at specified points. Reformism suggests that the system needs only to be adjusted. The call for revolution addresses the need for total, systemic change. It implies that the whole social order is fundamentally, if not irredeemably, flawed. It calls for the overthrow of the existing order by a seizure of power. Those who have held power must be dethroned. The powerless must be empowered—or rather, they must, through revolution, empower themselves.

In this sense, liberation theology is typically revolutionary and not reformist. Its slogan is provided, if not by Marx, by the Magnificat of Mary ("he has put down the mighty from their thrones, and exalted those of low degree; he has filled the hungry with good

---

[17]See, e.g., James H. Weaver and Marguerite Berger, "The Marxist Critique of Dependency Theory: An Introduction," in *The Political Economy of Development and Underdevelopment,* 3d ed., ed. Charles K. Wilber (New York: Random House, 1984), 45–64. Weaver and Berger cite the work of such Marxist writers as Bill Warren and John Weeks.

things, and the rich he has sent empty away"). Christians are called to fulfill the righteousness of God by turning things on their heads, utterly challenging the world's unjust power structures. The term "revolution" can, of course, mean different things to different people. Sweeping change can occur on one level, that is, a lower level, without greatly affecting power structures at other levels. One can speak of "revolutionary" change in the power structure of a political party which, however, leaves the overall constitutional structure of a society entirely intact. One can speak of revolutionary political changes (even at the constitutional level) which do not affect existing economic power structures, or of revolutionary changes in economic structures which do not affect political institutions substantially. What is "revolutionary" at one level of analysis may, in fact, be "reformist" at another level.

The point is not a trivial one, for what is revolutionary in the rhetoric of one thinker or form of liberation theology may not be to another. I am sure that most feminist theologians are not satisfied with the revolutionary agenda of much male liberation theology— for it can proceed with its economic and political agenda while leaving the inequality of women, the oppression of women (with its long historical and deep cultural roots) entirely unchallenged. The vanguard of the proletariat can be quite sexist, or even racist (though that may be less likely). So the rhetoric of revolution needs to be subjected to careful analysis.

Nevertheless, liberation theology in all its forms is consciously revolutionary in respect to what it perceives to be the oppressive powers that be, and it is generally critical of reformism. Reformism is suspected of being employed to shore up the power structures by deflecting criticism from the root causes of oppression in society. The criticism of reformism echoes the traditional Marxist challenge to every form of "revisionism." The latter, in fact, was often regarded as a worse enemy than the frank opposition of those clearly opposed to any change. Latin American liberationists can be especially critical of the process whereby particular leaders can be "elected" on a platform of reforms only to become hopelessly dependent upon the power elites, often invisible, who pull the real strings. The irony of Mexico, for instance, where the governing party (in power for half a century in self-perpetuating corruption) bears the name "revolutionary," is repeated with variations in many Latin American societies. Palace "revolutions" and *coups d'etat* of various kinds are regarded as neither revolution nor even reformist.

THE DELEGITIMATION
OF EXISTING POLITICAL INSTITUTIONS

The underlying political message of much liberation theology implies the delegitimation of entire existing power structures. Those who call for sweeping revolution do not recognize the legitimacy of current political leadership nor (often) of current political institutions. Insofar as those institutions have the form of democracy, it is considered to be a facade. Insofar as the leadership has been "elected," it is not understood to have a *real* mandate from the people.

Accordingly, the political task comes down to the seizure of political power and the restructuring of society at fundamental levels. This does not necessarily mean the nonparticipation in existing political institutions; it does at least mean that when one participates in existing political institutions it is with an eye toward ultimately bringing them down, or at least changing them fundamentally. The actual revolutionary movements of Latin America in the 1960s, '70s, and '80s typically were of the guerrilla type, modeled, more or less, on Cuban and Nicaraguan experience. Liberation theologians even in that era did not support all such movements in a blanket way (more on this below); but their support for this model of political activity and social change was considerable. When liberation theology calls for political activism, it issues a call to revolutionary change so that the present illegitimate political order can be replaced by one that is legitimate.

Two related points are worth noting. One could read through the work of many liberation theologians without finding much discussion of postrevolutionary political institutions. The immediate task of joining in revolution absorbs most of the energies. The later constructive task must be and can be postponed until the first task has been accomplished. The assumption is that postrevolutionary praxis will find a way to restructure the future, just as revolutionary praxis feels its way, partly by trial and error, to success in revolution. Indeed, too much preoccupation with the postrevolutionary situation could be seen as an impediment to revolution itself. Moreover, it can create divisiveness among people who have joined in making revolution from a variety of perspectives.

The other point is that the perspective is comparatively uncritical in accepting alliances with others in making revolution. The test is not some form of political or economic orthodoxy but the degree of one's commitment in and to the revolutionary struggle. Miguez Bonino notes that while Christians and Marxists have substantial disagreement at important points, they can come to better mutual understanding and perhaps ultimate reconciliation through the common struggle.[18]

AMBIVALENCE ABOUT DEMOCRACY

With this background, it is understandable why liberation theology has not always exhibited much faith in political democracy as such. Early Latin American liberation theologians were openly critical. It is not that they did not believe in human rights or broad political participation by all members of society. It is rather that they regarded fundamental power to inhere not in the visible political institutions but in the highly concentrated interests of elite groups in society. Political oratory may flourish, elections may be held, with results duly certified and officers properly installed in office. But fundamental power may continue exactly as it has all along. It is even possible that a Marxist may be installed in high office, as President Salvador Allende was in Chile. But in the final analysis, if fundamental interests are threatened, real power will be invoked and the democratic results will be set aside. (One should not be surprised that this happened to Allende.) Most of the time, fundamental interests are not even threatened by the process. But if real power is not affected by the processes of democracy, those who are concerned with the politics of real power will not encourage what they consider to be the illusions of democracy. One must not expect that real power will be handed over voluntarily, even in the unlikely event a revolutionary movement were to succeed in installing its leadership in office through the electoral process.

Much liberation theology has its roots in Latin America, where this mistrust of democracy has a good deal of historical basis. Many Latin American countries have had exemplary democratic constitutions for a century or more. But the realities of class oppression and the repetitive *coups d'état* and the persistence of official corruption are undeniably real. In that context a good deal of cynicism about political democracy is not only pardonable but necessary among people who care about what actually happens to marginalized people in a society.

---

[18]That is a major thesis in Miguez Bonino's *Christians and Marxists,* which he not inappropriately subtitles *The Mutual Challenge to Revolution.*

But liberation theologians do not restrict their mistrust of the illusions of political democracy to the Latin American context. They are deeply suspicious of the pretensions of North American democracy as well. From Gutierrez on, these theologians have criticized the imperialistic relationships between dominant economic interests in North America, Europe, and Japan (but especially those of the United States) and the economies of the Third World. They have witnessed firsthand the imposition of serious North American power to shore up oppressive Third World regimes protecting North American economic interests. They are impressed by the relationships between economic power elites of North America and their counterparts in the Third World. They easily conclude that political democracy exists only as a facade for the real power of such elites even in the North American democracies.

Still, the progress of numbers of Latin American countries toward real democracy and the shifting tides of economic circumstance—such as the North American Free Trade Agreement (NAFTA)—have introduced a certain ambivalence among Latin American liberation theology movements, while progress on several fronts has dampened the harshness of rhetoric in North America as well.

THE PROBLEM OF VIOLENCE

The call to revolution and the skepticism about democracy inevitably raised the question whether liberation theologians considered violence to be a moral problem for Christians. Clearly some do more than others, and there is no longer much of the romanticizing of violence that marked the revolutionary rhetoric of the 1960s and 1970s. But the movement has generally been very far from being pacifist in the usual sense. Violence has sometimes been pictured as more or less inevitable in the struggle against oppressive powers that will be defended, to the end, violently. As a matter of fact, liberation theologians typically remind us that an unjust order is itself inherently violent. Thus, Gutierrez quotes with approval the statement of the Second General Conference of Latin American Bishops (Medellin, 1968) that Latin American exploitation constitutes "a situation of injustice that can be called institutionalized violence," resulting in the death of thousands of people.[19] Even the church, in

---

[19]Gutierrez, *Theology of Liberation,* 108.

Gutierrez's view, is implicated, for "in many places the Church contributes to creating 'a Christian order' and to giving a kind of sacred character to a situation which is not only alienating but is the worst kind of violence—a situation which pits the powerful against the weak."[20]

Liberation theology shares many social justice concerns with leading pacifist thinkers. But in the concept of institutionalized violence, or the violence of the unjust order, there is implicit a searching criticism of much pacifism. To the extent that pacifism is predicated on the moral demand that Christians must not compromise or corrupt themselves by engaging in violence, the liberation theologians have a ready answer: you cannot avoid it as long as you live in an unjust society. "No one," writes James Cone in the North American context, "can be nonviolent in an unjust society."[21] He continues,

> The essential fallacy of the much debated issues of violence versus nonviolence is that the proponents of the latter have merely argued that issue from a perspective that accepted the oppressors' definitions. Too often Christian theologians have made the specious distinction between violence and force. . . . This distinction is false and merely expresses an identification with the structures of power rather than with the victims of power. I contend that every one is violent, and to ask, "Are you nonviolent?" is to accept the oppressors' values. Concretely, ours is a situation in which the only option we have is that of deciding whose violence we will support— that of the oppressors or the oppressed.[22]

Disagreeing with Martin Luther King Jr.'s "conceptual analysis of violence versus nonviolence," Cone argues that "his distinction between these terms did not appear to face head-on the historical and sociological complexities of human existence in a racist society."[23]

The point is not simply that nonviolence is ineffective as a revolutionary method in many oppressive contexts—though many liberationists plainly believe that. The deeper point is that true nonviolence is not even possible in such places. For if we do not join the

---

[20]Ibid., 265.
[21]Cone, *God of the Oppressed,* 219.
[22]Ibid.
[23]Ibid., 221.

struggle against oppression with every means at our command, we shall in effect be strengthening the hand of the oppressor. Thus Cone can argue above that we can only choose between supporting the violence of the oppressor or that of those who are struggling to break free from oppression. An African liberation theologian, Canaan S. Banana of Zimbabwe, argues in effect that in the struggle for liberation, violence, not nonviolence, is the moral norm. King "had to be content" with the nonviolent methods dictated by his historical situation. By contrast, however, "in the developing countries of the Third World today the historical context is different and the choice of armed revolution has been made possible."[24] Implicit in Banana's and Cone's interpretation of King's nonviolence is the belief that King's program was essentially reformist and not revolutionary. King did not seize power and destroy the roots of oppression. He dealt in specific reforms, good in themselves, but not the root of the violence suffered daily by the oppressed.

This argument has considerable merit if one accepts the assumption that ruling groups do not voluntarily relinquish power and that they have the means available to protect their interests. Advocates of nonviolence, such as John Howard Yoder and King, contend that nonviolent means can bring the system to a halt. That position, too, has merit. At least there have been numerous historical instances of success in achieving massive social change through use of nonviolent means.[25] The distinction between "revolution" and "reform" can be ambiguous, but some of the successful instances of change through nonviolence appear to have been more on the revolutionary than the reformist side. Still, the liberationist insists on a hard analysis of actual power relationships leading to the use of the means necessary for real revolution. Liberationists will not accept the notion that an ineffective nonviolence at least avoids the evils of violence, for they believe violence already to be present in the system of oppression itself.

The point was sharpened in a discussion of the problem of violence by Miguez Bonino.[26] Engaging the thought of Yoder, Miguez

---

[24]Banana, *The Theology of Promise*, 93.

[25]See especially Gene Sharp, *The Politics of Nonviolent Action* (Boston: Porter Sargent, 1973).

[26]See Miguez Bonino, *Toward a Christian Political Ethics,* and idem "Violence and Liberation," *Christianity and Crisis* 32, no. 12 (1972): 169–72. Some of the other Latin American liberationists, such as Juan Luis Segundo and Dom Helder Camara, could also be cited as warning against the evils of violence in the struggle for liberation, although I think it is fair to say that most liberationists are less sensitive to that point.

Bonino acknowledges the force of the latter's integration of a radical commitment to social justice with an equally radical commitment to a nonviolent witness and a theological understanding of the church as the locus in history of God's liberating activity. His problem with Yoder's position is that it forecloses serious discussion within the church of "the concrete issues and options of the outside world" and of "the questions of power and injustice within the community [the church] itself." "The hard reality of power refuses to submit to general principles or moral norms."[27] There can be no Christian alternative to confronting the realities in the concrete situation. Thus the question of violence cannot be treated in the abstract apart from the circumstances of its appearance: "Violence should not be divorced from the conflict situation in which it is exercised—as if it were an entelechy to be analyzed in itself."[28] For example, there is a difference between calculated use of violence by revolutionaries and the spontaneous outbreaks of violence within an oppressed community—just as there is a distinction to be made between the violence of the unjust order and the violence of the oppressive system.

Still, Miguez Bonino acknowledges the moral seriousness of violence even when undertaken in behalf of liberation. In tantalizingly brief allusions to the just war tradition, he implies that the presumption should be against the use of violence: "The Christian will certainly be concerned that the use of violence be kept to the minimum in any case."[29] "The traditional criteria elaborated in discussions of a 'just war' still have their relevance."[30] The brevity of this allusion seems, however, to be derived from his conviction that the issue of violence will be resolved in a morally satisfactory way in "a living relation between the leaders and the people" in which "the 'sense' of what is right at any given moment can prevail." The place of more theoretical "tentative ethical formulations" is to be regarded as "resources in the struggle." Clearly Miguez Bonino does not wish to impose Christian reservations about violence upon the liberation movement. Such an elaboration of ethical principle from outside the context of the struggle

[27]Miguez Bonino, *Toward a Christian Political Ethics*, 33–36.
[28]Ibid., 109.
[29]Miguez Bonino, *Christians and Marxists*, 129.
[30]Miguez Bonino, *Toward a Christian Political Ethics*, 109.

can deflect the movement from confronting hard power realities and dealing with them realistically. Moreover, Miguez Bonino plainly trusts the moral sensitivities of those engaged in the struggle.

THE UNIVERSALITY OF SIN

Do Miguez Bonino and other liberation theologians trust the moral goodness of those engaged in the struggle too much? And by the same token, do they locate moral evil in those against whom the struggle is being waged—or, more precisely, in the structures and powers upheld by those against whom the struggle is waged?

Such questions may be very important for those seeking to relate Christian faith to politics. In the first place, the answers one gives may determine the degree to which any particular actors in the political drama can be trusted with power or whether some actors should be denied political power altogether. In the second place, the answers may suggest the extent to which moral evil, or sin, can be banished altogether from human existence. A classical Marxist approach to human evil highlights both issues, for the tendency there is to locate evil objectively in the structural realities of class oppression. This, to a considerable extent, identifies the struggle against class oppression as the definitive battle against evil itself—that is, evil will be vanquished when class oppression is brought to an end. And, thereby, those who are engaged in that struggle are clearly understood as alone being worthy of exercising real political power. Such people are alone capable of exercising political power on behalf of the masses—whether the masses are conscious of this or not. By contrast, a view that located evil entirely in the personal sinfulness of individuals might conclude that it is a waste of time to change social structures without first redeeming individuals from their sinfulness.

Liberation theologians obviously do not take this last view, but neither do most of them adopt the classical Marxist conception uncritically. To them, evil is objectively real in the concrete structures and relationships of human social history. Indeed, the hallmark of "liberation" theology is to liberate human beings from oppressive structures. And the moral credentials of revolutionary liberation movements are clearly very high.

Later, we will examine more closely the views of Christian political realists who emphasize more directly the relevance of a Christian doctrine of original sin. But here we may note that Miguez

Bonino and some other liberation theologians have heard the criticism that they neglect that doctrine to their peril. In his principal work on Marxism, Miguez Bonino makes the point that "no human group or class can be made the exclusive and definitive bearer of evil in history." This is not because all people are equally sinful but because "wherever there is a human face there is evil and hope." Christ has unleashed in human history the power to overcome evil. At a particular time in history a class or nation can be "the typical and dominant representative"[31] of evil. But still, human alienation from God is so deeply rooted that it will be present until the end of history. Thus, the "process of redemption becomes a history of struggle which will not cease until the end." But, "when Christ's lordship becomes finally visible and totally operative, man will be really man, the solidary and creative creature that God created."[32]

Miguez Bonino's portrait of sin is complex. As an expression of human alienation and self-centeredness, it has overtones of the classical Marxist position, especially that of the early Marx. But as a separation from God and the divine purposes of creation, it is set in a theological context that is foreign to Marxism. Moreover, Miguez Bonino's assertion of our need for redemption from outside ourselves at the initiative of God—through Jesus Christ—heightens the emphasis on sin and evil as theological realities of greater than worldly importance. Nevertheless, the concrete expression of sin is within human history and in terms of human oppression. And the concrete expression of redemption is also within human history, in the struggle to overcome oppression. The struggle is to create the basis for a new humanity, expressing our true nature. The fact that Miguez Bonino, like other liberation theologians, discusses sin and redemption in social and not individual terms does not, thus, necessarily deprive these theological understandings of a basis transcending the purely historical plane. Institutionalized evil has a basis that is deeper than the institutions themselves, and redemption cannot come simply through institutional change. The revolution cannot be expected to offer a permanent cure to the reality of sin; sin is deeper than that. But, still, redemption lies in the struggle against sin—God's struggle first, and then ours as we are

---

[31]Miguez Bonino, *Christians and Marxists,* 129.
[32]Ibid., 110.

called through Christ to join in God's struggle. And that struggle is fought out on the plane of human social history.

As we join in that struggle, against the forces of injustice and oppression, are we invited to become self-righteous?

LIBERATIONIST ATTITUDES
TOWARD POLITICAL OPPONENTS

It might seem so. If (in Miguez Bonino's words) "a class or a nation can be the typical and dominant representative of [evil] at a certain point in history,"[33] and if one does not belong to that class or nation, could one be tempted toward self-righteous attitudes toward those who are identified as representing evil? We are partly saved from this conclusion by the Marxist revolutionary ethic, which inculcates a certain pressure of doubt about one's own revolutionary selflessness,[34] and there are parallels to that attitude in other movements such as the feminist and gay-lesbian liberation movements. One cannot, at least, become complacent in one's self-righteousness. For one is always under the judgment of history oneself. We are also partly saved from such a conclusion by the distinctly social understanding of righteousness shared by liberationists and non-Christian Marxists alike. *Self*-righteousness—like any other form of self-centeredness—is excluded, at least in principle. The sinfulness of those who belong to an oppressor class can indeed be judged, but only from the standpoint of the redemptive and liberating forces at work in history—not from the vantage point of anybody's personal moral superiority.

But that is not all that can be said. The liberationist, along with the follower of classical Marxism, understands the overcoming of oppression to be in the interest of the oppressor as well as of the oppressed. Gutierrez expresses this strikingly. He is clear that "class struggle means to decide for some people and against others." But at the same time "universal love is that which in solidarity with the oppressed seeks also to liberate the oppressors from their own power, from their ambition, and from their selfishness."[35] It is, in

---

[33]Ibid., 129.

[34]Asked in private conversation what her deepest theological criticism of the Communist party of her country might be, an Eastern European theologian acquaintance of mine commented on the striking inability of Marxists to receive and accept forgiveness.

[35]Gutierrez, *Theology of Liberation,* 275.

fact, an act of love for the oppressor to help liberate them "from their inhuman condition of oppressors."[36] But, he continues,

> this cannot be achieved except by resolutely opting for the oppressed, that is, by combating the oppressive class. It must be a real and effective combat, not hate. This is the challenge, as new as the Gospel: to love our enemies. . . . In the context of class struggle today, to love one's enemies presupposes recognizing and accepting that one has class enemies and that it is necessary to combat them. It is not a question of having no enemies, but rather of not excluding them from our love.[37]

It may be difficult to combat and love the same people at the same time. But to consider the act of opposing oppression as an affirmation of the oppressor clearly imparts a new moral quality to the struggle. This at least sets the stage for reconciliation, while implicitly calling into question every dehumanization of the adversary in one's rhetoric or action.

That point is also lifted up in Ruether's insistence that the liberation of the oppressed must also contain the liberation of the oppressor. In a book surveying several important spheres of human oppression, Ruether cautions against forms of liberation that constitute a mere reversal of the unjust relationship. One cannot, she writes, "dehumanize the oppressors without ultimately dehumanizing oneself. . . . By projecting all evil upon the oppressors and regarding their own oppressed condition as a stance of 'instant righteousness,' they forfeit finally their own capacity for self criticism."[38] And "only when protest and response remain in dialogue in such a way that the society which is condemned is also addressed as a community which has fallen away from its own authentic promise, can there be a liberation without ultimate violence; a liberation that can end in reconciliation and new brotherhood."[39] The issue of female/ male relationships, which Ruether addresses powerfully in this book, can almost be treated as paradigmatic of this understanding of liberation as the basis of the true humanity of both the oppressor and

---

[36]Ibid., 276.

[37]Ibid.

[38]Ruether, *Liberation Theology*, 13.

[39]Ibid., 15. In more recent writings Ruether has, of course, abandoned use of male-oriented metaphors (e.g., "brotherhood") as reflecting the domination of women by men.

the oppressed. Women and men truly need each other, and for men to dehumanize women is clearly to dehumanize themselves. If anything, as this example might suggest, those who oppress others are likely to be injured more severely than their obvious victims. But the larger truth is that all suffer together from the various forms of social alienation.

Not all liberation theologians have defined things in this way. For example, Cone cautions that "a word about reconciliation too soon or at the wrong time to the oppressors only grants them more power to oppress black people."[40] He admonishes black theologians to ask, "*not* about black people's reconciliation with white oppressors, but about our reconciliation with each other."[41] And he concludes with a stern warning that "we must let white oppressors know that we are on the 'battlefield of the Lord,' and are determined through God's grace to fight until we die. We must make clear to them that we will not be distracted from our liberation with their obscene talk about 'love' and 'forgiveness.'"[42]

THE ACCOUNTABILITY OF POWER

While the attitudes of liberation theologians toward political adversaries thus varies to some extent, two political conclusions of some importance emerge from this discussion. The first, which we have already seen, is that the adversary (whether or not regarded also as the victim of the adversary's own acts of oppression, whether or not the object of the drive for reconciliation) is not one to whom one would willingly cede any amount of social power. Indeed, they already have quite enough of that! The problem is to relieve them of power, not to provide legitimation for the power they have.

The other point is that the relevant liberation movement—defined and located in varying ways by different liberation theologians—is fundamentally accountable to itself and to the oppressed, not to a wider constituency, and certainly not to the oppressor. Liberation thinkers vary in the degree to which they believe the leadership of liberation movements should be formally accountable. Some are at pains to avoid elitism. Some appear to hold leadership

---

[40]Cone, *God of the Oppressed,* 243.
[41]Ibid., 245.
[42]Ibid., 246.

accountable only to objective results and to the liberating God. And some have comparatively little to say on the subject.

Understandably, the subject has more than academic interest among those who are defined as oppressors, particularly if they do not define themselves as oppressors and particularly if they feel threatened. Insofar as liberation theology presents itself as a quest for equality of formal political power (one person, one vote), the question may be unimportant. For those who seek to obstruct this can scarcely object to it on the basis of the values of democracy and political accountability. But liberation theologians are generally more interested in the substance of oppression—in economics, in race relations, in the relationships of men and women—than in the institutional forms of political democracy. The latter are typically regarded by them as facade anyway.

CONTRIBUTIONS AND LIMITATIONS

One's assessment of the contributions of the various forms of liberation theology will rest, no doubt, on whether one takes their fundamental protests seriously. *Is* society basically divided between oppressors and oppressed? Do the rich oppress the poor? Do white people oppress people of other racial groups? Do men oppress women?

Clearly, the answer to such questions is not only an emphatic Yes, but it must also include a reminder that such forms of oppression have long histories. Economic exploitation, racism, and sexism are also deeply embedded in human culture, not excluding the cultural forms of Christianity itself.

One's assessment of liberation theology also rests on whether one regards such forms of oppression as antithetical to Christian faith. Here, the protest of the liberationists against otherworldliness and detached pietism have a special resonance. For the liberationists are surely right in insisting that the gospel is not about individual transactions between human beings and God, having nothing to do with the way life is ordered in this world. And they are also right in emphasizing God's special concern for the poor and oppressed, not because God does not love everybody but because the poverty and oppression represent the breakdown of God's overall intention for human existence. The implicit claim—liberation theologians do not always trouble themselves about making the case for this explicitly—is that people are fundamentally equal in value, that they are created for mutuality in relationship, and that mutuality is not possible so long as some are in a position to dominate others. While the case against oppression can be made in most obvious terms where physical suffering is involved, most liberation thinkers also recognize the dehumanization involved through alienation within the human community.

On such matters they make common cause with the pacifists whom we discussed in chapter 4. But the liberationists part company with such pacifists on the question whether it is important to seize power to effect actual change and on the question whether coercive means, including violence, may legitimately be employed. Their implied criticism of the pacifists is that the latter suffer from ideological taint. By refusing to endorse revolutionary violence, the pacifists implicitly condone the violence of the unjust order. Pacifists themselves vigorously protest such an assessment, citing their devotion to nonviolent forms of protest (sometimes undertaken at great cost and personal risk). But the liberationist will press the question to the "bottom line": What are we to do when nonviolence does not work? And the liberationist will not allow her/himself to be inhibited from use of revolutionary means that are ultimately necessary to achieve revolutionary objectives. Least of all will liberationists be impressed by the insistence of a Yoder or a McClendon that Christians should not attempt to manage the course of history. That is precisely what liberationists have set out to do!

But liberation perspectives, despite certain recent refinements, remain troubling at three points. First is the question of sin. Is sin fundamentally located in social relationships and institutions or in personal dispositions or both? Miguez Bonino and others have attempted to address the charge that liberation theology treats sin as altogether structural or institutional by asserting a human need for redemption that transcends institutional reforms as such. But the relationship between the two needs more careful statement. That is not for the sake of theological abstraction but because the degree to which concrete political objectives should be absolutized rides on the outcome. The institutionalization of sin creates a strong theological motive toward institutional change. But the personal self-centeredness of individual human beings limits both the permanence and the quality of any institutional changes.

The second troubling point about the liberationist perspective is its tendency to absolutize diagnostic tools of limited range. Marxism may have much greater value as an analytical tool than most North Americans and Western Europeans are prepared to acknowledge, and even though Marxism is currently in eclipse in most parts of the world, we should not be surprised to see aspects of Marxist thought surfacing from time to time in the decades to come. But there is room for doubt whether the Marxist perspective provides an adequate basis for analyzing even economic forms of oppression much less those based on racism and sexism. At this point, the question is whether liberation theology is open enough to presentations of empirical truth that are not filtered through unquestioned ideological lenses such as those of Marxism.

The third and concluding question is whether the liberationist perspective is willing to *listen* to its adversaries. It is one thing to acknowledge the humanity of the adversary and to insist that the overcoming of oppression is as important for the oppressor as for the oppressed; on this, the best forms of liberationist perspective have truly opted for moral high ground. But it is quite another to acknowledge the humanity of the adversary by taking seriously the possibility that even the oppressor may have some part of the deeper human truth to share. Politics is important—let no reader of this book mistake my intent on that point!—but when human beings are fundamentally and persistently defined as allies or adversaries, as oppressors or oppressed, the tendency is to lose sight of their humanity. A good test question to ask ourselves is whether we think we have anything of importance to learn from our opponents. Not all liberation theologians have thought that they do.

6

Neoconservative Christian Perspectives

The United States of America is the primary bearer of the democratic possibility in the world today. The Soviet Union is the primary bearer of the totalitarian alternative. For better and for worse, each is a global force and between them there is no pattern of smooth convergence but of real and potential conflict. . . . More profound than the conflict of military and political forces, however, is the conflict over the dignity and destiny of the human person, and the societal order appropriate to that dignity and that destiny.
—*Institute on Religion and Democracy (1981)*[1]

"Judgment" is a word that is out of favor these days, but it remains a cornerstone of democratic self-government. It is what enables us to hold ourselves, and our leaders, to high standards. It is how we distinguish between right and wrong, noble and base, honor and dishonor. . . . It is the price—sometimes the exacting price—of citizenship in a democracy.
—*William J. Bennett (1998)*[2]

---

[1]*Christianity and Democracy* (Washington, D.C.: Institute on Religion and Democracy, 1981), 10. The statement was drafted by Richard John Neuhaus and adopted by the Institute's Executive Committee.

[2]William J. Bennett, *The Death of Outrage: Bill Clinton and the Assault on American Ideals* (New York: Free Press, 1998), 9.

A third generating center of recent Christian political thought poses still more questions. I refer now to the conservative reaction of thinkers such as Richard John Neuhaus, E. R. Norman, Paul Johnson, Ernest W. Lefever, Michael Novak, and William Bennett—and to the work of study centers such as the Ethics and Public Policy Center,[3] the Institute for Religion and Democracy, and the American Enterprise Institute. While representing a wide variety of positions on a number of issues, these writers and institutions were defined initially by their strongly held anticommunist position, an interest in legitimizing American power and presence in the political world, a commitment to democratic political institutions, and (for most) a conviction that healthy democratic government requires the presence of a rich fabric of "mediating structures" to foster group life at face-to-face levels uncontrolled by the state.

The collapse of the Soviet Empire and the virtual end of the Cold War removed anticommunism as a driving force for such thinkers and institutions, and the neoconservatives found themselves shifting gears. For some, the focus shifted toward the social and cultural agenda. The mood remained "anti," but the communist target was replaced by feminism, abortion, homosexuality, pornography, and the perceived liberalism of Protestant denominations and councils of churches. For others, the focus shifted more toward economic libertarianism and an emphasis upon limited government. On the whole, neoconservatism is more difficult to define, but it remains an important generating center of Christian political thought.

It was especially important in earlier years to refer to this as *neo*-conservatism. The prefix "neo" implied that they were, taken as a whole, not only conservative thinkers and institutions, but some *new kind* of conservative. The term conservative was clearly appropriate, if we think of a conservative as one who is especially concerned to preserve institutions and values considered to be in imminent danger. Soviet power and communist expansionism were the first major perceived dangers. The emphasis has shifted, and now there are other threats and dangers. But the "neo" prefix is also

---

[3]Not to be confused with the Churches Center for Theology and Public Policy, a study center reflecting the moderate to liberal orientation of mainstream denominations and theologians.

a helpful reminder that such thinkers are not from the same mold as a previous generation of theological conservatives.

For one thing, most of these thinkers are not biblical fundamentalists. For another, several of them have come to their conservatism by liberal, or even radical, routes. Lefever was originally a pacifist. Neuhaus was strongly opposed to the use of U.S. power in Vietnam (he was one of the founders of the primary religious anti-war organization, Clergy and Laity Concerned) and well to the left on most social and political questions. Novak first gained national prominence as a voice of the Catholic left, with essentially socialist views. Moreover, most of them continue to espouse aspects of a more liberal politics. Their views tend, therefore, to be complex. Their conservatism, thus, is partly a reaction against views they once held. But it also reflects their own struggle to voice creative new ideas and not simply to be reactive. Their complex new positions may also reflect a desire to support conservative political forces on the ascendancy since the late 1970s (such as the governments of President Reagan in the United States and Prime Minister Thatcher in Great Britain and conservative congressional leadership in the 1990s), while sometimes avoiding the extremes represented by those forces. Amidst the complexities, then, several important themes stand out.

THE AFFIRMATION OF DEMOCRACY

We have already taken note of the skepticism of the pacifists and liberationists concerning political democracy. On this question the neoconservatives wish to be *very* clear. To them democracy is the definitive political value. The point is not—at least not necessarily—that democracy has become for them the center of all value. As theologians, most of the Christian neoconservatives wish to be clear about the transcendence of God in Christ above all political systems, including democracy. But they are persuaded, nevertheless, that the theological case for the superiority of democracy among possible political systems is irrefutable.

These two aspects of neoconservative thought about democracy are illustrated in the foundational statement of the Institute on Religion and Democracy (IRD; an organization that was founded by neoconservatives and remains a principal outlet for many of them). The transcendence of God is afffirmed in the declaration that "every earthly sovereignty is subordinate to the sovereignty of Jesus

Christ"[4] and in the acknowledgment that even democracy is limited and imperfect.[5] But these points having been registered, the theological case for democracy is that "it is precisely the merit of democracy that it reminds us of this truth and sustains the possibility of humane government in a necessarily unsatisfactory world."[6] Democratic government respects the independent integrity of other aspects of culture (a point to which we will return). Its openness allows for the working of realities other than politics, especially those reflecting our ultimate grounding in a faith perspective.

In another writing, Neuhaus (who was also author of the IRD statement) speaks of the failure of the churches to supply "a theological and a moral reconstruction that will for the first time ground the democratic experiment in biblical faith." While acknowledging that the original sources of democracy (Greek, Cromwellian, French Revolutionary, and American) "were marginal to or even hostile to Christian faith," Neuhaus contends that "the fundamental notions of democracy—of the dignity of the human person, therefore of the necessary limits of the state, of the discrete spheres of influence of economics, political, and cultural life—are rooted in Christianity."[7] Democracy, while not ultimate in the religious sense, is certainly important enough to warrant dying for and killing for—a way of putting the matter that clearly underscores the difference between his position and that of the pacifists and (for different reasons) the liberationists!

J. Brian Benestad grounds similar judgments in the theological foundation of the dignity of the human person: "Catholic principles lead people to choose the form of government that most effectively allows, and even encourages, the human person to develop his spiritual and social nature."[8] While much Catholic tradition prior to recent years might not seem supportive of democracy, neoconservative Catholic thinkers like Benestad can lay hold of Vatican II and recent papal encyclicals to ground this point. And they can well argue

---

[4]*Christianity and Democracy,* 1.

[5]Ibid., 5.

[6]Ibid.

[7]Richard John Neuhaus, "A Crisis of Faith," in *Ethics and Nuclear Arms: European and American Perspectives,* ed. Raymond English (Washington, D.C.: Ethics and Public Policy Center, 1985), 62.

[8]J. Brian Benestad, *The Pursuit of a Just Social Order: Policy Statements of the U.S. Catholic Bishops, 1966–80* (Washington, D.C.: Ethics and Public Policy Center, 1982), 18.

that Catholic teaching has always at least implicitly affirmed the importance of human dignity, which in turn can be taken to support the case for democracy.

Neoconservative support for democracy has not been unqualified. The Ethics and Public Policy Center resisted liberation movements in South Africa and what is now Zimbabwe, and a number of neoconservative thinkers were critical of the Chilean government of Salvador Allende—despite the democratic process by which he came to power—because he was Marxist, and uncritical of the subsequent regime of General Pinochet because he was not. Moreover, neoconservatives are cautious in their support for the civil rights and civil liberties of minorities.

THE LIMITED STATE

But what is democracy? Since the term is commonly used by representatives of virtually all points on the ideological spectrum, the neoconservative case for democracy necessarily depends in part on what neoconservatives mean by it. The IRD statement emphasizes the importance of certain foundational rights, including freedom of speech, assembly, and publication: "What in our country [the U.S.A.] is represented by the Bill of Rights is not only constitutionally mandated but is theologically imperative." And the transfer of political power in a democracy includes "maximum consultation and participation by the people governed."[9] To this end, popular elections are important. Elections must be "regular," "contested," and "decisive." The IRD notes that "nowhere today is there democratic governance in the absence of regular, contested, and decisive elections."[10]

A striking feature in the neoconservative understanding of democracy is its emphasis upon the limited state.

> The state is not the whole of society, but is one important actor in the society. Other institutions—notably the family, the Church, educational, economic and cultural enterprises—are at least equally important actors in the society.... These spheres have their own peculiar sovereignty which must be respected by the state.[11]

---

[9]*Christianity and Democracy,* 7.
[10]Ibid., 8.
[11]Ibid., 4.

The meaning of this, particularly for Roman Catholic neoconservatives, is suggested by the Catholic doctrine of subsidiarity. First enunciated clearly by Pope Pius XI in the encyclical *Quadragesimo Anno,* the doctrine of subsidiarity holds that (in the words of that encyclical) "one should not withdraw from individuals and commit to the community what they can accomplish by their own enterprise and industry" and "it is an injustice and at the same time a grave evil and a disturbance of right order, to transfer to the larger and higher collectivity functions which can be performed and provided for by lesser and subordinate bodies."[12] In Catholic tradition, subsidiarity is a recognition of the organic character of society. Every part of society has its own intrinsic validity or end, and it is a violation of the moral order to treat any aspect of society simply as a means for the accomplishment of the purposes of society as a whole.

The doctrine of subsidiarity did not, of course, develop as a Catholic definition of or defense of democracy. Quite the contrary, it emerged during the reign of Pius XI as a part of a strong reaction against what certain popes had taken to be democracy. That reaction, which included Pius IX's *Syllabus of Errors* (1870) and Leo XIII's *Rerum Novarum* (1891), was against the excesses of the French Revolution and Marxism, both of which included the notion that society could remake itself in revolutionary fashion from the ground up. The doctrine of subsidiarity emerged as a defense of the integrity of lesser aspects and institutions of society. The state is not everything. Even for the state some things are off-limits.

Thus, a definition of democracy emphasizing the doctrine of subsidiarity could not be based solely upon majority rule—and neoconservatives clearly do not believe in a democracy of that kind. They would insist, however, that subsidiarity is not against democracy. Genuine respect for the political rights of every member of the community must necessarily include respect for the inviolability of the lesser groups and institutions of which we are a part.[13]

Peter L. Berger and Richard John Neuhaus emphasized the point in their work, *To Empower People: The Role of Mediating Structures*

---

[12]*Quadragesimo Anno,* para. 79.

[13]An important part of the task of liberal Roman Catholic political thought prior to Vatican II was to distinguish between the totalitarian forms of "democracy" against which the encyclicals had properly reacted, and those forms, such as the Anglo-American, which included protection of subsidiary rights.

in Public Policy.[14] Their point was that real democracy is not possible where social transactions are carried out directly between vast institutions, such as the state, and atomized individuals. To be human and to have real power we need smaller-scale institutions and groups in which to function. The principle is not limited to the relationship between individuals and the state; it includes our need for mediating structures standing between individuals and other large-scale collectivities, such as giant corporations, labor organizations, and even religious bodies. But the state is the sine qua non of totalitarian possibilities, for it is invested with coercive power as well as mass size. Special care must therefore be given to foster the well-being of social mediating structures vis-à-vis the state.

In a conception of the limited state that has proved influential among neoconservatives, Michael Novak contrasts unitary and pluralistic societies.[15] Most societies in the past have been unitary. By this, Novak means that the principal aspects of society are united in a single structure of power and meaning. The ideal of the unitary society is to link all people in a common expression of purpose based upon common values. Traditional societies are unitary, based upon myths and traditions held in common by all of the people and implemented by an overarching order. That was the case with medieval Christianity and ancient empires, as with isolated traditional tribes. That is equally true of socialism, which strives after a post-Enlightenment form of unitary order—even one based on materialistic atheism, in the case of Marxian socialism. Whether or not any given order has been precisely successful in achieving a fully unitary society is not the point; the point is that that has been a generally shared objective.

By contrast, according to Novak, a pluralistic society has no one set of myths and values, no one unified structure of political and economic power. "In a genuinely pluralistic society, there is no one sacred canopy. *By intention* there is not. At its spiritual core, there is an empty shrine."[16] In a democratic capitalist society three principal aspects of society are distinguished and deliberately kept

---

[14]Peter L. Berger and Richard John Neuhaus, *To Empower People: The Role of Mediating Structures in Public Policy* (Washington, D.C.: American Enterprise Institute, 1977). See also Michael Novak, ed., *Democracy and Mediating Structures: A Theological Inquiry* (Washington, D.C.: American Enterprise Institute, 1980).

[15]See especially Michael Novak, *The Spirit of Democratic Capitalism* (New York: Simon & Schuster, 1982).

[16]Ibid., 53.

separated: the political, the economic, and the moral-cultural. Each of the three affects and helps define the other two, but each possesses its own separate integrity and cannot be totally dominated by or reduced to one of the other two. The resulting checks and balances help preserve the creative freedom of the whole society. As Novak puts it,

> This differentiation of systems sets individuals possessed of the will-to-power on three separate tracks. Political activists may compete for eminence in the political system, economic activists in the economic system, religious activists and intellectuals in various parts of the moral-cultural system. But the powers of each of the three systems over the others, while in each case substantial, are firmly limited. It is not likely that one person or party can gain complete dominance over all three systems, and should such misfortune come to pass, there remain plural roads by which offending forces may attack each pretender at his weakest points.[17]

The import of this for politics is that economic life and the "moral-cultural system" must not be subordinated, at least not very much, to political purposes. The power of the political order over the other two aspects of society must be expressed in the somewhat ambiguous "not very much," as I have done here, because Novak does not provide us with a very precise way of delineating the separations from the interactions of his three spheres.

THE INDISPENSABILITY
OF CAPITALISM TO DEMOCRACY

A key point of application is the relationship between democracy and capitalism. Most, if not all, of the neoconservatives are deeply committed to capitalism. Most believe it to be superior in doing what economic systems are supposed to do: provide adequate material well-being for the world's people. Even though several of the neoconservatives have come to this judgment out of a prior background as critics of the capitalist system, most no longer consider the socialist alternative worth serious consideration. For example, Berger has recently written that "we know, or should know, that socialism is a mirage that leads nowhere, except to economic stagnation, collective poverty, and various degrees of tyranny. We also know that

---

[17]Ibid., 56.

capitalism has been dramatically successful, if in a limited number of underdeveloped countries."[18] But the commitment by neoconservatives to capitalism is not grounded solely on their views of its greater economic efficiency. Most are equally convinced that there is an inextricable connection between capitalism and democracy. Novak argues the point in various of his writings that democracy is possible only in predominantly capitalist environments, even though such environments do not necessarily produce democracy. We can have capitalism without democracy, but apparently we cannot have democracy without capitalism. The IRD picks up this theme as well. The organization's statement reaffirms its primary concern to be the preservation and strengthening of democracy. Nevertheless, it also expresses the view that "the personal and institutional ownership and control of property—always as stewards of God to whom the whole creation belongs—contributes greatly to freedom." And it notes "as a matter of historical fact that democratic governance exists only where the free market plays a large part in a society's economy." A market economy "may therefore be a necessary condition for democracy" even though "it is obviously not a sufficient condition for democracy."[19] Paul Johnson goes further in writing that "capitalism tends to promote—and in my contention, *must* promote—liberal-democratic political systems."[20] In his judgment, political freedom cannot exist without economic freedom. And "the notions of political and economic freedom both spring from the workings of the Christian conscience as a historical force."[21]

Few of the neoconservatives wish to banish the state altogether from economic life. (Novak explicitly affirms its regulatory functions, and my impression is that some neoconservatives would go further than he in affirming welfare-state functions.) But most now see an inextricable linkage between democracy and capitalism.

The neoconservatives, therefore, do not simply prefer to have their democracy mixed with capitalism; they do not think they can have it any other way. Therefore, they view the prospects for

---

[18]Peter L. Berger and Michael Novak, *Speaking to the Third World: Essays on Democracy and Development* (Washington, D.C.: American Enterprise Institute, 1985), 29. See also Peter L. Berger, *The Capitalist Revolution: Fifty Propositions about Prosperity, Equality, and Liberty* (New York: Basic Books, 1986).

[19]*Christianity and Democracy,* 6.

[20]Paul Johnson, "Is There a Moral Basis for Capitalism?" in *Democracy and Mediating Structures,* 56.

[21]Ibid., 57.

democratic socialism as essentially nil. Some consider the case already closed; others seem more open to further data demonstrating that socialism can be combined with democracy. In either case, their message to those who are committed to socialism is either that that commitment must be abandoned or that there is no use seeking to create or maintain democratic institutions at the same time.

It is interesting to observe that Christian neoconservatives have at least this in common with many liberation theologians: both are skeptical that democracy can stand as a meaningful (and morally supportable) political order apart from a particular kind of economic system. Both are unwilling, ultimately, to separate the case for democracy from the case for a particular economic system. But, of course, they draw exactly opposite conclusions as to which economic system can be combined with democracy, just as they differ in their understanding of democracy itself.

Thus, we are not surprised that the neoconservatives were initially prompted by their opposition to world communism. Their views on capitalism directly contradict the economics of communism, for which they have only disdain. Their views on democracy, with emphases upon freedom, human rights, and pluralism, are in sharp conflict with the unitary totalitarianism and flagrant denial of human rights which they perceived in Marxian communism. Add to this a whole range of theological conflicts, including Marxist atheism and Marxist understandings of human nature. Given the points of disagreement, one is not surprised by neoconservative opposition to Marxism. Still, the absoluteness in which neoconservative anticommunism was expressed was striking. The impression is left that communism is not simply a flawed, even deeply flawed ideological system; rather, it is the enemy in every respect, the prime example of social, political, economic evil in our time. The IRD could assert that "Christians must be unapologetically anti-Communist. Anti-Communism is not a sufficient political philosophy, but it is an indispensable component in discerning the signs of the times."[22] People who do not understand this "have not recognized the bloody face of our age."[23]

---

[22]*Christianity and Democracy,* 4.

[23]Such statements, drafted for the IRD by Neuhaus, may be compared with his words as published in another volume the same year: "The usefulness of the idea of 'the free world versus the Communist world' as the inclusive model for understanding international affairs has long since expired. In relating to other countries, U.S. policy should be deliberately indifferent to ideological labels" (*Christian Faith and Public Policy: Thinking and Acting in the Courage of Uncertainty* [Minneapolis: Augsburg, 1977], 81).

THE LEGITIMATION OF AMERICAN POWER

Given such themes, it is not surprising that neoconservatives support a strong U.S. political and military presence on the world scene. Faced, during the Cold War, by the world-historical reality of communism, headquartered in the USSR, the United States was seen to represent the only prospect of an adequate countervailing force in the modern world.

Neoconservatives do not like the United States to be or even appear to be weak militarily. Ernest Lefever has emphasized this point for some years, though not always with the candor displayed in a statement quoted by the press in 1986 (on the occasion of the Reagan administration scandal involving sale of arms to Iran with proceeds transmitted to "contra" revolutionaries in Nicaragua): "We've had enough rhetoric and blame. . . . We must get on with the business of being a great power. The president must do something in the real world that is bold, that involves the use or threat of military force."[24]

And neoconservatives do not exclude nuclear deterrence from the inventory of morally permissible military means. The British historian Edward R. Norman is representative in arguing that nuclear war is not fundamentally different. In his view, even the wars of ancient empires were "total"—entailing the total destruction of the lives, property, and civilizations of the vanquished. People fight not just over greed but over ideas and values. Traditional Christianity has known that "the history of the civilized world . . . was a history of conflict to secure values against competitors" and it understood that "whatever the evil of conflict, it was preferable to the surrender of values, for God had entrusted values to mankind—the treasure was in earthen vessels—and preserving these values was what life was all about."[25] It is, in Norman's view, a theological error to sacralize human life, as we do when we make human survival into an ultimate norm. Only God is sacred. And human beings are ennobled by the willingness to sacrifice even life itself in the pursuit of values. Ultimately, force is the arbiter: "Most of the great historical changes have occurred through force of arms, and the future is unlikely to be any different in this respect." And once the decision has been made to defend values by force, "then the enormous

---

[24]Quoted by Sidney Blumenthal, "Conservatives Fear for Contras," *Washington Post,* November 28, 1986, p. A32. Lefever went on to suggest that "the most logical place [for a display of force] would be in Central America."

[25]Edward R. Norman, "Christian Morality and Nuclear Arms," in *Ethics and Nuclear Arms,* 113.

destructive potential of nuclear weapons does not add anything new." And Christians should not delude themselves that nuclear deterrence can be used without a readiness to use nuclear weapons in the event of necessity. In such an event, "the possibility of an actual resort to nuclear conflict will always remain." Norman believes that "it is the duty of Christians to face that prospect clearly and to decide about its morality."[26] And he hopes Christians will make that decision in favor of the morality of nuclear weapons should such a situation arise.

Running through the writings of neoconservatives is the complaint that "left-leaning" churches and church leaders have seriously eroded the legitimacy of American power in the contemporary world. By treating U.S. power as a primary source of evil in the contemporary world, such people have weakened the will of the West to defend its civilization and its values against the threat, previously of Soviet aggression and presently of repressive regimes such as North Korea, China, and Iraq. The maintenance of a strong military is essential to the defense and furtherance of democracy and market economics in the contemporary world.

THE CHURCH AND POLITICAL WITNESS

As we have observed, the neoconservatives are in sharp opposition to liberationists at many points. It is noteworthy, however, that most of the neoconservatives join the liberationists in the view that the churches and individual Christians need to be engaged in political life, if only to diminish the totalitarian tendencies afoot through much of the world. That is in itself a remarkable development, given the historic tendency of many conservatives to oppose church involvement in social action. But at this point, at least, neoconservatives remain in touch with the earlier, more liberal commitments many of them had to church social action. While vigorously, some would say unfairly, criticizing the churches for one-sidedness and naivete in the *way* in which mainline churches and councils of churches have responded to political issues, neoconservatives do not, in the main, repudiate church involvement with such issues. In that, they also agree with a number of representatives of the religious right wing, whom we will discuss in the next chapter.

Some of the neoconservatives remain critical of church involvements in politics, however. In a diatribe against the World Council

---

[26]Ibid., 120.

of Churches' political activism (in particular blaming the WCC for fostering Western guilt over the Vietnam War),[27] Lefever goes further than most neoconservatives in questioning the churches' institutional role:

> [I]t is morally wrong and politically unwise for the church to identify itself or Christianity with any political cause, movement, party, or regime. . . . Identification deprives the church of the critical distance essential for judging the behavior of any human institution or program in the light of eternal and universal principles.[28]

By contrast, he writes that "individual Christians *as individuals* can and should participate in partisan political causes, supporting those that show some promise of advancing justice, freedom, or order."[29] While the view of the church, or ecclesiology, underlying these judgments is not too clear, even Lefever does not appear to dispute the idea that justice has theological importance—and, therefore, that Christians have theological reasons for seeking to advance "justice, freedom, or order." The problem with church involvement, in his mind, appears to relate to more practical considerations. Church involvement suggests a more serious judgment by the community of faith that a particular course of action is theologically correct. If individual Christians make mistakes in such judgments the world is not as likely to be misled about the character of Christian faith than it can be when the church makes mistakes. But even Lefever does not appear to question the theological importance of the issues themselves. Nor do most of the other neoconservatives.[30]

---

[27]Ernest W. Lefever, *Amsterdam to Nairobi: The World Council of Churches and the Third World* (Washington, D.C.: Ethics and Public Policy Center, 1979), 26.

[28]Ibid., 53.

[29]Ibid., 54 (emphasis added).

[30]Dutch theologian H. M. Kuitert has concluded that the church in our time is far too politicized. See H. M. Kuitert, *Everything Is Politics but Politics Is not Everything,* trans. John Bowden (Grand Rapids: Wm. B. Eerdmans, London: SCM Press, 1986). Kuitert reserves the possibility of church political action in extreme circumstances where there is no other recourse for oppressed people (e.g., apartheid-era South Africa). But he is generally opposed to the church playing a political role: "I mistrust politics through the church; that makes the churches lose their nature; as a result politics becomes devalued and it is not inconceivable that Christians socialize their faith" (p. 5). "And a church which has nothing to talk about but social and political solutions and views is hardly worth the trouble" (p. 163). While his conclusions about the church and politics are conservative (in the older sense), I do not classify him among the neoconservatives since his views on most of the subjects discussed above appear to diverge from theirs.

If the witness of individual Christians is theologically mandated—as most of the neoconservatives, including Lefever, affirm—then it is not clear why the weight of Christian corporate witness should not be thrown on the scales of political debate as well.

RELIGION AND MORALITY IN PUBLIC

Part of the stock in trade of the "new right" evangelicals (whom we are to discuss in the next chapter) has been their insistence that the United States is a Christian nation and their desire to see that recognized in various symbolic ways.[31] When, at the Republican National Convention of 1992, Pat Buchanan announced that the United States is in a "culture war," his views were embraced by some and regarded with embarrassment by others. Behind Buchanan's statement lay debates on public standards of sexual morality and related problems of abortion, sex education in the schools, homosexuality, and the preservation of traditional social roles for women. Neoconservatives are not easily characterized about such matters.

Some, like Novak, are largely committed to a secular conception of the public order: "Christian symbols ought not to be placed in the center of a pluralist society. They must not be, out of reverence for the transcendent which others approach in other ways."[32] Other neoconservatives, such as Neuhaus, believe that a democratic society such as the United States depends for its moral foundations upon values derived from Christian faith. He wishes to resist the secularism he sees advancing in American public life. "Intellectually, what is now called neoconservatism not only represents disillusionment with earlier liberal policies but in many cases stands as a challenge to reigning assumptions of the secular Enlightenment, including the exclusion of moral, metaphysical, and religious vision from the public arena."[33] While noting that the conservative political tide is

---

[31]See Erling Jorstad, *The Politics of Moralism* (Minneapolis: Augsburg, 1981); Peggy L. Shriver, *The Bible Vote: Religion and the New Right* (New York: Pilgrim Press, 1981); Jerry Falwell, *Listen America* (New York: Doubleday, 1980); and David G. Bromley and Anson Shupe, eds., *New Christian Politics* (Macon, Ga.: Mercer University Press, 1983).

[32]Novak, *Spirit of Democratic Capitalism,* 70.

[33]Richard J. Neuhaus, "From Providence to Privacy: Religion and the Redefinition of America," in *Unsecular America,* ed. Richard J. Neuhaus (Grand Rapids: Wm. B. Eerdmans, 1986), 60.

largely "a populist protest against the undemocratic imposition of a secular and secularizing definition of American life,"[34] Neuhaus is critical of the religious new right for wanting "to enter the political arena making public claims on the basis of private truths."[35] By doing so, it becomes an ironic collaborator with secular humanism in separating religion from the public sphere. The acknowledgment of the indispensability of religion in public life must be rational accountability. Religion cannot simply be imposed, although neither can it be ignored. Explicitly criticizing Novak's "reverential emptiness," Neuhaus remarks that the attempt to banish religion from public life can only be a "transitional phenomenon." Such a state of society "is a vacuum begging to be filled." And it will be filled "by the agent left in control of the public square, the state."[36]

Other neoconservatives, such as Buchanan and William J. Bennett, are even more critical of what they see as an advance of libertarianism in American culture. A defining moment for most neoconservatives was the controversy over the impeachment of President Bill Clinton in 1998–99. Most were bitterly critical of the president and disheartened by the failure of two-thirds of the American people (in repeated public opinion polls) to share their outrage. William J. Bennett shared his own sense of outrage in a small book attacking the president and, derivatively, the public who were disinclined to remove him from office.[37] To Bennett this was evidence of the loss of virtue in the public culture. He writes:

> In living memory, the chief threats to American democracy have come from without: first, Nazism and Japanese imperialism, and, later, Soviet communism. But these wars, hot and cold, ended in spectacular American victories. The threats we now face are from within. They are far different, more difficult to detect, more insidious: decadence, cynicism, and boredom.[38]

In a similar vein, most of the authors in a volume published at the height of the impeachment controversy were deeply critical, not only of the president but of the culture and of religious leaders who

---

[34]Ibid.

[35]Richard J. Neuhaus, *The Naked Public Square: Religion and Democracy in America* (Grand Rapids: Wm. B. Eerdmans, 1984), 36.

[36]Ibid., 86.

[37]Bennett, *The Death of Outrage.*

[38]Ibid., 130.

seemed to have granted him too easy an absolution for his sins.[39] "Is this where we have arrived as a culture?" asks Jean Bethke Elshtain. "Shouldn't our public leaders work to counter this sort of antinomianism rather than play to it?"[40] Similarly, Matthew L. Lamb decries the "nihilistic indifference" that "spreads like a cancer that erodes the very fabric of family and social life." "This indifference," he warns, "seeps into all facets of American life." It includes especially a wrong-headed individualism in sexual relationships of all kinds and the "indifferent abstractions of a secular humanism [that] replace concrete human beings making real decisions."[41]

While responses to the controversy varied widely and did not always correlate with ideological or political orientations, it is striking how readily neoconservatives seized upon that moment to express alarm over the drift of American culture. Their alarm was only deepened by the president's acquittal in the impeachment trial.

CRITICAL ASSESSMENT

It would appear, on balance, that the greatest contribution of this generating center of Christian political thought lies in what brought it into being: its reaffirmation of democracy and its warnings about totalitarianism. Against many of the liberation theologians as well as many of the pacifist/anarchists, it was able to recognize that democracy provides protections against human pretensions and idolatries while affording greater opportunity for the creative possibilities of human freedom to emerge in the political arena. Neoconservatives were, I think, also prompted by their reaction against what they perceived as the dishonesties of the ideologues of the left who always seemed to overstate their positions. Neoconservatives proved capable of overstatement themselves, but their reactions to "knee-jerk" liberalism or socialism were not unhealthy.

The concept of mediating structures, especially as applied to the churches, needs to be examined rather more carefully. On the face of it, this is a helpful reminder that democracy remains abstract if it does not include freedom of association and the possibility of generating an

---

[39]Gabriel Fackre, ed., *Judgment Day at the White House* (Grand Rapids: Wm. B. Eerdmans, 1998).

[40]Jean Bethke Elshtain, "Politics and Forgiveness: The Clinton Case," in ibid., 17.

[41]Matthew L. Lamb, "President Clinton and the Privatization of Morality," in ibid., 37–38.

organized political opposition and a realm of life not subject to politicization. But on the other hand, the state must be strong enough to enact the end results of a thoroughly democratic process while fully respecting the continued freedom of opposition. For the church to be a mediating institution in the political order does not mean that it should only be a refuge from that order. Even more, it should be a center of creative thought and action to affect what that order does.[42]

The point is that the limited state is not necessarily a responsible state. Those areas of life that are marked off as being beyond the limits of the state's power need to be examined very carefully, for they represent powers that are removed from the political reach of the people. No doubt there are aspects of human society that should thus be placed out of the reach of the political process. The neoconservatives make that point, although they are by no means the only ones to do so in the contemporary political discussion. The question remains, what forms of human power should be removed from political accountability? That question will occupy us later in this book. But, for now, the judgment can be entered that the neoconservatives have an inclination to limit the state at some points where it ought to have more power and at other points, perhaps, to give it too much power.

One is struck by the extent to which many neoconservatives wish to mark economic life off as an area for noninterference by the state. What this means, practically, is that an area of human life that profoundly affects everybody is removed from democratic accountability. The issue here is not just whether or not Christians should support socialism or capitalism. It is the extent to which the economic order should be made accountable to the people whose welfare is affected by it. Most of the arguments advanced in behalf of democracy would seem, at the same time, to be arguments for democratic control of the economic sphere. Such democratic control is, in principle, consistent with modified forms of capitalism. But the issue is raised with full force when we ask whether democratic socialism is even a conceivable option.

To say, as many neoconservatives do, that democracy depends upon capitalism is to argue that the economic sphere should be governed primarily by private forces in the marketplace—that economic life should be primarily if not altogether referred to mediating structures. This is to place the burden of proof very

---

[42]I have explored these points further in "The Church as Mediating Institution: Theological and Philosophical Perspective," in *Democracy and Mediating Structures*, 69–81.

heavily against governmental involvement in economic life. But if government is encouraged to absent itself from the economic sphere, does this not leave ordinary people without the capacity to affect the broad outlines of their society's economic destiny except insofar as they can acquire power through market economics (as few can)? Moreover, if we are to believe (as Reinhold Niebuhr evidently did)[43] that the theological case for democracy is more compelling than the case for Western capitalism, then there must be a basis for dialogue with socialists that entertains the possibility of a democratic socialism and not only a democratic capitalism.

The neoconservative anticommunist theme presents further difficulties. Insofar as this is simply a criticism of the totalitarian history and tendencies in many Marxist societies it may be a good reminder that Christians need to be wise as serpents as well as innocent as doves. And, indeed, by century's end the neoconservatives could justly claim to have been right about the flaws in Marxism. The collapse of the Soviet Empire around 1990 revealed profound internal defects that were economic and political, but also philosophical and religious. Neoconservative thinking anticipated that, even though most of them were as surprised as everybody else by the suddenness of the collapse.

But some of the neoconservatives went much further than that. Their rhetoric suggested not only that all Marxist societies are in principle totalitarian and, ultimately, the same in their totalitarianism; it further implied that Marxists themselves were incapable of anything else as long as they remained Marxists. There was an almost Manichean tendency here to absolutize an adversary. And it is well to remember, theologically, that the absolutizing of an enemy is as much a form of idolatry as the absolutizing of any person or movement we wish to affirm. One clear and present danger in absolutizing an adversary is that it can so easily lead to self-righteousness.

Aside from being a spiritual danger, self-righteousness in the political sphere in turn easily leads to the legitimating of cruel means to combat the evils we have identified. I am not here referring to the neoconservative insistence upon legitimating American power in the contemporary world. On this I am in agreement that American power often has been a force for good, that the extent of its malevolence in the contemporary world has been overstated in much of the

---

[43]Reinhold Niebuhr, *The Children of Light and the Children of Darkness* (New York: Charles Scribner's Sons, 1944).

rhetoric of liberation theology, and that it is possible to use American power as a force for good and to correct those areas where that power has been a force for injustice and evil. I am referring, rather, to the tendency to define the problem of combating forces such as communism in primarily military terms and to justify preparations for military destructiveness utterly out of proportion to any known evil—including totalitarianism—on earth.

Nuclear war, to which this of course refers, poses dilemmas for all Christians. The case for retaining some nuclear deterrence, though strongly opposed by many Christians, is by no means limited to the neoconservatives. But the absoluteness of the latter's anticommunism led them, it seems to me, to a too-easy escape from the dilemmas. It made the evils and risks of nuclear war appear too modest in relation to the perceived evils of communism.

If an important needed corrective here is theological, another needed corrective may be a more careful reading of history. The neoconservatives thought of communism as inevitably totalitarian and totalitarianism as essentially irreversible. But perhaps they could have attended more carefully to the actual history of communism since the Russian Revolution. While that history records many inhumanities, it also reveals variations and changes, such as the Soviet *glasnost* of the 1980s and the extraordinary role of Mikhail Gorbachev. On the basis of neoconservative stereotypes one could scarcely have predicted the earlier rise of the Alexander Dubcek government and the Czech reform movement in 1968—changes occurring, first, *within* the Czech Communist party. Nor could one have predicted Salvador Allende's commitment to democracy in Chile. Such changes do not represent the arrival of the kingdom of God on earth; they do suggest that communism was a more human phenomenon than the neoconservatives gave it credit for being. President Ronald Reagan famously referred to the USSR as an "evil empire." He was certainly right in that there was a good deal about it that was evil—but not all. Part of the problem with demonizing a historical force is the spillover effect upon all of its leaders and even the ordinary people who make it up and who also come to be treated as evil. But such people are not just evil; indeed, some of them, individually, may be quite as good as those who call them evil.

Similar points can be made about the reactions of neoconservatives to moral problems in contemporary culture. Any thoughtful Christian can observe evidences of moral laxity in Western culture, and it does not hurt to be reminded of that from time to time. But the neoconservatives here, as with communism earlier, have a tendency to paint with

121

a very broad brush. There are also evidences in the culture of morally positive things. When, for example, current divorce rates or teen pregnancy or the spread of pornography are cited as examples of the society being much worse morally than it was thirty or forty years ago, it is forgotten that we had the most vicious imaginable examples of systemic racism then, along with systemic discrimination against women.

Thus, while contributing some useful correctives, neoconservatism may ultimately be too reactive, too defensive to provide a suitable framework for serious Christian thought about politics. Neoconservatives so often seem to be clearer and more passionate about what they are against than what they are for, forgetting Santayana's dictum that we are more likely to be right in the things we affirm than the things we deny. Neoconservatives are usually pretty bright. But, in theological terms, they are better at law than at grace—and grace, more than law, is where God, as revealed in Christ, is to be found.

The point became clearer during the impeachment controversy of 1998–99. There was little dispute that what the president had done was sinful and wrong—he himself was very clear about that. The question was what should be done about it and, in particular, whether this was a moment when a whole country could respond with something like grace. Neoconservatives, as exemplified by William Bennett and most of the authors of *Judgment Day at the White House,* were openly critical of such a response. Their desire to punish was much more evident than their desire to heal.[44] In this, and in other respects, their reactive views need to be supplemented.

---

[44]My own role during that period was not simply that of disinterested academic observer. As a pastor to the president as well as a Christian ethicist, I felt that I needed to participate in the national debate, and I did so by appearing extensively in the media and by writing *From the Eye of the Storm: A Pastor to the President Speaks Out* (Louisville, Ky.: Westminster John Knox Press, 1998). I argued in that book that the controversy confronted the nation with conflicting alternatives: Either we could respond primarily in a legalistic and vindictive spirit or we could extend forgiveness and seek the healing of the nation. Since the heart of the president's problem—and that of the culture in general—was the loss of connection between caring, committed love on the one hand and sexual expression on the other, it seemed clear to me that such a problem could not be healed in an unloving way. In contrast to those who called for a return to public virtues by punishment and public shame and to those who considered forgiveness and love to be weak and sentimental, I felt that love is in fact the foundation of all other virtues. It is the virtue without which there can be no other virtue. As I write these words now, I cannot conclude that the country has achieved perfect healing in this matter, nor that it ever will. Nevertheless, I am persuaded that the good sense of a majority of the American people is what prevailed and that the nation's public life is stronger for that and not weaker.

7

Evangelical Perspectives:
Right and Left

But let us not stop short until there is a complete restoration of the time-honored traditions of this nation, the complete fall of liberalism, and God's blessings are once again upon the land.

—Pat Robertson (1993)[1]

Whether they are religious or not, most Americans are hungry for a deeper connection between politics and moral values; many would say 'spiritual values.' . . . But for too long the so-called Religious Right has dominated that discussion in the mainstream media. The result is that many people who have religious or spiritual con cerns, but don't feel represented by groups like the Christian Coalition, feel left out of the conversation. These people must be brought back into the public discussion. We need them.

—Jim Wallis (1996)[2]

Christian evangelicalism emerged as a new force in American political life during the closing decades of the twentieth century. In some respects, it parallels the development of religious conservatism in

---

[1]Pat Robertson, *The Turning Tide* (Dallas: Word Publishing, 1993), 302. Cited in Justin Watson, *The Christian Coalition: Dreams of Restoration, Demands for Recognition* (New York: St. Martin's Press, 1997), 95.

[2]Jim Wallis, *Who Speaks for God? An Alternative to the Religious Right—A New Politics of Compassion, Community, and Civility* (New York: Delacorte Press, 1996), xi.

many countries—and in several very different religious traditions.[3] Fundamentalism can be known by its absolute commitment to certain sources of religious authority, especially sacred writings interpreted with uncompromising literalism, along with doctrines that are held undeviatingly and with the assurance that those who disagree are dead wrong. There are fundamentalist subgroups in each of the major world religions. In recent years, many of these have played a forceful, sometimes fanatical role in the public life of particular countries.

American evangelicals are not so easily characterized in that way. For one thing, the word "evangelical" is subject to varying definitions. Some who describe themselves as evangelical are fundamentalists, as I have used the term above. Others, while deeply devoted to the Bible, are not absolutist in their thinking. Sometimes they might better be called pietists. Still others are somewhere in between, sometimes appealing to taking particular scriptural passages literally and applying them rigidly, sometimes treating parts of the Bible with greater flexibility.

But if our purpose is to identify "generating centers" of political thought, we may not have to define "evangelical" very precisely. Instead, we can note the views and actions of individuals and groups who describe themselves by that term or are generally accepted as "evangelicals" by others.

We immediately notice that evangelicals (spoken of loosely in that way) have become a significant factor in American public life. No longer is it expected that a true evangelical will be so concentrated on his or her individual "spiritual" life that politics is considered unworthy. We also notice that evangelicals do not think alike on political issues. Many evangelicals are very conservative in their political views (as that term is used), while others have much more in common with liberals (as *that* term is commonly used). How are we to understand the evangelicals of the right and the evangelicals of the left as generating centers of Christian political thought?

EVANGELICALS OF THE RIGHT

The evangelical right has attracted by far the most notice. Through its increasingly sophisticated use of mass media—particularly television and radio—its effective organizational techniques,

---

[3]See Martin E. Marty and R. Scott Appleby, eds., *Fundamentalisms and the State: Remaking Politics, Economics, and Militance,* The Fundamentalism Project, vol. 3 (Chicago and London: University of Chicago Press, 1993).

the charisma of its top leaders, its direct effect on many elections from local to national, and its penetration of party structures, particularly those of the Republican Party, the religious right has emerged as a highly visible part of the American political scene. In the 1980s and 1990s such evangelicals so dominated public attention that they were often taken to be the *only* expression of evangelical Christianity. Christians from mainline denominations had, in fact, come to fear that such evangelicals were becoming the visible spokespersons for *all* Christians.[4] These evangelicals may not have been the monolithic force they were sometimes perceived to be, but they clearly signaled that evangelical Christianity could no longer be considered aloof from public life.

Some of its forms were clearly extreme—an embarrassment to other evangelicals. Operation Rescue, made up of evangelical Protestants and a fringe group of Roman Catholics, achieved much public notice through disruptive tactics at abortion clinics and other kinds of street demonstrations. Hate demonstrations and literature targeting homosexual persons by other individuals and groups similarly expressed the extremes of evangelical Christianity. The violence directed against abortion clinics and doctors and against gays and lesbians committed by evangelical extremists was repudiated by more responsible evangelicals.

Reconstructionism appeared as an effort to translate biblical commandments literally into contemporary American law. While repudiating violence, the reconstructionists called for the structuring of government upon strictly biblical lines. "Christians," declared reconstructionist leader Gary North, "are called by God to exercise dominion."[5] The movement's principal founder, Rousas Rushdoony considers his strictly laissez-faire economic views to be the only reasonable expression of God's will: "Social progress comes with the accumulation and development of *wealth*. Wealth comes, in a free

---

[4]The national Interfaith Alliance was created during 1994, in part as an effort to correct that image and to reclaim a place in the national media for more "mainstream" religious perspectives. As the name implies, the Alliance includes participation by non-Christians, including Jews, Muslims, Hindus, and Buddhists.

[5]Gary North, *The Theology of Christian Resistance* (Tyler, Tex.: Geneva Divinity School Press, 1983), 60. Quoted by Nancy T. Ammerman, "North American Protestant Fundamentalism," in Martin E. Marty and R. Scott Appleby, eds., *Fundamentalisms Observed,* The Fundamentalism Project, vol. 1 (Chicago and London: University of Chicago Press, 1991), 50. See also successive issues of the movement's *Journal of Christian Reconstruction.*

economy, as a product of *work and thrift*—in short, of character. Capital is often accumulated by inheritance, a God-given right which is strongly stressed in the Bible."[6] Rushdoony insists that the "roots of the free market . . . rest on the doctrine of God. . . . The battle for the free market is but one facet of a battle against idolatry."[7] Rushdoony carried his reconstructionist views to the extreme of advocating literal obedience to the divine command to kill recalcitrant children.[8]

Notwithstanding the diversity of views on the evangelical right, certain themes unified the dominant organizations and leadership.[9] These themes include

> An easy identification of Christian values with the founding principles and traditions of American nationhood. This is a Christian nation, and we need to restore it to the golden age of past Christian Americanism.
>
> The Restoration of prayer and Bible reading in the public schools, the posting of the Ten Commandments in schools and other public places, and the inclusion of more explicitly biblical content in textbooks and actual instruction (for example, in the teaching of biblical creationism alongside of, or in replacement of, the theory of evolution, and in the challenging of what is perceived to be a dominant, parallel religion of secular humanism).
>
> Opposition to the legalization of abortion in any form (though some evangelicals are willing to make the life of the mother an exception), including the effort

---

[6]Rousas J. Rushdoony, *The Politics of Guilt and Pity* (Fairfax, Va.: Thoburn Press, 1978), 236–37. Quoted by Laurence R. Iannaccone, "The Economics of American Fundamentalists," in Marty and Appleby, *Fundamentalisms and the State,* 348.

[7]Quoted by Iannaccone, "Economics of American Fundamentalists," 348–49.

[8]Ammerman, "North American Protestant Fundamentalism," 52. Rushdoony's literalism, thus vividly illustrated, led numbers of his followers to seek a more moderate application of ancient biblical commands.

[9]Popular literature, including pamphlets, voter guides, statements on the Internet, and fundraising letters, emphasize these themes recurrently, though in variant forms. Among useful studies of the Christian Coalition, the most prominent of the organizations, see Justin Watson, *The Christian Coalition,* and *The Christian Coalition's 'Road to Victory': A Report on the Political and Policy Agendas of the Christian Coalition* (Washington, D.C.: Interfaith Alliance Foundation and Americans United for Separation of Church and State, 1995).

to reverse the Supreme Court decision in *Roe v. Wade* by the Court or by constitutional amendment and, barring that, to secure laws and policies making actual abortions more difficult.

Opposition to the moral or legal normalization or legitimization of homosexuality, including opposition to recognition of homosexual unions and recognition of homosexuality in classroom settings. The evangelical right has no doubts about this: homosexuality is condemned by the Bible and should be severely condemned by church and society. Homosexual persons, by turning to Christ, can be saved from this sin.

Opposition to the display of pornography in the media, cinema, Internet, or literature, with particular concern about the access of school children to pornographic materials.

Alarm over the presence of liberals and secular humanists (the two generally equated) in positions of power and authority.

Opposition to legalization of drugs and gambling.

Readiness to join other, more secular groups in such political causes as tax reduction, dismantling or weakening governmental welfare programs and federal involvement in education, a weakening of governmental regulatory programs (such as the federal Environmental Protection Agency), resistance to gun control, support of stiff criminal penalties, including capital punishment.

Such positions are stated and pursued with great passion.[10] Ralph Reed, when he was executive director of the Christian Coalition, wrote of his and other movement leaders' objectives in an essay he summarized as follows:

---

[10]When I attended a session of the Christian Coalition's annual "Road to Victory" conference in 1995, I was struck by the unswerving conviction (and oratorical effectiveness) of many of the speakers, but even more by the sheer passion of the thousands in attendance. The crowd was on its feet, thundering its approval of the call for more capital punishment and less social welfare. By contrast, a more moderately conservative speech by Senator Robert Dole—soon to become the Republican nominee for president—was greeted with polite hand-clapping.

The essay included a call for balanced budgets, term limits, school choice, lower taxes on the family, laws against abortion and euthanasia, and reforms of the divorce laws so that married couples with children could divorce only if there were such grounds as adultery or abuse. In addition, I called for a constitutional amendment allowing for greater religious freedom, a nationwide ban on state sponsored gambling, and a transfer of welfare functions to churches, synagogues, and local communities. One-third of the functions and spending of the existing federal government would have been returned to state and nongovernmental organizations.[11]

Reed, like most other movement leaders, does not attempt a theological analysis of such positions. In part, that is because the movement relies upon the intellectual capital of other, mostly earlier, conservative theologians as well as secular political thinkers whose support for limited government these leaders incorporate into their arguments. In his book, *Active Faith,* Reed called for a "new theology of political activism for religious conservatives." His own comments about that emphasize limited government (especially limitations on the federal government) and the importance of political activism. Political activity is "a spiritual obligation." He writes that "there is simply no biblical basis" for the belief, previously held by many conservative Christians, that politics is a worldly distraction from the essential work of evangelism.[12] Reed's example illustrates that the evangelical right places much more emphasis upon activism in political life than upon theological reflection.

ASSESSING THE EVANGELICAL RIGHT

How are we to assess the evangelical right as a generating center of Christian political thought? It certainly is a generating center of political *action.* As we have noted, it clearly marks the end of an era when most evangelicals were politically passive. In that sense, it is a strong affirmation that this is God's world and what we do about it matters. Consciously or unconsciously, the evangelical right is in-

---

[11]Ralph Reed, *Active Faith: How Christians Are Changing the Soul of American Politics* (New York: Free Press, 1996), 192.

[12]Ibid., 256.

fluenced by Calvinist ideas (quite consciously in the case of the reconstructionists). In terms of H. Richard Niebuhr's *Christ and Culture* typology (not consciously employed by any of the evangelicals, to my knowledge), these evangelicals are more definitely transformationists.[13] The movement, moreover, also contains a considerable strain of political realism, in contrast with the unrealism of some Christian idealists, although there is room for questioning the political goals to which that realism is devoted.

It is more doubtful how much of a theological contribution the conservative evangelical movement will make in the long run. The very certainty with which positions are held and defended suggests that these evangelicals are neither inviting nor contributing much thinking. Their literature is bent upon exposing and condemning the views of the liberals and secular humanists. One does not encounter much careful exploration of the connections between Christian faith and the political, social, and theological positions they advocate. Standing behind some of those positions is the work of such conservative theologians of a previous generation as Francis Schaeffer, Cornelius Van Til, and Carl F. H. Henry—each very conservative, but each also much more open to dialogue with theological opponents. Major figures of the new Christian right, like Pat Robertson, Jerry Falwell, and Ralph Reed, are not theologians as much as they are activists, even though several are very effective as orators. Where positions of the evangelical right provide intellectual depth, that is generally supplied by secular thinkers, such as the economists and social philosophers who make the case for a virtually unrestrained economy. So it may be a bit of a stretch to characterize the evangelical right as a generating center of *Christian* political thought.

Moreover, their stance is primarily reactive: a setting forth of the things to be against. Any theological position is likely to contest opposing views, but a mark of mature theology is the clarity with which it sets forth its own positive views. What it is *for* is more important than what it is *against*. The lack of well-thought-through positions or of openness to dialogue with alternative views means that this movement is not—at least not yet—a strong generating center of Christian political thought.

---

[13]H. Richard Niebuhr, *Christ and Culture* (New York: Harper and Row, 1951). The fact that this is a point of similarity with the social gospel movement and figures such as Walter Rauschenbusch would make neither the social gospelers nor the evangelicals very happy!

Even its stance in respect to political action is generating increasing criticism from other evangelicals. Most remarkably, two prominent evangelicals, syndicated columnist Cal Thomas and pastor Ed Dobson have challenged the evangelical right's political behavior.[14] Their criticisms are especially noteworthy because both were leaders of Jerry Falwell's Moral Majority and are widely read and respected by evangelicals. Thomas and Dobson are alarmed by the extent to which religious conservatives have lost sight of the main objective, which is to transform people. "Power," writes Thomas, "is the ultimate aphrodisiac. People may have wealth, position, and fame, but unless they have power, many of them believe their lives are incomplete. Power cannot only seduce, but also affect judgment. It can be more addictive than any drug. . . . "[15] The seductive effects of power were experienced in the early days of the Christian Coalition, of which he was then a leader: "Who wanted to ride into the capital on the back of an ass when one could go first class in a private jet and be picked up and driven around in a chauffeured limousine? Who wanted the role of a servant when one could have the accolades given to leaders?"[16] Even so, Thomas and Dobson remark throughout the book on the failure of the movement, for all its appearances of power, to advance its agenda very much. Dobson notes that twenty years after the emergence of the Moral Majority,

> Even a casual observation of the current moral climate suggests that despite all the time, money, and energy—despite the political power—we failed. Things have not gotten better; they have gotten worse. . . . Crime is still rampant, judging from the overcrowding of our prisons. Drugs are even more readily available to our children than they were twenty years ago. Pornography has moved from the back shelf to the television sets in our living rooms. The number of abortions performed each year has declined only slightly. Homosexuality is shrugged off as an acceptable, alternative lifestyle. And even within our churches, divorce rates continue to climb, mirroring those of people who do not attend church.[17]

---

[14]Cal Thomas and Ed Dobson, *Blinded by Might: Can the Religious Right Save America?* (Grand Rapids: Zondervan Publishing House, 1999).

[15]Thomas and Dobson, 50.

[16]Ibid., 26.

[17]Thomas and Dobson, 42–43.

As this quotation suggests, neither Thomas nor Dobson questions the basic objectives of the evangelical right nor even its effectiveness in placing its agenda before the nation, but they have had serious second thoughts about its political activism, centering on the acquisition of power. Dobson is particularly concerned about methods that demonize opponents and fall far short of the Christian ethic of love.

It is striking that such voices are now being heard among evangelicals who have heretofore been prominent in right-wing organizations and causes. That kind of soul-searching may indeed lead this activist movement to generate more positive contributions to Christian political thought.

EVANGELICALS OF THE LEFT

While the evangelicals of the right have dominated public perceptions of the term "evangelical," an important generating center has developed in recent years centering around the combination of evangelical theologies with left-leaning politics. Such figures as Ronald Sider, Tony Campolo, and Jim Wallis have adhered to a more conservative theological orientation while pressing a more liberal political agenda. The latter is not so true of their views on such social issues as abortion and homosexuality, where they have remained more conservative (though even on such issues, they are notably more irenic than the evangelicals of the right). Their liberalism is expressed more vigorously on economic issues, civil rights, prison reform, and international peace.

At the center of much of this has been the Sojourners community and magazine, whose leader is Jim Wallis. Founded in the 1970s, Sojourners was principally responsible in the 1990s for an evangelical "Call to Renewal" whose purpose was "to offer an alternative to the Religious Right and to help forge a new politics in America"[18] and was, in part, a direct response to the religious right. In the introduction to a publication setting forth the movement's basic purposes, the editors express concern that "the image of Christianity in America is increasingly associated with narrow, right-wing partisanship and vicious ideological attacks on the poor, liberals, women, homosexuals, immigrants, and others—all in the guise of reclaiming

---

[18]Wallis, *Who Speaks for God?*, ix.

America's 'godly heritage.'" The editors deplore the fact that "too many people forget the American religious community's historic role in the abolition of slavery, the struggle for civil rights, anti-war and nuclear disarmanent efforts, and human rights support around the world."[19] Writing in this publication, Tony Campolo comments,

> If I were asked to summarize quickly the beliefs of this re-defined group of Christians, I would lay out the following: (1) We are a people who believe in the doctrines of the Apostles' Creed. (2) We are a people who hold to the infallibility of scripture. (3) We are a people who are committed to the social vision articulated by Martin Luther King Jr. in his famous 'I Have a Dream' speech.[20]

The Call to Renewal, while initiated by evangelicals, includes participants who are more liberal theologically—which suggests a more irenic spirit of openness than the religious right. It also suggests a commonality of political purpose with many who are more traditional liberals. The principal focus has been upon poverty issues (with particular criticism of the Welfare Reform Act of 1996) and a desire to make government more responsive to the plight of poor people in America. The Bible, Wallis reminds his readers, "*insists that the best test of a nation's righteousness is how it treats the poorest and most vulnerable in its midst.*"[21] Wallis indicts the nation for its callous neglect of the poor:

> If we have been fiscally irresponsible as a nation, why are we blaming the poor? If we have spent too much money on weapons and war, why are we blaming those who need the most protection? If we have been too generous with large public subsidies to big corporations, why are we blaming the people at the bottom? And if the welfare systems we have set up are not working very well, why are we blaming the recipients? Why is it that the poor, and especially poor women and children, will bear the biggest brunt of budget balancing and deficit reduction, instead of the Pentagon, the *Fortune* 500, and the middle class?[22]

---

[19]*Recovering the Evangel: A Guide to Faith, Politics, and Alternatives to the Religious Right* (Washington, D. C.: Sojourners, n.d.), 2.

[20]Tony Campolo, "Faith in Search of a Home: The Lost Meaning of 'Evangelical,'" in *Recovering the Evangel*, 24–25.

[21]Wallis, *Who Speaks for God?*, 42. His italics.

[22]Ibid., 44–45.

With similar rhetoric, Wallis and others in this movement emphasize the importance of overcoming the legacies of racism by continuing the commitment to affirmative action.

It is interesting that while the evangelicals of the right and the left both purport to base their political views on the Bible, those of the right more generally cite prescriptive laws of the Old Testament governing sex and other social matters, while those of the left characteristically refer to the prophets and Jesus. Evangelicals of the left emphasize God's special concern for the most vulnerable members of the human community. In that respect, they have much in common with the pacifist and liberationist perspectives which we have already examined.

One subset of the evangelical left is worth noting, not because it has become prominent publicly but because its views are evolving creatively and in dialogue with other Christians. This is the frankly sectarian Bruderhof community. The Bruderhof (sometimes called Hutterians) live in a half dozen small communities, emphasize close family life, ground their faith in very conservative biblical views, and avoid participation in electoral politics. In large measure, this community seeks to influence the wider society more by example than by playing a direct role in politics.[23] In recent years it has become much more involved in direct peacemaking (such as in relation to Iraq, the Balkans, and Cuba) and in the struggle to end capital punishment in America.

ASSESSING THE EVANGELICAL LEFT

The evangelicals of the left can be taken more seriously as an intellectual force than their counterparts of the right. They are, for one thing, more consistently biblical in that they are less captive to nonbiblical ideological perspectives such as the economic philosophy of the Austrian school of laissez-faire capitalism. Moreover, their biblical perspective is less a matter of proof-texting (although they are not above doing that as well) and more an attempt to get at the central core meanings of scripture. Their biblical methodology would not be very compatible with that of more liberal

---

[23]Johann Christoph Arnold is the leader and principal theologian of this movement. Among his many writings, *Seeking Peace* (Farmington, Pa.: Plough Publishing House, 1998) illustrates many of the concerns of the community.

Christians, but they may have more affinity with liberal Christians about what ultimately matters and what does not.

Among the values of the evangelical left is its spirit. While that in itself does not constitute an intellectual force, it is by no means to be despised when we assess this movement as a generating center. That point can be made historically as well as logically. Great evangelical movements of the past, such as the Great Awakening in the eighteenth century and the evangelical revivals in the nineteenth century, were not primarily intellectual movements. But they generated enormous energy around social and political causes and, in the end, greatly affected political thought as well. The blending of nineteenth-century evangelicalism (as expressed by Charles Finney, among others) with theological liberalism would not have been possible if there had been no evangelicalism! We do not know precisely where these currents of evangelicalism will lead in the twenty-first century, but a generating center is never fully predictable. The fact that the left-leaning evangelicals have much in common with the mainstream liberals we are about to consider means that there may be more creative blending ahead.

Still, in assessing the evangelicals of the left, one is struck by a certain lack of clarity about the meaning of politics. The Call to Renewal seeks a creative third way between the traditional politics of right and left, but that remains ill-defined except in respect to its motivations. Moreover, while this evangelical movement seems more open to cooperation with non-Christian religious groups, the theological grounds for that are unclear. Is God also at work in those groups? If so, how and with what limits?

The fact that much of the movement (though not all) is committed to pacifism raises the usual questions that historically have been pressed by nonpacifists. Lurking behind those questions is the deeper one of whether the movement can affirm the actual exercise of political power—and whether it fully understands the consequences of power vacuums. Even within a democratic society, such as in the United States and the United Kingdom, the movement does not appear to be thinking constructively about the role of political parties as power centers needing criticism but also affirmation. Still, the evangelical left may have very important contributions to make in the years to come.

8

Mainstream Liberal Christian Perspectives

The Christian strives to make the kingdom more present in this world, but the fullness of justice and peace will never be here. I maintain there can be some truly human progress in history, but such progress is ordinarily slow and painful.

—*Charles E. Curran (1982)*[1]

A . . . merit of avoiding absolutes is to remind one of the role of prudence in political decision making. Since at least the time of Aristotle, political ethics have underscored the imperative of seeking to find the mean between extremes. Being less than certain about the truth—recognizing the ambiguities of all political situations—tends to dampen one's excessive trust in any particular policy solution.

—*Donald E. Messer (1984)*[2]

Biblical thought is quite aware of oppressive forces against which the government must act. In an industrial society such forces appear in groups holding concentrated economic and social power and in environmental factors such as disease and hunger.

---

[1]Charles E. Curran, *American Catholic Social Ethics: Twentieth Century Approaches* (Notre Dame, Ind.: University of Notre Dame Press, 1982), 284.

[2]Donald E. Messer, *Christian Ethics and Political Action* (Valley Forge, Pa.: Judson Press, 1984), 105.

Here justice often requires an expanded role for the state.

—*Stephen Charles Mott (1982)*[3]

The fourth generating center of Christian political thought is what I will broadly term "mainstream liberalism." Labels are misleading, and this one perhaps more even than the others. "Mainstream" suggests a majority point of view, but the mainstream liberals may be a majority only among theologians and ethicists. It may also suggest a relationship to mainstream Protestantism in the United States, but among the mainstream liberals I will speak of are such Roman Catholic thinkers as John Coleman and Charles Curran. The term "liberal" is used here in its American popular connotation—definitely not in the classic economic sense, where liberal meant a believer in laissez-faire economics. Many of the liberal political thinkers can also be classified as theological liberals, but not all. Biblical evangelicals, such as Stephen Mott and Richard Mouw, are political liberals as I am using that term. Such writers in some ways resemble the evangelicals of the left discussed in chapter 7.

Indeed, most of the Christian writers on politics in North America and Great Britain, if not also on the European continent, can be classified as political liberals. But such labeling has become more difficult in the United States for yet another reason. The term "liberal," once embraced with enthusiasm by many, has come under a cloud in a public arena dominated in recent years by more conservative viewpoints. Many who previously would have been called liberal now prefer to be described as "moderate." I expect these linguistic fashions to change along with political fortunes in the years to come, and it will not surprise me if even the word "liberal" is restored to full respectability. But again, our purpose is not to classify thinkers but to be aware of generating centers of Christian thought about politics. Several themes stand out in this one.

THEOLOGICAL CONVICTIONS

It is said (perhaps apocryphally) that reporters covering the electoral campaigns of the late New York governor and U.S. vice-president Nelson Rockefeller simply wrote down the letters "BOM-

---

[3]Stephen Charles Mott, *Biblical Ethics and Social Change* (New York and Oxford: Oxford University Press, 1982), 193.

FOG" when he came to a certain point in his typical stump speech. That stood for "Brotherhood of Man under the Fatherhood of God" and expressed his somewhat less than precise political objectives for the long run. The expression is also reminiscent of the language of the social gospel era, and it may be no accident here that Rockefeller's boyhood pastor was Harry Emerson Fosdick, who was himself deeply influenced by that period.

Many—perhaps most—of the Christian political liberals can also acknowledge at least an indirect influence from the social gospel movement. Their theological orientations, while much more carefully nuanced than "BOM-FOG" conveys, still have a certain affinity. Most, though not all, believe in a personal God whose act of creation and whose profound love form the basis of human community—so that the family metaphor is not inappropriately applied to humanity as a whole. Thus, a deep, formative theological conviction, underlying the work of many political liberals, is the view that we are all sisters and brothers because God is our common parent.

Such root metaphors, drawn from the most intimate, caring aspects of human life, are accompanied by the view that the reality of our fellow humanity can be realized to some extent in human history. Indeed, this reality defines the meaning of human history and the purposes of God for human history. Consequently, the struggle to overcome all that denies this reality is central to the life purposes of Christians. The ethical orientation of such thinkers accordingly has a strong *consequentialist* cast. They are concerned about what actually happens in human history; they are eager to help make things happen. As the term "consequentialist" is often used by its critics, it suggests somebody who believes that means are justified by ends. In part that may be a fair characterization of many of the political liberals, but only if one remembers with them that means affect ends. Bad means can contaminate good ends so that they are no longer good. But most political liberals are impatient with a style of ethics that concentrates on the goodness of actions while ignoring concrete results. If good ends do not necessarily justify bad means, it is equally true that good means do not justify bad ends. It matters what happens. And it is not enough to avoid contaminating oneself morally if our inaction contributes to evil results.

The theological perspective of mainstream liberalism has been deeply influenced at this point by the realism of Reinhold Niebuhr, particularly in its understanding of sin. The Niebuhrian conception of "original" sin as universal and perennial, based ultimately on human insecurity, is accompanied by a recognition that human life is also capable of justice and benevolence. This view that we are both good and evil in the root of our being has two consequences in the political ethics of many mainstream liberals. First, it contributes to the view that all political solutions are provisional and limited. We are not going to be able to establish the kingdom of God on earth, as some of the earlier liberals had supposed, because God's rule will continue to be frustrated by the fact of human sinfulness until the end of history. Political ethics is therefore a matter of degree and relativity. Absolute good is never a concrete possibility, but neither is absolute evil. Thus, the truly important ethical questions in politics, as in other realms of human experience, are the relative questions of better or worse, of provisional good and limited evil.

The second consequence of this view of sin is that mainstream liberals find it difficult to separate humanity along moral lines, dividing the good people from the bad people. Original sin is a great leveler. We are all unworthy. No individual or group has grounds for self-righteousness. In the political competition of one group with another, one side may represent goodness and justice more—even much more—than the other, but in no simple way can political contests be reduced to a struggle of the forces of righteousness against the forces of evil.

In these two respects, mainline liberalism tends to differ from the four generating centers of political thought we have already examined. Each of the four takes sin seriously, to be sure, and it would not be exactly accurate to say that any of them thinks it possible for any human being to escape sin altogether. But the pacifists come close to the simple notion that it is possible to avoid sinfulness—and therefore that a kind of moral separation can be made between those Christians who accept the pacifist orientation and those who do not. The liberationists come close to locating evil historically in particular classes and institutions—therefore effecting a kind of moral separation between those who have identified themselves with the revolutionary cause, serving it wholeheartedly, and those who are guilty of economic oppression or accept its existence complacently. The neoconservatives come close to a division of humanity between the forces of freedom, honor, and decency and the forces against which they largely define themselves. The evangelicals of the right have a clear division between the saved and the unredeemed, and even those of the left often make a sharp division between Christians and non-Christians and between Bible believers and those who supplement the Bible with other sources of authority.

All of these are only tendencies, to be sure. The mainstream liberals themselves identify with causes and range themselves in opposition to institutions and movements that obstruct those causes. But their theological conception of the universality of sin and its coexistence with the possibility of righteousness in the soul of every person leads them to draw the lines less sharply. Among the mainstream liberals there are, of course, very great theological differences. Evangelicals such as Mott and Mouw are more deeply biblical in their orientation, and exegesis accordingly plays a more important role in their method of approach to political questions. Such evangelicals do not allow proof-texts to settle questions, but a clear biblical precedent or injunction carries great weight with them all the same. Roman Catholics such as Curran or Coleman continue to honor the natural law tradition, although they no longer approach it with scholastic rigidity. Like the other (non-Catholic) liberals, they take sin and grace seriously, and they make much more use of scripture than previous generations of Catholic moral theologians. The other Protestants also differ among themselves on a variety of theological points.

THE ECUMENICAL CHURCH AUDIENCE

The audience of the mainstream liberals is generally the mainstream church. That includes specific denominations (most of these writers have deep commitments to particular communities of faith and serve their churches in a variety of ways). But most of them are also deeply committed to the ecumenical church. In writing for this audience, these thinkers clearly accept its legitimacy, though often they engage in a kind of lover's quarrel with it. A number of them, such as Roger Shinn, Ronald Preston, and the late John Bennett have served as consultants or commission members for the World and National Councils of Churches. Denominational and conciliar documents on political questions often are influenced or even drafted by them. Father Bryan Hehir was a principal drafter of the U.S. Roman Catholic bishops' 1981 pastoral on peace and a frequent consultant for the bishops in subsequent years, and David Hollenbach and Daniel Finn played an important role in the 1986 pastoral on the U.S. economy. Alan Geyer was principal drafter of the 1986 United Methodist bishops' pastoral on nuclear war, *In Defense of Creation.* Roger Shinn, Max Stackhouse, and Charles West have played a similar role with United Church of Christ and Presbyterian documents, as have Larry Rasmussen and Glen Stassen for

Lutherans and Baptists. Thinkers and writers associated with the other generating centers often have some influence on ecclesiastical statements as well, but the influence of pacifists, liberationists, neoconservatives, and evangelicals is more characteristically exerted from the periphery. Neoconservatives, in fact, put more energy into criticizing denominational and interdenominational statements than into formulating them.

The underlying conception of the church is also a "mainline" one. The church exists in the midst of a larger society and an important part of its mission is to impact what happens in the larger arena. The church cannot settle for a sectarian conception of itself or an aloof attitude toward society at large. Thus, Messer will write that "particularly needed is for the church to highlight the vocation and avocation of politics as an appropriate means for Christian witness and participation in the world."[4] And while Mott emphasizes that the church should "maintain a separate and distinct identity from the surrounding society" (in order "to have a corrective impact" upon it), he also cites the importance of the church contributing to social change.[5]

On the surface at least, that is also the attitude of the other positions we have examined. But the first has sectarian tendencies, the second questions the theological legitimacy of a mainline church that has become captive to dominant class interests, and the third is alienated from churches and ecumenical bodies considered insufficiently committed to capitalism, national interests, democracy and (for some) traditional moral standards. The evangelicals exhibit varying forms of ecclesiology and church commitment. But as with the others, the implied audience is not the mainstream churches and ecumenical movement.

The church addressed by mainstream liberals is understood to have a leadership role in the wider society. In the terms of H. Richard Niebuhr's *Christ and Culture* typology, it is definitely "Christ transforming culture." In addressing a church audience on political questions, such thinkers are implicitly seeking to influence a wider public. Indeed, that wider public is sometimes indistinguishable from the church constituency, although the case presented in behalf of particular viewpoints may often depend, ultimately, upon Christian theological commitments.

---

[4]Messer, *Christian Ethics and Political Action,* 34.
[5]Mott, *Biblical Ethics and Social Change,* 133.

In such respects the mainstream liberals assume a church that is not radically discontinuous, in principle, from the larger society of which it is a part. In this respect, the mainstream liberals are fully in accord with Michael J. Perry's view that "neither legislators nor other public officials nor even citizens should rely on a religious argument about the requirements of human well-being unless, in their view, a persuasive secular argument reaches the same conclusion."[6] This does not mean that such thinkers have capitulated to culture, however, in the sense of Richard Niebuhr's "Christ of culture." They may be and often are deeply critical of contemporary culture and social institutions. But they do not draw a sharp line between the surrounding culture and the church. The people inhabiting both are often the same people. Appeal can be made to values in the surrounding culture that have their origin in Christian influence. And many of the resistances to be overcome are within the churches as well as in the surrounding culture. So the lines are not so easily drawn. Mainline liberals no doubt sometimes slip into naivete in their assumption that they can address a church audience and a wider audience at the same time. The question is whether even the mainline churches have become marginalized in the Western cultural setting. The high visibility and political successes of the evangelical right in the closing decades of the twentieth century suggest that may be so.

Mainline liberals assume that that has not yet occurred—at least not decisively. They are not prepared to concede that their churches and ecumenical bodies no longer occupy a place of influence and respect in Western society—although most would readily acknowledge that that society is pluralistic and that the mainline churches can no longer determine, in any simple way, the core values of the surrounding culture. Moreover, mainline liberals are more prepared to redefine the cultural high ground. If it is no longer the exclusive preserve of mainline Protestantism, it is now becoming a pluralistic environment in which Protestants can enter dialogue and work together with like-minded Roman Catholics and Jews along with adherents to other faiths such as Islam, Hinduism, and Buddhism. The emergence and rapid growth of the Interfaith Alliance in the late 1990s signaled a largely mainstream liberal effort to resist the evangelical right but at the same time to forge positive new interfaith relationships in American public life.

---

[6]Michael J. Perry, *Religion in Politics: Constitutional and Moral Perspectives* (New York and Oxford: Oxford University Press, 1997), 79.

A REFORMIST ATTITUDE
TOWARD CHANGE

Mainline liberals are more typically reformist than revolutionary in their attitude toward politics. This may, of course, be as much a function of location as anything else. The same writers, transplanted from North America into more repressive Third World settings, might be more revolutionary. Their writings on public policy questions are certainly saturated with unhappiness with things as they are. They want change. But in the setting for which they write that does not necessarily mean immediate revolutionary change. In a discussion of different approaches to social change, Mott has emphasized the radical demands for justice in the biblical perspective. But at the same time, he suggests a reformist or incrementalist strategy for implementing them:

> But there is another type of reform. It is built on the premise that many social changes, even revolutionary changes, come only through a cumulative series of partial steps. Here the reformer's goals are dissonant with the current social structures, but he or she recognizes that these goals cannot be achieved all at once. One accepts concrete solutions to specific problems but only on premises that question the assumptions of the present order and only as leading in the general direction of a new order. The Christian reformer first of all has a vision of the new order of the Reign of God but also realizes that the Reign will be only partially realizable in history. The Christian also operates with a vision of a community in history which is not the Reign of God but which is more proximate to the Reign than is the present society.[7]

While such a vision remains radical and even revolutionary, its reformist character is revealed clearly enough by contrasting it with most of the liberation theologians.

Writing from a very different theological orientation, John Bennett could similarly speak of a "radical imperative" while counseling basically reformist measures to achieve the radical results.[8] Implicit here is a recognition that there are important values in existing institutional structures that need, if possible, to be preserved.

---

[7]Mott, *Biblical Ethics and Social Change,* 202–3.
[8]John C. Bennett, *The Radical Imperative* (Philadelphia: Westminster Press, 1975).

Even where sweeping changes are needed, continuity in the process of change may be important. Historical circumstances sometimes justify out-and-out revolution. Writers such as Mott and Bennett are well-enough aware of that. But they avoid the illusion that a postrevolutionary situation will represent perfect justice and social harmony. Thus, Bennett, while also expressing great appreciation for the work of the prominent black theologian James Cone, suggested that

> it would be good if Cone were to put a theological message in a sealed envelope to be read at some future time when black people gain more power, when blacks are seen to be oppressors of other blacks or of whites. This is especially important because black theology is a call to revolution, and revolutionaries, whatever form the revolution may take, are greatly tempted to a passionate self-righteousness which distorts the mind and spirit.[9]

Bennett argued that liberation theology in its various forms has made important contributions to Christian political thought in the late twentieth century. And he recognized that the call to revolution is sometimes valid, sometimes urgently needed. Yet his recognition of the relativities of good and evil in all historical circumstances contributed to a reformist orientation—while preserving openness to sweeping change when injustices are severe enough and when opportunity for revolutionary change exists.

Similarly positive in his assessment of the world-transforming agenda of liberation theology, Ronald Stone also insists that the kingdom of God transcends political change even while being relevant to it. Therefore, the reformed theology to which he is committed "cannot give up its insight that politics is ambiguous while calling for a theology of politics to serve the poor." Such a theology "insists upon a religious reservation about politics that disinclines it from affirming utopian politics while affirming a politics for change inspired by the Kingdom of God."[10]

---

[9]Ibid., 128.

[10]Ronald Stone, "Introduction," in *Reformed Faith and Politics,* ed. Ronald Stone (Washington, D.C.: University Press of America, 1983), 9. In his earlier book, *Realism and Hope* (Washington, D.C.: University Press of America, 1977), Stone discussed the confusing variety of conceptions of revolution and suggested a series of criteria to govern Christian participation "in continuity with the tradition of Christian ethics concerning just war and with the liberal-democratic tradition of the right of revolution" (p. 168).

Most of the thinkers here characterized as mainstream liberals would probably agree with Alan Geyer's observation that the great differences between political cultures and systems make ethical generalization about politics difficult. Radical social change may be required in some situations while, "in other societies, Christians are rightly concerned to conserve, improve and redeem an existing political system so that it may serve the common good more adequately."[11] It is a mistake, specifically, for Americans to "export if not impose their own models of constitutionalism or political parties on cultural environments in which those models are inappropriate or untimely." But at the same time, Americans should not "import models of revolution or liberation which are not responsive to indigenous political culture in the USA."[12]

Writing, as most of them do, in a context where they do not consider revolution appropriate, mainstream liberal thinkers are concerned with a wide variety of specific reforms. The struggle to overcome poverty and unemployment is not least among them. Mainstream liberals do not accept the neoconservative prescription of more and better "democratic capitalism" as solution, but neither do they urge a Marxist revolution to replace capitalism with socialism. Despite the clear ascendancy of global capitalism at century's end, some may still fairly be characterized as "democratic socialists"—advocates of bringing socialism in through democratic means and keeping it accountable to democratic government. But most mainstream liberals accept the broad outlines of a "mixed economy" in which private and public sectors coexist and in which specific efforts are made to ensure adequate income and employment for all. They can be found, therefore, in the political struggles for more adequate public welfare programs, full employment and job training programs, and a more progressive tax structure. A related concern is with adequate health care delivery, particularly in the United States and other countries where medicine has remained a predominantly private practice and where even health insurance programs are privately funded and administered. The failure of the health care reforms proposed by the Clinton administration in 1994 did not, for them, settle the issue.

---

[11]Alan Geyer, "Towards an Ecumenical Political Ethics: A Marginal American View," in *Perspectives on Political Ethics: An Ecumenical Inquiry,* ed. Koson Srisang (Washington, D.C.: Georgetown University Press, 1983), 131.

[12]Ibid.

Mainstream liberals have been in the forefront of the struggle for environmental protection and energy conservation—again, seeking to implement such concerns through specific reforms. See, for example, James Nash's theological analysis of environmental issues[13] and Larry L. Rasmussen's *Earth Community Earth Ethics*.[14] Significantly, both of these thinkers have done their work in a specifically ecumenical context: Nash with the Churches' Center for Theology and Public Policy and Rasmussen with the World Council of Churches.

Similarly, mainstream writers have sought additional protections of public safety, such as legislation to require more safety features on automobiles and greater caution in the development of nuclear reactors. In addressing such problems, they are often forced to wrestle with real dilemmas, for instance, when the industrial growth needed for new jobs threatens increased environmental pollution.

Mainstream liberals were and are in the midst of civil rights struggles. They have been a part of the struggle for desegregation and affirmative action for women and members of marginalized ethnic groups. They have supported the civil rights of unpopular religious groups, liberalized immigration laws, and the freedom of public school teachers to approach their subject matter without harassment from conservative religious groups. Again, they have confronted dilemmas, such as the difficulty of defining the basis for affirmative action while articulating a principled case for nondiscrimination, or the question whether there should be limits to the freedom of expression for groups (such as the Ku Klux Klan) who preach hatred for minority groups.

At the international level, mainstream liberals have often (though not always) supported disarmament negotiations, an increased role for the United Nations, more generous foreign aid programs (and less generous military assistance), pressure for human rights in authoritarian societies, greater regulation of transnational corporations, and trade policies that better serve the interests of developing countries of the Third World. The list of specific reforms is very long, even if restricted to the concerns of mainstream liberals in recent years. Sometimes the list emphasizes needed changes—

---

[13]James Nash, *Loving Nature: Ecological Integrity and Christian Responsibility* (Nashville: Abingdon Press, 1991).

[14]Larry L. Rasmussen, *Earth Community Earth Ethics* (Maryknoll, N.Y.: Orbis Books, 1996).

things to be done. Sometimes it is a question of *preventing* changes from occurring—for instance, resisting encroachments on the Bill of Rights in the United States, resisting the reversion of public enterprises to the private sector in the United Kingdom, or resisting cutbacks in social welfare benefits, the development of more nuclear reactors, and the dismantling of affirmative action programs. So the reformist perspective is not always oriented toward change, per se; it can be conservative where mainstream liberals perceive the need to protect social values.

The reformist orientation is easily misunderstood. That is, I suppose, partly because mainstream liberals themselves sometimes are in disagreement on specific questions. (For instance, some support while others oppose the right of women to elect abortion, and some support while others oppose the concept of guaranteed annual income.) The orientation is also, but mistakenly, treated as revolutionary by ideological conservatives. And radical structuralists, such as socialists, often characterize reformism as an implicit support for existing systems of injustice because the reforms only serve to make the systems more palatable. But mainstream liberals remain unpersuaded by the arguments at either end of the ideological spectrum except as these may help to illuminate particular issues and problems.

THE ROLE OF GOVERNMENT

Mainstream liberals have generally taken a positive attitude toward government, even to the point of being accused by neoconservatives as "statists." I have already cited Mott's comment that justice "often requires an expanded role for the state."[15] Joseph L. Allen argues similarly that "in any effective program for social justice toward the most needy, government will necessarily play the key role."[16] Such remarks do not imply a "statist" outlook; they are less ideological than practical. Things need to be done for the sake of a theologically based understanding of justice. And if these things are to be done, the state will have to be more active.

Noting a certain bias in American culture against government,

---

[15]Mott, *Biblical Ethics and Social Change,* 193.

[16]Joseph L. Allen, *Love and Conflict: A Covenantal Model of Christian Ethics* (Nashville: Abingdon Press, 1984), 177.

the members of a Theology of Politics study group at the Churches' Center for Theology and Public Policy argue that

> the anti-political animus of American political culture makes the restatement of the case for *positive government* a prime task: that government really can and must serve the people in that range of human need which will never be justly served by private action. What a mature religious faith must do is not only to offer prophetic principles from which to criticize government: it must lift up the most creative human possibilities of achieving the common good through government action.[17]

The (mostly) mainline liberal thinkers making up this working group express a consensus view: government is not a predominantly negative force but a positive one. Mainline Catholic writers have long expressed this view, but usually in the form of the doctrine of subsidiarity (which we have already cited in chapter 6 on neoconservatism). Built into this doctrine is a certain presumption against invoking the power of government to deal with human problems. But when needed, that power is to be seen in positive, not negative terms. Some Catholic writings early in this century—responding in part to the aftermath of the French Revolution and Marxism— tended to emphasize the negative implications of the principle. More recent writings, including Pope John XXIII's encyclical *Pacem in Terris* and the American Catholic bishops' 1986 pastoral letter on the U.S. economy, have emphasized the positive.[18] Pope John noted the virtual political anarchy existing among nation-states at the international level and asserted the need for new forms of governmental organization at that level that might contain the conflicts. The American bishops noted the failure of laissez-faire capitalism to deal adequately with poverty and unemployment and asserted the need for effective governmental action. These documents echo the writings of many mainstream Catholic moral theologians.

While mainstream liberals generally support a stronger government role in dealing with societal problems, a significant number urge a greater role by nongovernmental institutions, a major

---

[17]Quoted in *Perspectives on Political Ethics,* 147.

[18]For the latter, see *Economic Justice for All: Pastoral Letter on Catholic Social Teaching and the U.S. Economy* (Washington, D.C.: National Conference of Catholic Bishops, 1986).

emphasis in the thought of the late James Luther Adams.[19] Adams was not in any sense opposed to a positive role of government, nor could he have been characterized as a neoconservative in any sense. But he was convinced that nongovernmental institutions are fundamental in a healthy democratic society. That theme has more recently been emphasized by Max L. Stackhouse, who questions the priority of politics in some Protestant Christian thought:

> The deeper presuppositions of Protestantism see society as prior to politics. Centered in the life of faith, but taking shape in the formation of the family, the community, the school, the arts, and the economy, as well as the government, it treats government as but one of the several malleable arenas or sectors of practical human association.[20]

In a number of his writings, Stackhouse has sought especially to reclaim a positive moral basis for the vocation of corporations, a point he would have in common with the neoconservatives. But despite his affinity at several points with the neoconservatives, Stackhouse remains (in my judgment) essentially mainstream liberal in his basic views. His own assessment of neoconservatism is instructive:

> The problem with neo-conservatism is that it does not want to give an account of why the traditional practices and classical wisdom are the only things that can preserve the vital aspects of freedom without succumbing to anarchy. Traditional practice and wisdom may indeed be valuable, but tradition is dynamic and ongoing. It changes and develops. And wisdom has never been confined to one tradition or period of the past.[21]

This generating center is, as we have seen above, committed to an activist conception of the church in the world—not simply a "witnessing" church, but a church prepared to be an actor in the public sphere, working for concrete change or defending humane laws and institutions from erosion. Each of the generating centers is activist

---

[19]See James Luther Adams, *On Being Human Religiously* (Boston: Beacon Press, 1976) and "Mediating Structures and the Separation of Powers," in Michael Novak, ed., *Democracy and Mediating Structures: A Theological Inquiry* (Washington, D. C.: American Enterprise Institute for Public Policy Research, 1980), 1–33.

[20]Max L. Stackhouse, "Christian Social Ethics in a Global Era: Reforming Protestant Views," in Max L. Stackhouse, et al., *Christian Social Ethics in a Global Era* (Nashville: Abingdon Press, 1995), 27.

[21]Ibid., 40.

to a certain extent; each wishes to impact attitudes and events. But the mainline liberals are particularly affirmative about a political role for their denominations and the ecumenical organizations in democratic societies. This does not generally extend to seeking the direct endorsement of candidates or parties in electoral campaigns. Mainstream liberals are not reticent about offering such personal endorsements themselves, or about personal participation in political campaigns. But only rarely do they propose such actions by churches as such. They do encourage church efforts to educate their memberships on important political issues and to translate this into influencing decision making by legislators, executives, and even judges. As a matter of fact, mainstream liberal thinkers often participate as members of or consultants to the boards, commissions, and committees of their denominations or of the councils of churches performing such political roles. (A generation ago they had to spend more time justifying this role by the churches—a defensive role that has less point now that their critics and the more conservative churches have become much more politically active themselves.)

Implicitly, the encouragement of mainline church bodies to accept a leadership role in national political life is an answer to Richard Neuhaus's charge in the preceding chapter that these churches have delegitimized American democracy. The most convincing way to confirm the basic legitimacy of the political order is to *assume* its legitimacy while going on to discuss how the church can be most effective in using the channels it provides. The Roman Catholic thinker John A. Coleman is typical in providing a variety of suggestions for this, ranging from use of liturgy to concrete forms of social action to express the church's witness in the political order.[22] Bennett provides a thoughtful analysis of the different levels at which Christians and their churches and ecumenical bodies can become engaged in political life, with different possibilities and limitations involved in each.[23]

THE SPECIAL PROBLEM OF VIOLENCE

Some of the thinkers whom I would consider to be a part of this generating center—such as Walter G. Muelder, Paul Deats Jr., and John Swomley—are pacifists. Such a classification is another

---

[22]John A. Coleman, *An American Strategic Theology* (New York: Paulist Press, 1982).
[23]John C. Bennett, "Church and State in the United States," in *Reformed Faith and Politics,* 128–31.

reminder of how insecure any "typing" of thinkers can be! I locate them here rather than in chapter 4 because of their clear acceptance of the legitimacy of the democratic state, their insistence upon the accountability of political power to the people affected by it, and their openness to a role for police protection.

Nevertheless, most mainstream liberals are not pacifists. At the same time, they are deeply critical of unrestrained violence and social coercion. They perceive more ambiguities in the uses of violence in revolutionary struggles than do many of the liberationists, especially those most influenced by Marxism. And they are more in earnest about the understanding of and reconciliation with national enemies than the neoconservatives usually appear to be. Violence, to them, is a sometimes necessary but always tragic recourse in civil society. It is always a frustration of God's intentions for civil society. Even when violence or coercion must be used against a clear wrongdoer, the Christian must act with restraint and avoid self-righteousness.

Joseph Allen, following the late Paul Ramsey, believes that "perpetrators of injustice" must be restrained. And if it comes down to a choice between supporting the interests of victims or those of wrongdoers, the former must clearly have priority. Nevertheless, he writes that

> once we view the conflict of wrongdoers and wronged from the perspective of God's inclusive covenant, we do not have the option of rejecting the wrongdoer. Both victim and wrongdoer are children of God and thereby have equal human worth. It is not as though once one person has seriously, even grievously, wronged another, we are then free to wash our hands of further respect for the wrongdoer's worth.[24]

Allen is typical of many mainstream liberals, then, in employing a restatement of the classical Christian just war criteria to determine when violence is morally to be preferred as a lesser evil. Such thinking places a clear burden of proof against the use of violence, while recognizing it as a moral possibility under some circumstances.

Nonpacifist mainstream liberals have sometimes been challenged to demonstrate their good faith by opposing actual wars or

---

[24]Allen, *Love and Conflict*, 181–82.

other forms of violence sponsored by their governments.[25] Some who are theoretically opposed to indiscriminate violence have indeed found it difficult to confront their own governments in an actual case. But a large number of the mainstream liberals have not hesitated to apply their principles in controversial ways. That was certainly true of many who, like Bennett and Reinhold Niebuhr, resolutely and publicly opposed U.S. involvement in the Vietnam War. Others have publicly resisted U.S. support for counterrevolutionary guerrillas in Central America, the British waging of war in the Falkland Islands and, more recently, the Gulf War, the conflict in the Balkans over Kosovo, and continued military enforcement of economic sanctions on Iraq. Mainstream liberals can be found on both sides in assessing such military involvements, but they tend to employ similar just war tools of analysis in their assessments. Many mainstream liberals have publicly rejected the use of nuclear deterrence, increases in military budgets, and other examples of what they consider excessive militarism.

But mainstream liberals have also taken the positive tasks of peacemaking seriously. For instance, most mainstream liberals support the United Nations, positive efforts to further economic and social development in Third World countries, and other efforts to lay the foundations for global peace with justice. Many of them would subscribe to the ecumenical call for a "just, participatory, and sustainable" world society in the belief that peace is more than the absence of war.

THE MAINSTREAM LINK

Taken as a whole, the recent literature of mainstream liberalism does not provide startling novelty so much as a reflective gathering together of insight from a variety of intersecting traditions of Christian thought about politics—combined with a creative attempt to cope with awesome new dilemmas posed by the politics of the late twentieth-century world. Such thinkers sometimes appear to be eclectic or even fuzzy, and they are easily criticized by their colleagues from the other generating centers. The pacifists are critical

---

[25]See John H. Yoder, *When War Is Unjust* (Minneapolis: Augsburg, 1984). I do not believe that Yoder sufficiently acknowledges the extent to which ethicists subscribing to the just war tradition have in fact opposed military actions by their own countries which they considered in violation of the standards imposed by that tradition.

of their acceptance of violence. The liberationists mock their reformism, sometimes attributing it to the privileged social location of most mainstream liberals. The neoconservatives consider them to be too idealistic about the sinful realities of the actual world and too naive about the threats to democratic society. Evangelicals, especially those of the right, are critical of their nonliteral approach to scripture and their tendency to be too accepting of abortion and homosexuality.

Each of the generating centers of Christian political thought we have considered in these five chapters has, as we have noted, some contributions to make. The first reminds us that all human values must be subordinate to a transcendent center of value and that Christians can never take the purposes and pretensions of ordinary political life simply at face value. In particular, it reminds us that violence and coercion are, on the face of it, antithetical to the way of Christ. Our use of violence and coercion in the political order can never be regarded as morally good or even morally neutral. Mainstream liberalism may (and usually does) disagree with the pacifist view that violence should never be used. But it is well reminded that such means should never become routine.

The second generating center reminds us that suffering humanity constitutes the most urgent agenda for the politics of Christians. Liberation theologians argue well that the oppressed of the earth define Christian political purpose more clearly than anything else save, to be sure, the urgency of avoiding thermonuclear war. They will not allow the church to be defined asocially or apolitically. Nor will they permit its proclamation of the good news to be treated as an escape from grappling with the hard realities of human suffering. If liberationists tend to be less critical of violence, they are at least a reminder to pacifists that there is violence in the unjust order. And they remind us all that injustice may not always yield to expressions of love alone.

The third center is more defensive in character. It is less sensitive to the horrors of war and the dehumanization caused by poverty, racism, and sexism. Still, its commitment to democracy is a reminder that humanity has a very great stake in institutions protecting freedom of expression and guaranteeing the rights of participation in the political process. It will not allow the church to forget the disillusionments and deepened suffering that have so often accompanied even successful revolutions. Nor will it overlook the illusions of Marxism, whatever value we may gain from specific Marxist insights.

The evangelical centers, right and left, remind us of the deep foundations of scripture for all Christian thought and the importance of personal transformation, even though the evangelicals—especially those of the right—can justly be criticized for the extreme narrowness and divisiveness of their message.

Having recorded these points, it remains that mainstream liberalism is possibly best prepared to link all of these insights into a faithful and feasible Christian political perspective. Certainly the writers who share this "location" in Christian ethics have attempted to take seriously what writers associated more with the other generating centers have to say, even though the former may be more persuaded than the latter to hold these insights in tension. Thus, Bennett, while not opting for thoroughgoing socialism in the manner of many of the liberation theologians, still urges Christian ethics "to press the socialistic questions even though they do not accept ready-made socialistic answers."[26] A similar point could be made in this spirit about the need to press pacifist questions even though one may not accept ready-made pacifist answers. And we can speak of the need to press the human rights questions, and the questions about democratic accountability, and the questions about world order.

These and other questions will be dealt with in the chapters that follow. I do not intend to present a *radically* new Christian perspective on politics here. Nor do I wish to "put down" the work pouring forth from the generating centers described in these last five chapters. Wherever serious Christians wrestle with urgent political questions they are likely to bring forth insights to which all of us must attend. None of us have all the answers; none of us will *ever* have all the answers. The discerning reader will note quickly enough—if she or he has not already done so—that my own affinities are more with the last of the generating centers than with the other four. But in what follows I gratefully acknowledge insights gained from these others as well.

---

[26]Bennett, *Radical Imperative,* 156.

PART 3

Christian Convictions and the Political Order: A Constructive Statement

Introduction

The work proceeding among Christian thinkers in the various generating centers discussed above suggests that many Christians consider their faith to be relevant to politics. It also suggests that their differences will not be easily overcome. The differences may, in fact, be healthy. Each of the perspectives we have discussed has much to contribute. Each may also have blind spots. The vigorous debate among the viewpoints helps keep the contributions before us while also illuminating the blind spots.

In the chapters that follow, we will examine more closely the relationship between basic theological convictions and a broad conception of the political order. I am confident that this will not end the worldwide debate over Christianity and politics! What follows is informed by that debate and hopes to contribute to it, but with an understanding that the last word will not, cannot, be spoken.

9

Theological Entry
Points and Political Ethics

> Back of the contemporary discussion of these many po-
> litical problems there is the whole history of Christian
> thought. Much of this history that has the greatest rel-
> evance to our problems today is more fundamental and
> broader than Christian political theory. It deals with
> God's purpose for our life, with the nature of man and
> society, with the political symptoms of sin, with the di-
> rect and indirect political effects of the redemption me-
> diated to us by Christ, with the essential nature of the
> Church and its role in society.
> —*John C. Bennett (1958)*[1]

These words, written forty years ago by a leading Christian theologian, apply equally well today. A number of the problems discussed
in Bennett's *Christians and the State* take a different form today,
and there are new issues besides. Meanwhile, there have also been
interesting developments in theology, some of them contributed by
Bennett himself. But still, it is not as though successive generations
of Christians had to reinvent Christianity. In a sense, we all go back
to the same well, understanding it to contain (in the biblical
metaphor) the water of life. The subject, like a good well, is inexhaustible. After we have said everything, there is still something
more to be said. After we have drawn forth all the resources, there
are still more to be found by others. But the inexhaustibility of
Christian faith should not inhibit our drawing upon its resources for

---

[1]John C. Bennett, *Christians and the State* (New York: Charles Scribner's Sons, 1958),
1:xvi–xvii.

understanding life in political society. And the complexity of political problems and our inability to say the last word about them should not prevent us from struggling with those problems as best we can.

In this chapter, I wish to discuss the problem of how to relate fundamental Christian convictions to politics.

THE POLITICAL RELEVANCE
OF CHRISTIAN FAITH

There are those who hold that Christian faith, as such, does not provide us with the essential grounding needed for political ethics. One seeks, instead, for that grounding in universal reason. Western Christians are the beneficiaries of great traditions of political philosophy which can be expressed without reference to Christian ideas. One thinks of such particularly influential philosophies as those of Plato, Aristotle, the Stoics, Hobbes, Locke, Rousseau, and Marx—each of which, at some time or other, has influenced Christian political thought. Not infrequently, Christian thinkers have used such philosophies as their governing conceptions, adding the theological element as a merely inspirational appendage. Nor are Christian thinkers limited in this respect to the Western traditions. There are very important traditions of political organization in Africa, recovered in our time by such leaders as Julius Nyerere, which can form the basis of a political ethic. And in Asia where, after all, Confucius and other thinkers had important things to say about social organization.

Such "secular" traditions are important. They contribute immeasurably to our understanding of political life, and Christians should at least draw upon them freely.

Nevertheless, any political philosophy remains incomplete unless it has reference to a vision of what is ultimately true and ultimately good—that is the contribution of theological traditions. In particular, a political ethic must finally be validated by a conception of value that is central to all other values. And theology expresses, at bottom, what it is that we *worship*—what is finally of value to us. Relating political philosophies to theology is no simple exercise, but it is finally a necessary one.

In another sense, one does not have to linger over whether Christian faith is relevant to politics. We have already seen in chapter 2 that anything that people believe or value can have political consequences. There are certainly religious beliefs and values in the contemporary world that can be considered superstitious nonsense, and some religious beliefs may in fact be terribly destructive. But that does not mean they are not *relevant* to politics. In a sense, anything that has political consequences is relevant to politics.

But I speak of relevance in a different way. I have in mind the capacity of religious ideas to bring political problems into perspective, to illuminate them, to help us resolve them in ways we find satisfactory. Another way to raise the question is to ask whether we can be deeply Christian and politically active without self-contradiction. Indeed, the fact that we are inescapably political (in the sense suggested in chapter 2) forces us to confront the question in yet another way. Given the fact that we are political beings, is Christian faith itself sustainable? If, to be political, we must put our Christian identity with its values and beliefs resolutely aside, that may suggest that we cannot, ultimately, be Christian. On the other hand, the relevance of our Christian convictions to politics may be such that we are forced to change our way of thinking about politics and the ways in which we practice politics.

A full assessment of these tensions requires serious grappling with what it means to be Christian. Clearly it means more than church membership, though I doubt that it can mean less than that (a point to which we will return in the next chapter). It also means more than a mechanical search of the Bible for political directives. Even fundamentalists are sometimes embarrassed by what they find there in their search for direct guidance on the issues of the day. Are we to approve of war? Fundamentalists may justify war by the precedents of the wars of the people of Israel, as chronicled in Hebrew scriptures. But can we be content with the portrait of a God who commands the annihilation of every man, woman, and child of the enemy peoples (as suggested in 1 Sam. 15:3 or Josh. 10:40)? Are we to approve of capital punishment? Fundamentalists may advocate this on the basis of the laws and commandments of Hebrew scripture specifying that miscreants be put to death. But can we inflict such a penalty for all of the infractions for which it is specified in the scriptures (including religious apostasy, incest, adultery, and even disobedience to one's parents)? In some cases, scriptures may say too little; in other cases, too much. But in all cases, one must dig deeper than literal proof-texting (using a particular scriptural text to "prove" a point) permits.

One must also dig more deeply than a modeling of one's life, attitudes, and actions on the historical figure of Jesus. Jesus Christ is obviously important to Christians. Indeed, he is absolutely central to the faith. But it is in a sense that is more profound than using him as a specific model for life. Christians maintain that Jesus Christ is the best revelation we have of the character of God.[2] Through the person of Jesus Christ we are brought into awareness of the source and power of all being and value. Our problem is less one of copying Jesus and more one of coming to terms with the God, who is our God, who is revealed in Christ.

Obviously the historical character of Jesus himself is not irrelevant to this. John Howard Yoder has a certain point in arguing that through the resurrection God has identified the way of Jesus as normative for Christians.[3] But one drawback in stating the matter in that way is that we may be led to absolutize particular ways of acting because Jesus acted in that way, or particular teachings about what to do because we believe the teachings truly to have been those of Jesus and in the exact form in which we have them. However, much of Jesus' behavior and many of his teachings must be seen in light of the historical-cultural setting, and all of our records of Jesus' life and ministry come to us through the interpreting witness of early Christians and the early church. This record must still be taken seriously by Christians, of course, for if Jesus Christ is understood as revelation of God, then his historical presence and teaching are of no small importance.

But it is the nature, the character of God, and God's relationship to the world that is central. I cannot imagine a credible version of Christian faith that regarded the particular life and teachings of Jesus as being an inauthentic human response to God. But as we confront the reality of God in the person of Jesus Christ, we are forced to distinguish between the essential meaning of the revelation and the ways the early church (and Jesus himself) addressed the particular historical setting. There are commonalities in history and culture. The ancient world was not different from our world in every respect. We can learn much from Jesus' own practice and from the practice of the church at the beginning and in subsequent centuries. Moreover, there is a certain presumptive rightness in whatever we know to have been Jesus' way of responding to his situation

---

[2]I have discussed the meaning of revelation and the centrality of Jesus Christ more fully in *Faith and Fragmentation: Christianity for a New Age* (Philadelphia: Fortress Press, 1985), 41–64.

[3]See John H. Yoder, *The Politics of Jesus* (Grand Rapids: Wm. B. Eerdmans, 1972) and chap. 3 of this volume.

and in what we know of the church's subsequent moral teaching, based on the moral experience, in the light of faith, of Christians through the centuries. But still, it is the character of God that stands ultimately behind it all, and it is to God that Christians respond in faith and action.

The whole tradition speaks to this. Christian scriptures, the original witness and the original theological interpretations, form the seedbed of tradition and ultimately stand as a check upon pure inventiveness in Christian theology. The subsequent flowerings of tradition and the work of seminal theologians is not inconsequential, however. This later work helps one understand the meaning of the scriptures themselves, and it also elaborates the meaning of tradition in the light of new questions and changing circumstances. The very vastness of the traditions and theological reflections of twenty centuries of Christian experience means that the well is deep indeed! But it is not just the tradition that is deep. If that tradition is right in pointing to the God revealed in Jesus Christ as the center and source of all being and value, then the meaning of God is itself as inexhaustible as "all being" can be.

And it is the deep reality of God, as revealed in Jesus Christ, that is relevant or irrelevant to politics. How are we to go about translating our convictions about God and God's ways with humanity and the world into a meaningful political ethics or theology of politics?

THEOLOGICAL ENTRY POINTS

There is an understandable tendency among Christian writers on politics to build the edifice of their thought on some one doctrinal emphasis (or at least a very limited number of theological points of emphasis). Thus, Jacques Ellul (to some extent following Karl Barth) stresses the importance of Christian freedom, and the liberation theologians have based their work on the exodus metaphor. Reinhold Niebuhr emphasized the doctrine of original sin and the tensions between love and justice. Walter Rauschenbusch and others of the social gospel era built their work around the kingdom of God. Joseph Allen develops a covenantal conception, as, in fact, have many reformed theologians for generations. In our time a number of writers have based their work on the multiple meanings of the Hebrew word *shalom,* which conveys a deep sense of the peace that contains justice and the harmony of God's intended creation.

All of this is helpful. There is a certain two-sided risk in trying to place too much weight on any one theological point. On the one hand we may contribute to fads and the early obsolescence of perfectly valid insights as the theological procession moves on to some new emphasis. On the other hand, we may overlook insights that are better illuminated by other symbols or doctrines than the ones we have chosen. We may even find ourselves *opposing* theological views that are not so much contrary to our own as they are complementary.

But how, then, to bring order out of the vast number of Christian symbols and doctrines that are potentially relevant to politics? It is well to remember that the many and varied Christian symbols and metaphors and doctrines point toward unity, even if it is a unity that cannot finally be grasped by any of us. Or, to put this in another way, every authentic symbol, metaphor, or doctrine helps us, in principle, understand all the rest a little better. We can, in a sense, begin at any point and find that it leads us to the other points. But some points may illuminate certain political questions or issues more clearly than others do.

We can call these "theological entry points."[4] The idea is not that there is only one grand theological conception that must be applied to politics, nor even that only one conception is helpful in illuminating any one particular problem. But it remains that certain theological concepts or symbols or metaphors or doctrines may be particularly relevant to particular problems. It is often true that politics poses questions for us which evoke particular theological answers (as Paul Tillich understood with his method of correlation).

I wish here to anticipate the remainder of the book by identifying several particularly promising theological entry points. I do not mean by this selection that these are the only theological conceptions having political relevance. Given the breadth of both politics and theology, I would suppose almost *any* theological idea to be relevant in some way to politics—just as any aspect of politics is subject to theological analysis. The selection is dictated by the judgment that these entry points may be among the most useful. Here, then, are ten such theological entry points.

The Sovereignty of God

In answer to the political question, to what power do we owe ultimate allegiance? the only possible Christian response is *God*. In saying that they must obey God rather than human authority (Acts

---

[4]I am indebted to Walter G. Muelder for this felicitous term.

5:29), Peter and the other apostles spoke for all Christians everywhere on this matter of ultimate loyalty. When any human authority is in clear conflict with the divine authority, it is the latter, not the former, that is sovereign. This is the basis for Jacques Maritain's insistence that no human authority be considered to be "sovereign," for none possesses absolute supremacy.[5] I have already disagreed (in chapter 2) with his view that human sovereignty is not a useful term of reference. But, theologically speaking, every human sovereignty is subordinate to the sovereignty of God. Needless to say, Christians have had to face the conflict between the two in virtually every epoch of human history. And that is a particularly relevant theological entry point in the era of the totalitarian state.

Even apart from the stark conflicts posed by totalitarian states, the sovereignty of God is a caution against idolatries. The ancient Hebrew commandment "You shall have no other gods before me" expresses an enduring theological conviction of Christians (as well as Jews and Muslims). It certainly applies to the worship of material things—always a tendency in materialistic cultures. It also applies to the deification of social groups, including the nation. Whatever appreciative things may be said about patriotism or civil religion, nothing less than God can be turned into an ultimate objective of devotion.

The Transcendence of God

There is an immediate problem, however. How are we to *know* the will of the sovereign God? What appears to some to be a conflict between God and human authority may appear to others an instance of human authority implementing the will of God. Some believe that the state should prohibit women from having abortions, others consider abortions sometimes to represent the will of God. In the first tragic world war of this century, the British, French, and Americans clearly understood that "God is on our side," but in the opposing trenches the Germans were equally clear about "Gott mit uns!" Some sociologically Christian nations have been organized as virtual theocracies, on the assumption that an identifiable religious elite had privileged access to understanding the will of God. Smaller dissident groups of Christians in such societies have had to pay a heavy penalty for sticking by their conflicting interpretations of

---

[5]Jacques Maritain, *Man and the State* (Chicago: University of Chicago Press, 1951), 38, 44.

God's will. If we could be very sure we knew the will of God or that we could identify those who did, the political problem for Christians would be enormously simplified—however much the plight of non-Christians might be complicated.

But in answer to the question of our knowledge about God, the relevant theological entry point is the transcendence of God. God is sovereign, but God is also beyond full human comprehension. God, as center and source of all being and value, the Lord of all ages and before all ages, is always more than anything any of us can identify or manipulate. It would be meaningless to speak of the will of God if there were no basis whatsoever for asserting that any course of action reflects that will, but the transcendence of God injects an element of principled humility into the equation.

Human Finitude

The same point, seen now from the human or anthropological standpoint, is that human beings are limited beings. We are, to be sure, enormously clever beings, capable of all sorts of surprising things. The fund of human knowledge is, in its totality, impressive. But even adding it all up—which no individual human being can do—it still falls vastly short of the comprehension of all reality. The wider the expanding periphery of human knowledge, the greater our exposure to the frontiers of our ignorance! We live very briefly. Indeed, the whole human enterprise occupies thus far but the smallest fraction of the history of the universe. The fact of human finitude is evident quite apart from a Christian theological orientation. But it is a point of reference in that theology as well. For we understand people to be creatures and not the Creator. Recognition of our finitude reinforces the point that we cannot so easily identify the judgment of any human being or groups of people with the will of God.

Covenant

The covenantal conception is at the heart of Hebrew as well as Christian understandings of God. God is understood to have formed a covenant with the people of Israel: "I will be your God and you will be my people." The covenant is formed and expressed in the great moments of Israel's history: the exodus, the giving of the law at Mount Sinai, the giving of the promised land. It is used by the great prophets to criticize the unfaithfulness of the people and to expand the nation's consciousness of the covenant's meaning. At bottom, the covenant expresses the view that the people derive their meaning from their relationship with God. God has created this relationship; their role is to respond loyally and obediently.

The political importance of the covenant is twofold: first, to reinforce the sovereignty of God. God is the author of the covenant; the covenant is about God's ways with humanity (and the rest of creation). The unfolding of the purposes and possibilities of the covenant contains the meaning of life. But second, the covenant is what creates the community. Israel has its being as a result of the covenant. It is the relationship that the people have in common with God that makes them *a* people and not just people.

The Christian theological conception does not abandon the covenantal notion. Christianity also is about the covenant, for it is about the relationship of people to God. But it understands the meaning of the covenant to have been disclosed most profoundly in Jesus Christ. In Jesus Christ the depth of God's covenantal love is revealed. And in Jesus Christ we understand that the covenant is universal. It is with and for everybody; it is not limited to a particular historical community. Thus, the New Testament letter to the Ephesians addresses people (Gentiles) who had not been included in the Hebrew conception of community: "Remember that you were . . . separated from Christ, alienated from the commonwealth of Israel, and strangers to the covenants of promise, having no hope and without God in the world" (2:12). But now Gentiles are included: "For he is our peace, who has made us both one, and has broken down the dividing wall of hostility" (2:14).

The suggestion here that the community of reference for all people is the inclusive, universal community has political consequences on the face of it. No people can be understood as total aliens—not even clear political adversaries. All political divisions based upon city, nation, or empire are relativized by the covenantal notion when it is applied in this universal sense. On the other hand, whenever the covenant is limited theologically to a particular, identifiable group of "chosen people," the political consequences of that are also very important.[6] Such a limited community of

---

[6]This point is argued persuasively by George W. Buchanan, *The Consequences of the Covenant* (Leiden: E. J. Brill, 1970), although I believe he has overstated the degree to which such covenantal narrowness dominates the entire biblical canon. At the end of the twentieth century extreme forms of political Zionism in Israel, racism in South Africa, and anticommunism (with a crusading attitude toward the military defeat of specific communist regimes) can be related to narrow versions of covenantal religion. Of course, the concept of covenant can lead to toleration and compassion when expressed in universal terms.

reference permits its members to treat nonmembers as creatures of lesser value and to regard its adversaries as the enemies of God. While these attitudes are not easily reconciled with the full sweep of Christian theology, they have been expressed with some frequency throughout history.

The Theology of the Cross

The Christian symbol of the cross is understood as an expression of Jesus' free acceptance of painful, ignominious death on that implement. Jesus' death is taken as a maximal expression of human evil— the killing of one who embodied the goodness of God—and as a maximal expression of that goodness itself. The cross portrays human sin and divine love—in the most vivid possible contrast. The contrast is heightened by the fact that the love was expressed for those responsible for the evil. Translated into relevant political terms, the theology of the cross can point to the contrast between the altogether positive, self-sacrificial expression of love on the cross and the negative uses of violence and coercion in "power politics." Seen in that light, it is something of an irony that the symbol of the cross was employed by the medieval crusaders and—in the contemporary world— by the racist Ku Klux Klan. The deep meaning of the cross challenges every designation of people as the enemies of God, and it places a question mark before the use of political methods that are violent and coercive. In the cross, God—through Christ—did not choose to force or manipulate humanity, but rather to *appeal* to humanity.

Justification and Grace

Related to the doctrine of the cross is the theological understanding that God's love is a free, unmerited gift. Salvation is not something we are called upon to earn. Set initially in the context of the various requirements of Hebrew law, which must be observed if one is to merit good standing in the covenant with God, Saint Paul's understanding of God's love was that such requirements are not a precondition to God's favor. Indeed, Paul is impressed by the impossibility of observing the law in all its particulars. But through the cross we are given to understand that the law has been set aside. God's love is direct and unqualified. Paul has much to say about the moral demands implicit in our response to God's grace, but it is important whether these demands are a precondition or a response. Paul's notion is that we are fully accepted by God, even in our imperfection. And while this gift can be lost through our willfulness and rebellion, the gift itself is never withdrawn. There is nothing we could possibly do to make God no longer love us.

The doctrine of grace has political relevance in relation to the question, whenever raised, of who does or does not *deserve* specified political benefits. Attitudes toward public welfare programs or "the dole" clearly are involved here. The concept of grace is a kind of leveler: we are all, ultimately, dependent upon God's free gift of love, unmerited, undeserved. Translating that into policy detail can be very difficult, of course. But the relevance of grace to such political questions is challenging all the same.

The Doctrine of Creation

By this I refer to all tangible aspects of existence. The view that the natural universe and those who inhabit it were created by God is central to Christian (and Hebrew) theology. Particular mythological conceptions of how this came to be are not the point; often those conceptions represent a fairly primitive effort to understand things in prescientific terms. The important point is that the material universe has an indispensable role to play in the unfolding of God's purposes for life. Seen in relation to the doctrine of the covenant, as Barth has done, the work of creation can be understood as a necessary condition for the realization of the meaning of the covenant.[7]

Again, the political consequences of the way we view creation are potentially enormous. Perhaps the material world is only an illusion, as some religious tendencies suggest. If so, then whatever appears to be important in that world is also only an illusion. Perhaps what happens in that world is real, but of no moral consequence one way or another. If so, why should one care about what happens? Perhaps the world is fundamentally evil, the work of a malevolent deity, or totally ruined by the "Fall." If so, how could any good thing be done in such an environment? Such religious attitudes toward the physical world could logically lead us to conclude that hunger and poverty, illness, economic exploitation, slavery, or even physical torture are not *moral* problems for us. We can

---

[7]Barth's formulation of this is to refer to "Creation as the External Basis of the Covenant" and "The Covenant as the Internal Basis of Creation" (*Church Dogmatics,* vol. 3, *The Doctrine of Creation,* part 1 [Edinburgh: T. & T. Clark, 1958]).

live our lives on a purely "spiritual" level—whatever that might mean. The material level of existence might literally no longer concern us. And by the same token, the significance of political power itself would be sharply relativized. What would be worth struggling for in the political arena?

But suppose, on the other hand, that there are important human values that can be enhanced or frustrated by what happens in the material realm. Suppose severe hunger and malnutrition have a negative effect on our development as human beings or that debilitating disease can defeat God-intended possibilities. Suppose the acquisition of physical skills is related to the fulfillment of those possibilities. Suppose the terrors of war and the agonies of political and economic oppression undermine the possibilities of human community as God intends it to be. In a word, suppose there are physical conditions that help and physical conditions that hinder divine intentions for human life and for the welfare of other beings. Then the political struggle may be very important, for it maintains or changes the circumstances of human existence. When Barth refers to "creation" as the basis and precondition of the "covenant," his point is not that the physical realm is the center of value for Christians. Rather, his point is that the physical realm helps or hinders the realization of the things that do matter. And it logically follows from this that public policies, arrived at through the political process, are decidedly relevant to all a Christian hopes for in this world.

In the debate between pacifist and nonpacifist Christians, the doctrine of creation can be pivotal. Is there anything that is worth fighting for—that is, are the stakes of any struggle important enough to justify the moral risks and losses of the struggle itself? Most pacifists are convinced of the importance of engaging in social struggle by nonviolent means, so the question must be recast: Is there anything that is worth fighting for violently, even lethally? Or is the use of violence invariably an evil greater than any other evil that can possibly befall humanity in this world? In the contemporary world these are not purely academic questions! A doctrine of creation that emphasizes the moral importance of the things that can be fought over correspondingly increases the possibility that the fight itself may not be the greater evil. That same doctrine of creation, however, also can be taken to emphasize the evil of war itself—for war, particularly modern war, is profoundly destructive.

Original Sin

Traditional Christian thought generally portrays human nature as seriously flawed by sin.[8] The doctrine of original sin is easily caricatured, particularly when taken as a literal consequence of Hebrew/Christian mythological events or of the sexual transmission of human life. It can also be considered a threat to moral freedom and responsibility if it is portrayed as *requiring* human beings to do evil deeds. People certainly cannot be blamed for doing things they are already "programmed" to do. But the idea of original sin has deeper meaning than all of this. As understood by Reinhold Niebuhr, this tendency does not result from any natural necessity; it is rather a consequence of our anxiety in the face of our own finitude. The only "cure" for original sin is deep trust in the goodness and grace of God. We do not have to shore up our own selfhood or self-esteem; we can count on God for our ultimate significance. Some versions of Christian theology imply that there can be complete release from original sin in human existence, while other versions stress the continuing struggle between the fearful, anxious, self-centered force of sin and the attraction of goodness and love.

In any case, one's view of sin can have very great political consequences. Who should govern? What constraints are needed to hedge the exercise of power? To what extent does human nature limit public-spiritedness and the construction of positive institutions?

If human nature is as profoundly sinful as Thomas Hobbes supposed in *Leviathan* ("every man is enemy to every man . . . and the life of man, solitary, poor, nasty, brutish, and short"), we may wonder whether any positive thing can be achieved through the political process—or whether, as he thought, government can only be an expression of the mutual self-interest of selfish people who need a power greater than any of them just to protect a tolerable level of human security. On the other hand, if human nature is as benevolent as Leo Tolstoy thought, then one scarcely needs to have a restraining, order-maintaining government at all: we can count on innate human goodness to keep the peace in a just society. But if we, like Reinhold Niebuhr, think of all people as sinners while still recognizing the

---

[8]The best theological presentation of the doctrine of original sin remains, in my judgment, that of Reinhold Niebuhr in *The Nature and Destiny of Man* (New York: Charles Scribner's Sons, 1943).

possibilities of goodness in human nature, our view of politics is likely to be more nuanced. We can seek to develop a political society that protects all against the sinful tendencies of each, while also providing institutional support for the more creative, positive, community-building possibilities to assert themselves. Or if, like many people, we think it possible to identify some people as sinners and other people as good, then it makes sense to allow only the good people to govern. But if disproportionate political power falls into the hands of sinful people, they will have disproportionate opportunity to harm others.

The suggestion that all of us are both sinful and benevolent, combined with the belief that only the sovereign God finally knows the extent of our sinfulness or benevolence, has a leveling political effect. No individual's or group's pretensions should be taken entirely at face value. Nobody has theologically privileged ground in the political order. And political ethics must be especially careful about questions of distribution of power. Clearly our attitude toward sin has great political consequences.

Eschatology

Doctrines of eschatology refer to theological conceptions of the ends of history, not simply in the sense of the termination of history but also its fulfillment. A doctrine of eschatology that emphasizes the realization of divine purposes in history is open to an important role for politics, while if history has no ends or prospects of fulfillment that may mean, correspondingly, that politics does not matter. More to the point here, if one's eschatological conception envisages the fulfillment of history altogether as the work of God—without any direct contribution by human action—then politics can be taken either to be irrelevant or to be a part of the "principalities and powers" that God must and will overcome. When a Yoder argues that it is not the responsibility of Christians to seek to manage the course of history (as noted in chapter 4), an eschatological claim has been made. The claim may either simply be that no Christian or group of Christians can possibly undertake to manage *all* events and assume responsibility for *all* outcomes. Or it may be the more sweeping claim that Christians are not accountable before God for the effort to *make* any desired thing come to pass. In either case, the ultimate power of God as consummator of human history is registered. At the other extreme, as in the work of William R. Jones,[9] it can be declared that everything that happens in human affairs must either be the result of purely natural forces or human action. Such an eschatology generally places a very high premium on political responsibility. But every eschatology has political consequences. It is, of course, possible to conceive of deep involvement by a personal God in the directing of human history toward its fulfillment, while at the same time emphasizing that God works in human history only through the responsiveness of human beings. That, too, would heighten the theological importance of politics.

Ecclesiology

Finally there is the doctrine of the church. The church, understood as the community of faith and its institutional structures, can be conceived in different ways with correspondingly different political consequences. As Ernst Troeltsch and those influenced by his work have maintained,[10] it is possible to think of the church ideally as the incorporation of everybody in a whole society into one vast religious community—an ecclesiastical unity of civilization. Or, at an opposite pole, one can understand the church as the company of the truly committed—a sectarian island of holiness or redemption in the larger sea of secularity or fallenness. There are many possible variations at both ends of the spectrum (and Troeltsch himself also documented a third "type"—mysticism—which deemphasized any tangible institutional manifestation of church while emphasizing the higher end of spiritual fulfillment). But any variation is likely to have political consequences. The first type is likely to have a positive conception of the state as the temporal aspect of a civilized order of which the church represents the spiritual aspect. The second type, the sectarian, is

---

[9]William R. Jones, *Is God a White Racist? A Preamble to Black Theology* (Garden City, N.Y.: Doubleday, 1973). Jones contends that the traditional Christian theistic conception of God cannot be reconciled with divine benevolence in the face of the realities of human suffering—particularly those occasioned by racism. His own preference is to replace that theistic conception with a humanistic view, thereby placing full responsibility in human hands.

[10]Troeltsch's early twentieth-century work *The Social Teaching of the Christian Churches* (London: George Allen & Unwin, 1931 [1911]) has had vast influence on subsequent work in Christian social ethics and sociology of religion even though his specific typology of social forms of religious expression (church, sect, and mysticism) has been refined endlessly. Among Christian ethicists, H. Richard Niebuhr's typology in *Christ and Culture* (New York: Harper & Brothers, 1951) has exerted widest influence.

likely to envisage the church as withdrawn from the political realm.[11] Of course, a sectarian religious group can think of itself as an important instrument in God's hands for the achievement of justice in the social sphere—which would entail an activist political orientation. But such a group might not be altogether sectarian, for it would necessarily be less negative about the possibilities of the achievement of goodness through the processes of political life in society at large.

We could almost endlessly add to this list of Christian doctrinal options, illustrating their political consequences. Christian doctrines of the Trinity, resurrection, Holy Spirit, vocation, stewardship, sanctification, and so on—all very important—could readily be added to the list. But enough has been written here to illustrate the point that theological doctrines provide entry points of different kinds into the political realm. It is, in fact, difficult to imagine a theological doctrine without political ramifications, just as the various theological doctrines all point toward the central reference point—the reality of God.

THE FORMULATION OF THEOLOGICAL
PRESUMPTIONS FOR POLITICS

It is easy enough to demonstrate the relevance of theological entry points to politics. But how exactly are we to *apply* theological insight? Sometimes a given theological view seems to have very clear political implications, as though we are absolutely committed to some particular political policy once we have adopted its corresponding theological precursor. Some theologians and church leaders seem eager enough to draw such airtight conclusions on occasion: For example, God is the source and sustainer of human life and value, so therefore the state should prohibit women from having abortions. Or, God treats us graciously regardless of our undeserving, and therefore welfare benefits should be provided without tests for need or other requirements. Or, all people are sinners, and therefore it is a mistake to try to give institutional form to goodness in human history.

But the effort to draw a straight line between given theological doctrines and given political conclusions generally falters in face of the complexities of life. We may not know as much about the real

---

[11]Contemporary Jehovah's Witnesses illustrate the apolitical tendencies of withdrawal rather clearly. Such sectarian groups are of course less than pure in their sectarianism to the extent they are involved in the normal economic and social life of the community

situation as we think we do. Or, a direct application of Christian doctrine may have unintended and undesired consequences.

In light of this complexity and uncertainty, it may be better (as I have proposed elsewhere)[12] to treat Christian doctrines as presumptive rather than definitive in the guidance of specific human action. By that I mean that a theological view with clear political ramifications should lead us to adopt those ramifications provisionally but with openness to the possibility that they should be set aside for sufficient reason. Theological entry points can help us define initial presumptions in the political realm. We can commit ourselves to follow those presumptions unless or until it is clear (beyond reasonable doubt) that more will be lost than gained. For example, it may seem clear (I trust it *does* seem clear) that war is contrary to various theological commitments. Our presumption may therefore be (I trust it *must* be) against any particular war. But in a given and exceptional historical situation, the burden of proof may be met by those who believe that military action would be more in accord with the ultimate commitments of Christians than a refusal to pursue such action would be. In that case, the presumption against war would have to be set aside. The approach suggested here is something like that of a court of law in the Anglo-Saxon tradition, where an accused person is *presumed* to be innocent unless and until proven guilty beyond reasonable doubt. The most direct line of application of a given theological doctrine is presumed to be the right one to pursue unless and until it is shown, in fact, to lead to deviation from real Christian faithfulness.

Sometimes, of course, theological reflection presents us with seemingly contradictory signals. A given doctrine may have one set of apparently logical political consequences, but these may be in conflict with the equally compelling ramifications of a different theological doctrine. How are we to deal with the apparent conflict between presumptions?

We should remember that every particular doctrine (or entry point) is an expression of deeper truth. Confronted by apparent contradiction we are challenged to think more deeply as we struggle to reconcile the conflict. The implication of this way of putting the matter is that truth is ultimately one. All being has its source and unity in God. God is not self-contradictory, but our views of God may be. Deeper reflection may show that one approach is right and the other wrong, or it may show that both are wrong, or it may show that

---

[12]See *A Christian Method of Moral Judgment* (Philadelphia: Westminster Press, 1976).

there is some rightness and some wrongness in each, or it may show the rightness of each but the greater factual promise of one than of the other.

The fact of human sin and human limitation can function to set aside the theologically grounded presumption. The most direct route from theology to political practice may not be a possible route because of the intervening reality of sin. There may be real theological as well as practical wisdom in Luther's insistence that it is not always possible to govern the world "in a Christian and evangelical manner." If that is so, it is not because there is anything inherently faulty in the expression of Christian love as such. It is because sin resists goodness; therefore action to confound the effects of sin may be the most loving possibility available, even though such action appears not to be an expression of love. On the other hand, it may be more possible than Luther ever supposed to be direct and loving in our political actions. The initial presumption should be in that direction. But the doctrine of original sin should also lead us to expect that the direct, positive presumption will have to yield to reality at some points.

In the pages that follow, I shall seek to use theological entry points in this kind of way—by attempting to define the political presumptions that appear to flow most directly from Christian commitment. A first step in this direction will be to explore the fundamental question of the legitimacy of the state. In the following chapter I shall do so by exploring the apparently conflicting loyalties to church and state.

10

The Confessing Church
and Civil Society

> But outside [the] sphere of personal morality, the evangelical church has little to say about wider social commitments. Indeed, the sect draws together those who have found a personal relationship to Christ into a special loving community, and while it urgently seeks to have everyone make the same commitment, it separates its members off from attachment to the wider society. Morality becomes personal, not social; private, not public.
> —*Robert Bellah et al. (1985)*[1]

In many ways, the first political question to be asked by Christians concerns our community of reference. We belong to the church; that is given with our being Christian. We are also subject to the state; that is given with our being human in some society or other. But exactly how our belonging to the church affects our belonging to the state is not at all clear theologically. Members of "mainline" or "establishment" churches in Western countries do not often have to face the question, because in such settings the church and the wider society involve the same people, the same culture, the same basic values, the same history. That is even true in religiously pluralistic societies, such as the United States, where any one denomination constitutes but a small fraction of the total population. Even in such a situation there may be little to distinguish between the mainline churches and the dominant culture. Most people are not United Methodists, or Presbyterians, or Episcopalians in the United States.

---

[1]Robert N. Bellah et al., *Habits of the Heart* (Berkeley and Los Angeles: University of California Press, 1985), 231.

But to be a member of one of those denominations is, in a sense, to be like most people—at least, most people who make up what is often considered to be the mainstream of the culture. Members of such churches can readily transfer to similar denominations, and the difference between their lives as church members and the rest of their existence often is not readily discernible.

This is all the more true of the members of establishment churches in countries such as the United Kingdom and Sweden, where citizenship and church membership are virtually the same thing. Ernst Troeltsch and others have explored the ramifications of the "church-type" encompassing of a whole society into the ecclesial framework, noting that the complementary encompassing of the church into the broader social framework often occurs at the same time.

The problem facing us now is whether this virtual identity of the church community with the rest of the culture is possible without abandoning the real meaning of Christian faith.

To put this in political terms, it is a question whether Christians can interact with non-Christians within the same civil society in such a way that the wider civil society is affirmed by all as a community of reference.[2] Are there values that can be held in common, on the basis of which political objectives can be defined and debated? Is there a common history that can be affirmed by both Christians and non-Christians? Is real cooperation possible? Do Christians have anything to learn from non-Christians—not only about factual or technical questions but about values and meanings? In a word, can Christians and non-Christians constitute an authentic *community?* Or is such a society a pluralism of communities, interacting on the basis of group interests and mutual endeavors at conversion or proselytism, but not on the basis of an affirmed commonality?

The importance of these questions, already anticipated in Part 2, continues to grow in a cultural setting of increasing pluralism.

---

[2]The term "community of reference" is suggested by sociological "reference group" theory, which has established the profound importance to all of us of the groups with which we identify ourselves. Its members are the persons whose respect and affection we most wish to have, and its values are the ones we accept for ourselves. The community of reference may be any kind of group. For many but by no means all people, a religious group will be the primary community of reference. Whether religious or not, a community of reference serves largely to provide our basic identity.

THE FAITHFUL CHURCH
AS COMMUNITY OF REFERENCE

A group of contemporary theologians, reacting strongly against what they perceive as the cultural captivity of the church in liberal Western societies, calls for greater ecclesial identity. The church must be the *church*. It must be clearly distinguishable from the world that is not the church. A number of these theologians, influenced by the narrative or "story" approach to theology, emphasize that Christian identity is formed within the church. Nurtured in and accepting the Christian story—the narrative of God's action in Jesus Christ and its subsequent unfolding in the life of the church through history—Christians are formed in their basic character. To be a Christian person with integrity is to have one's life formed on the basis of the Christian narrative. The character of Christians, thus formed, is different from the character of non-Christians. The community of faith, the church, is not at all the same thing as the broader society—although acting in faith the church may well seek to be a model to the rest of society of what human life ultimately and "truthfully" is invited to be.

James Wm. McClendon and Stanley Hauerwas are prominent among those who pursue this understanding. Hauerwas explores a series of ten theses intended to express the social meaning of the gospel. A number of these theses express radically this sharp distinction between the church and the wider society. For example:

> The primary social task of the church is to be itself—that is, a people who have been formed by a story that provides them with the skills for negotiating the danger of this existence, trusting in God's promise of redemption. [and]
>
> Christian social ethics can only be done from the perspective of those who do not seek to control national or world history but who are content to live "out of control." [and]
>
> In our attempt to control our society Christians in America have too readily accepted liberalism as a social strategy appropriate to the Christian story. [and]
>
> The church does not exist to provide an ethos for democracy or any other form of social organization, but stands as a political alternative to every nation, witnessing to the kind of social life possible for those that have been formed by the story of Christ.[3]

---

[3]Stanley Hauerwas, *A Community of Character: Toward a Constructive Christian Social Ethic* (Notre Dame, Ind.: University of Notre Dame Press, 1981), 10–11.

There is some ambiguity in these and the other theses, but it is at least very clear that Hauerwas wishes to sharpen the distinction between the church and the world beyond the church. Moreover, he does not see the task of the church to be the reform of that world. In commenting on another of the theses ("The ability to provide an adequate account of our existence is the primary test of the truthfulness of a social ethic"), Hauerwas questions whether any society "can be just or good that is built on falsehood." And he argues that "the first task of Christian social ethics, therefore, is not to make the 'world' better or more just, but to help Christian people form their community consistent with their conviction that the story of Christ is a truthful account of our existence."[4] Thus, the church's story is "truthful" while that of the rest of society apparently is not. And thus (presumably) there can be little genuine sharing of common values, except in the sense that those within the community of faith seek to witness to their "story" and to live out their ethic within that community, trusting its attractiveness to others to be based on its truthfulness.

Indeed, to understand the church's story, we must be formed by it. The heart of that story is Jesus, and to understand who Jesus is "we must be formed by the kind of community he calls into existence."[5] The truth of Jesus is universal truth. But this cannot be known except "through learning the particular form of discipleship required by this particular man."[6] The universality of Jesus "is manifested only by a people who are willing to take his cross as their story, as the necessary condition for living truthfully in this life." Those who are willing to take this cross as their story "become the continuation of that ethic in the world, until all are brought within his Kingdom."[7] Therefore, Christians are called into a polity "based on that power which comes from trusting in the truth."[8] Hauerwas thus makes clear that those who are within the community of faith—those who are formed by the Christian story and their discipleship in the cross—do not really have a basis for openness in dialogue and mutual cooperation in the common endeavors of the political order with

---

[4]Ibid., 10.
[5]Ibid., 40.
[6]Ibid., 41.
[7]Ibid., 44.
[8]Ibid., 46.

those who are outside that community in the wider society. The political point is emphasized in such comments as: "the kingdoms of the world derive their being from our fear of one another; the rule of God means that a community can exist where trust rules" and "the service that Christians are called upon to provide does not have as its aim to make the world better, but to demonstrate that Jesus has made possible a new world, a new social order,"[9] and

> by making the story of such a Lord central to their lives, Christians are enabled to see the world accurately and without illusion. Because they have the confidence that Jesus' cross and resurrection are the final words concerning God's rule, they have the courage to see the world for what it is: The world is ruled by powers and forces that we hardly know how to name, much less defend against. These powers derive their strength from our fear of destruction, cloaking their falsehood with the appearance of convention, offering us security in exchange for truth. By being trained through Jesus' story we have the means to name and prevent these powers from claiming our lives as their own.[10]

The church does have a contribution to make to that world: It is that of giving the world a "contrast model" by means of which it can come to know the "oddness of its dependence on power for survival," or the "strangeness of trying to build a politics that is inherently untruthful."[11]

At one point Hauerwas goes so far as to say that "the church and Christians must be uninvolved in the politics of our society and involved in the polity that is the church." But in some way we may still be called upon "to negotiate and make positive contributions to whatever society in which we may find ourselves" on the basis of the experience and skills we have gained within the church.[12] But it is clear enough that whatever dialogue Christians might have with the world is a one-way street.

---

[9]Ibid., 49.

[10]Ibid., 50.

[11]Ibid.

[12]Ibid., 74. There is some irony in Hauerwas's further observation that "any radical critique of our secular polity requires an equally radical critique of the church"—for "the church has not been a society of trust and virtue" (p. 86). If not, one might ask, where has the nurturing or formation of character occurred on the basis of which such a radical critique could be offered?

McClendon, while acknowledging indebtedness to Hauerwas, heightens the contrast between the church and the world beyond the church. With a radically pluralistic model of society, McClendon argues that "there is no single form of social whole to be designated 'society.'"[13] To him, therefore, the conception of a "civil society"—a larger society containing all the smaller subunits and focused in the institutions of state—is empirically unfounded. It is not just a question of competing claims between the church and its story, on the one hand, and the "world" of the wider society and culture, on the other hand. The latter simply does not exist. Instead, the church is but one of many communities of reference, each possibly offering its own "story," each perhaps forming the character of its own people in some way.

McClendon also insists that the church be a deeply committed fellowship, limited to those who have made the total and conscious commitment of themselves to this company. Consequently, as we have seen, McClendon repudiates infant baptism. Infants and children are under the care and nurture (and formation) of the church, but they do not become truly a part of the church until they are prepared to make a very conscious decision to do so. The church is a confessing church; its people stand in sharp contrast to those who identify with other communities. There would seem to be little to share, little basis for mutuality between confessing Christians and those whose identity is formed by other communities.

Are such views sectarian? Some, including James Gustafson and Paul Nelson, have suggested that possibility.[14] That depends upon one's definition of the term, and such a classification lies mostly beyond the scope of this book. If by "sectarian" we mean an attitude of total detachment from the world, then the label would not seem to apply. For both Hauerwas and McClendon believe in the active witness of Christians in the world and even engage in forms of resistance to what they perceive to be evil. On the other hand, both—following John Howard Yoder—disavow efforts by Christians to assume responsibility for managing political history. Both clearly do not attach great importance to the participation by Christians in the

---

[13]James Wm. McClendon, *Ethics: Systematic Theology* (Nashville: Abingdon Press, 1986), 1:171.

[14]Neither Hauerwas nor McClendon would wish to be classified as sectarian since the popular connotation of that term suggests total withdrawal from secular society.

civil society on the basis of the shared story, meanings, and values of that society.

We may pause to note a certain swinging of the pendulum. Some readers will recall the considerable splash made by the "secular" theologies of the 1960s, when the new freedom of "man come of age" was celebrated. Whether in the form represented by Friedrich Gogarten's theology or the prison writings of Dietrich Bonhoeffer (or the popularization by Harvey Cox and others), the emphasis was upon how Christians were liberated through Christ from the "sacralizing" of culture so they could truly and authentically attend to society in its own terms. The movement was attended by substantial engagement with social reform and with a great deal of optimism about the possibilities of such reform. The political effect of the movement was activist. It did not disavow the church. But it emphasized the full, wholehearted participation by Christians in the world on terms set by the world.

The irony is that the underlying basis of the theology of the secular theologians was not all that different from that of the Hauerwases and McClendons. Both movements emphasize the effect of the gospel in freeing us from the mystifying powers represented by false cultural values. Both see humanity freed by the gospel to be authentic and lucid (or "truthful," as Hauerwas would say). But their ecclesiologics arc almost diametrically opposed. And where the secular theologians emphasized the need for Christians to participate wholeheartedly in the shaping of human social and political history—fully engaged in the give and take of political and social life—the more recent writers we are considering are preoccupied by the internal life of the church and by the character and identity of Christians as individuals formed in that communal context.

THE CHRISTIAN AS CITIZEN

We could linger speculatively over the question whether these theological tendencies of the 1960s and 1980s are somehow an expression of the climate of the times. In any case, we are left with the question with which we began: Does Christian faith entail so radical an identification with the church per se and so sweeping a detachment from the larger civil community? Or are there theological grounds for legitimizing the larger civil society and its political and governmental institutions?

The case for an alternate perspective on these questions has been made in the writings of Robert Bellah, a prominent American sociologist who is also a personally committed Christian. Beginning with a 1967 essay, "Civil Religion in America,"[15] Bellah has called attention to the importance of a legitimizing ground of transcendent beliefs to give meaning to American political society. The term "civil religion" is often employed pejoratively by theologians as a synonym for the idolatry of nationalism—worshiping the state or nation as God. Such theologians have ample illustration of their fears in the writings of Jean Jacques Rousseau and others who have advocated use of a contrived "religion" to further the unity of the state, the obedience of subjects, and other political objectives. Such a civil religion is, needless to say, the very apotheosis of what writers such as Yoder and Hauerwas and McClendon mean when they characterize the "principalities and powers" holding sway over the culture that knows not God.

But, in fairness, Bellah means something quite different. The idea of civil religion is not a set of beliefs and rituals used by the state for its own ends so much as it is a body of beliefs and values with transcendent sources held in common by the people of the civil community. To speak of "transcendent" sources is to say that the civil religion has its grounding *beyond* the state, not derived from it. The civil religion, as understood by Bellah, cannot function as such unless it can in fact stand in *judgment* of the state. It provides the "symbolization of an ultimate order of existence in which republican values and virtues make sense." It provides "a purpose and a set of values."[16] It can be the basis on which prophetic leaders call the nation back to its authentic existence. It can also, Bellah acknowledges, be used to rationalize injustice:

> It may be a sobering thought, but most of what is good and most of what is bad in our history is rooted in our public theology. Every movement to make America more fully realize its professed values has grown out of some form of public theology, from the abolitionists to the social gospel and the early socialist party to the civil rights movement under Martin Luther King and the farm workers' movement under

---

[15]Robert N. Bellah, "Civil Religion in America," *Daedalus* 96 (Winter 1967): 1–21; reprinted in Robert N. Bellah, *Beyond Belief: Essays on Religion in a Post-Traditional World* (New York: Harper & Row, 1970).

[16]Robert N. Bellah, "Religion and the Legitimation of the American Republic," in *Varieties of Civil Religion,* ed. Robert N. Bellah and Phillip E. Hammond (San Francisco: Harper & Row, 1980), 12.

Cesar Chavez. But so has every expansionist war and every form of oppression of racial minorities and immigrant groups.[17]

Bellah considers Abraham Lincoln to have been the foremost American civil theologian because of the depth of Lincoln's grasp of the accountability of the nation to the God who is the source of justice and charity, and his capacity to understand the meaning of public tragedy in the light of a reality transcending the nation.

In an illuminating discussion of the legitimizing values of the American republican experiment, Bellah suggests that there have been two traditions, fundamentally contradictory, existing side by side from the beginning. One, which he attributes (perhaps too simplistically) to the principal founders of the American republic, perceives the civil society as a political covenant of citizens bound together in a common commitment to and pursuit of the public good. The other, which he associates with eighteenth- and nineteenth-century liberalism, conceives of the state as a set of institutions designed to govern the exchanges of a community of self-interested people. The former conception seeks to inculcate virtue in its citizens, specifically the virtues of public-spiritedness and self-sacrifice. The latter (that is, the liberal tradition) assumes the reign of freedom and the beneficence of the end result of the exchanges of self-interested people. The former is the basis on which a genuine republic can be developed and maintained. The latter is based on illusion:

> Though formulated by some of the toughest minds in the history of modern philosophy—Hobbes, Locke, Hume, and Adam Smith—this [liberal] tradition gave rise to what would appear to be the most wildly utopian idea in the history of political thought, namely, that a good society can result from the actions of citizens motivated by self-interest alone when those actions are organized through the proper mechanisms.[18]

Bellah believes that the liberal tradition, with its emphasis upon individualism and its invitation to self-centeredness, finally undermines the moral foundations of a republican political order. People

---

[17]Ibid., 15.

[18]Ibid., 9. It should be noted that Bellah's use of the word "liberal" here is the nineteenth-century sense of laissez-faire capitalism and utilitarianism—not in the sense of "New Deal liberalism" in the usual American connotation.

185

become corrupted by self-indulgent materialism. They are no longer committed to the well-being of the society as a whole. They are willing to settle for whatever will preserve their personal self-interest, above all their material way of life. Conflicting self-interests threaten finally to tear society apart, and to the self-interested citizenry some form of despotism may even seem inviting so long as it can assure the preservation of those interests. The society founded on that kind of liberalism thus points toward its own degeneration into some form of despotism. Bellah cites the warning of the aged Benjamin Franklin at the conclusion of the U.S. Constitutional Convention in 1787 that even the new Constitution, which he fully supported, could lead to despotism "when the people shall have become so corrupted as to need despotic Government, being incapable of any other."[19] And Bellah expresses his own fears in this way:

> Corruption . . . is to be found in luxury, dependence, and ignorance. Luxury is that pursuit of material things that diverts us from concern for the public good, that leads us to exclusive concern for our own good, or what we would today call consumerism. Dependence naturally follows from luxury, for it consists in accepting the dominance of whatever person or group, or, we might say today, governmental or private corporate structure, that promises it will take care of our material desires. . . . And finally ignorance, that is, political ignorance, is the result of luxury and dependence. It is a lack of interest in public things, a concern only for the private, a willingness to be governed by those who promise to take care of us even without our knowledgeable consent.[20]

Bellah notes, with Alexis de Tocqueville, that the real school of political virtue in America has been the churches. They have provided the grounding for a republican polity—a transcendent source of legitimation and criticism of government and a disposition toward responsible, even self-sacrificial citizenship. And they have been a school for political practice, making it possible for large numbers of people to participate in the public order. The churches, thus, have been indispensable in the grounding of the civil religion. But Bellah does not suggest that they have, thereby, lost their own identity or integrity.

---

[19]Quoted in ibid., 19.
[20]Ibid., 19–20.

The widely noted volume *Habits of the Heart,* written by Bellah and four colleagues, develops the civil religion theme from a different sociological angle.[21] Here, Bellah asks whether the individualism of American culture has created an unbridgeable gulf between personal life and public responsibility. Has human fulfillment in this culture come to be defined so completely in individual terms that participation in the shaping of the common life is no longer an essential part of it? Bellah notes two dominant forms of contemporary individualism: "expressive" and "utilitarian" individualism. The former characterizes human fulfillment in terms of our feelings. (The contemporary way of expressing this is that we should "get next to our feelings" or that we should feel good about ourselves.) The latter characterizes fulfillment in terms of pursuit of our self-interest, with major emphasis upon economic success. Both forms of individualism can be found in small groups or institutions, such as the family, church, business, and so on. But Bellah and his colleagues depict an American culture in which these forms of individualism cut one off from public life. They do not form public-spirited kinds of character. They do not cultivate the civic virtues.

That is even true of religion. Religious practice increasingly focuses upon mutual support and fulfillment within the religious group. But the group is distant from the public sphere, and the practice of the religious group is neither preparation for nor encouragement of participation in that sphere. That is clearly true of the more sectarian church groups: "The sect draws together those who have found a personal relationship to Christ into a special loving community, and while it urgently seeks to have everyone make the same commitment, it separates its members off from attachment to the wider society. Morality becomes personal, not social; private, not public."[22] But that is also true of large numbers of ordinary churches.

> There are thousands of local churches in the United States, representing an enormous range of variation in doctrine and worship. Yet most define themselves as communities of personal support. A recent study suggests that what Catholics

---

[21]The Bellah team made use of a method of sociological investigation in this study that has not been viewed favorably by all commentators. I am among those who think it a fruitful and promising approach, but that is not our concern here. For our purposes, Bellah's philosophical and ethical viewpoint is what is interesting.

[22]Ibid., 231.

look for does not differ from the concerns of the various types of Protestants we have been discussing. When asked the direction the church should take in future years, the two things that a national sample of Catholics most asked for were "personal and accessible priests" and "warmer, more personal parishes." The salience of these needs for personal intimacy in American religious life suggests why the local church, like other voluntary communities, indeed like the contemporary family, is so fragile, requires so much energy to keep it going, and has so faint a hold on commitment when such needs are not met.[23]

Even in the religious sphere, people are likely to use abstractions such as "communication" in speaking of their needs. Substantially lost is "a language genuinely able to mediate among self, society, the natural world, and ultimate reality."[24] In this and other writings, Bellah asks whether a recovery of biblical language might provide this mediating cultural form.

Our purpose here is not to agree or disagree with Bellah's assessment of contemporary American culture. Like other sweeping sociological generalizations, it is doubtless partly true and partly false—as Bellah and his colleagues would themselves unquestionably attest. The question is whether it is the *business* of the church to provide this mediating linkage between people and public responsibility. Bellah and his colleagues ask, "Is it possible that we could become citizens again and together seek the common good in the postindustrial, postmodern age?"[25] Their own vision, in response to that, is that of a common life grounded in a deep religious sense.

> Perhaps enduring commitment to those we love and civic friendship toward our fellow citizens are preferable to restless competition and anxious self-defense. Perhaps common worship, in which we express our gratitude and wonder in the face of the mystery of being itself, is the most important thing of all.[26]

---

[23]Ibid., 232.
[24]Ibid.
[25]Ibid., 271.
[26]Ibid., 295.

And we must ask, in turn, have they raised the right question? Is there a "common good" that can be addressed meaningfully by the whole company of citizens ? Or is that only a fiction in the pluralism of the contemporary world? Can other people who are not a part of our own confessing church truly be fellow citizens in any meaningful way? Or is the only meaningful community the confessing church, the only meaningful history the salvation history that is disclosed in the "story" of our own community of faith?

WHO IS RIGHT?

We have seen, thus, what appear to be radically contradictory answers to such questions: on the one hand, the maximum claims for the confessing church; on the other hand, the call for a recovery of civil identity, with an accompanying religious commitment held in common by all.

But while these two approaches are indeed in deep conflict, we should not pass over their points of agreement. Both are deeply concerned about the profound corruption they perceive in contemporary culture, specifically in America, but also in the rest of the world. Materialism, self-centeredness, self-indulgence, competitiveness—both are aware of these as alien to our true humanity. Both emphasize the importance of the traditions (or stories) of the community in establishing the identity of its people. Both, above all, emphasize the centrality of character and the kind of virtues constitutive of our being in human society. Both see religious faith in more than socially or politically manipulative terms; neither would have much patience with the cultural accommodation of profound religious faith, or "culture religion" as it is sometimes called. People like Hauerwas and McClendon would be deeply suspicious of any kind of "civil religion," of course, but in fairness to Bellah they might at least acknowledge his attempt to delineate this in transcendent terms. Perhaps Bellah's project might finally come down to some kind of "Christ of culture"; but clearly that is not his intention. Indeed, at this point Bellah's own serious commitments to the church may be as relevant to his perspective as his stature as a sociologist.

Bellah does not write as a theologian, and the perspective he and others have suggested needs to be examined theologically. But before turning to that, certain hard practical and sociological questions need to be put to those who, like Hauerwas and McClendon, so strongly emphasize the separate cultural existence of Christians. I wish to pose two such questions.

First, how are we to do justice here to the fact that all of us are simultaneously participants in *many* communities of reference, each with its own "story" and cultural forms? One possible answer— not proposed by such thinkers and certainly not by me—is to allow our existence to be fragmented, to be in and of the church part of the time, in and of our jobs part of the time, in and of the political order part of the time, in and of various interest and recreational groups part of the time, with each of these settings kept quite distinct. That might fairly characterize much of modern existence, but that is hardly a way to become whole in our being.

Another way is to be radically sectarian; to hew to one's community of faith and keep other social, economic, and political contacts to the absolute minimum. That hardly works today even for the Old Order Amish and other explicitly sectarian groups such as the Bruderhof communities, for the conditions of modern life practically guarantee that everybody will have much contact with others. That certainly is not a solution for others who live in modern cities and do their work in company with people who are not of their faith community. Presumably the preferred answer of a Hauerwas is that one's character should be formed in the story-bearing community of faith and be and act in that character in all the other settings of one's life. There is much to be said for that. But our cultural existence is fed by many streams, and all of those streams play some role in making us what we are.

In Jesus Christ we may be liberated from the cultural idolatries of any age. But that does not mean we will not interact with others, who are not of our faith community, on the basis of a great diversity of immediate values. We may share with others an appreciation for the values of health, beauty (in various forms), family life, physical comfort, adequate community facilities (utilities, sewerage, etc.), literature, honesty, the quest for scientific truth, and so on. These and other values can be transformed into idolatries, but Christians are not the only ones who do not treat specific values as idolatries. The ultimate frame of reference of Christians, if truly Christians, will set all specific values in a theological context. But that does not mean that Christians should, or even can, function in a totally unique cultural atmosphere so far as values are concerned. We do and will find ourselves interacting with others, holding views and values in common, despite differences in our ultimate grounding.

The second question grows out of the perspective on politics suggested in chapter 2. If the state represents society acting as a whole, how on earth is one to escape doing whatever the state is doing? I can readily appreciate the effort to transform what the state is doing by various forms of witnessing, including even civil disobedience. But the reality of the state cuts deeper than anything we can be conscious of at any point in time. I may, for example, be so outraged by the vast public expenditures for military purposes that I join others in attempting physically to block the transport of such materials (perhaps lying down in front of the trucks or pouring concrete on the railroad tracks), or at least I can withhold my taxes, accepting in the spirit of the cross whatever penalties the state may choose to inflict. Well and good. But insofar as I am a functioning participant in the economy, whether or not I myself even pay taxes directly, I am contributing to the sum of wealth from which the state's capacity to act is derived. That is even true if what I am doing is writing theological books and giving theological lectures. In other words, like it or not, I am a participant in the civil society that extends beyond my confessing church. And in some measure I will do what that civil society is doing, whether or not I wish to do so.

In this perspective, it seems clear that Christians should acknowledge their belonging to the civil community and their shared responsibility for what it is or does.

GOD'S ACTION IN HISTORY

It is not immediately clear, however, how Christians should understand this theologically. In what sense, if any, is God at work in the activities of the wider civil community? Is God's action exclusively or primarily through the confessing church—or is it, in some sense independent of that community of faith, also to be found in the political process of the state?

In the first place, one must be cautious about identifying God's actions anywhere too readily. Christians affirm the action of God in Christ. That is their faith, their commitment, their "story." But who can truthfully claim to know the exact meaning of even that event, much less the whole course of subsequent human history? Christians, as well as other people, continue to be haunted by the words of Isaiah: "Woe to those who call evil good and good evil, who put darkness for light and light for darkness, who put bitter for sweet and sweet for bitter!" (Isa. 5:20). We do not always know the difference. We live by trust and limited knowledge, not by certainty. The crusaders were sure God was on their side, but Saint Francis was not so certain. And are there not numbers of churches claiming themselves to be the "one true church" while condemning the rest?

Particular leaders have been identified as God's anointed, only later to be revealed as world-class scoundrels. Some who were despised in their time have come to be regarded as saints and saviors by a grateful humanity of later generations. Christians do well to be both confident of God's actions in human history and humble about their own ability to discern the details.

The claim that the church is *exclusively* the bearer of God's redemptive action in human history is doubly questionable. On the one hand, it does not take the sinfulness of the church itself seriously enough. On the other hand, it restricts the power of the God of all the ages to be present in and through the lives of non-Christians.

Most Christians will readily acknowledge the sinfulness of the church. How could they fail to do so, given the plain evidence? But not all Christians understand the importance of the point. The corruptions of the church's cultural environment invade the church, it sometimes seems, like water through a sieve. In our own time, the materialistic idolatries, the vanities, the chauvinisms, the self-centeredness so typical of Western culture seem quite at home in most Western churches—and not just Western culture and Western churches either! If we are to regard the church as the essential sphere of God's political activity, where the story is told and where the faithful are formed by that story to be persons of character, then we need to know where that church is.

Almost any church to which we are pointed manifests some evidence of faithfulness, with some saints who witness quietly and humbly to the power of good they have discovered in the life of their master and in the fellowship of the faithful. Almost any church also illustrates the potency of unfaithfulness and corruption. Nor can we be so sure that the difference between faithfulness and corruption is contained in the ecclesial polity. When high standards of membership are set, people may conform to them as the price paid for acceptance in the group. Are the various religious cults and communes of our time not full of people who need desperately to belong to a caring group? And almost regardless of the particular doctrines or "stories" of the group, will they not conform to belong? Can we be so sure that a "saint" in a (regrettably) culturally accommodated church is less Christian in character than the members of a church that rigorously protects its boundaries from "the world"?

It is important for the church to be faithful. And when it is unfaithful, as to some extent it usually is, it needs to be called back to its true identity as the "body of Christ." It is called to manifest in its own life what it proclaims God's intentions to be for the world.[27] I believe that a vast number of churches, of many denominations and in many lands, manifest this reality to some degree—just as I believe that none of them manifest it perfectly.[28]

What of God's activity beyond the church? Is God's activity beyond the church always *through* the church? That is a perennially troubling question for theologians to answer. On the one hand, Christians affirm the redemptive power of Jesus Christ as true revelation of the absolutely gracious love of God. There is, to Christians, no deeper truth. And the fellowship of the church is precisely the place where Christians are nurtured in the reality of that gracious love, where they are formed in their very being by it. On the other hand, there seem to be clear reflections of that same love at work in other cultures and religious traditions. In some respects the Christian views this reality beyond the church through the prism afforded by her or his tradition. But in another sense, the Christian also views this wider reality with some expectancy that the richness of God's being may speak through it in unanticipated ways.

Vatican II's Declaration on Non-Christian Religions (*Nostra Aetate*) marked a breakthrough, not only for Roman Catholicism but for much of the rest of the Christian community as well. Referring to non-Christian religions, that document said:

> The Catholic Church rejects nothing which is true and holy in these religions. She looks with sincere respect upon those ways of conduct and of life, those rules and teachings which, though differing in many particulars from what she holds and sets forth, nevertheless often reflect a ray of that Truth which enlightens all men.[29]

The document therefore exhorts Roman Catholics "prudently and lovingly" to enter into dialogue and collaboration with persons of

---

[27]The point was made strikingly (if with sexist language) by the message of the First Assembly of the World Council of Churches: "We have to make of the Church in every place a voice for those who have no voice, and a home where every man will be at home" (*Man's Disorder and God's Design*, ed. John C. Bennett [New York: Harper & Brothers, 1948], n.p.).

[28]I have written more extensively on the church in *Faith and Fragmentation: Christianity for a New Age* (Philadelphia: Fortress Press, 1985), 141–70.

[29]"Declaration on Non-Christian Religions," in *The Documents of Vatican II,* ed. Walter M. Abbott, S.J. (New York: Guild Press, America Press, Association Press, 1966), 662.

other religions and "in witness of Christian faith and life, acknowledge, preserve, and promote the spiritual and moral goods found among" these persons of other religions "as well as the values in their society and culture."[30] The point of this statement is that Christians can be full participants in the wider community, and that in that participation they should anticipate learning from non-Christians as well as from those who also belong to the confessing church. They must, in that wider context, expect to find themselves in agreement with the non-Christians about many specific values and political objectives, for which both can work cooperatively together.

Implicitly, the Declaration on Non-Christian Religions affirms that God is at work in these non-Christian contexts as well. The declaration also acknowledges that we cannot be uncritical in our acceptance of the values and beliefs which are affirmed by non-Christian faiths. All values and beliefs are to be judged in the light of Jesus Christ, but then that principle of criticism is also an important one to direct toward the specific teachings and practices of any branch of the Christian church. Jesus Christ, ultimately, is the criterion by which it is all measured. And since Jesus Christ has been and is a living presence, such a criterion is open and dynamic. On the one hand, we can never be sure we have got it all. On the other hand, it suggests the presence of the life of God, to some extent, in all human contexts.

There is, frankly, a real divide among Christians on this point. Some locate the redemptive activity of God solely within the context of "salvation history"—the history of Israel and the church. Others understand that redemptive activity to be at work, at least in some respects, everywhere. In casting my lot with the latter, I wish also to affirm the critical principle: Not everything that is believed is true; not everything that is worshiped is good. Jesus Christ, as revelation of the depth of the love of God, remains the point of reference. But who of us can claim full understanding of the depth of that love? Who of us would deny the power of that love when it is manifested in other, non-Christian settings?[31] Do we not all gain from

---

[30]Ibid., 662–63.

[31]The debate between those who regard the gulf between Christianity and other world religions as absolute and those who see this more relatively continues to rage. See *Faith and Fragmentation,* chap. 10.

mutual sharing and mutual criticism across all lines that separate human beings from one another, including religious lines? Does not the presence of God everywhere in the world constitute theological grounds for affirming that we are ultimately one community, not just a plurality of communities?

RECONCILING THE TWO COMMUNITIES

Simply put, the point I have sought to make in this chapter is that there is no *necessary* conflict between the commitments Christians have in and to the church and their commitment to the wider civil society. The insights and values gained in the former can enrich the latter. At the same time, there is no necessary conflict between loyalty to the community of faith and openness to the insights and contributions of others in the civil society who do not belong to the same faith community. It is possible to belong to the faith community and the wider civil community simultaneously and in good faith.

I have not suggested that the best way to do this is by seeking out some lowest common denominator of general beliefs and values that might be shared by all, regardless of religious persuasion. To do so is to lose the depth, the transcendence that persons of differing faith traditions may have to contribute. Though I am not a Buddhist, I am more interested in encountering a Buddhist fellow citizen from the center of his or her faith than at some superficial level we might immediately share. If civil society is to be taken seriously as the sphere of God's activity in human history, it must somehow be grounded in the deepest sources of human meaning and purpose. The ends of civil society must be at a level beyond the improvement of sewerage systems and paved streets, important as such commonly desired facilities may be. If the civil society has a claim upon the commitment of Christians at the center of their being, it must reflect more than trivial consensus.

Of course it is also true that even at the lowest-common-denominator level there is not likely to be complete consensus in any modern community. Any political purpose imaginable will be opposed by some people. Perhaps we do best to recognize this frankly and be all that we are in the civil as well as the faith communities to which we are committed. If we can believe that God is at work in both spheres, we may trust that our contributions in both spheres will resonate with the moral seriousness of other people.

A CONCLUDING
ILLUSTRATION: SELMA, 1965

Those who stress the importance of narrative in theology are certainly correct in emphasizing that we grasp truths more deeply when we see them as an outgrowth of recalled events. We understand truths more readily when they come in story form. It may help to summarize the conclusions of this chapter if we can visualize a situation in which they were illustrated.

Toward this end, I offer one of the luminescent moments in the American civil rights struggle—the march from Selma to Montgomery, Alabama, in March 1965.[32]

The Southern Christian Leadership Conference (SCLC) and the Student Nonviolent Coordinating Committee (SNCC) had focused on Selma in 1964–65 as a place to dramatize the disenfranchisement of southern black people. (Of Selma's fifteen thousand African American citizens, scarcely three hundred were allowed to vote.) The campaign built in intensity, with nonviolent demonstrations and jailings attracting increasing national attention. As a dramatic gesture recalling Gandhi's salt march to the sea, the SCLC decided to lead a march from Selma to the Alabama state capital, Montgomery, to present the grievances of black citizens and demand the right to vote. The nonviolent march began on Sunday, March 7, and was brutally repulsed by local and state police. A courageous NBC cameraman managed to film scenes of the brutality, and the contrast between the violence of the law enforcement officers and the peaceful deportment of the marchers was displayed on millions of television sets across the nation that very evening. The movement leadership announced that the march would go on and sought a federal district court injunction to restrain Alabama authorities and to require federal protection. The movement's leader, Dr. Martin Luther King Jr., appealed to people of good will from all parts of the nation to come to Selma to join in the march. Meanwhile, President Lyndon B. Johnson went before Congress to urge enactment of a federal Voting Rights Act to protect the right of all citizens to vote.

The court injunction was obtained, and the march was rescheduled for Sunday, March 21. It occurred under the protection of the

---

[32]This section is based on personal recollection (Selma was an unforgettable part of my own "story") and on Charles E. Fager, *Selma 1965: The March That Changed the South* (Boston: Beacon Press, 1985 [1974]).

U.S. Army and federalized National Guard units. The Voting Rights Act was adopted by Congress, with enormous effect in changing the political power structure of the southern states.

The civil rights movement's objectives were, of course, thoroughly political. The goal was the right to vote and, with that, the opportunity for black people to remove the political repressions they had suffered for generations. The movement was predominantly Christian in character, with many of its leaders ordained clergypersons and most of its participants active members of churches. But part of the drama of the Selma campaign was the thoroughly ecumenical, even interreligious character of the people who worked together for a common political objective. During the weeks preceding the final march to Montgomery, the participants in the movement engaged in a series of demonstrations in Selma designed to probe the defenses of the segregation system and to dramatize the realities for the national and even worldwide audience. People came to Selma by the hundreds, and ultimately thousands, from all over the country. They represented many Christian denominations, Jewish congregations, and secular organizations. The center of movement activity was the Brown Chapel African Methodist Episcopal Church, a large brick building in the black section of the city. Combination prayer meeting/rally-and-strategy sessions were held once or twice daily. At these meetings people shared insights drawn from their own particular religious heritages, with appreciative listening from others and sometimes applause. (A small group from New York even was applauded when its spokesperson announced that he wished to offer a contribution from "us atheists.")

The week before the march, a peaceful demonstration at the county courthouse was based around prayer, with participation from different segments of the ecumenical spectrum. Two days later, Friday, March 19, three hundred demonstrators were arrested and spent that night in detention. A group of rabbis conducted a Jewish sabbath service that night, inviting all to participate. The next morning, the three hundred detainees were released and returned to Brown Chapel in time to participate in an Episcopalian eucharistic service, conducted in the open air (since the Episcopalians had been denied access to the local Episcopal church). Each of these services was conducted in the full integrity of its own tradition. Yet each somehow also spoke to all of the other people, of other traditions, about the depth and seriousness of their common endeavor.

Was this a matter of "using" religious beliefs and practices for "secular" ends? I do not think so. The lasting impression was rather that the occasion made it possible for the greater depth of each tradition to be expressed with an integrity far greater than routine expressions of faith permit. Religious faith was alive and profound in its expression, and the occasion evoked a kind of interreligious dialogue cutting much deeper than superficial consensus about desirable common goals.

The movement, of course, represented but one side in the political controversy. Was there a sense in which the faith perspectives of the participants entered into dialogue with their adversaries in the broader political field of the conflict? Superficially, at least, the answer is no. Episcopalians in the movement were not in rapport with local Selma Episcopalians, who even denied them use of their church. Methodists in the movement had virtually no contact with their local counterparts. The same, essentially, applied to other faith communities. The movement participants from other parts of the country were considered to be "outside agitators." But despite this, communication was occurring at a serious level. The movement's strategy was a strategy of communication—to the local power structures and to the nation and world at large.

What was being communicated? A striking part of the communication was love of the adversary. It was a moving experience for participants, onlookers, reporters, and (perhaps) the local adversaries themselves to hear the words "We love [Sheriff] Jim Clark in our heart" or "We love [Governor] George Wallace in our heart" sung lustily by hundreds of voices. The nonviolent commitment by movement participants was itself an expression of the desire by the oppressed for a more civil, humane level of communication with the oppressors. But the communication was also about the quality of the community as a whole. The struggle for voting rights was a struggle by an oppressed people and their allies to remove the reality of "second-class citizenship." Equality of voting rights is equality of formal power, and equality of voting rights was understood to be necessary to full participation in the life of society. The religious commitments by the movement participants gave greater depth to that. The deeper meanings of community could be voiced through religious expression with greater power than through simple political rhetoric. In a religious perspective, the political community could be understood to be more than an association of convenience or mutual self-interest. In those unforgettable days in Selma, under the glare of international publicity and under the pressure of intense confrontation, the oppressed and their allies broke down the barriers to full participation.

The campaign obviously would not have been successful if the oppressed had kept to their churches in sectarian fashion, rehearsing their story and anticipating a happier time in the "sweet bye-and-bye." I think it might also have been unsuccessful if a way had not been found to communicate to the conscience of the nation on the level of values more basic than those of routine politics and economics. Some might wonder whether the fact of the movement's nonviolence was ultimately a judgment against the state as such—for the state, as we have seen, exercises coercive power. It is an intriguing question, and the fact that it can be raised in relation to the powerful story of Selma means that there is at least a judgment here against casual coercion and violence by the state.

But the movement did not hesitate to seek an injunction from a U.S. district court *requiring* local authorities to respect the march to Montgomery and *requiring* the U.S. government to afford whatever necessary protection to ensure its safety. Those who participated in the march as it set forth on a bright Sunday must have sensed the irony: Here was a nonviolent demonstration being conducted under the protection of an awesome display of military power! But the irony was not contradiction. The movement was not denying the legitimacy of such state power, if responsibly exercised in the support of justice. Such power was a threat to no one who did not break the peace. The issue for the movement was not the existence of such power but the question of how it should be exercised. Its own commitment to nonviolence was both principled and pragmatic. Principled, because it entailed a recognition that it must act in love and not take physical power into its own hands. Pragmatic, because it recognized the futility of deepening the cycles of violence in an already too-violent society.

If, as I believe, a compelling case can be made for full Christian participation in the civil as well as ecclesial communities, the question remains what *kind* of civil community is most in accord with Christian understanding. The Selma story suggests the importance of a civil society based on participation by all. This is a question we are now ready to address more fully.

11

Christian Support for Democracy

The church does not exist to provide an ethos for democracy or any other form of social organization.
—Stanley Hauerwas (1981)[1]

Modern democracy requires a more realistic philosophical and religious basis, not only in order to anticipate and understand the perils to which it is exposed; but also to give it a more persuasive justification.
—Reinhold Niebuhr (1944)[2]

Man is created and called to be a free being, responsible to God and his neighbour. Any tendencies in State and society depriving man of the possibility of acting responsibly are a denial of God's intention for man and His work of salvation. A responsible society is one where freedom is the freedom of men who acknowledge responsibility to justice and public order, and where those who hold political authority or economic power are responsible for its exercise to God and the people whose welfare is affected by it.
—World Council of Churches (1948)[3]

---

[1]Stanley Hauerwas, *A Community of Character: Toward a Constructive Christian Social Ethic* (Notre Dame, Ind.: University of Notre Dame Press, 1981), 12.

[2]Reinhold Niebuhr, *The Children of Light and the Children of Darkness* (New York: Charles Scribner's Sons, 1944), xiii.

[3]World Council of Churches, *The Church and the Disorder of Society* (New York: Harper & Brothers, 1948), 192.

Does it indeed matter at all what *kind* of political system people live under? Hauerwas is but one of several contemporary Christian writers who emphasize that the church does not exist to provide an ethos for any particular form of social organization, such as democracy. Are these critics right? Should Christians invest their energies in any form of political order?

There is some truth in the claim that Christians have no stake in any particular system. Christians have functioned in every conceivable political environment over the past twenty centuries. Indeed, they have *thrived* in some of the most unlikely settings, for "the blood of the martyrs is the seed of the church." The Neros, Hitlers, and Stalins have made life uncomfortable. But ultimately they have been powerless to contain the winsome power of the gospel. It seemed for a time that it might be otherwise in the aftermath of the Chinese Cultural Revolution. But even there, after the smoke had cleared, it became evident that large numbers of Christians had maintained underground the witness and worship of the church.

Nor could one say that oppressive rule has forced the church into a defensive "survivalist" mode. Often Christians have humanized the worst political settings by reaching across the barriers of power and privilege to touch the real humanity of officials. A Christian friend in one of the Eastern European countries during the period of totalitarian rule relates how the churches were regularly infiltrated by government spies—until the government discovered it was losing too many of its agents through conversion. Another Eastern European Christian pastor reports that, notwithstanding the official antireligious stance, some governmental officials found they could trust the public-spiritedness of Christians more even than that of many party members.[4] The effectiveness of nonviolent resistance in a variety of oppressive political settings owes much to Christian witness, at the heart of which is an appeal to the essential humanity of the oppressors themselves.

So Christians can act like Christians wherever they are. Moreover, nondemocratic systems of government are not necessarily oppressive ones. Hereditary monarchs have been known to be benign

---

[4]These observations are based on visits with church leaders and pastors in several Eastern European countries. For background on the situation of the churches in those countries, see Trevor Beeson, *Discretion and Valour: Religious Conditions in Russia and Eastern Europe,* rev. ed. (Philadelphia: Fortress Press, 1982).

and wise. Would one prefer being governed by a democratically elected Senator Joseph McCarthy or by a Queen Elizabeth I, who was designated by hereditary right? Was Juan Peron, when elected president of Argentina, preferable to the Roman emperor Marcus Aurelius? Was Richard Nixon better than King Wenceslaus?[5] So what difference does it make which system we live under?

It can make a *very* great difference! To say that it does not matter what kind of political order one lives under is to ignore very great relative differences. The same logic might lead us to say that no oppressive institutions, laws, or systems should matter to Christians because Christians have lived with and under all kinds of problems: slavery (which the letter to the Ephesians somehow managed to come to terms with), segregation and apartheid (which Christians of the American South and South Africa somehow managed to live with), customs and institutions subordinating women (which Christian women have managed to live with nearly everywhere), militarism, or various systems of economic exploitation. Some who question the importance of Christians investing much in the struggle to achieve or sustain democracy wish, at the same time, to engage in witness against economic and social oppression. But if it is important to weigh other kinds of institutions for their effect on people, why not systems of government? Indeed, systems of government may be even more important because of their great effect on everything else. Of course, Christian witness can help humanize even bad systems of government—just as Christians can humanize slavery or other forms of exploitation—and good or bad rulers can be brought forth with good or bad results in almost any political system. But that too is true of other forms of institutional order: There were benign and wicked slaveowners. There have been compassionate and unfeeling business leaders. There are decent spouses and those who behave like tyrants. Under segregation and apartheid there were decent white people and insufferable racists. But we are concerned here with *systems*. Does it not matter, in terms of the concrete

---

[5]I must acknowledge the ambiguity of such illustrative comparisons. For example, the Roman emperor Marcus Aurelius, while generally a wise ruler of unquestionably noble character, figures in the pages of church history as one of the more diligent persecutors of Christians. And Richard Nixon while president undoubtedly accomplished a number of useful things during his administration such as the regularization of diplomatic relations between the United States and China. But despite such ambiguities, the point remains that some authoritarian rulers have been relatively enlightened and some democratic rulers have been corrupt and shortsighted.

human results (and regardless of the benevolence of the people involved), how the system itself is constructed? Paraphrasing Walter Rauschenbusch, does not a bad system make even good people behave worse than they would have in a good system?[6] And does not a just system make unjust people behave better than they want to? Is that not more likely to be the case in respect to the political order than any other aspect of human life?

THE COVENANTAL
REALITY OF THE STATE

Recalling the understanding of the state set forth in chapter 2, we cannot very well avoid contributing to the success of whatever the state is up to at any moment. There truly is a sense in which the state is all of us acting together. But not every political system makes it possible for people to participate in the process of determining what the state (and therefore they themselves) will do. Like it or not, we are doing what the state is doing. Whether we can affect policy very much is another matter. That depends very largely on how political institutions are ordered. A democratic political order (as we shall define it shortly) makes it possible for people to participate in determining what they will, as members of society, be committed to do.

The tradition that the state essentially belongs to all of the people has very ancient roots. The Greco-Roman and biblical traditions are very different in most respects, yet both contain elements of this. The biblical tradition includes what some have called the "royal theology,"[7] with the glorification of the legacy of King David and the institutions of monarchy. But it also includes the prophetic criticism of the royal theology and a sturdy defense of the rights of the people.[8] It even includes, in the case of the period of the judges, the no-

---

[6]Rauschenbusch wrote that "an unchristian social order can be known by the fact that it makes good men do bad things. It tempts, defeats, drains, and degrades, and leaves men stunted, cowed, and shamed in their manhood. A Christian social order makes bad men do good things. It sets high aims, steadies the vagrant impulses of the weak, trains the powers of the young, and is felt by all as an uplifting force which leaves them with the consciousness of a broader and nobler humanity as their years go on" (*Christianizing the Social Order* [New York: Macmillan Co., 1912], 127). Were he writing today, I am sure Rauschenbusch would use inclusive language.

[7]See, e.g., Walter Brueggemann, *The Prophetic Imagination* (Philadelphia: Fortress Press, 1978).

[8]Ibid.

tion that the leadership of Israel should be validated by the recognition of leadership charisma by the community as a whole. The New Testament is not the tradition of a political community in quite the same way. But its affirmation of the significance of common people to God at least means that people are accountable to an authority higher than the state—with the implication that nobody should be considered to be *only* a "subject" to the human authority of others. I shall have more to say about that below.

The Greco-Roman traditions of political philosophy were grounded in early democratic practices. While neither Athenian nor Roman democracies were perfect, coexisting as they did with slavery and with lower status for women, they did recognize the accountability of political power to the citizens. At least as early as Plato's dialogue *The Crito,* mutual political accountability was formalized in a kind of contract theory. In that writing, Socrates is quoted in support of mutual consent as a principle of political order:

> [The laws of Athens] proclaim and give the right to every Athenian that if he does not like [the laws] when he has come of age and has seen the ways of the city [and become acquainted with the laws], he may go where he pleases and take his goods with him; and none of [the laws] will forbid him or interfere with him. . . . But he who has experience of the manner in which [the laws] order justice and administer the state, and still remains has entered into an implied contract that he will do as [the laws] command him.[9]

The Stoic tradition, especially embodied in the work of the Roman lawyers, emphasized the equality of all people (possessed, as all are, by the faculty of reason) and denied the right of any to rule without the consent of the governed. Since the Stoic writers did most of their work after the Roman Empire was already well established, emperors and all, their conclusions might have seemed directly contradictory to current Roman practice, for few of the emperors tarried long over the niceties of consent and accountability (though all were still formally accountable to the Senate). But as we have seen, the Stoic thinkers resolved the conflict by a doctrine

---

[9]Plato, *Crito,* trans. Benjamin Jowett, Harvard Classics (New York: P. F. Collier, 1937 [1909]), 2:40. Plato was not a supporter of democracy per se, and we can only speculate about Socrates. But the contractual understanding of our relationship to the laws—and the affirmation of our freedom to leave the contract—is one of the important theoretical foundations for subsequent democratic theory.

of implied consent. Sovereignty is possessed by all; this has been delegated by all, by implication, to the emperors who govern in behalf of all.

Even medieval Europe, authoritarian as it is in historical stereotype, managed to preserve some of this. The vigorous, if unsuccessful, conciliar movement of the fourteenth and fifteenth centuries illustrates how ideas can burst forth from historical traditions. That movement, which sought to democratize the life of the church (to some extent), owes something to the covenantal traditions spawned in the ancient world.

Most Western democratic notions trace their direct origins to the seventeenth- and eighteenth-century "contract" thinkers, especially Hobbes, Locke, and Rousseau. If recognition of the great antiquity of some of their ideas demythologizes their pure originality to some extent, there can be no question that these Enlightenment thinkers established the covenantal understanding of the state more systematically and powerfully. To these thinkers, the state is a product of human decision: We have decided to be a civil society; our "pooling" of our private powers is for the sake of greater gains; for the sake of these greater gains we accept the obligation to obey the laws adopted by our magistrates, and we indicate our willingness to suffer the penalties prescribed for those who do not obey. We renounce the use of private force in order to gain the greater advantages of collective security.

This last idea is expressed most bluntly by Thomas Hobbes, who viewed the state as a contract entered into by essentially self-centered but fearful people. In a world dominated by mutual fear, the state becomes the only means of assuring peace and security. We pool our powers in order to create one power great enough to hold all others in check. The root conception of human nature underlying Hobbes's conception is, of course, thoroughly pessimistic, thoroughly in harmony with the most sweeping versions of the doctrine of original sin. Its relevance to political thought among Christians is perhaps contingent upon the importance they themselves attach to that doctrine.

In any case, John Locke's version of the contract theory—with a less pessimistic view of human nature and a more positive conception of the possibilities of the state—still understands the "contract" to be a delegation of real power by the people to a central authority. Locke is clearer than Hobbes in concluding that in the exercise of that power the central authority should remain directly accountable to those who have delegated it. Locke is therefore the primary progenitor of most contemporary political democracies, especially those of the Anglo-Saxon world.

To complete this brief historical sketch, Jean Jacques Rousseau's version of the contract is more ambiguous but, at the same time, more deeply social. The "contract" is apparently more than an agreement among essentially independent beings. It appears with him to be the basis of a new social whole from which we receive back a more completed selfhood.[10]

At the most elementary level, the contract tradition speaks to the question whether the struggle for power in human society can be conducted by means other than brute force. The fiction of an original covenanting process, as though human beings at some time and place came together and decided to form the political contract, should not be taken as literal truth. But the real truth to which the fiction points may lie deeper than mere fact. Is there, in the reality of the state, an unconscious agreement by people that they will be a civil community?

Some of the brutal political conflicts of the late twentieth century have helped illustrate the power and consensual realities to which the contract tradition has pointed—sometimes because the contract is effectively present, sometimes because it is not. Note, for example, how the acrimonious debates and bloody conflicts of the Middle East and Central America dramatize the primal covenant-creating or covenant-denying realities of the political order. These conflicts have ripped aside the facade more easily maintained in a settled political order to remind us that underneath it all there truly is a covenant about what the people are agreed the state should be. In some of these conflicts the base question is whether one's political opposition is to be given some ground to stand upon, some way of pursuing its political goals by means other than brute force. Seemingly intractable conflict has divided Serbs from Albanians and Croats in the Balkans, various tribal groups from one another in Central Africa, Protestants from Catholics in Northern Ireland, Israelis from Palestinians in the Middle East—the list goes on and on, illustrating the importance of the political covenant by demonstrating the effects of its absence. Invariably, such conflicts are resolved by arriving at some mutually agreeable covenant embodying

---

[10]One can with some plausibility trace the more communitarian, less individualistic political theories of Hegel and Marx to the influence of Rousseau.

mutual respect and the right of all to participate in the governance of society.

The contract tradition asserts the formal equality of all persons in civil society. This implies two things: (1) Equal formal power or majority rule. If all are equal, then the vote of none should count for more than the vote of any other. And a majority of votes therefore counts for more than a minority of votes. (2) Equal formal rights of expression, access to the political process, and overall equality before the law. All are equally free to express their views on any subject and to enlist support for political positions. This includes freedom to organize political forces and to be free from legal harassment by those currently in power.

Translated into a definition of democracy, these conceptions mean that democracy implies majority rule. But it also implies minority rights. Indeed, unless political minorities are free to express themselves (even if it is a minority of a single person) and to organize a political drive to become the next majority, even the term "majority" is not meaningful.

The post-Marxian world poses yet a third question: Can democracy function as such in the absence of an adequate material base? Are there conditions of health and material well-being in the absence of which the first two orders of rights are deprived of meaning? When the political covenant is agreed to in democratic terms, does that require not only formal tolerance and legal opportunity but also the material conditions in the absence of which political participation may be quite empty? By referring to this as a question posed in the post-Marxian world I do not imply that the question is uniquely a Marxian one. Indeed, the neglect of the first two aspects of democracy in most Marxian theory and practice suggests that the third aspect may not even attain its fullest expression in Marxian thought. But the question does arise out of the Marxian critique of political democracy: Can real democracy exist in a society where there is dire physical need—when there is inadequate food, clothing, shelter, and medical care at even the most rudimentary levels? And can there even be real democracy where people differ greatly in their command of those economic resources that are easily translatable into political power?

These last questions must be deferred for now. At this point we are concerned with the more limited issues of formal equality and formal rights of expression and political organization. Should Christians seek democracy when democracy is understood in those terms?

POPULAR SOVEREIGNTY AND
THE SOVEREIGNTY OF GOD

We return to the question of sovereignty. The distinctive mark of covenantal theories of the state is their insistence that all people share equally in sovereignty; all are, alike, sources of the ultimate power. We have already noted (in chapter 2) the objections of Jacques Maritain to any notion of human sovereignty, whether of the popular, oligarchical, or monarchical variety. "In the last analysis," he writes, "no earthly power is the image of God and deputy for God." Only God "is the very source of the authority."[11] Does this invalidate or make irrelevant the question of what *human* power is ultimate?

There surely is a sense in which the sovereignty of God is the primary theological entry point on political questions, for the sovereignty of God at least means that God is ultimately in charge of the whole creation. God, the center and source of all being, has created it all. The whole creation is responsive to God's purposes. The Christian doctrine of sin implies human power to frustrate divine intentions. But even the reality of sin does not set aside the point that the will of God ultimately governs. When humanity, through sin, resists the will of God it is not without consequences. The sovereignty of God does not have to be expressed in prescriptive (or deontological) terms. We do not have to think of God as "governing" by static law. Even a "process" understanding of God can depict God as the One who has initiated creation, who has opened up the possibilities and invited humanity to participate in the ongoing work of creation.

Whatever the understanding of the meaning of divine sovereignty, it is at least the beginning point for the criticism of political idolatries. No ruler or system of government, no program or ideology can be invested with the ultimate loyalty of Christians. If the sovereign God is ultimate, there is room for no other final loyalty.

Does this, in itself, imply the superiority of democracy? Not necessarily. For one thing, democracy cannot be made into an ultimate. It is a human thing; it is not God.

Even in relative terms, the case for democracy would evaporate if (and it is a big "if") a select group of people can be shown to be

---

[11]Jacques Maritain, *Man and the State* (Chicago: University of Chicago Press, 1951), 50.

God's chosen deputies. If such an elite exists, then it logically follows that they should govern—in which case we would have some form of theocracy in place of democracy. There are not many unchallenged illustrations of that in the contemporary world (and not all that many unambiguous examples of theocracy in the last twenty centuries of Western history for that matter). The contemporary government of Iran, which is clearly dominated by the mullahs, may illustrate the possibilities, however. The mullahs really are understood by faithful Shiite Muslims to represent the mind of Allah (or God) better than ordinary folk. And so it is not illogical for the mullahs to be allowed to make the pivotal political decisions. But the whole case for this depends upon the privileged access of such religious figures to the mind of Allah and the trustworthiness of these same figures as dependable agents of the divine being. Zealous fundamentalists in America raise similar points. So eager are they to ensure that only Bible-believing, born-again Christians are elected to office, always assuming that such people alone can be trusted to translate the eternal will of God into the governance of the affairs of this world. The logic of this is clear if, but only if, we can be assured that such people really do have such a direct channel to the Almighty than their less anointed sisters and brothers.

But, on the other hand, if God transcends and relativizes the human sphere, a better case can be made for skepticism concerning all human powers. God is always greater. God is always better. God is always the transcendent source of judgment holding all human life in tension. No human agent can be absolutized as divine; God transcends them all.

The transcending sovereignty of God also means, on the positive side, that the source and center of all being and value also has unique, immediate access to *all* people. All people must therefore be presumed to be God's chosen deputies for the governance of the world. People are subjects as well as citizens; but the unique, immediate access of God to all people means that nobody can be treated as *only* a subject. And so, as the World Council of Churches' 1948 statement put it, human beings "must never be made a mere means for political or economic ends." Each of us "is created and called to be a free being, responsible to God and [our] neighbour."[12]

---

[12]World Council of Churches, *Church and Disorder of Society,* 192.

These statements are simply incomprehensible apart from faith in the transcendent sovereignty of God. But in the light of that faith, any political arrangement subjecting some people absolutely to others is equally incomprehensible.

Moreover, in light of the transcendent sovereignty of God, there is much to be said for a political system that is self-criticizing and self-correcting. Lacking final answers to any human questions, it is well to keep the possibilities open. Perhaps, as the process theologians say, the future is open even to God. In any case, human beings cannot lay claim to enough wisdom to set political arrangements in concrete. It is well to have a system with built-in checks and balances, one in which everybody is free to criticize present imperfections and to organize a more perfect future.

HUMAN SINFULNESS
AND HUMAN GOODNESS

A theological analysis of human nature yields similar conclusions. The point was registered classically in Reinhold Niebuhr's small book on democracy, *The Children of Light and the Children of Darkness*. According to Niebuhr, the case for democracy is based upon both the human disposition toward sin and the human capacity for goodness. In his familiar prefatory aphorism: "Man's capacity for justice makes democracy possible; but man's inclination to injustice makes democracy necessary."[13] The fact that human beings can be counted upon to be sinful means that nobody is to be trusted too much. But a nondemocratic society does not control its rulers sufficiently. By contrast, a democratic society erects a fabric of controls, of checks and balances. Above all, it guarantees the right of all people to be critics of those in power and also, if they wish, to seek to replace the rulers.

On the other hand, if people were *totally* evil there would be no positive basis on which to construct even a democratic society, for democratic institutions depend upon substantial reservoirs of public-spiritedness and voluntary compliance with the will of the majority. The unrelieved pessimism of a Hobbes cannot really form the basis of democracy, as Hobbes himself well knew. It is not by accident that Hobbes's civil contract, unlike Locke's, places ultimate

---

[13]Niebuhr, *Children of Light and Children of Darkness*, xiii.

211

power in the hands of an essentially unrestrained monarch. The best the profoundly self-centered subjects who inhabit Hobbes's kingdom can hope for is a strong ruler who has enough power to keep them from eating each other alive. And since that ruler also is evil, they had better make it in his or her self-interest to play the role! Such people can hardly be expected to cooperate, to enter into dialogue, to persuade, to volunteer their services, and all the other things a thriving democracy depends upon.

Undergirded as it is by Niebuhr's careful analysis of the doctrine of original sin,[14] the negative side of his support for democracy is a relentless critique of the union of power and sin that is potential—and even pervasive—in all human institutions. People who have unlimited power will always be tempted to use it in the service of self-interest. And since the roots of self-interest are much deeper than simple venality, there is a persistent danger that power will be used by insecure people to buttress their self-esteem and ultimately their assurance of the lasting significance of their lives.[15]

The positive side of the argument can be constructed from two theological entry points: the doctrine of creation and the doctrine of grace. The human capacity for justice can be grounded in the biblical notion that humankind is created in the image of God so long as original sin is not understood to have effaced that image altogether. God did not create human beings to be evil. Apart from God (or in rebellion against God) people are sinful, but even in their sinful state people are also attracted by goodness. Some versions of the doctrine of original sin are compatible with Hobbesian pessimism, but most are not. Historically, the most substantial Christian traditions recognize the warmth and decency that are possible to human beings even in their completely natural state.

Theology also recognizes, apart from this, the workings of redemptive grace: the penetrating love of God that reaches across the barriers of anxious self-centeredness to evoke trust and love in response. The power of God's grace in human history opens up constructive possibilities even in theological contexts overemphasizing the doctrine of original sin.

If we are to follow Niebuhr in identifying the human "inclination

---

[14]Reinhold Niebuhr, *The Nature and Destiny of Man* (New York: Charles Scribner's Sons, 1941), see especially vol. 1, chap. 7.

[15]This point is made strikingly by Ernest Becker, *Escape from Evil* (New York: Free Press, 1975).

to injustice" and "capacity for justice" as the basis for democracy, we do well to observe one cardinal point: These positive and negative attributes of human nature are to be presumed to be present in *all* people. If good people and bad people could be identified with certainty, then the rational thing would be to let the good people rule and to keep the bad people as far away from power as possible. Marxism is among the political movements that have tended to make such neat divisions, with oppressive exploiters and class-conscious proletarians representing the evil and good respectively. Christians have also made such divisions from time to time, as have persons in other religions. When this is done, it is presumed not only that objective differences exist between good and bad people but that these differences can be observed with sufficient certainty to rest the divisions of power upon them. Such differences do, no doubt, exist *relatively*. Some people no doubt are "better" or "worse" morally. But even those who are morally "better" cannot be presumed to have escaped sinfulness altogether, and they may yet be corrupted by too much unrestrained power. On the other hand, even those who are morally "worse" cannot be understood to be totally devoid of any shred of human decency and totally impenetrable by divine grace. And on the question of how to locate and separate the "better" from the "worse" in human affairs, the judgment of the whole community is more to be relied upon than the judgment of any self-appointed elite.

The Christian case for supporting democracy could possibly be enlarged by reference to other theological entry points. Those we have referred to here are actually quite interrelated. The sovereignty and transcendence of God emphasize the relativity of the human. At the same time, the conception of human nature as sinful emphasizes, from the human standpoint, the distance from the human to God—and the conception of human goodness emphasizes the power and inclination of God to manifest the divine presence in human life and history.

ACCEPTING RESPONSIBILITY
FOR THE FUTURE

It bears repeating here that democracy is the system of government best assuring opportunity for all to assume part of the responsibility for the future course of human history. We all affect the future through our actions, whether we intend to or not. When it is said that Christians should not attempt to manage the course of history it is forgotten that we cannot help participating in the events that shape history. Whatever the political order under which we live, we contribute to its success through the routines of ordinary life. Whatever the state is doing, we are doing. Much that the state does is not planned, at least not well planned. But public policy is consciously directed by people who rule. In a democratic system, everybody has some opportunity to share in the framing of public purposes. That is not "shaping history" in the broadest sense, for nobody can do that. But democracy does make it possible for everybody to contribute.

To illustrate the point: Many Christians are opposed to capital punishment. Even so, they are a part of the act of execution in societies that engage in this practice—for whatever the state is doing, we are doing. A democratic system at least makes it possible to assume some direct responsibility for changing the course of the state when we believe it is on the wrong course—or to help keep it on the right course. Christians can assume historical responsibility even in nondemocratic political systems, as through acts of civil disobedience. But democracy provides the most direct opportunity.

INDIVIDUAL AND COMMUNAL
IDENTITY IN TENSION

Some late twentieth-century criticisms of democratic liberalism attribute it to a one-sided Enlightenment individualism, contrasting this with Christian commitments to community. The criticism is not altogether unfair. The contract theories of Hobbes and Locke emphasize, even exaggerate, an understanding of the state as a grand covenant between individuals. And the slogans of the American and French revolutions certainly emphasized individual freedom above all other values. Nineteenth-century philosophical support for democracy—as expressed, for example, by such utilitarians as John Stuart Mill—clearly picked up the individualistic theme. In our own time, excessive individualism is illustrated in extreme libertarianism and even in the more moderate union of laissez-faire capitalism with worldwide crusades for democracy. The increasing tendencies for public life to be conducted via the mass media suggest a breakdown of group life into an atomized individualism.

Against this, Burkean conservatives continue to make the case for custom and tradition and a sense of one's rank and place in the inherited social scheme. And the neoconservatives remind us of the importance of "mediating structures." At the same time, members of ethnic minority groups and other definable minorities insist that social participation is fundamentally through one's group identity.

Christians must agree with those who insist upon the importance of community. We are not just individuals by nature and calling. We are born into communities, and we are called into communities. We cannot live without communities. The whole covenantal understanding of biblical religion is communitarian through and through.

But the biblical covenant also supplies the basis for the emphasis upon our identity as individuals. Because our primary being is from the transcendent God, no human group commitment (not even our commitment to humanity as a whole) quite captures our full identity. We are individuals in the deepest sense of the word because we belong to God more than we belong to the group. And we are also members of community in the deepest sense because we all have our being *together* from God. Christians thus recognize the theological roots of the drive toward community while not allowing the imposition of false community to dissolve their individuality. Christians are critical of tendencies toward social idolatry, by which group loyalties are given ultimate status. And Christians see the importance of resisting conformity for the simple sake of conformity. The group is important, but it is not God.

Individual rights, as embodied in democratic constitutions, can therefore exist as a protection against false community with its idolatries and its pressures toward conformism. The rights of freedom of speech or press cannot simply be the rights of groups, with individuals within the groups subjected to tyranny by the groups themselves. Civil rights—those rights recognized and protected by the state—necessarily reach across the lines of group identity to protect individuals within groups. Among those rights, the right to vote is particularly important. Within a democratic society, that right is an *individual* right. Other groups within society cannot speak for their members in the formal political sense without their consent. Thus, power questions in a democratic society cannot be resolved on the basis of compromises among the constituent groups—unless the individual rights of the memberships of the groups are fully protected. In that sense, the democratic state must assert a connection with the individuals of the society that is prior to their relationships to other groups.

The meaning of this is easily misunderstood. This does not mean that people are only creatures of the state. It does not mean that our social identity is established by the state more than it is by family or religious groups. What it means is that no other group in society can claim to speak for the individual politically without the individual's consent and that the individual has rights that are protected by the state.

A DEMOCRATIC
UNDERSTANDING OF JUSTICE

That point has important implications for our view of justice. If society were simply a contract among self-centered individuals, each pursuing her or his self-interest, then justice would amount to little more than a proper ordering of the necessary rules of the game. Above all, justice, in that setting, must carefully apportion to each what is her or his due as a partner in the contract. Each must be rewarded or punished on the basis of her or his behavior and deserving. The theory of justice implied by Locke's social contract has this as an important element. A primary purpose of the contract, in his view, is to protect our claims to the property we have accumulated through our labor. Justice is preserving to us what we have made, and it is punishing those who violate the terms of the social contract.[16] That understanding of justice relates very well to retributive conceptions, according to which, above all, people should get what they deserve.

I suppose that when most people speak of justice, at least in the more individualistic Western societies, this is largely what they mean. But there is a very different way of seeing it. From a more communal point of view, justice is the community's guarantee of the conditions necessary for everybody to be a participant in the common life of society. Ultimately that notion has theological roots. If we are, finally, brothers and sisters through the providence of God, then it is *unjust* to treat people as though they did not belong. And it is *just* to structure institutions and laws in such a way that com-

---

[16]Locke's theory of property as belonging to individuals by natural right as a result of their act of withdrawing things from the state of nature (or mixing their labor with the state of nature) played an important role not only in the development of his view of the contract but also in the subsequent unfolding of capitalist economic doctrine. Mill, who made important contributions to the latter, is also noteworthy for his emphasis both on civil liberties and on social reform. Contemporary libertarians, such as Robert Nozick, are strongly influenced by Locke's view of property when they define governmental taxation as theft—and Locke, no doubt, would have been horrified by the extremes to which the libertarians have gone in delegitimating government.

munal life is enhanced and individuals are provided full opportunity for participation.

I have spoken of this as a notion with theological roots. Ultimately that is so because our relatedness stems from our common relationship to the source of all being and value. And that relationship is finally interpreted through religious traditions. But does this mean that such a theory of justice is the work of the churches and not an appropriate subject for discussion in the secular environment of the state?

To the contrary: Justice, as even the ancients well understood, is the *primary* topic for civil discourse. Unless civil society limits itself to triviality, it is concerned above all with the question of what its own life as a community means and with how its institutions and practices can best preserve and enhance that conception. When John Courtney Murray refers to civilization as, at its best, "men locked together in argument,"[17] that is what they are arguing about (though Murray wants to be sure we understand that we shall never arrive at true ultimates through the political process as such). The state, as I shall suggest later, cannot espouse any version of the religious ultimate. But its conception of its own life can be enriched by the insights flowing from all who participate in that dialogue. The theological meaning of our belonging to one another must finally elude the state as state. But a profound civil consensus that we are, above all, a community can register politically even as it is fed by streams of thought and devotion that transcend that consensus. Most theologians are cautious about the construction of a "civil religion," or even a "public philosophy," for the subject smacks too much of the cultural accommodation of religious truth to the idolatries and goals of the political process. But when justice is truly the subject matter, and when the deepest—and not the most trivial—insights of great theological traditions are plumbed to explore the meaning of justice, then even these terms take on a deeper pertinence. For how can those who are grounded in theological traditions fail to participate in the community's consideration of what it means to be a community? We cannot avoid being a community of some kind or other. Cannot the theological traditions be brought to bear

---

[17]John Courtney Murray, S.J., *We Hold These Truths: Catholic Reflections on the American Proposition* (New York: Sheed & Ward, 1960), 6. Murray credits Thomas Gilby, O.P., *Between Community and Society* (New York: Longmans, Green & Co., 1953), with this expression.

in helping the community discover what it means to be caring and protective, venturesome and creative?

DEMOCRATIC PROCESS
AND ITS OUTCOMES

Whether or not the community does discover such things in its search for justice depends on many things, including the degree to which ordinary human self-centeredness dominates the political process.

But even democracy does not guarantee a just outcome to the political process. George Bernard Shaw once remarked that while democracy may not be the best form of government, it is that form of government under which we can best guarantee that people will get what they deserve. Such a witty observation may be unfair to the losers in the process, but there is insight there all the same. Democracy is a way of clarifying responsibility and of spreading responsibility throughout the whole populace. When the populace as a whole—or at least a decisive portion of it—is dominated by greed or meanspiritedness, that is bound to affect the outcome.

Sometimes, as we have seen, benevolent monarchs or aristocrats have done better by the people than the people's own elected representatives. Sometimes democracy facilitates evil. Every nation's history is a record of moral unevenness. Sometimes, as in the McCarthy era in the United States or the Nazi period in Germany, large numbers of people allow themselves to be swept up in tides of hysteria with tragic results. The closer the populace as a whole is to the actual levers of power, the more readily hysteria is enabled to move those levers. That is the risk of democracy.

On the other hand, there are times when a people can be profoundly moved by caring. Then, too, democracy facilitates the public will. Woodrow Wilson noted that only once in a generation is a society capable of rising to idealism in its politics. Applied to some countries that may be too generous an estimate. But his point is well taken: Peoples are capable of "rising to idealism," and they will do so periodically. Wilson had a chance to see (and give some leadership to) the Progressive Era in early twentieth-century American public life, while observing how it followed on the heels of the "Great Barbecue" when ruthless competition and cynicism reigned. His own presidency, marked (and somewhat flawed) by idealism, was to be followed by the era of Warren G. Harding and Calvin Coolidge, which was anything but idealistic. That period, in turn, was succeeded by Roosevelt's New Deal, and so on. Similar turns and twists of the moral compass can be observed in the histories of other lands. Democracy promises no end to the ups and downs; it certainly does not portend the coming of the kingdom of love and righteousness on earth.

Nevertheless, even the shabby times can be improved by clear access by reformers to popular opinion and to the levers of power. One could not describe the Nixon presidency in the United States as a time of moral nobility. Yet the existence of a free press and a potentially arousable populace committed to its Constitution was important to the prospects for reform. In nineteenth-century England, when a somewhat corrupted leadership was inclined to support the slaveholding South in the American Civil War, it was the direct moral appeal to the ordinary workers (who themselves had a material stake in the cheap cotton provided by the slave system) that at least made it impossible for the leadership to take that route.

Democracy does not guarantee good results, but it does keep things open. It does provide channels for criticism and for change. Its people are not saints, but they are challenged by the opportunities and responsibilities of self-government. Indeed, the most corrupt periods in the histories of democratic societies seem also to be those times when people are least interested in exercising their opportunities and responsibilities.

Western democracies at the turn of the new millennium must grapple not only with the flawed outcomes of democratic process but with imperfections in the process itself. Mass society, with communication increasingly mediated through nationwide television and other mass media, tends to erode the health of the necessary mediating structures where people find identity and clarify their purposes. Political institutions that are democratic on one level may even work against democracy on other levels. For example, in the United States the committee structure of the Congress gives power to committee chairpersons far out of proportion to the size of the electoral constituencies sending them to Washington, sometimes allowing such politicians to exercise capricious power over national policy. Or, to cite another example, the fact that black people, while the largest single racial or ethnic minority group in the United States, are not a numerical majority in any state is one reason that there have been so few black members of the United States Senate (where election is by states). At the present time of writing there are no black U.S. senators at all, even though there are more than twenty-five million black people in the country. Or, to cite still another example, the lack of proportionate representation in parliamentary constituencies in the United Kingdom means that one party can gain a very large absolute majority in Parliament on the strength of much less than 50 percent of the votes cast—a circumstance that occurred twice in the U.K. during the 1980s, when three major parties contended for power.

Such problems (many more could be cited) are not valid arguments against democracy. Nor do they mean that democracy has utterly broken down in the contemporary world. But they are a reminder that democracy, like the church, must continually purify itself with reform and that those who care about its health will attend to it steadfastly.

In the next chapter, we shall want to examine more closely the contributions Christian faith can make to the character of the people of a democratically governed society. For the *degree* of public-spirited caring represented by those people obviously affects the political outcomes very much.

A CHRISTIAN "PRESUMPTION" FOR DEMOCRACY

May we conclude, however, that Christian faith implies support for democracy and that democracy expresses the Christian spirit? In a remarkable chapter in one of his books, the social gospel leader Walter Rauschenbusch came close to making such a flat assertion:

> A fourth great section of our social order which has been christianized is the political life. . . . The fundamental redemption of the State took place when special privilege was thrust out of the constitution and theory of our government and it was based on the principle of personal liberty and equal rights.[18]

Rauschenbusch surrounded this declaration with caveats (for instance, "of all corrupt things surely our politics is the corruptest").[19] But plainly he believed the democratic constitution, if not all democratic practice, to be a part of the "christianized" social order.

My own observations in this chapter concur with Rauschenbusch

---

[18]Rauschenbusch, *Christianizing the Social Order,* 147–48.
[19]Ibid.

on the basic point that this kind of political order—embodying equal civil rights and participation in political power—is more fully in accord with Christian insight than any alternative. But political history in the decades following Rauschenbusch's death may require greater care in the way we express Christian support for democracy.

Clearly, much depends on *how* a democratic order is structured and upon the character and culture of the people who make it up. And much depends upon the actual development of the history of a society and character of the challenges it faces. It may be best, therefore, not to treat democracy as an absolute. Some situations may not be ready for it. Some crises may be so severe that greater centralization of power—or even outright autocracy—might be needed to see society through. Even so committed a believer in democracy as Abraham Lincoln took steps at the outset of the Civil War that ran roughshod over constitutional rights and liberties. Had he not done so, it is more than likely that the Union would have been dissolved, slavery perpetuated, and a protracted era of deep conflict in North America begun. History does not disclose its alternatives, but in such extraordinary situations it does seem advisable to have modified the canons of democracy.

On the other hand, there are many historical illustrations of resort to despotism in the face of crises that pose less danger than the despotism itself. The incarceration of Japanese-Americans at the outset of World War II is a clear case in point. No interpretation of the U.S. Constitution could possibly have warranted the herding of these citizens and lawfully resident noncitizens into concentration camps. The move was prompted by hysterical fear of Japanese invasion and of the possible disloyalty of the Japanese-Americans. Both fears were absolutely unfounded, and it seems evident, in retrospect, that the hysteria owed as much to racism as to objective assessment.

In a number of Third World countries in our own time it is asserted that the historical situation is not yet ripe for democracy. Even such non-Marxist countries as Zambia and Tanzania—both led by presidents of deep democratic sensibility—maintained one-party political systems on the supposition that the lack of supporting culture and the lack of a sufficient pool of leadership made this necessary for a generation or so. The results were not impressive. Even so, a case can sometimes be made that a country simply is not yet ready for real democracy.

It is too easily forgotten in the Western democracies that it took a long time for democracy to take root in all of them, and that all of these more settled democratic societies continue to have problems.

But the cultural background of a people and its actual historical situation do make a difference. Sometimes democracy is not immediately attainable.

But, conceding that point, our commitment to democracy should be firm enough to force all exceptions to face the hard questions, and to continue to do so until democracy is achieved: Are the people truly incapable of governing themselves? Faced with competing ideas, are the people unable to sort out the truth? Will the rule of a nondemocratic leadership be *temporary?* Will such leadership resist corruption over the long haul? Will it be wise enough? Will it find ways to avail itself of the best thinking among all the people of the society? Will it be able to motivate people to seek the common good? Is there any way for it to test the proposition that "people do not want democracy"— when the proposition itself is predicated on democratic values?

What this means is that we should have a *presumption* in favor of democracy. Governmental systems that are less than democratic should be required to face a continuing burden of proof [20] to show that it is not yet possible to be democratic. I am reluctant to name such situations in the contemporary world, partly because such designations quickly become obsolete in the moving tides of history and partly because I would offer no encouragement to those who wish, for self-interested reasons, to postpone what is already possible. In every situation the presumption must be that a society is ready for democratic reform unless it can be shown otherwise to the satisfaction of people whose commitment to democracy is beyond question.

WHEN MAY DEMOCRACY
BE POSTPONED?

What, then, are the circumstances that justify *not* organizing a society democratically? How do we know when the burden of proof has been met?

The general answer is, of course, that democracy is to be avoided when it would do more harm than good. That is, in general, when democracy works against and not for justice and human well-being. It is possible to be more specific in suggesting standards or criteria to be used when thinking about specific situations. I wish now to

---

[20]I have explored the use of "presumptions" in Christian moral judgment in my book, *A Christian Method of Moral Judgment* (Philadelphia: Westminster Press, 1976).

suggest five questions that can be used to test whether a given situation justifies deviation from the democratic norm.

1. *Is the temporary use of authoritarian or autocratic methods necessary during a time of disaster to assure the meeting of basic needs for the populace?* Most legal systems provide for a declaration of a state of emergency to set aside normal legal constraints for the sake of public safety. Thus, in the vicinity of a forest fire, public authorities can sometimes draft able-bodied persons on the spot to help fight the blaze. Martial law can be declared during a major earthquake or during a time of civil rioting. The executive can assume authoritarian powers for the duration of the emergency. An important test of the compatibility of such authoritarianism with the fundamental commitment to democracy is whether provision for it is made in law and whether mechanisms to terminate the extraordinary powers upon conclusion of the emergency are clearly spelled out.

2. *Is the temporary use of authoritarian or autocratic methods necessary to preclude a greater or more permanent despotism?* In a deeply unsettled situation, an undemocratic leader or movement might be able to exploit the confusions of an election campaign and full access to public opinion to rise to power, and once there use the police and military powers at its disposal to cut off civil liberties and further electoral politics. Hitler's Nazi party thus made adroit use of the electoral process to gain power—and then to destroy that process. Having noted this possibility, however, it must be remembered that democracy may actually be a better defense against such threats than authoritarianism. In any event, we must be aware of the ease whereby this rationale for temporary use of authoritarianism can be used as a rationalization. Some neoconservative leaders, such as former U.S. ambassador to the United Nations Jeane Kirkpatrick, have made too much of the distinction between "totalitarian" and "authoritarian" regimes. The former are described as despotic and permanent, the latter as less democratic and temporary. Such a distinction has sometimes been employed to justify authoritarian regimes in countries such as South Korea, Argentina (under the generals), and Chile (under Augusto Pinochet Ugarte) as a defense against the alleged communist totalitarian threat. But some of the authoritarian governments have themselves been both despotic and long-lasting, and some of the communist regimes finally proved capable of moving

toward democracy. U.S. support for authoritarian dictators in a number of countries during the Cold War hardly met the test implied by this question. Still, history does sometimes confront us with the need to be authoritarian over the short run in order to pave the way for democracy over the long run.

3. *Is the (short-term) authoritarian leadership governing by law and committed to observing its own laws?* Recognition of its own accountability to law at least demonstrates a commitment to avoid using power for corrupt gain and provides a clear basis by which the government and its leaders can be judged (as well as laws which can be assessed and debated). This is so even though the laws as such may be quite undemocratic.

4. *Will the (short-term) authoritarian government honor and protect as many elements of democratic rule as possible under the conditions of emergency?* If elections are temporarily out of the question, will freedom of expression still be honored? If one-party rule seems necessary, will people still be free to organize an opposition to the extent of conducting meetings and formulating criticisms? Will advisory councils be formed, where possible on an elected basis, so the popular will can more readily be consulted?

5. *Will the (short-term) authoritarian government commit itself to specific times for review of the temporary arrangements and for the institution of real democracy?* And in the implementation of this, will it refer part of the decision-making process about when to commence or return to real democracy to persons or groups having no self-interest in the perpetuation of authoritarian rule, such as disinterested international panels?

All of these questions can be used as rationalizations by people of bad faith. But such questions may at least help us determine whether a given authoritarian "exception" to the norm of democracy is truly desirable and whether it is in fact a true exception. Thinking clearly about such exceptions helps us remember that they are *exceptions* to the norm and that, for Christians, the norm is democracy. When a society is forced to settle for something less than democracy, it must be understood to be something *less*. And Christians have, as we have seen, compelling theological reasons for moving on as quickly as possible to develop and maintain democratic political institutions.

In the next chapter I shall raise the question whether there may be more specific resources in Christian tradition to help undergird those who seek to participate in the democratic political process.

12

Democratic Rights
and Democratic Disciplines

A republic as an active political community of participating citizens must have a purpose and a set of values.
Freedom in the republican tradition is a positive value
that asserts the worth and dignity of political equality
and popular government. A republic must attempt to be
ethical in a positive sense and to elicit the ethical commitment of its citizens. For this reason it inevitably
pushes toward the symbolization of an ultimate order
of existence in which republican values and virtues
make sense.

—Robert N. Bellah (1980)[1]

Love is patient and kind; love is not jealous or boastful;
it is not arrogant or rude. Love does not insist on its
own way; it is not irritable or resentful; it does not rejoice at wrong, but rejoices in the right. Love bears all
things, believes all things, hopes all things, endures all
things.

—1 Cor. 13:4–7

The relationship between Christian faith and political democracy
needs to be pursued in yet a different way: on the personal level.

We have surveyed the relationship at the systemic level, and we

---

[1]Robert N. Bellah, "Religion and the Legitimation of the American Republic," in *Varieties of Civil Religion,* ed. Robert N. Bellah and Phillip E. Hammond (San Francisco:
Harper & Row, 1980), 12.

have concluded that a democratic system of government is more nearly compatible with Christian theological insight than any other except when historical circumstances justify the *temporary* expedient of more authoritarian rule. But what difference does it make when the citizens of a democratic society are themselves Christians? Should they claim individual political rights for themselves in the same way as non-Christians? Do they as Christians have any special contributions to make to a democratic society? Does being a Christian make a difference in the exercise of citizenship and leadership in such a society?

CHRISTIANS AND THE
RIGHTS OF CITIZENSHIP

Some of Christianity's most famous critics have held that Christian character is too passive, too submissive, too preoccupied with otherworldly and spiritual matters to function effectively in the sphere of worldly politics. The virtues of Christian life appear to such critics to be incompatible even with the capacity to claim and exercise one's own rights. Jean Jacques Rousseau, for example, referred with contempt to the political effects of the piety of Christians: "Christianity preaches only servitude and dependence. Its spirit is so favorable to tyranny that it always profits by such a regime." "True Christians," he adds, "are made to be slaves, and they know it, and do not much mind; this short life counts for too little in their eyes."[2] A century later, Friedrich Nietzsche condemned the church for preaching a gospel that was against the assertion of life. It has, he wrote, "at all times laid the stress of discipline on extirpation (of sensuality, of pride, of the lust to rule, of avarice, of vengefulness)." "But," he continued, "an attack on the roots of passion means an attack on the roots of life."[3]

This kind of statement is extreme. But one might still wonder whether the kinds of virtues listed by Saint Paul at the head of this chapter should inhibit Christians from insisting upon their own po-

---

[2]Jean Jacques Rousseau, *The Social Contract,* trans. Willmoore Kendall (Chicago: Gateway, 1954), Book 4, chap. 8, pp. 204–23. Quoted in Bellah, "Religion and Legitimation," 5.

[3]Friedrich Nietzsche, *Twilight of the Idols,* in *The Portable Nietzsche,* ed. Walter Kaufmann (New York: The Viking Press, 1954), 487.

litical rights: "Love does not insist on its own way." "Love bears all things." Is this not a prescription for political passivity?

Later in this chapter I shall consider the other positive—even indispensable—contributions the Christian virtues have to offer to the democratic political order. But here it is important to remember that the surrender of one's own political rights is not a very good way to help maintain a healthy system of such rights for a whole society. There are, no doubt, times and places where one has no alternative but to accept tyranny, while continuing to bear whatever witness one can under the circumstances. But love does not mean the denial of one's own personhood. To be a Christian human being is to be active, creative, even assertive. When Christians mistakenly allow the denial of their own basic civil rights (such as freedom of speech, freedom of the press, freedom of worship, freedom from arbitrary arrest and detainment, and the right to vote) they weaken such rights for others. For democracy to function, it is important to insist upon the rights of all, including oneself.

It is sometimes a risky, courageous act to insist upon exercising one's rights or to challenge some new encroachment by the state or powerful private organizations. For instance, during the McCarthy era in the United States, Methodist Bishop G. Bromley Oxnam had been accused of being a communist sympathizer (or dupe) by the House Un-American Activities Committee. The committee claimed to have a lengthy file of materials documenting its charges. The bishop insisted upon a public opportunity to confront the committee, hear its evidence, and have an opportunity to reply while accompanied by legal counsel. The committee reluctantly agreed, and the eyes of the nation were riveted upon a congressional hearing room for hours as Bishop Oxnam replied point by point to the committee's allegations.[4] The hearing fully vindicated the bishop. But more than that, his insistence upon exercising his rights helped clear the air of the stifling conformism of the McCarthy era. It would have been a total misunderstanding of Christian love for the bishop to have accepted ill-treatment by Congress passively. Similarly, when Christian women and members of ethnic minority groups have insisted upon their rights, they have served the deeper interests of *everybody*. On this basis, the civil rights movement of the 1960s, prompted very largely by its own understanding of Christian

---

[4]G. Bromley Oxnam, *I Protest* (New York: Harper & Brothers, 1954).

love, expressed that love by insisting upon exercising rights that had been denied for many generations. Is this insisting upon one's own way? In a sense, to be sure. But in a larger sense, it is an act of great courage offered as a gift to all other people within a society—for all are blessed by the existence of a well-defined, well-respected system of civil rights.

Fundamentally selfish people usually find ways of accommodating themselves to any regime. If it is despotic, they will find ways to get into the good graces of the tyrant. If it is corrupt, they will manage somehow to become corrupted. If it is sustained by the prejudices or hysteria of the multitude, they will generally conform. Under such circumstances, it can be an act of incredible unselfishness to insist upon the exercise of one's own rights! Some, no doubt, do so out of psychological exhibitionism. But Christians sometimes do so out of self-giving love.

THE DISCIPLINES OF DEMOCRACY

I noted above (as have many writers) that democracy is not good enough to operate *automatically*. The majority, even when it respects the rights of minorities, can still be unwise in the exercises of political power. Majority rule can be a prescription for disaster if most people are self-centered and corrupt. The late American congresswoman Edith Green, who was recognized by many as an unusually wise political leader, remarked that she could tell much about the character of the people of a state on the basis of those whom they sent to Congress as their representatives.[5] (On that basis, one could have commended the people of the State of Oregon for their political maturity.) Similarly, one can tell much about the people of a democracy at any given time on the basis of governmental policies and priorities. There *is* a connection between the character of a people and its politics, and democracy tends more to emphasize that connection than to lessen it.

Perceptive interpreters of democracy have often stressed this connection. Democracy can be said to work better than other political systems, but that does not make it easy. Democracy is hard work. It is relatively easy to get along under authoritarian rule. All one

---

[5]Personal interview, Washington, D.C., April 1960.

has to do is to obey. Self-government requires greater self-discipline from its people.

What are the disciplines required of a people in order to make democracy work? We may recall the half of Reinhold Niebuhr's aphorism stating that "man's capacity for justice makes democracy possible." Does this "capacity for justice" suggest a basic attitude upon which democracy depends? The other half of the aphorism, about human sinfulness, means we must not assume too much about human virtue. Nevertheless, democracy entails cooperation in the pursuit of common purposes and a willingness to accept the legitimate rights of others. People who are entirely corrupt, altogether self-centered, are a threat to such a system. There must be some degree of commitment to a common good transcending individual interests and some willingness on the part of participants to sacrifice those individual interests. Apart from this, it is hard to see how a democratic state could resist disintegration. Most such societies have enough experience with periods of corruption to illustrate the disintegrative effects of selfish spirit. In the United States, the Gilded Age of the nineteenth century was such a time, as were the post-World War I period of the 1920s, the 1950s, and perhaps the 1970s and 1980s. In such periods, prevailing cultural values have stressed individual wealth and success, and many people have taken shortcuts to attain their goals. Inevitably, respect for law, as the common agreement of a free people, has eroded, and high office has not been associated with deep integrity. There has been comparatively little commitment, during such periods, to the plight of marginalized people or to making the nation a genuinely constructive force in world affairs. Fortunately, at least thus far, such periods have given way to more idealistic times. During the Progressive Era, or the New Deal, or the New Frontier—whatever we might think of the specific goals and policies adopted—the health of the system was renewed through the deep personal commitments of large numbers of people. And we are reminded again of the great importance of our capacity for justice. Unless there is some kind of commitment to the greater social good, and some ability to act on such a commitment, a participatory form of government can fall apart.

We have referred to the disciplines of democracy. These are the habits of mind and heart that dispose us to cooperate with one another toward the common good. The classical virtues (such as the temperance, courage, prudence, and justice of Greek thought) were partly framed as a statement of the personal qualities needed for

229

the well-being of the commonwealth.[6] And such virtues clearly are relevant to the well-being of a democratic state. *Temperance* refers to control of the senses and reminds us that when people are corrupted by excessive sensuality or materialism they cannot be counted upon to think and act in the public interest. *Courage* refers to the control of fear so that one can speak or act in accordance with the common good in spite of the prospect of physical or social harm to oneself. *Prudence,* or wisdom, refers to the capacity to anticipate probable consequences and to avoid foolhardy actions or policies. And, in the Platonic tradition, *justice* is in the proper relationship between all aspects of the personality (the appetitive, spirited, and rational "faculties") and the different classes of society. Neither Plato nor Aristotle was a democrat, strictly speaking, but both had a high conception of the civil community as a community of discourse and action in which those who are capable of participation are called upon to do so. Their discussions of virtue therefore remain useful to those who wish to understand the disciplines needed for democratic society. But much more needs to be said about democratic disciplines.

The classical virtues do not immediately bring to mind some of the disciplines and skills without which democratic political practice must falter. For instance, all political practitioners in such a society speak of the importance of compromise, so that conflicts between individuals and groups do not have to be resolved by raw force. The capacity to treat political opponents with respect is basic to the effective functioning of legislative bodies whose memberships include sharply opposing viewpoints and interests. The ability to win or lose with grace, recognizing that another day will come in which today's victory will turn to defeat and today's defeat to victory, is a necessary trait. The political practitioner must also demonstrate the independence to recognize and resist demagoguery—and

---

[6]Plato's conception of the relationship between personal virtues and the proper ordering of the commonwealth is complex. Each of the virtues corresponds to one of the three human faculties—the appetitive (or sensual), the spirited (the vital physical force), and the rational—and represents its perfection. The commonwealth is divided generally into three classes of people, based upon which of the faculties predominates within them. Thus, the artisans, farmers, etc., are predominantly appetitive in nature. The warriors are predominantly spirited. The philosophers are rational. Just as the rational should ultimately govern the appetitive and spirited faculties within individuals, so the philosophers should govern the well-ordered commonwealth. Plato did not regard our particular natural endowments as specifically hereditary; consequently, class membership itself is not hereditary. Nevertheless, his view could not be characterized as democratic in the sense we are using the term in this volume.

the restraint to avoid employing it—as well as the grace to recognize the limitations of one's own views and interests combined with the courage to defend views and interests one considers valid.

Democracy depends upon the observance of such disciplines. Some disciplines amount to the graceful habits of courtesy that make group conflict-resolution tolerable. Others have deeper roots. But such disciplines imply personal commitments transcending the political process itself along with deep commitment to that process.

CHRISTIAN CHARACTER AND
THE DEMOCRATIC DISCIPLINES

Does being a Christian contribute anything to the democratic disciplines?

There is always the danger that Christians may so overemphasize individual character that the justice or injustice, the wisdom or folly of large public policies will be neglected. The personal Christian virtue of a public figure or a group of citizens may overshadow the need to examine carefully what they actually stand for. John Bennett makes the point with the observation that it is a "major error"

> to stress the personal character or piety of a candidate without taking into account the forces which support him or the wisdom of his policies. The personal character of our leaders in public life is of great importance, but the primary emphasis should be placed upon integrity in the discharge of public responsibilities. The error appears when the private character or religious habits of a candidate become a front for interests and policies which are not examined.[7]

Bennett wishes to affirm the importance of morality in politics, but he reminds us that "neither personal virtue nor sincere piety are any guarantee of social wisdom."[8]

---

[7]John C. Bennett, *Christians and the State* (New York: Charles Scribner's Sons, 1958), 296.

[8]Ibid. Bennett's point reminds me of a political associate in the 1960s. As a member of the California legislature, this individual successfully sponsored landmark legislation benefiting many people and could be counted upon in support of the great social justice causes that have stood the test of time. Regrettably, his own personal life was in some shambles—with an alcohol problem, a shaky marriage, and some hints of material corruption. I grieved over the characterological problems on one level while celebrating the quality of his leadership and vision on another level. Many people reacted similarly to President Clinton's difficulties in 1998–99.

It is a happy thing when a virtuous life is also a politically saga-cious one. In more than thirty years of life and work in Washington, D.C., I have had ample opportunity to observe political leaders who combine personal virtue and piety with public vision of a very high order. I am not sure I would even describe the combination as rare. But at the same time, one cannot fail to notice the genuinely pious and personally virtuous political leaders who, for whatever reason, seem utterly lacking in historical grasp and commitment to social justice. At the other pole, there are those whose personal lives seem more seriously flawed, but whose public leadership is exemplary. It seems a pity that real life must present such unevenness in the dis-tribution of virtue and wisdom, though we should perhaps not be surprised in light of the prevalence of sin among human beings![9]

But our concern here is at a different level. It is with the rela-tionship between Christian virtue, when it is truly authentic, and the kinds of democratic virtues we have been discussing. Does Christian virtue make a contribution?

We have seen in chapter 10 that Christian character and virtue, as fruits of commitment to the Christian "story," can be depicted as the form of Christian life in an *alternative community*. Seen in this way, the quality of the life in such a community is a great blessing to people who are its members and a source of great attractiveness to those who are not. It is even relevant politically in the sense that it presents humankind with a basis for claiming their independence vis-à-vis the pretensions and tyrannies of the "principalities and powers" of the present world darkness. But seen in those terms, Christian life is not understood to be a direct contribution to the po-litical process as such—certainly not on its own terms. Christian virtue can, thus, be attached to a sectarian conception of the rela-tionship of church and society.

But virtue can also be understood as a support for our participa-tion in the wider political community. Christian faith is more than

---

[9]The impeachment controversy of 1998–99 evoked much soul-searching by Americans at exactly this point. How were we to measure flawed personal behavior against the lead-ership of an accomplished president? No reasonable person, including the president him-self, condoned the behavior. But he was an effective president and, indeed, in most aspects of his life a man of personal sensitivity and character. It struck me that the efforts to re-move him from office were based upon too narrow a moral assessment and that no small part of this effort was politically motivated. My analysis of the issues, written in the midst of the national debate, is in J. Philip Wogaman, *From the Eye of the Storm: A Pastor to the President Speaks Out* (Louisville, Ky.: Westminster John Knox Press, 1998).

its contributions to that community, but its contributions are undeniably powerful.

Recognizing that non-Christians can also make such contributions to the commonwealth, it can still be said that mature Christian character certainly does so. I wish to illustrate the possibilities by taking one of the classic biblical texts on Christian virtue, the thirteenth chapter of 1 Corinthians, and noting the pertinence of several of the central virtues listed there to the disciplines needed in democratic society.

THE THEOLOGICAL VIRTUES

When Thomas Aquinas wished to distinguish between those virtues understandable by reason and those which are a gift of revelation, he used the classical Greek virtues (in their Aristotelian form) for the former and the summary verse of Paul's 1 Corinthians 13 for the latter: "So faith, hope, love abide, these three; but the greatest of these is love." All three of these seem terribly general, even platitudinous, but each may have specific contributions to make to the disciplines needed in a democratic society. Consider:

1. *Faith* can be understood as our ultimate trust that we belong to God, who loves us at the core of our being. Such a grounding of our lives means that we do not have to surrender to egoism or ambition and that human pride and pretension are no longer attractive to us. Egoism, in fact, is seen in a new light as a compensation for our deepest anxieties. Many politicians appear motivated less by commitments to public interest and more by the propping up of their egos through publicity, votes, and applause. It is almost as though one were in search of a sense of self-worth. Political defeat therefore appears as personal defeat; one has been rejected as a person. The political struggle therefore becomes a highly personal struggle with absolute stakes. One could not observe the tragedy of Senator Joseph McCarthy without some conception of how fragile his personal sense of self-worth really was. His campaign against communism possibly had very little to do with that historical movement and very much to do with whether he could be successful at the center of the public stage. When he was finally (and one might say belatedly) censured by his senatorial colleagues, he could not survive the blow psychologically, and his death followed within three years. There was possibly some of that in the career of former president Richard Nixon, as well as in the race-baiting of former Alabama

governor George Wallace.[10] Similar comments could be made about more recent politicians, including some still holding office, whose position on issues is often framed solely upon attracting votes or (even worse) campaign contributions. By contrast, former senators George McGovern and Barry Goldwater (to frame the matter in nonpartisan fashion) were both willing to take unpopular positions they believed in, even though it was to court defeat. Two political adversaries of the 1990s, President Bill Clinton and Speaker Newt Gingrich—both much maligned by political opponents—clearly had things they wished to accomplish politically and seemed capable of absorbing defeats without loss of a sense of self.

Doubtless some element of egoism appears in the political ambitions of every successful politician. Reflecting on a lifetime of experience in politics, Senator Mark O. Hatfield remarked that "any honest politician would have to admit to the ambition and ego that motivate his or her journey in public life. . . . The allurement of power and honor subtly but malignantly grows within the politician, often gaining control of one's whole being before it is discovered."[11] Some may even doubt that democratic politics could exist without egoism and ambition. But that is not so. A life that is grounded in faith can, where appropriate, offer itself for service in a leadership role. And persons who are not so consumed by ego needs can make enormous contributions to the health of the democratic process. Hatfield, who had to struggle with the conflict between ego and the deeper promptings of faith, speaks of the crisis when he came to understand that "service to others, solely for their own behalf and even entailing deep sacrifice, is the true essence of leadership and the ultimate form of power." He began to feel liberated, he records, "from the idolatry of power and given over more deeply to a whole new vision of prophetic witness, faithfulness, and servanthood."[12]

---

[10]Wallace appears to have been a political moderate—at least not at all a racial demagogue—in his first unsuccessful run for statewide office in Alabama. But upon being defeated by a racist opponent, he is reputed to have remarked that that was the last time he would ever be "out-segged" by anyone (i.e., the last time anybody would be able to appear more of a racial segregationist than he). For many years he was remarkably successful in the fulfillment of this prediction.

[11]Mark Hatfield, *Between a Rock and a Hard Place* (Waco, Tex.: Word Books, 1976), 15–16.

[12]Ibid., 26, 30.

The virtue of faith is important for ordinary democratic citizenship as well. The egoism of people can be fed not only by leadership roles but by identification with abstract ideologies and winning causes. A quite ordinary citizen, who would be shocked by the thought of personally running for public office, may still corrupt the public life through fanaticism. The victory of certain abstract values (racism, prohibition, anticommunism, prayer in the public schools, right-to-life, or their opposites) can become one's personal victory. On a more ordinary level, one can so identify with a particular candidate or party that electoral success or failure is one's own personal success or failure (just as it might be with one's favorite athletic team). Again, one's ego is being shored up in compensation for not being very well grounded. The effect is basically damaging to the democratic political process.

A democratic society is well served by a citizenry not fanatically attached to single issues or causes but capable of rounded judgments and a careful weighing of ambiguous alternatives. That maturity is grounded, first, in a secure sense of personal worth. It is at that point that the personal faith of Christians is a distinct contribution to democratic disciplines.

2. *Hope* can be understood as belief in the possible fulfillment of God's intended good in the future. Christian faith entails both a "long-run" eschatological hope in God's ultimate victory over sin and death and a "short-run" hope for the achievement of particular objectives in human history. The "long-run" perspective helps to relativize particular objectives. Because the hope of Christians is set beyond history, they are not as prone to absolutize particular goals. They are therefore more prepared to enter into the give-and-take of political process with its necessary compromises. On the other hand, because the hope of Christians is also within history, they are able to work vigorously for attainable historical goals—and even to entertain hopes long abandoned by the disillusioned and cynical. That relative historical hope is necessary to motivate serious political endeavor for, as Samuel Taylor Coleridge observed, "Work without hope draws nectar in a sieve, and hope without an object cannot live."[13]

It is difficult to think of a single political reform of consequence that

---

[13]Samuel Taylor Coleridge, "Work without Hope," in *The Literature of England,* 3d ed., ed. George B. Woods, Homer A. Watt, and George K. Anderson (Chicago: Scott, Foresman, 1948 [1825]), 2:190.

has not been dismissed as impossible by people incapable of entertaining this kind of historical hope. The nineteenth-century British chartist movement had to confront a heavy weight of hopelessness about the attainability of universal suffrage, as did the antislavery movement about its goals. The twentieth-century American civil rights movement fought a constant battle against the widespread conviction that it could not succeed. Efforts to discipline major corporations, to establish ecological safeguards, and to achieve adequate nutrition for the world's hungry people all have had to contend first of all with a dead weight of hopelessness. The virtue of hope thus enlivens politics with a sense of the achievability of worthy purposes.

3. *Love,* the crowning Christian virtue, can be understood in this context as a deep recognition of one's belonging to other human beings as to a family and an utter devotion to the good as God's good.[14] Who of us is capable of fulfilling such a sweeping conception of love? Yet this is the summary virtue of a Christian character, and growth in the maturity of Christian love has always been understood by Christians to be possible.[15] And where embodied in the character of participants in the political process, it is surely relevant to their observance of the democratic disciplines. For one thing, it leads one to respect the humanity of one's political adversaries, a point to which we shall return below. For another thing, it leads one to care very deeply about the consequences of the political process in the lives of actual human beings. For still another thing, it leads one to pursue political purposes that contribute to a community in which all are valued participants.

Is it possible for a political community as a whole to exemplify this virtue? Some commentators question this. Robert Jewett writes of "the distinction between a private ethic of forgiveness and a public ethic of honor," and Jean Bethke Elshtain remarks that "forgiveness is not a political term."[16] But is that so? Was not the Truth and Reconciliation Commission of South Africa a stunning example

---

[14]I have discussed the meaning of Christian love more fully in *A Christian Method of Moral Judgment* (Philadelphia: Westminster Press, 1976), 85–93, and *Faith and Fragmentation* (Philadelphia: Fortress Press, 1985), 87–89, 102–4.

[15]John Wesley's doctrine of Christian perfection in fact goes rather far in affirming that one can be made perfect in love in this life. By this, Wesley did not mean that one could be free from error or even from the unintentional committing of sin; he did mean that one's character could be wholly formed by love. See Thomas S. Kepler, ed., *Christian Perfection, as Believed and Taught by John Wesley* (Cleveland: World Publishing, 1954).

[16]Robert Jewett, "Confession and Forgiveness in the Public Sphere," in Gabriel Fackre, ed., *Judgment Day at the White House,* 56.

of forgiving love at work in the political sphere representing, at least to some degree, a national purpose framed by love? Is that not also true in acts of amnesty or pardon, and is it not so when international aid programs from country to country are prompted by a generous spirit and not simply national self-interest?

In a thoughtful study of forgiveness in politics, Donald W. Shriver Jr. offers a number of well-developed illustrations, setting forth his purpose in these words:

> Can whole nations repent? Forgive? Engage in processes that eventuate in collective repentance and forgiveness? Rather than arguing theoretically for an answer of "yes" to these crucial questions, the rest of this book will examine at length the history of three twentieth-century enmities that have profoundly shaped the lives of every living American: our wars with Germany and Japan and our centuries-old internal struggle for just relations between African Americans and the country as a whole.[17]

Notwithstanding his modest disclaimer, Shriver's carefully developed illustrations make it clear that "yes" is the only possible answer to the question whether whole nations can forgive—and, in a manner appropriate to a vast collective of people, love. But for that to happen generally presupposes leadership that is itself prompted by love. The virtue is more rare than we might wish, but it is not altogether missing either.

Christian love, like the other theological virtues, points beyond any concrete human characterization. And, like the other virtues, one cannot expect to find it perfectly manifested in any actual human being—although Christians affirm the full embodiment of love in the person of Jesus Christ. But such virtues, insofar as they can be and are formative of the character of people, can make such contributions to the health of the democratic process.

VIRTUES IN DETAIL

The fact that the theological virtues, which I have briefly discussed, are as general as they are suggests the importance of a somewhat more detailed understanding of virtue. This is a truly

---

[17]Donald W. Shriver Jr., *An Ethic for Enemies: Forgiveness in Politics* (New York and Oxford: Oxford University Press, 1995), 71.

dangerous thing to suggest, for every "virtue," once identified, can so easily become the ground for a new legalism that is the deadly enemy of real virtue! Nevertheless, when virtue can be understood in its full grounding in faith, hope, and love, it can be helpful to see how a more detailed understanding of virtue also contributes to the observance of democratic disciplines.

Here we can also turn to 1 Corinthians 13 for splendid illustration, noting in particular the lively relevance of verses 4–7 (which also appear at the beginning of this chapter). Each of these more specific comments on the virtuous life is grounded in love. Each has implications for political practice. Observe:

1. *Love is patient.* Patience, in this context, clearly does not mean not caring whether desirable goals are ever achieved in politics. One is not "patient" with the continued hurt suffered by oppressed people or the preventable hunger of people without food. Such things lead to a love that is *not* patient! But the patience that is grounded in love is the virtue of being willing to invest as much time as necessary for the achievement of worthy goals. For instance, patience does not mean acceptance of oppression. To the contrary, it means a commitment to use as much time as necessary to overcome it. The veteran Quaker lobbyist Raymond Wilson—for many years leader of the Friends Committee on National Legislation in Washington, D.C.—used to remark that every major legislative reform takes at least twenty years. If the objective is an expression of justice and the common good, then patience is the price love is willing to pay to accomplish it. Patience is taking the time necessary—no more, no less. Clearly democracy is well served by patient people.

2. *Love is kind.* Translated into political terms, kindness might include a specific concern for the well-being of others (including adversaries) that transcends the immediate interests of the struggle itself. To be kind is to care about people, to be sensitive to their hurts and needs, never to inflict pain needlessly, and whenever the inflicting of pain is unavoidable, to seek to mitigate its harshness. A touching story is told about then-President Richard Nixon's going out of his way to express sympathy with Senator Edward Kennedy after the tragic and politically ruinous Chappaquiddick event in 1969. Whatever Nixon's motives may have been (and one should not simply be cynical about them as a matter of course), that was apparently received as a genuine kindness. Political defeat can be rendered less personal when victors make thoughtful gestures of friendship with losers. Such kindnesses can help enormously to maintain community solidarity in the face of social conflict.

3. *Love is not jealous or boastful; it is not arrogant or rude.* Such attitudes, obviously inconsistent with Christian love, are equally incompatible with the demands of democratic group process. Jealousy makes cooperation difficult. It even inhibits clear communication, for those who are jealous of others can be counted upon to oppose them without exposing the real reasons for the opposition. To be boastful is to invite resentment. Arrogance and rudeness in politics, showing contempt for adversaries and allies alike, undermine group feeling and invite retaliation. All such attitudes lead to a personalizing of political conflict, while distracting the political community from consideration of issues and problems on their merits. Political participants who exhibit the virtue of love may not be immune from opposition, but their attitudes make inevitable conflicts tolerable and productive.

4. *Love does not insist on its own way.* This is a difficult "virtue" to defend. This almost seems to mean that loving people stand for nothing, that they are willing to struggle for nothing. Applied to the political process, it appears to identify the virtue of love with the disciplines of compromise. Indeed politicians, in characterizing the virtues and disciplines peculiar to their profession, are likely to emphasize *compromise* most of all. Compromise makes it possible for decisions to be reached which represent some part of the objectives of each of the contending interests and centers of power. Is compromise good or bad? T. V. Smith, who was a sagacious interpreter of democratic political life during the difficult days of the 1930s (when the great democracies had to confront economic depression at home and the looming dangers of fascist dictatorship abroad), had this to say in defense of political compromise:

> Clashes must be softened if bitterness and then violence are not to ensue, giving birth to subsequent coercion of groups who get the worst of it. So difficult to adjust are the conflicts of interest that furnish the problems for democratic politicians that dictatorship has again become in many erstwhile democratic lands the standardized method of dealing with them. It is precisely that outcome of intergroup conflicts which the democratic politicians shield us from.[18]

The disciplines of compromise are enhanced by the presence of people who do not insist on their own way. Is that really what love means?

---

[18]T. V. Smith, *The Promise of American Politics,* 2d ed. (Chicago: University of Chicago Press, 1936), 248.

Saint Paul may well have had in mind the kinds of people who must have their own way as a way of reinforcing their fragile sense of self-worth. Clearly it is a virtue to be secure enough in one's own selfhood that one can allow others to prevail in a contest of egos. Clearly this virtue helps lubricate the process of give and take that is so essential to the democratic political process. Is all compromise therefore desirable? Not necessarily. We have already noted that there are times when it is desirable to stand up for one's own rights as a way of protecting the rights of others. There are also compromises of principle that no Christian should consider virtuous. For example, to give public witness to values or beliefs one considers false as a way of maintaining power would be to lose the very reason for retaining power. During the 1950s a number of politicians in the American South signed declarations of support for the principle of racial segregation, even when they knew better, rather than lose office. Others, like the deeply Christian congressman Brooks Hays, recognized that this was a point where no compromise could possibly be consistent with the higher demands of love.

The kinds of compromises that are necessary to the democratic process involve the accommodation of power with power, where that is a preferable alternative to bloody confrontation.[19] In a democracy, one can always look forward to improving the present solutions. Moreover, compromises often involve recognition that one does not have all the answers. God may be speaking to and through one's political adversaries as well as through oneself. Compromise can pay tribute to the finitude of all human wisdom as well as to the prudence of avoiding the disintegration of the community over issues that are hardly worth such a price.

5. *Love is not irritable or resentful.* Irritability and resentfulness are personal characteristics that are not necessary in the support of great causes. Indeed, like arrogance and rudeness, they tend to get in the way of resolving objective political problems. Freedom from such personal "hang-ups" is a real contribution to group process.

---

[19]Even so committed a revolutionary as V. I. Lenin had a keen sense of the need for compromise, as his response to the more dogmatic "left-wing communists" in 1920 indicates. Defending his diplomatic compromises with European bourgeois politicians, Lenin remarks that "to reject compromises 'on principle,' to reject the permissibility of compromises in general, no matter of what kind, is childishness, which it is difficult even to consider seriously" (see Lenin's 'Left-Wing' Communism—An Infantile Disorder," in *The Lenin Anthology,* ed. Robert C. Tucker [New York and London: W. W. Norton & Co., 1975 (1920)], 563).

6. *Love does not rejoice at wrong, but rejoices in the right.* One of the most corrupting things in the political process is when politicians (or ordinary citizens) support or oppose particular policies not because of their merits but because of the political effects associated with winning or losing on the issue. "Rejoicing at wrong" might mean celebrating some evil if it helped defeat one's political adversaries. If, for example, an economic catastrophe might help unseat one's opponents who are currently in power, one might not want to join with them in preventing the catastrophe. On the other hand, the virtue of "rejoicing in the right" might lead those who are habitually constructive to join in common cause with political adversaries whenever possible for the public interest.

7. *Love bears all things . . . love endures all things.* A democratic society needs people who are fairly sturdy, who are not too fragile in the face of all the predictable abuse. Political leaders are likely to be treated as bloodless stereotypes by friends and foes alike, not as the truly vulnerable human beings they are. Most people who have taken political stands or run for office have been subjected to a certain amount of sheer hatred. Even if that were not so, they have to have a fairly high "frustration tolerance" in the face of defeats. To endure abuse and defeat because of a deep underlying love for those whom one's political action might serve can be an enormously important contribution in political life.

8. *Love believes all things.* This is not to make a virtue out of credulity! A Christian recognition of the realities of sin protects us from naivete. Perhaps a true sense of this is habitual faith in the possibility of good in human affairs. Love recognizes that people are sinners, but it also recognizes the possibilities of grace in the lives of individuals and the affairs of state. Such optimism, however qualified by realism, often appears naive. But as we noted above, history has often been changed by people who saw possibilities where others were only skeptical. A specific application of this point is one's attitude toward one's benighted adversaries. Believing that it is truly possible for people to change their minds is a positive contribution to political dialogue. Christian love, seen from this perspective, forms the habit of not writing people off.

9. *Love hopes all things.* In any event, loving people really *want* good things to happen, really *hope* they will. Love is consistent with realism about the tragic reality of sin, but love is utterly inconsistent with cynicism and despair. Christians do not abandon their hopes within history because they are formed by the larger hope set beyond history. They know that particular causes are rarely

successful at first blush and that, even when successful, particular achievements of justice and goodness in human affairs fall short of the ultimate good. Nevertheless, believing in the power of the ultimate good, Christians who are formed by hope do not despair of relative possibilities within history.

THE REALITY AND
APPEARANCE OF VIRTUE

We should perhaps remind ourselves that political wisdom cannot be inferred from the existence of Christian character alone—nor political folly purely from the absence of Christian character, for that matter. But democratic process does depend upon certain disciplines, and this discussion of Christian virtue may suggest what an important resource to any democratic society can be afforded by the presence of persons of genuine Christian character.

We must also remind ourselves that not everything that appears virtuous really is. Earlier we took note of Machiavelli's observation that the prince must always appear to be virtuous—but that the appearance is more important than the reality. We must here reverse that proposition and say that in a democratic society the reality is more important than the appearance. The more important Christian institutions and practices are to a culture, the more likely it is that contenders for popular approval and public power will clothe themselves in Christian appearances. In such a culture, public piety may readily substitute for deep theological integrity. Participation in "prayer breakfasts," while genuine with some, may be manipulative with others. Church attendance can be the dues one pays for political success. (One successful U.S. presidential candidate, not previously a church member, is alleged to have remarked upon having decided to stand for office: "Hell, I guess this means I've got to join a church.") Surely an equivalent situation existed in the culture known to Jesus of Nazareth, who warned his followers in language open to political as well as personal application: "And when you pray, you must not be like the hypocrites; for they love to stand and pray in the synagogues and at the street corners, that they may be seen by men. Truly, I say to you, they have received their reward" (Matt. 6:5–6). Instead, persons of integrity will pray privately to God and quietly receive God's blessings.

In this connection, it is interesting that the U.S. president most widely acclaimed (in retrospect) as embodying Christian virtue was one out of very few in all U.S. history who did not belong to a church!

While Abraham Lincoln was not formally a church member, he did attend services, and he did employ theological language—though clearly not for the cheap effects. For all his imperfections, of which he was possibly more aware even than his critics, his was a deeply formed character. The contrast between such a character and the outward piety of many political opportunists is instructive. Obviously, I do not record such thoughts in criticism of professions of faith and church membership by public figures. But if there is no connection between the forms of piety and the expressions of leadership, the integrity of both may be called into question.

The concluding comment in what must necessarily be an incomplete discussion should therefore be the scriptural reminder that Christian disciples are called to "be wise as serpents and innocent as doves" (Matt. 10:16). Such wisdom and such innocence are enduring contributions to the democratic polity under discussion here.

PART 4

Perennial Issues
in Christian Perspectives

Introduction

The political agenda, at any point in time, is crowded with many specific issues. They vary in importance and the length of time they command public attention. The public's attention span can, in fact, be rather short. A particular problem can burst on the scene, arouse intense public debate, be resolved or remain unresolved, while popular attention flits to some other subject. Some issues that appear crucial at the time this book is written may be nearly forgotten by the time it is published! But this lamentable fact is not a good reason for overlooking issues in such a book. Politics is, in large measure, about issues, and we must deal with them. In doing so, however, we do well to remember that some issues are broader and more enduring than others. For example, a particular approach to public welfare or unemployment might be debated vigorously at a particular time, then be resolved or forgotten with public focus moving on to other things. But the broader, enduring issues lying behind those debates have to do with the proper role of government in addressing economic life. Or, as another illustration, there might be great controversy over public sponsorship of particular religious observances (such as reciting prayers in public schools or placing religious symbols in public places at public expense). But here the more enduring issues have to do with the right way to conceive of the relationship between church and state. Or, as yet another illustration, a national debate might focus on particular disarmament approaches, while the deeper issues have to do with war and peace and with the question of nationalism itself.

It is not always easy to demarcate the line between the specific and transitory and the universal and enduring. But a book of this kind must lean toward the latter, while speaking of the former more as illustrative.

In the chapters that follow, I wish to consider some of the more perennial issues facing the public order in a modern democratic society. In doing so, it will prove impossible to avoid specific problems altogether, but these will serve as illustrations—and they will be chosen from other periods of history as well as our own. My intention is to serve the ongoing debate over public policy questions, including the issues of the future that cannot be anticipated here.

13

Church/State Relations

> Justice therefore forbids, and reason itself forbids, the State to be godless; or to adopt a line of action which would end in godlessness—namely, to treat the various religions (as they call them) alike, and to bestow upon them promiscuously equal rights and privileges. Since, then, the profession of one religion is necessary in the State, that religion must be professed which alone is true.
>
> —*Pope Leo XIII (1888)*[1]

> The right to religious freedom has its foundation in the very dignity of the human person, as this dignity is known through the revealed Word of God and by reason itself. This right of the human person to religious freedom is to be recognized in the constitutional law whereby society is governed. Thus it is to become a civil right.
>
> —*Second Vatican Council (1965)*[2]

As these two statements on religious liberty suggest, the relationships of church and state have been seen very differently by different people, even within the same ecclesial community. The earlier statement by Pope Leo XIII was grounded in a tradition holding that the state has a positive obligation to promote the true religion. The

---

[1]Pope Leo XIII, encyclical *Libertas Praestantissimum,* 1888.

[2]"Declaration on Religious Freedom," in *The Documents of Vatican II,* ed. Walter M. Abbott, S.J. (New York: Guild Press, America Press, Association Press, 1966), 679.

later one, reflecting deeper sensitivity to the pluralism of a shrinking world, speaks of the rights of all people, whatever their religious persuasion. Both statements are Roman Catholic, but both viewpoints (and other opinions as well) can be illustrated within many other religious communities. Sometimes the church views itself as the sole institutional embodiment of truth and goodness, and then it is indeed rational to seek special privileges from the state. But sometimes the church takes a broader view of God's redemptive purposes, recognizing the possibility that God may be at work in other religious groups, and then the church may prefer a neutral state.

DIFFERENCES OF NATIONAL TRADITION

Almost every conceivable relationship between religious groups and political authority can be illustrated historically—and many variations exist even within the contemporary world.[3] The complexity defies easy classification. But it may still help frame the broader issues for us to note four basic models of church/state relationship that have some importance in different parts of the world.

Theocracy

Here the state is under the control of religious leaders or institutions for essentially religious purposes. Theocracy can be illustrated by most primitive societies, by ancient Hebrew theocracy (particularly of the judges period), by traditional Tibet, by the Puritan establishments in colonial America, by early Mormon Utah, by Muslim territories at various times (including, to some extent, contemporary Iran). It can also be illustrated to some extent by medieval Catholicism and by modern Catholicism in some countries up to the time of Vatican II. It can be illustrated to some extent by Zionist Israel—although that country is *very* complex in its church/state patterns.

Erastianism

It is difficult to identify theocracy with certainty because what may appear to be a religious leadership controlling the state for religious purposes may, in fact, be exactly the opposite—political leadership controlling religion for purposes of state. As we noted in

---

[3]See Leo Pfeffer, *Church, State, and Freedom* (Boston: Beacon Press, 1953), or standard works in church history for historical material. See also *A Journal of Church and State* for contemporary information and analysis.

chapter 2 and elsewhere, religion is highly exploitable for political ends such as fostering unity within a society, providing a basis of legitimation for the state, and sanctioning war and other political policies. Most of the Roman emperors who commanded religious worship of themselves were not as vain as their decrees implied. They simply wished to foster some object of common loyalty within the empire that could be utilized to draw the diverse peoples into a politically workable unity. (The unwillingness of Christians to worship the emperors must have appeared as an act of treason or disloyalty to the commonwealth, not as an assertion of religious integrity.) The use of religion by the state has been termed "Erastianism" (after the sixteenth-century Swiss German Thomas Erastus, whose views are only loosely related to the attitude bearing his name). The Erastian approach of the state attempting to control the church has been followed to some extent by politicians in many countries who have sought, thereby, to advance political ends through religious means. It is especially evident wherever the state's control is legal or constitutional. Japanese Shinto worship was certainly more Erastian than theocratic, and that may be true of some of the Southeast Asian Buddhist societies. Joseph Stalin's sudden accommodation with the Russian Orthodox Church after the German invasion in 1941 owed more to his need for national unity at that time of crisis than to any softening of his generally hostile attitude toward religion. During World War I substantial efforts were made in the United States and other countries to rally religion behind the war effort. At certain periods of history, the English established church has taken on a largely Erastian relationship to the state.

Separation of Church and State—Friendly

In some countries, religious and political institutions have remained legally separate, but without hostility. Essentially that is true of the principle of separation in the United States. Despite the rhetoric of those calling for a closer relationship, the principle of the nonestablishment of religion in the U.S. Constitution is not to be understood as a negative one. I shall say more about this below, but nonestablishment can even be viewed as a positive support for the integrity and independence of religious bodies.

Separation of Church and State—Unfriendly

Decidedly unfriendly kinds of separation have developed, however, particularly in the last two centuries. French anticlericalism in the nineteenth century was of this sort. Anticlerical policies in

Mexico (where priests were forbidden to wear clerical garb) produced an unfriendly form of separationism. Most of the Marxist countries institutionalized a hostile stance toward religious institutions, perhaps most brutally expressed by the Constitution of Albania, which provided (before the end of the Cold War, of course) that

> The State recognizes no religion and supports and develops atheist propaganda for the purpose of implanting the scientific materialist world outlook in people. (Art. 36)

> The creation of any type of organization of a fascist, anti-democratic, religious or anti-socialist character is prohibited. (Art. 54)[4]

Albania aside, the unfriendly separationism of Marxist countries was not, even at the height of the Soviet empire, as absolute as commonly believed in the West. Indeed, in most such countries religious institutions, clergy, seminaries, and so on, were even provided with some public financing—along with a good deal of public control.[5] But the clear attitude in these countries was that religion is, at best, only to be tolerated until the populace has matured into a more scientific outlook. At century's end, religious groups continued to face difficulties (though not outright proscription) in the remaining Marxist countries.

In assessing the various national traditions it is important to bear in mind that actual practice can be very different from constitutional theory. Things are rarely all they seem to be. Moreover, what works in one society—with its unique historical traditions—may not work at all in another. And even in the most unlikely situations, Christians can somehow manage, bearing in mind that the blood of the martyrs is indeed often the seed of the church. Nevertheless, the unfriendly separation model is on the face of it contrary to what Christians hope for in civil society. The degree to which the state should support religious institutions and practices may be debatable. But it should not, in theological (and democratic) principle, be *opposed* to them.

---

[4]Quoted in Trevor Beeson, *Discretion and Valour: Religious Conditions in Russia and Eastern Europe,* rev. ed. (Philadelphia: Fortress Press, 1982), 322.

[5]Once, after I attended a worship service in Czechoslovakia during the period of the Cold War, the pastor apologized for not having invited me to preach. To have done so would have required a special governmental license; that was apparently only the tip of the iceberg of regulations under which churches had to function in that country. Preaching was the last thing on my mind that day, of course, but I joined the pastor in deploring the heavy-handed effort by the state to regulate the church's message.

THE ILLUSIONS OF THEOCRACY

Are there theological reasons for supporting one or more of the other models?

Theocracy has often been a peculiar temptation of people committed to a particular religious viewpoint. If one's religious perspective is true (and how many people believe their views to be false?), then why not enlist the powerful engine of state in its support? Few theologians have ever really thought it possible to force people to accept the faith. But state power can at least disable the competition and establish more favorable material conditions. That is exactly what happened in post-Constantinian Europe, where Christianity quickly changed from an occasionally harassed minority status into the dominant cultural force of the Roman Empire. State power did not exactly guarantee the spread of Christianity, but who would argue that it did not greatly facilitate it?

Few in our time suggest a wholesale theocratic union of church and state, but certain aspects of the theocratic model are indeed supported. Vestiges of the old religious establishment continue in a number of European and Latin American countries, whereby the established church receives by right certain benefits, not least the funding of clergy and certain public ceremonial rights. In the United States efforts are occasionally made by zealous evangelical Christians to have the nation constitutionally designated a "Christian nation" and to reintroduce religious observances in the public schools. While such largely symbolic actions fall far short of real theocracy, they do reveal a desire to give special political status to Christians. They may also reveal a latent desire to go as far in the direction of outright theocracy as the political climate will permit.

But that is a dangerous course for Christians to take. It is a way paved with illusions. Some of the illusions are practical and political. Those who seek to control the state for religious purposes sometimes discover, in the end, that it is the church, rather, that is being controlled by the state for political ends. The dividing line between theocracy and Erastianism is easily crossed, and it is the state that generally winds up in control.

There is also the practical problem of how to distinguish between sincere and insincere professions of faith in a society where a religious body has dominant power. Power has its rewards. How can the church tell the difference between those who profess faith out of pure religious devotion and those who are after the more mundane rewards? Ironically, that is the problem that confronted the

Communist party in many of the Marxist countries, where it paid to be a Marxist and where religious profession frequently led to social disability. For instance, young people wishing to enter universities and get on with their careers typically found they would do better as party members. So how was the party to know which young people joined out of their commitment to Marxism and which out of opportunism?[6] A theocratic state may proceed on the illusion that its many public supporters are religiously committed, when they may not be.

But the deeper illusion is theological. Theocracy exists on the supposition that the truth can be known well enough to make an a priori distinction between those who are "in the truth" and those who are not. The former are to be allowed to govern, the latter are legally disempowered. The illusion here is not simply that some of those appearing to be in the truth may only be opportunists taking advantage of the special privileges of believers. It is also that God, if God is truly the transcendent center and source of all being, cannot be *fully* known by *anybody*. To be sure, Christians hold their faith on the basis of beliefs about the transcendent God, and to exist in the faith they must be able to discern the character and purposes of God amidst the relative values and truth claims of a finite world. But a formal, legally established distinction between those who are and those who are not among the true followers of God denies the truth that may have been grasped by the outsiders.

In an earlier writing, I suggested that a reformed theological conception of the transcendent God helps establish a basis for the criticism of premature absolutes while at the same time creating a certain "expectancy" that the transcendent God may break in upon human society through *anybody*.[7] As we have already seen, this more open conception of God is a powerful general support for democracy. By the same token, it may be the strongest basis for rejection of theocracy, for theocracy has already decided who God can and cannot speak through.

---

[6]Sometimes the opportunists gain control from those who are more sophisticated intellectually and more deeply committed personally. In Czechoslovakia the genuinely committed Marxist philosopher Milan Machovec was dismissed from his university professorship and relegated to obscure library translation work after the collapse of the Czech reform movement of 1968.

[7]J. Philip Wogaman, *Protestant Faith and Religious Liberty* (New York and Nashville: Abingdon Press, 1967), especially chaps. 3 and 4.

THE IDOLATRIES OF ERASTIANISM

Similarly, the control of religious institutions by the state for political ends entails a formal rejection of the transcendence of God. The political ends themselves are absolutized. The state, in effect, becomes God—perhaps the most typical and at the same time most dangerous of idolatries. In our earlier discussion we noted that civil religion can be consistent with a transcendent conception of God—as in the utterances of Abraham Lincoln, where the state was understood to be under the judgment of God. Certainly Robert Bellah's call for a healthier civil religion is not Erastian, although he is concerned that there be a source of transcendent religious legitimation for the democratic state. For he, too, understands that the political order must stand under the judgment of God and not be a manipulator of religious institutions for purely temporal purposes: "Such symbolization [of an ultimate order] may be nothing more than the worship of the republic itself as the highest good, or it may be, as in the American case, the worship of a higher reality that upholds the standards the republic attempts to embody."[8]

When the state itself is treated as the highest good—as is usually the case with Erastianism—the integrity of religious organizations and institutions is fatally undermined. They can no longer be taken seriously in their own terms, that is, on the basis of the faith they profess. Now they are important only for their political utility. The loss of integrity seems obvious in extreme cases, such as the corruption of the "German Christian" movement by the Nazis in the 1930s, the control of the Church of England by King Henry VIII, or the political uses of the Dutch Reformed Church of South Africa in the era of apartheid. But Erastianism can also appear in small increments, with a gradual whittling away of the church's integrity. Episodically, the churches in the United States have occasionally been used by the state or individual politicians in this way, as in the use of churches to whip up enthusiasm for this or that war effort.[9] The current established church arrangement in England is hardly Erastian in the full sense of the term, but the church is legally

---

[8]Robert N. Bellah and Phillip E. Hammond, eds., *Varieties of Civil Religion* (New York: Harper & Row, 1982), 13.

[9]See Ray H. Abrams, *Preachers Present Arms* (New York: Round Table Press, 1933), for particularly egregious illustrations of the use of the pulpit to create support for a war effort (in America during World War I).

governed by Parliament, and the Crown is also constitutionally the head of the Church of England. To some extent, designation of top ecclesiastical leadership is subject to political forces outside the church, and even the liturgy is subject to those forces. In all countries where churches receive public, tax-supported funding, church decisions are to some extent subject to a broader political decision-making process with its own ends.

Some degree of Erastianism may in fact be unavoidable, for the church exists within society and will to some degree be governed by the state. That fact means that the integrity of the church must always be a matter for theological struggle. But full-blown Erastianism, with total control of churches by the state, is idolatrous in principle.

THE PRACTICAL IMPOSSIBILITY
OF TOTAL SEPARATION

The "friendly" version of separation of church and state is practiced to some extent in most of the Western democracies. It is an especially important part of the law and tradition of the United States, where the key constitutional provision is the requirement in the First Amendment that "Congress shall make no law respecting an establishment of religion, or prohibiting the free exercise thereof." That provision, which is the basis for the American tradition of "separation of church and state," has sometimes been interpreted in a very sweeping way. Thomas Jefferson's own interpretation, often repeated by other separationists, was contained in his famous letter to the Danbury Baptists Association:

> Believing with you that religion is a matter which lies solely between man and his God, that he owes account to none other for his faith or his worship, that the legislative powers of government reach actions only, and not opinions, I contemplate with sovereign reverence that act of the whole American people which declared that their legislature should "make no law respecting an establishment of religion, or prohibiting the free exercise thereof," thus building a wall of separation between church and state.[10]

---

[10]Quoted by Pfeffer, *Church, State, and Freedom,* 119.

The sweeping implications of the "wall of separation" metaphor (mistakenly regarded by many Americans to be a part of the Constitution itself) were developed by the U.S. Supreme Court in a 1947 decision holding that neither federal nor state governments "can pass laws which aid one religion, aid all religions, or prefer one religion over another."[11] Subsequent Supreme Court decisions have had to weave a somewhat torturous path in ruling on complex relationships between governmental and religious institutions. In doing so, the Court has not been able to follow the wall of separation metaphor literally. How could it? Church institutions exist as a part of society, occupying social and economic space. Public interests are bound to intersect with the temporal interests of religious institutions at many points. For the latter to be kept "separate" would imply the existence of a separate state with temporal as well as religious authority. The point may be clearer in the modern world than it was in Jefferson's time. The modern state has had to deal with issues in education, communication, health and welfare, commerce, and public safety that are far more extensive and complex than the requirements of two centuries ago. If the wall of separation metaphor were to be taken literally, it would serve as a bulldozer pushing more and more of the activities and interests of the churches out of the public sphere.[12] That might not be contrary to Jefferson's view. But his conception of religion as "a matter which lies solely between man and his God" is, from a theological standpoint, unacceptably individualistic. When religion is understood to be not only personal but social in its essential character, a "friendly" separation must be affirmative about its social as well as its individual expression.

Another point that is especially clear in a pluralistic society, where there can be very different kinds of religion, is that the state must supply a legal definition of religion. It may seem an unwarranted intrusion upon the internal integrity of a religious group for it to have to submit to definition by external legal authority—a gross violation of separation of church and state. But U.S. constitutional lawyer Charles M. Whelan is surely right in pointing out that the doctrine of separation itself would have no meaning if government had no way of knowing what a religion or "church" is. In order to

---

[11]*Everson v. Board of Education,* 330 U.S. 1 (1947).

[12]I have developed this theme more extensively in "The Changing Role of Government and the Myth of Separation," *A Journal of Church and State* (May 1963).

respect the First Amendment provisions, he writes, "government must also be able to recognize and articulate the basic differences between religion and other types of belief, and between religious practices and other forms of behavior."[13]

The problem is exquisitely difficult. Some religious leaders and theologians do not even like to be called "religious." Christian theologians Karl Barth and Hendrik Kraemer, among others, often distinguished between "Christian faith" and "religion"—reserving the latter designation for human efforts to find God and the former for grateful human response to the gift of faith resulting from God's reaching out to humanity in Jesus Christ. Presumably, however, both Barth and Kraemer—had they been citizens of the United States—would have wanted to include the witness and liturgical life of those exhibiting the faith as Christians under the protections of the First Amendment. And, no doubt, they would not have wanted government to harass "religious" people even though the latter have yet to yield themselves to the grace to be found in Jesus Christ. But the state, for its part, must be careful not to define "religion" in such a way as to create an opportunity for fraudulent exploitation of the law by persons or groups calling themselves "religious" only in order to take advantage of legal privileges peculiar to religion. (For example, if clergy are exempt from some kinds of taxes, it is always possible to form a new religious group to confer ordination for a small fee so the newly ordained "clergy" can enjoy the exemption. The law, for instance, might well require other evidence of how a religious group and its clergy are organized so as to fulfill their self-avowed religious precepts.)

Whelan notes, not surprisingly, that the U.S. government has not found it easy to define religion. In fact, there are different kinds of definition by different laws and different governmental agencies corresponding to different needs. Not surprisingly, the results are inconsistent and often philosophically naive. But this is further evidence of the difficulty, even the impossibility, of maintaining total separation of church and state.

As observed above, the U.S. Constitution itself does not even use the term "separation." A kind of neutrality or separation is indeed implied by the First Amendment. But the principle articulated

---

[13]Charles M. Whelan, "Governmental Attempts to Define Church and Religion," in *The Uneasy Boundary: Church and State,* ed. Dean M. Kelley, The Annals of the American Academy of Political and Social Science, vol. 446 (November 1979): 33.

there is the *nonestablishment* of religion. The term "establishment," with a peculiar Western tradition lying behind it, refers to direct legal sponsorship or funding of religious institutions. The term "separation" poses philosophical and sociological problems which may not attach to the term "nonestablishment." Nonestablished churches are still related to government in a variety of ways, but they are not its creatures—they continue to have independent roots.

THE PRIMACY OF RELIGIOUS LIBERTY

The point of separation of church and state (or the nonestablishment of the churches) is partly to protect religious groups from being corrupted by Erastian schemes of various kinds and partly to preserve the freedom of religious expression of the people. In some respects these are distinct points. But if religious liberty is taken in its broadest sense, this is the value that is ultimately at stake.

There are two senses in which that is true, and both point to the central theological point we have been emphasizing in this chapter. In the first sense, it is a corruption of the transcendent religious point of reference of a religious body for its institutional life to be used by the state for political purposes. State purposes and religious purposes may coincide, but if control is in the hands of the state, the values informing the group may now effectively come from outside. The theological integrity of the group may be fatally compromised. The freedom of the people to hold and express their deeper religious faith may be, however subtly, diminished by the need to conform to other values (or, from the church's standpoint, idolatries). That kind of corrupting can be present in the midst of the most generous kinds of public support, for support rarely comes unencumbered by aspects of control.

The other sense in which religious liberty is involved is when one's own group is not included in special privileges accorded to others. Then one's taxes are used to support views and values one does not hold; one is in the position of being forced to contribute to the success of a religious viewpoint other than one's own, which, I take it, is what the denial of religious freedom always comes down to in one form or another. That may even be true if government scrupulously avoids harassing the religious group that is not receiving the public support. Even in such a relatively benign situation, those whose groups are excluded are forced to contribute to the ones receiving special privilege.

But is that not the inevitable consequence of democratic government? Are we not always placed in a position of having to accept and even support (with our taxes and our conformity to law) policies and programs with which we disagree?

That is indeed true of the give and take of democratic life. But there is an important difference between winning or losing on a particular action or policy of government that is the outcome of legitimate democratic procedures and having one's transcendent conception of the meaning and purpose of life defined as true or false by a political process. Actions and policies reflect answers to the question, What is to be *done?* They do not necessarily suggest an answer to the question, What is ultimately to be *believed?* When government begins to address the second question it tampers with the very essence of the political covenant itself. For the essence of the covenant is that equal persons, acting in the deepest integrity of their being, join in a common enterprise. The participants in a democratic covenant cannot be treated only as things; the transcendent life of each must be respected. Each is subject to the law, and as subject must act in conformity to what has been decided corporately. But each is also a citizen. And as a citizen each is copossessor of the sovereignty of the whole. As a citizen-sovereign, each must continue to be a channel of meaning and value to the group—not only subject to the imposed meanings and values of others. From that standpoint, incidentally, it is possible to agree with those who hold that religious liberty is the fundamental human right upon which all other rights finally rest.[14]

What then of the civil religion? Is that finally a violation of the religious integrity of those who do not accept it? It certainly can be, if it takes the form of a set of tenets to which all must subscribe or a set of rituals which all must observe. But I think the essence of a defensible civil religion (if one must use that term) is the commitment by most if not all of the people to the proposition that people do have transcendent meaning and that society can have purposes that truly do matter. Such a common body of conviction includes the affirmation of the bonds uniting people within society.

It is possible to disagree with such beliefs. But it would be difficult to disagree and at the same time to affirm the democratic political covenant. Or to put it differently, it would be difficult to disagree

---

[14]See especially H. Emil Brunner, *Justice and the Social Order* (New York: Harper & Brothers, 1945), 57.

with such beliefs while justifying one's privilege to disagree on the basis of the democratic covenant. The covenant itself presupposes the underlying belief one intends to deny.

Let us try to understand this concretely. There are some kinds of fundamentalist Christians, Muslims, Buddhists, Sikhs, and Marxists who are convinced that they alone have the truth and that those who disagree are absolutely, not just relatively, in error. Such people dwell in democratic as well as in authoritarian societies. They could not be expected to agree with the proposition that all people have access to the transcendent and that the potential contributions of all should be respected in the common life of society. In a democratic society such people should be free to express their views and practice their worship. But the very existence of such a society stands as a contradiction of their exclusivism. And such a society could not silence them without, in turn, denying itself.

This may suggest that there are some kinds of official public symbolization of religion that are acceptable in a democratic society and some that are not. It is not acceptable for the state to define the ultimate or to exhibit symbols of one religious group in preference to others. In that sense, Richard Neuhaus's "naked public square" must remain "naked" in a democratic society. But it is another matter for the state to provide a common life (a "public square") that is open to the religious expressions of any and all. If the essence of democracy is its openness to political debate, behind which lies a dialogue over what really matters in the common life, then it would seem essential for such provision to be made. In that sense the arena of public discourse does not have to be secularized, but it must be equally accessible to all.

The importance of these distinctions was brought home to me several years ago when I was asked to testify in a U.S. federal district court case on the propriety of an officially sponsored Christmas display (a manger scene) near the national Christmas tree in Washington, D.C. A sign erected at the site informed the public that the display was not to be taken by the viewer as a "religious" exhibit but only as a portrayal of a part of the nation's cultural heritage. Dealing with this as a theologian I found myself objecting on two counts. First, the sign was demeaning to the tradition of those of us for whom the birth of Jesus *was* a religiously meaningful thing. But second, I knew that any number of my fellow citizens—including Jews, Buddhists, and so on—were excluded by this symbolization of what the nation is all about. Their faith was symbolically relegated to secondary status. So I spoke against the display in court that day. But on the other hand, I could have no objection to space for such a display being provided on public land (within limits imposed by time, space, and common decency) for exhibits by *all* religious groups.

LIMITATIONS ON RELIGIOUS LIBERTY

Clearly everything that calls itself "religion" cannot enjoy absolute freedom in civil society. Too much has gone by the name of religion! When a cult group (such as Jim Jones's People's Temple or the more recent and tragic Heaven's Gate, both of which ended in mass suicide) endangers life and violates laws essential to public well-being, then it must be restrained. And there may be limits beyond which even a religious majority can go in imposing its peculiar scruples upon others.[15]

Some rights of religious expression may be more absolute than others. The right not to be required to affirm what one does not believe or to engage in liturgical practices to which one objects may constitute a near absolute. It is difficult to think of any circumstance justifying such a violation of human integrity, although it has been violated often enough. (Such a violation occurred in the United States when public school children were required to recite particular prayers whether they wished to or not and even when Jehovah's Witnesses children were required, against their will, to recite the pledge to the flag.) Under such circumstances, dissenters at least have the right to remain silent. And it is highly questionable whether the state should ever officially place its citizens in a position where they may feel great social pressure to conform in the expression of beliefs they do not hold.

At a somewhat lower, but still very important level, the right to express beliefs through speech and publication should enjoy a near-absolute status. The freedom to speak and write is fundamental to democracy, even apart from the religious content. Here some limitations might be required insofar as speech or writing can inflict palpable damage on others and endanger the community. Being cloaked in religious rhetoric, for example, might not preserve libelous speech from legal accountability. And the incitement of a mob

---

[15]In U.S. constitutional law the principle has been invoked that a law must have "a clearly secular legislative purpose." See *Committee for Public Education v. Nyquist,* 413 U.S. 756, 773, 93 S. Ct. 2955, 2965 (1973) and my discussion of this principle in "The Churches and Legislative Advocacy," in Kelley, *Uneasy Boundary,* 57–59.

to riot could be grounds for prosecution, even if only words were used. Still, the burden of proof should weigh heavily against the limitation of speech and writing.

At yet another level, actions motivated by religion might well claim *some* privilege, though not as much, since *any* action can claim religious motivation. On this score, the U.S. courts and Congress have had a difficult time establishing what exactly the rule should be. The courts initially held that religious motivation for actions—even illegal ones—creates a privilege unless the state can show that a compelling state interest cannot be accommodated without restricting such religiously motivated actions.[16] Subsequently, this was reversed by the U. S. Supreme Court, which ruled that Congress alone can establish such a principle. Congress did exactly that, in the Religious Freedom Restoration Act (RFRA). But that, too, was ruled out by the Supreme Court. Most recently, Congress has tried again. Where this will end, I do not know at this writing.

The principle behind RFRA (and the earlier court position) struck me as good policy and defensible law. It is usually possible for the state to make a showing of compelling interest when truly necessary. But the requirement at least grants a certain presumption in favor of religious motivation and thereby pays tribute to the importance of such motivation. It means that the state must accommodate religious practices and observances where it can.

These three levels (which we may term freedom of conscience, freedom of religious expression, and freedom for religious action) each present different problems, though each is important in its own way.

POLITICAL ADVOCACY
BY RELIGIOUS GROUPS

In the United States, the doctrine of separation of church and state is sometimes understood to mean that churches (and clergy) are legally prohibited from participating in political activity. Such a view would be a philosophical and sociological absurdity, and it has in fact been rejected explicitly by the U.S. Supreme Court in forceful language:

---

[16]See the U.S. Supreme Court decision, *Wisconsin v. Yoder,* 406 U.S. 205, 219–20 (1972).

Adherents of particular faiths and individual churches frequently take strong positions on public issues including, as
this case reveals in the several briefs amici, vigorous advocacy
of legal and constitutional positions. *Of course, churches as
much as secular bodies and private citizens have that right.*[17]

Indeed, there is no legal or philosophical reason why a church could
not even form a political party if it wished to do so—although in current U.S. law it would then confront loss of some forms of tax exemption. There may be sound theological reasons why churches
should not go that far, at least under normal circumstances. But
when they do they do not violate the democratic covenant. People
are always free to vote against such a party in the privacy of the
election booth. The fact of being a party is not the same thing as "establishment." A party's status attaches to the political process; it is
not an organ of government.

Short of becoming a political party, there are compelling reasons
that Christian churches should engage in the political process quite
vigorously. We have already addressed that question as a general
theological matter. But it may be helpful here to assess briefly the
different levels at which the church's political responsibility can be
exercised. We shall proceed from the most indirect and general to
the most direct and specific.

Level 1: Influencing the Ethos

At the most general level, churches engage in political advocacy
by influencing the spirit of the times out of which political actions
spring. Public policies and programs are directed toward the realization of cultural values, and anything that confirms or challenges
existing cultural values may have at least some political relevance.
Lincoln is supposed to have remarked to the clergy that the church
sets the boundaries within which politics has to function. That may
overstate the influence of the church, at least in our time. But certainly the church is one of the influences setting those boundaries.
When the American churches eventually affirmed the equal humanity before God of persons of color they created a profound tension between the faith of Christians and their participation in a
racially segregated society. Eventually large numbers of Chris-

---

[17]*Walz v. Tax Commission of the City of New York,* 379 U.S. 670, 90 S. Ct. 1409 (1970)
(emphasis added).

tians—probably a large majority—came to believe that racial segregation was contrary to their deeper values and beliefs. If they were black, they were emboldened to act more vigorously in the political arena to demand equal rights. If they were white, they were less disposed to resist those demands—and in many cases they joined black people in the struggle. Even without specific church action, then, the proclamation of certain values had deep political effects. More recently, a similar conflict arose in South Africa where even the Dutch Reformed Church, traditional religious bastion of support for apartheid, began to question the theological grounds for racism. What happens on that level, where the church confronts the ethos, has great political effect.

Casual readers of history may sometimes puzzle over the reasons that the theological platitudes of an earlier era could have gotten people so excited. The point is that *in context* the platitudes may have represented values and beliefs in sharp contradiction to existing laws, institutions, and political interests. The famous 1934 Barmen Declaration of the Confessing Church of early Nazi Germany does not read, today, like such a radical document. It says nothing about Hitler. It makes no comment about particular laws or proposed laws. It supports no candidate or party of opposition. But it declares that Jesus Christ is the only Word of God, to hear, trust, and obey—and that, *in context*, challenged the idolatries and totalitarian pretensions of the Nazi era. In that setting, any affirmation of a source of value and authority transcending the German state had political implications. The Barmen Declaration did not have much effect in the struggle against all that Hitler represented, but it certainly helped lay the groundwork for a more constructive political climate in the post-World War II era.

Regardless of what churches feel prompted to do more specifically about politics, their responsibility to address the ethos, the cultural values, the spirit of the times, is very clear.

Level 2: Educating the Church's Own Membership about Particular Issues

One of the problems in restricting political witness to the first level is that oftentimes the true meaning of beliefs and values is not clear apart from application to concrete circumstances. Sometimes it is possible for people to be committed to contradictory values if one set is vague enough. In understanding the proposition that all people are equal, it helps to say that people are equal regardless of race, gender, nationality, or economic circumstances. And it may help to indicate further, somewhat more concretely, what the implications of such beliefs and values would be in the way life is organized.

At this second level, the church accepts responsibility to relate its more general faith to particular political issues. Most modern churches have a whole array of educational techniques available to help them get on with this educational task, and sometimes this is backed up by impressive technical analysis of the issues themselves. In the early 1980s, the U.S. Catholic bishops developed impressive study documents on such issue areas as nuclear war and economic life. While these were designed to influence the wider public, the immediate audience was the church itself. Similar documents on political issues have been developed by other church bodies, though rarely with the same degree of sophistication. The presumption behind such study programs is that lay church members, once suitably informed, will act appropriately as citizens and political leaders. Such educational campaigns have, in fact, been effective. A widespread Protestant educational campaign in the U.S. during the last years of World War II helped prepare a climate of political acceptance for the United Nations. A thoughtful study program on race relations helped make a generation of Methodist women and young people a source for change in American race relations. Given the inherent power of ordinary people in the democratic political process, efforts to inform them on the factual and theological aspects of public issues can have importance in the long run.

Are there theological objections to this? I can see none. It could be objected that the churches run the risk of being wrong in their analysis of particular issues. But they can be wrong about *anything*, including their more basic statements of faith, their exegeses of scriptures, their portrayals of church history, or the implications of their canon law or liturgies. The church is a fallible human institution, populated and led by sinners of limited intelligence. It is God's "earthen vessel." If the church had to limit itself to actions and proclamations concerning which it could be certain, what could it do or say?

The objection is a good reminder, however, that in its analysis and education on political issues the church should inform itself as competently as possible. Indeed, the more controversial an issue is, the better prepared the church needs to be.

Level 3: Church Lobbying

Moving beyond the education of its own membership, churches can make direct attempts to influence public decision. Lobbying itself functions on several levels. The term conjures up images of paid lobbyists buttonholing legislators in the halls of Congress or Parliament, attempting to influence their votes on critical measures. Some church advocacy is indeed that direct, including testimony offered before legislative committees and the less-visible efforts to affect policy rulings by executive agencies and judicial rulings by the courts. A somewhat less direct, but often more effective technique is for the legislative advocate to alert a broad constituency to deluge legislators with communications on particular proposals. That can create the impression, sometimes the illusion, that the position advocated is supported by a vast public.[18]

What is to be said, theologically, about direct church lobbying of these kinds? In the process of joining directly in power struggles over issues, there is always some risk that those who lead the effort may become more oriented toward power per se or even corrupted by it. We have already discussed this in relation to the agenda of the religious right, but corruption is a matter of neither left nor right. There is also a possibility that people may become so caught up in the minutiae of particular policies or legislation that the broader picture is lost or that short-term gains are traded for long-term losses. The legislative process involves compromise—not a bad word, as we have seen. But there is some danger that the church, by advocating a bill or policy embodying compromise, may appear to support the bad aspects of the proposal as well as the good. Politicians are expected to do this and are honored if they do it well. But

---

[18]An acquaintance, who was engaged in religious lobbying with the U.S. Congress in the mid-1960s, provides an interesting illustration of this. While supporting an important bill in the War on Poverty program, the lobbyist encountered resistance from a key senator. The senator professed his personal support for the program, but noted that he had had nothing but opposition from constituents. The lobbyist spent several hours on the telephone and managed to generate a substantial flow of mail from the senator's state in support of the bill, whereupon the senator voted for the bill. The artificially generated support was not, however, very representative, and the senator's vote on the bill almost cost him the next election! Politicians do understand, however, that support or opposition for a particular measure may be very intensely concentrated in a relatively small group which is interested in *only* that measure. A majority may be opposed to the small group's position, but less intensely so. Sometimes the intense feelings of a small group matter more politically than the lukewarm feelings of the vast majority.

churches are expected to keep their message as clear and truthful as possible.

Furthermore, some kinds of lobbying (including the mass-mailing kinds) imply a kind of political threat. The message to a legislator is, If you do not vote with us on this bill we will oppose you in the next election. The appeal, thus, is to power as much as to the merits of the issue. In the United States, the early twentieth-century Prohibition movement often resorted to naked appeal to power, as did the late twentieth-century Right to Life movement. Both movements succeeded in removing uncooperative legislators from office. But that can be theologically troubling.

Such objections do mean that church lobbying should be done with great technical competence and maturity. People who are not thoroughly grounded in the faith and of unimpeachable integrity should not be entrusted by the church with that responsibility. Lobbying does entail compromise and it does involve power, often extending beyond the immediate issues themselves. Those who do it should be capable of seeing the wider picture and of conveying accurately where the compromises lie.

A refusal to undertake lobbying because of such objections may, however, suggest an illusory conception of the possible purity of the nonlobbying church. Just by existing as an institution the church is involved in compromises, some of them more hidden and possibly more serious than those entailed in legislative advocacy—including the patterns of church investments, property holdings, and employee relations, as well as the compromises over decision making within the life of the church itself.

I am concerned at another point. A democratic society urgently needs informed participation by groups having a broader, more disinterested view of the common good than the powerful organized interests populating the corridors of Parliament or Congress. The churches may be, often will be, wrong about public policy issues. But if their views are seriously grounded in theological perspective and informed by competent technical judgment, they have a contribution to make that is sorely needed. As corporate bodies, churches have a weight considerably greater than that of individual Christian citizens. As churches, they have greater objectivity than most other organized lobbies.

Level 4: Supporting Particular Candidates for Office

Churches, as such, rarely do this in the Western democracies. There is no reason in either theological or juridical principle why they should not if circumstances warrant it. In the United States, ethnic local churches have sometimes given direct support to candidates with the best records in civil rights. Historically, ethnic churches were the one form of social institution directly controlled by ethnic minority members, and it is not surprising that they should have played such a role.

An argument can be made that other churches should likewise support candidates with positive records on civil rights and other social justice issues. On the other side of the political spectrum, groups such as the Christian Coalition and Focus on the Family come very close to endorsing or opposing particular candidates and encouraging like-minded churches also to lend their support or opposition.

The problem is that a new complexity enters the political equation when the conflicting ambitions and careers of candidates are considered. And for all the difficulty of sorting out the complexities of political issues themselves, it is that much worse to have to judge the true character of aspirants for public leadership. Without ruling out this level of political involvement altogether, the burden of proof should weigh heavily against it.

Level 5: Becoming a Political Party

The existence of Christian Democratic parties in a number of European and Latin American countries attests that even this level of political involvement has some history—although such parties generally were formed by lay Christians acting in concert and not by the churches as such. Again, if circumstances seem to warrant it, there is no reason in democratic political theory why this cannot be done. But it remains problematical for the church to become a political power configuration, seeking to gain power for itself, installing its own people in office, and gathering in the rewards, even though the ends in view may be quite laudable. Political parties inevitably have to take positions partly on the basis of what will get the votes. Churches, when they take positions, should be free to advocate policies that may not persuade a majority of voters for years to come. Churches should also stand more aloof from the struggle of conflicting personal ambitions (though admittedly much of that already occurs within the churches themselves!) and remain in a position to minister to and influence people in all parties.

Again, one could conceive of extraordinary circumstances where a church should categorically condemn a particular party (such as the Nazis) or even become a party. But the circumstances should be truly extraordinary.

Level 6: Civil Disobedience

Here and there in earlier sections of this book, we have noted the possibility of Christian witness through acts of civil disobedience, particularly as it relates to the orientation of Christian pacifists. While such civil disobedience sometimes implies a view that the state is not legitimate, it can simply represent Christian conviction that a particular law or policy of state is so far out of line that the only effective Christian recourse is to disobey it. When Christians like Martin Luther King Jr. and his followers engage in civil disobedience the act is generally quite open, nonviolent, and with no attempt to evade the legal consequences. Under such discipline, civil disobedience can even be portrayed as a confirmation of the legitimate authority of the state—coupled with the strongest possible effort to induce those in authority to change objectionable policies. Such actions have generally been undertaken by Christians as individuals or in nonecclesial groups, though in principle there is no reason that a church as such could not engage in civil disobedience. Sometimes church groups have done so (for example, in the sanctuary movement of the late 1980s).

Sometimes civil disobedience is undertaken to establish that a specific law or ordinance is unconstitutional, in which case it may not prove to be civil disobedience after all. But what is one to say of the theological status of incontestably illegal behavior undertaken as Christian witness? It is, to be sure, a violation of the civil covenant. And since the civil covenant has important theological status, as we have seen especially in chapters 10 and 11, the presumption should be against civil disobedience. It should never be undertaken casually, as though the civil covenant had little moral claim upon Christian conscience. The fact that a given state policy or law embodies what one perceives to be evil may not be sufficient grounds to warrant breaking the law, since almost any law, custom, or policy is likely to embody *some* evil in this fallen world! The purpose of civil disobedience, when undertaken by Christians, is not to be pure. In *that* sense, nobody can be pure in this world. The purpose is rather to communicate, in the most urgent way, that the law or policy is unusually or egregiously contrary to Christian conscience, or to frustrate the effect of the law or policy when the human consequences are perceived to be deeply intolerable. The act should be reserved for unusual circumstances.

Should civil disobedience always be subject to the discipline of openness and willingness to accept the consequences of the action? That has become so generally accepted in the literature as a necessary condition of morally responsible civil disobedience that I must pause to dispute it. Normally, such a discipline does confirm respect for the legitimacy of civil authority. But some situations where civil disobedience is warranted may require secrecy for it to be effective. I have in mind the Underground Railway in pre-Civil War America, where openness would have defeated the purpose of attempting to aid runaway slaves from the South, or the more contemporary example of efforts by U.S. churches to provide sanctuary for illegal aliens fleeing oppressive conditions in Central America in the 1980s. These are exceptions, to be sure, but they make the point.

Level 7: Participating in Revolution

Each of the other levels implies the legitimacy of the democratic political order in which the church finds itself. This level alone does not. Revolution is the most serious level of political involvement because it entails a total reconstituting of the political covenant itself. For Christians it is also deeply serious because it typically entails resort to violence as well. Clearly, in the perspective of this book, revolution—and even violent revolution—can be undertaken by Christians only in truly extreme circumstances. Such circumstances of intolerable repression have existed historically. (Has there ever been a time when such circumstances did not exist somewhere on the face of the earth?) I am aware of situations, such as the civil war in Zimbabwe, where church groups cooperated with revolutionaries. And in several African and Latin American situations in the late twentieth century, individual Christians felt called, *as Christians*, to participate in revolution. We have already noted this as a theme in the writings of some of the liberation theologians. Some of the neo-conservatives accused the World Council of Churches of actively sponsoring revolution through its Programme to Combat Racism, a charge that is scarcely sustainable on the basis of fact.

But in any event, the church as such should be very cautious about embarking on such a course. It can champion human rights and the importance of participatory democracy, and that very advocacy can align it with revolutionaries if the old order is unwilling to change. But revolutionary causes tend to absolutize themselves, and the church must always be in a position to remind people that there is no absolute except God. Even the most promising revolution will yield disillusionment and need criticism. Even the forces of repression may contain some redeeming possibilities. The church may need to identify overall with the cause of the former, while still being in a position to help the latter yield with greater grace.

In the final analysis, the church is committed to political

involvement. It is a part of the civil society, as are all other groups. Whatever the state is doing at any time will involve the church as well as individual citizens, like it or not. This discussion of the various levels of church involvement cannot do justice to the complexities. But it does suggest the importance of weighing the complexities carefully at every stage.

RELIGION AND CIVIL DISCOURSE

These more or less formal principles may help religious groups sort out the different possible levels of political involvement, each with possibilities and limitations appropriate to different historical circumstances. Such principles do not quite tell us how religious groups should go about making their case in the public arena. The problem is especially important in a pluralistic society, where there are many different religious groups seeking to influence public debate and action and where, besides, many people are thoroughly secular in viewpoint. I believe the problem is also real in religiously homogeneous societies as well, for the dominant religious group must still be understood in order to be effective.

Two disciplines can helpfully be observed by religious groups as they seek to influence public policy. The first is that they should show respect for those who do not share their religious presuppositions. A religious group does not *have* to do that—and may fanatical churches or movements (in all religions) do *not* show such respect to those who are considered to be sinful, unjust, and wrong. In our time there have been both left- and right-wing versions of such incivility. The Christian perspective informing this book, however, bases such respect both upon love for others and upon humility before God. We hold the truth in clay jars, as the apostle Paul puts it; we do not necessarily have all the answers. We should respect those who disagree, partly because we love them and partly because in some respects they may be right and we may be wrong. Even if that is not the case, showing respect for others is often more effective politics. It definitely is more conducive to peace and harmony within the community.

There is a second discipline, suggested persuasively in a recent volume by Michael J. Perry. Those who seek to express the implications of their faith in the public arena should be able to provide secular reasons—not just an assertion of claims based upon their own special revelations. Writing in the context of the American Constitutional principle of nonestablishment of religion, Perry concludes that "neither citizens nor even legislators or other public officials

violate the nonestablishment norm by presenting religious arguments in public political debate, but that a political choice would violate the norm if no plausible secular argument supported it.[19]

Quite apart from the nonestablishment clause of the First Amendment to the U.S. Constitution, is this a good principle? Does it mean
that only the secular arguments really count, while the religious arguments are pious window dressing? I do not think so. Perry's point is
that the reasons we give when we seek to influence public policy and
events should *make sense* even to people who do not necessarily share
our faith perspective. We may believe that God has revealed to us,
more or less directly, what should be done. The question is, *why* has
God revealed this to us?

Theologically speaking, the secular issues facing us in the real
world are also profoundly related to our faith. Faith-based viewpoints can usually be translated into secular language, where they
can be argued up and down. For instance, my own faith entails grat-
itude for God's love and recognition that God loves all humanity, and
that all humanity is ultimately a single community or "family" to
God. That viewpoint is shared by many who are not Christians,
based upon the conclusions of other religious or philosophies. It is a
viewpoint that competes with extreme forms of individualism, such
as those proposed by an Ayn Rand or the libertarians. Ultimately it
can be defended on the basis of a whole lot of empirical observation.
To say, with John Donne, that "no man is an island" is very Christian, but it is not exclusively Christian. Vast political consequences
flow from such a religious base, but one does not have to argue the
case on the basis of a purely Christian assertion.

Any religion that is not totally other-worldly should be able to
"make sense" of its views. In doing so, the case for this as an attractive religion may become more persuasive as well.

CONFRONTING CHURCH/STATE ISSUES

There will always be new problems of church/state relations to
test every set of principles. In this chapter we have mainly sought
to locate principles on the basis of which new and recurring specific
issues might be addressed. At the beginning of the third millennium, the docket is crowded with many new and recurring problems

---

[19]Michael J. Perry, *Religion in Politics: Constitutional and Moral Perspectives* (New
York and Oxford: Oxford University Press, 1997), 6.

of church/state relationship in many countries. We do not know what new problems lie ahead, but it is safe to predict that there will be many unanticipated ones. When John C. Bennett wrote his thoughtful book *Christians and the State* forty years ago, the American landscape on church/state issues was dominated by the effects of Protestant/Catholic tensions. Issues such as religion in the public schools and the propriety of diplomatic recognition of the Vatican were fought out in the courts and legislative halls, with hidden stakes at deeper cultural levels. Vatican II ushered in a new ecumenical era largely removing the animus behind such issues. But new cultural realities in an increasingly pluralistic world have yielded new problems.

The deep anxieties experienced by many people confronting cultural changes of unprecedented magnitude have given rise to defensive fundamentalism in many parts of the world and within most of the great world religions. This in turn has led to new efforts by fundamentalists to shore up their threatened cultural positions with state power, leading in turn to a new crop of religious liberty problems. Meanwhile, the broader and deeper concerns for social justice, also unleashed in many parts of the world and within most of the great world religions, have put religious bodies on a collision course with the narrower interests of nationalism and political expediency. This, too, has given rise to new issues. The increased expression of pluralism and the rise of new cult groups (themselves often a product of cultural insecurity) confront even the most mature democracies with dilemmas.

In face of this, Christians do well to keep faith with a preference for a democratic political system, and within such a system to insist upon the deep respect for the transcending religious identity of every person. That will not automatically solve all the problems, but it provides a basis without which they cannot be solved. The Christian faith in the transcendent and caring God is deeply supportive of that basis.

14

The Economic Role and Responsibility of Government

> The political community must have the ultimate authority in handling economic power relationships.
> —*Walter G. Muelder (1953)*[1]

Muelder's words ring strangely in the ears of a generation schooled to believe that economics is a totally independent sphere of human life. Yet he writes from the grand tradition of political economy that was formative of this civilization. Neither the Greek philosophers nor the Hebrew prophets thought of economics as a self-contained aspect of civilized life. In the grand tradition economic life was understood to be accountable to the community—to its laws, to its customs, to its well-being. Ultimately, the rulers—such as they were—had to be concerned about the economic welfare of the society. What would Plato or Aristotle, Amos or Micah have made of the doctrine of laissez-faire, the notion that government should keep its hands off the economic sphere? What would they have thought of Adam Smith's strange notion that an "invisible hand" will guide the workings of the free market toward the public good when those who act in that market think only of their own self-interest? To be sure, Smith's free market did not exist in the ancient world, and the ringing denunciations of the prophets against riches and exploitation did not have modern capitalism in mind. But it seems inconceivable that the great philosophers or prophets would have accepted easily the notion that economic affairs should be conducted without accountability to the community as a whole.

---

[1]Walter G. Muelder, *Religion and Economic Responsibility* (New York: Charles Scribner's Sons, 1953), 169.

THE THEOLOGICAL CONTEXT

Seen through the eyes of faith, that community is the community or family of God. Every theological point that has been made in the preceding chapters is relevant to defining the character and disciplines of that community. It is rooted in the creative purposes of God and in God's gracious love. For it to find fulfillment, it must come to terms with those creative, loving purposes as well as with the reality of sin and the need to preserve communal life from moral disintegration. Clearly this means that the community must attend to the basic material necessities of life, without which people suffer and die. Christians are not unique in their hardheaded perception of this economic reality that has faced every human society throughout history. But they may have peculiar insight into the moral obligation to ensure that *all* people should have access to such necessities since *all* people alike belong to God and are encompassed by God's love.

Christians may also have unique theological insight into the economic significance of the doctrine of grace. If grace means that humanity is accepted by God despite its undeserving, that may also mean that fundamental economic necessities—the condition of our physical existence as human beings on earth—should not be made contingent upon anybody's conception of who does or who does not "deserve" to live.

Most people quickly grasp the importance of physical well-being, and reasonably compassionate people will not let their fellows suffer and die if there is anything that can be done to prevent it. But relatively few people seem aware of the intimate relationship between economic relationships and the moral or spiritual life of society. Yet insofar as economic life fosters greed or despair, it is spiritually dangerous. Insofar as it provides opportunities for people to be creative as stewards of the material world and their own talents, it contributes to spiritual fulfillment. And insofar as it helps provide a basis for constructive community participation, it helps facilitate what Christians take to be God's intentions for humanity as the family of God on earth.

THE ROLE OF GOVERNMENT

Such a theological perspective on economics does not, in itself, require any particular conception of the economic role of government. It is even conceivable that the perspective might be shared by people with widely diverse conceptions of government. Still, in the context of everything that has been said about government and democracy in this book thus far, one might well question whether economics should be placed outside the sphere of political accountability. To do so is to make an abrupt departure from the "grand tradition," as we have said; it is also to suggest that in this all-important sphere of human life, the community may not take on responsibility for its own life. It is more than questionable whether a society can be what Christian theological insight sees it to be if it detaches economic questions from the political process.

Such a detachment was virtually unthinkable until the relatively recent past. Indeed, economics did not even exist as a separate intellectual discipline or science until the early years of the Industrial Revolution, about two centuries ago. Then Adam Smith, David Ricardo, and other intellectual giants of early capitalism advanced the notion that independent private enterprise acting in a free market is the engine of ever-increasing prosperity for all. Government, to some extent, has been on the defensive ever since. Still, faced with the actual ups and downs of economic life in the industrial age, the people have often pressed government into an activist role in spite of capitalist doctrine. Muelder summarizes the problem:

> Left to itself, private economic activity will fluctuate, and when it contracts it is inevitable that there will be intervention of some sort. Thus, it is no longer a question of government versus no government; it is a question of the community accepting responsibility for the general welfare. Moreover, it is becoming more and more apparent that when official government keeps its hands off, there would still be the unofficial types of *de facto* government which have grown up within "private" economic structures, in big business, agriculture and the trade unions. These "private" spheres of control make collective decisions which deal with rights, wrongs and coercive remedies.[2]

Muelder's views, as expressed in the book from which this quotation is taken, were neither laissez-faire nor socialist. He argued the case for a "mixed economy" in which particular economic problems are solved privately or governmentally on the basis of what is pragmatically most appropriate. But the underlying criterion of the

---

[2]Ibid.

well-being of persons in community strongly reinforces the idea that the community itself must ultimately decide, using government as its political instrument.

This was a typical view in the 1950s, although Muelder's version was markedly more socialistic than those more common in the U.S. during the Eisenhower era.[3] In recent years, the mixed-economy Keynesian orientation has been challenged from both right and left. We have already noted this in characterizing the generating centers of liberation theology and neoconservatism. But the left, whatever its view of mixed-economy (or social-market) capitalism—which it generally despises—does not challenge the legitimacy and importance of a strong governmental role in economic life. To test that role, we have to turn to the libertarians of the right.

THE LIBERTARIAN CHALLENGE

Real libertarians, such as Robert Nozick, David Friedman, and Walter Block, reduce the economic role of government to the barest minimum. To them, it is a serious mistake to turn to government for solutions to economic problems; to them, government *is* the problem!

They express the point in both moral and technical terms. Morally, they consider it simple theft for government to tax the income or property of the people. That is particularly so when the resources of some are taken coercively by government to be given to others. Such transfer payments are just as larcenous as if one private group of citizens forcibly robbed another. Private citizens ought to be generous with the needy, but generosity cannot be forced upon people.[4] Underlying the conception that taxation is theft is the libertarian conception of property. Following John Locke,[5] they con-

---

[3]Note in particular the eleven volumes in the series on the Ethics and Economics of Society, sponsored by the National (previously Federal) Council of the Churches of Christ in the U.S.A., and written by a number of Christian ethicists, theologians, and business and labor leaders.

[4]President Ronald Reagan expressed something of this view in his famous remark that "the taxing power of government must be used to provide revenues for legitimate government purposes. It must not be used to regulate the economy or bring about social change." But Reagan, a pragmatist as well as an ideologue, accepted a good deal more governmental activity than the extreme libertarians.

[5]See John Locke, *Second Treatise on Civil Government* (1690).

sider property to be derived from labor. According to this view, property is created by the work of those who improve upon nature or, as Locke put it, mix their labor with nature. Once created, one kind of property can be exchanged for another, or it can be given away or passed on to others at one's death. But those who originally create the property are the ones who have the moral right to its use or disposal. For government to take it from them (or from their heirs) really just amounts to some people using the coercive power of government to rob other people. Most libertarians accept some government for the protection of property, though some, like David Friedman, do not even allow for taxation to support the police force or fire department. The more extreme libertarians insist that all such services, as well as highways and parks, must be maintained by private associations. To deprive people of the property they have created, or have exchanged for, or have been given, is theft—and the commandment against stealing is a moral absolute, even when it applies to the acts of government.

Libertarians support their views with technical economic arguments as well.[6] They conceive of the unregulated market as an intricate, self-adjusting mechanism for allocation of resources, accurate determination of costs and prices, provision of full employment, and overall creation of new wealth par excellence. The market, in their view, does a better job of "planning" than any government bureaucracy could possibly do. Government only impedes the free decision making of the real wealth creators, while also making it more difficult for consumers to order up and buy the goods and services they really want at the lowest possible prices. Libertarians attribute most economic difficulties to governmental interventions in the economy. To them, unemployment is a result of minimum-wage laws and governmental support for unions, housing shortages result from rent control and zoning regulations, inflation from governmental spending. A sluggish economy is, to them,

---

[6]Ludwig von Mises, F. A. von Hayek, and Milton Friedman have been particularly influential among libertarians (although Friedman's version of libertarianism is qualified at important points). See von Mises, *The Free and Prosperous Commonwealth: An Exposition of the Ideas of Classical Liberalism,* trans. Ralph Raico (Princeton: D. Van Nostrand, 1962 [1927]); idem, *The Ultimate Foundation of Economic Science: An Essay on Method* (Princeton: D. Van Nostrand, 1962); Friedrich A. von Hayek, *The Road to Serfdom* (Chicago: University of Chicago Press, 1944); idem, *The Constitution of Liberty* (Chicago: Henry Regnery, 1960); and Milton Friedman, *Capitalism and Freedom* (Chicago: University of Chicago Press, 1962).

caused by high taxes that take money for nonproductive public purposes that could have been invested in productive new ventures. Third World poverty is partly caused by policies inhibiting free trade and the investments of multinational corporations, and by foreign-aid programs that destroy local incentives, especially in agriculture.

Despite the germ of truth in some of this (all ideas contain *some* germ of truth), the debate over libertarianism is essentially a sterile one. Most people know intuitively that the extreme of dismantling *all* governmental economic activity would be terribly destructive. Most of the governmental policies and programs now criticized by libertarians came into being historically to correct the flaws in pure free-enterprise capitalism.[7] A case can be made that the trade policies of several nations had much to do with the Great Depression that swept the world in the 1930s. But it is also clear that it took governmental economic activism (some of it related to World War II) to mitigate the human suffering and finally bring the depression to an end. There is room for debate over particulars, but if the total sweeping agenda of the libertarians were to be adopted—with the abolition of all kinds of public programs, protections, facilities, and amenities—it would surely be a disaster of epic proportions.

Ironically, it may be that fact that keeps libertarianism alive as a philosophy. The fact that no society is ever likely to adopt the whole sweeping vision means that the libertarians will always be able to claim that it would work if only it were tried! Even a strong policy movement in that direction, such as in the 1980s by the Thatcher government in the United Kingdom or the Reagan administration in the United States, could be said by the libertarian purists to be fatally flawed by the unwillingness to go *all* the way. All economic problems can still be attributed to that alleged failure of nerve. Ideological absolutes of this kind are rarely ever faced with a full empirical test because people are generally wise enough not to adopt them in their absoluteness as public policy. Still, the libertarian absolute provides a helpful backdrop for a more positive consideration of the role of government in economic life.

---

[7]Karl Polanyi, in his insightful study of the origins of capitalism, *The Great Transformation* (Boston: Beacon Press, 1944), cites the enormous costs in human suffering attending the beginnings of the Industrial Revolution and the rise of capitalism in England. It is noteworthy that even in those early years government found it necessary to adopt policies and programs (such as the Speenhamland experiment, whereby the income of destitute people was subsidized by government) to reduce social dislocation and human misery.

THE DEFINITION AND PROTECTION OF PROPERTY

There is no better place to begin than with the question of property. That is the centerpiece of the libertarians' moral understanding of economic life. Libertarians are not alone in this, for property is involved in most legislation, and it is at the center of *every* economic philosophy. The libertarians in fact appear to understand everything about property except the first thing—what property is. Following Locke, they think property is a relationship people have with *things*. We have made a thing, and therefore it is ours; it would not even exist but for us, so who else could possibly lay claim upon it? And if we have made it, it is ours to give or sell or bequeath to somebody else—and then it is theirs. It is all very simple and absolute, our relationship to this thing that we have made, or bought, or had given to us, or received as an inheritance.

Of course, practically it is not so simple as all that. Some of what we have, such as land, was stolen at some point in time. And even if that were not so, it is extraordinarily difficult to determine exactly how any particular thing has come into being. If I pick up a piece of wood and with my pocketknife whittle it into a beautiful wood carving, I might be able to argue that this highly individualistic work of creation really did establish my absolute ownership—although even here I must not overlook the participation of the unknown hands that provided me with the necessary tool. Most objects are created through highly complex processes of production involving the cooperative work of large numbers of people. Free market enthusiasts argue that market transactions provide us with *exactly* the amount of wages corresponding *exactly* to the contribution we have made to this process and that with these wages (or the return of investments, etc.) we can purchase objects which are *exactly* ours.

The economic analysis standing behind this vision of reality is troublesome enough, but what stupendous *moral* claims must be made for such a conception to remain credible! One must take the gigantic step of assuming that each and every factor involved in the production of objects and in the allocation of wages has been properly accounted for and exactly rewarded. For if that is not so, then some unknown portion of what we "own" *really belongs to somebody else!* There had best be no market imperfections in the chain of circumstance yielding our present possessions, no thievery (indeed, no unearned governmental benefits!), no inaccurate calculations by employers of what we have earned and deserve.

Even if all this could be worked out with satisfactory exactitude, the conception of property would be superficial. For this absolute view of property pertains to a finite world. There is more than irony in the adage "you can't take it with you." No relationship between a person and an object can be absolute because it cannot be permanent—not even our relationship with our own body. So much less the objects outside ourselves where "moth and rust consume." The fitting biblical word to the absolute property claims of the libertarians may well be that spoken in one of the parables of Jesus: "Fool! This night your soul is required of you; and the things you have prepared, whose will they be?" (Luke 12:20). The point of the parable was not, I take it, that we should be sure to prepare a will prior to that night when our soul is required of us. The point was that there can be no absolute relationship between persons and things. Of course, the theological point underlying this is, in the opening words of Psalm 24, "The earth is the Lord's, and the fulness thereof, the world and those who dwell therein." Ultimately all things belong to God.

The theological point does not immediately settle the economic and political point. Granted that all things, and we ourselves, ultimately belong to God, how are *earthly* property questions to be resolved? I know of no serious thinker, Karl Marx included, who believes literally that there should be *no* property rights or that *all* things should be held in common. Marx did not oppose private property in consumer goods—and that would include considerably more than one's own personal toothbrush. Most writers on political economy, who are neither doctrinaire socialists nor libertarians, would include the possibility of some private ownership of productive assets as well as consumer goods. But we are concerned here with the *source* of property and how it is related to the state.

Walter Muelder's understanding of property rights is much more profound than that of the libertarians. He understands property to consist, not first in our relationship to things, but in our relationship to one another and to the community in respect to things. "Property," he writes, "is not primarily a relation of individual persons to material things, but of rightful claims of persons on each other with respect to some scarce value." He continues.

> A right is a moral claim of the person on the community for some value which is essential to the actualizing of personality, i.e., for the satisfaction of some common need in human nature. Property rights, then, have to do with moral claims of members of a community on each other, or of groups of persons on other groups, with respect to scarce instrumental values. For property rights to be effectively implemental

the community must make them legal, i.e., they are dependent for all practical purposes on government.[8]

Thus, as R. M. MacIver has put it, there is a sense in which "*it is
government that creates property.*"[9] Or more properly, it is the
community, acting through government, that determines what
property is. Property is first, then, a relationship we have with other
people and with the community as a whole, determining what
claims to "scarce values" will be respected and, in the event of
threat, protected.

Even a casual perusal of all the things that constitute property in
a modern society suggests just how relative all this is and how dependent upon the current state of the law. I may own my toothbrush
more or less absolutely, but my ownership of patents or copyrights,
of drilling rights, of air rights, of options to buy, of commodity fu-
tures, of a co-op apartment, of a second mortgage, of a tenured academic post, of a share in "community property," and so on, is all
much more complex and socially defined.

In the Hobbesian or even the Lockean "state of nature" each of us
lays claim to what is his or hers and defends it against marauders
privately as best we can in the war of each against all. In the political community, however, we create a common authority empowered
to protect the legal rights of each member of society. This obligation
to defend rights presupposes the need to define them, to determine
what is to be defended.

This is not to say that property rights as defined and defended by
the political community are *morally* the right ones. No person of
moral sensitivity would have much difficulty in locating seriously
objectionable property rights. It is the political community that defines and enforces a system of property rights and with it, one might
say, a whole economic order. But responsible citizens, including
Christians and their churches, have a moral obligation to subject
the property system to serious ethical scrutiny. Ultimately, the
property system will embody a community's whole system of values,
its whole understanding of the good life and the good community.
When communities in the past practiced chattel slavery, that spoke
volumes about their understanding of human life and relationship.

---

[8]Muelder, *Religion and Economic Responsibility*, 135–36.
[9]Quoted in ibid., 136. See R. M. MacIver, *The Web of Government* (New York: Macmillan Co., 1948), 126.

When medieval societies were structured hierarchically, with persons bound, more or less permanently, to inherited social roles and obligations and with property institutionalized accordingly, that, too, revealed a conception of social good. So, too, the modern capitalist or socialist state embodies a vision of what persons and societies ought to be.

Political societies typically are engaged in profound internal struggles over such issues, and the definition of property lies close to the heart of the struggle. It is no answer at all to say that this should be renounced as only a *political* struggle, as the libertarians seem to want us to do. That only returns the question to the Hobbesian jungle, in which naked power determines outcomes. Nor is it much of an answer to say that we have clear divine guidance about property in the Sixth Commandment. True enough, we ought not to steal. But first we must decide *what property is* before knowing that it is something that should not be stolen. The decision about such things must be taken by the community, although, as in all political decisions, the wisdom and morality of the decisions taken depend upon the deeper theological wisdom brought to bear.

For Christians, this necessarily means that the definition of property hinges upon what we believe God's intentions are for people and their communities.

THE RIGHT TO INCOME
AND EMPLOYMENT OPPORTUNITY

Here we must return to a question touched upon earlier: Should the "bill of rights" by which the rights of citizenship in a democratic society are established include specifically economic provisions? In addition to the formal rights of freedom of worship, speech, association, and the like, without which even majority rule is meaningless, should there be listed the right to the meeting of one's basic economic needs?

The point is raised in the 1987 Pastoral Letter on *Catholic Social Teaching and the U.S. Economy* issued by the Roman Catholic bishops of the United States. This far-reaching document posed the problem of economic rights in the context of the conditions necessary for meaningful participation in the life of the community. The ultimate criterion of economic justice is whether the economy enables all persons to be full participants. It is not enough to speak simply of civil and political rights, such as freedom of speech and worship. It is not enough for government to restrain itself from gross invasions of the dignity and freedom of its sovereign citizens. They also need to be empowered materially if their participation is to be more than abstract. Echoing Pope John XXIII's encyclical *Pacem in Terris* (1963) and the United Nations' Universal Declaration of Human Rights, the bishops call for both kinds of rights:

> Both kinds of rights call for positive action to create social and political institutions that enable all persons to become active members of society. Civil and political rights allow persons to participate freely in the public life of the community, for example, through free speech, assembly, and the vote. In democratic countries these rights have been secured through a long and vigorous history of creating the institutions of constitutional government. In seeking to secure the full range of social and economic rights today, a similar effort to shape new economic arrangements will be necessary.[10]

At the time of its publication, some of the bishops' critics made the obvious point that for such "positive rights" to be implemented, more is required than the governmental restraints implied by the civil liberties of the U.S. Constitution's Bill of Rights.[11] Any government at any time in history can, presumably, refrain from infringing upon freedom of speech and assembly so long as those in power are willing to run the attendant risks of being cast out of office. But economic rights depend upon the availability of material resources, job opportunities, and so on, for their fulfillment. The distinction is, of course, valid up to a point. But a right still represents a moral claim upon the community which the community recognizes and endeavors to honor. If there are economic preconditions to real participation in the life of the community, is it illogical for a democratic society to make the commitment to *do all in its power* to ensure the access of all its citizens to those preconditions?

I can even imagine a society defining such economic rights under circumstances of dire want—such as a communal decision made by

---

[10]*Economic Justice for All: Pastoral Letter on Catholic Social Teaching and the U.S. Economy* (Washington, D.C.: National Conference of Catholic Bishops, 1986), p. 43, para. 82.

[11]See, e.g., Walter Block, *The U.S. Bishops and Their Critics: An Economic and Ethical Perspective* (Vancouver, B.C.: Fraser Institute, 1986), 5–11, and Michael Novak, "Toward Consensus: Suggestions for Revising the First Draft, Part I," *Catholicism in Crisis* 3, no. 4 (March 1985): 7–16.

the occupants of a lifeboat on the high seas or a party of explorers in the wastelands of Antarctica to share and share alike from their meager resources. Apart from such a decision, freedom of speech or freedom of assembly would be as empty as the stomachs of those denied their fair share! Modern industrialized states all do, as a matter of practice (though not necessarily as a matter of constitutional principle), assure some kinds of economic entitlements to needy citizens. But rarely are these sufficient to ensure real continued participation by these citizens in the common life. What *is* sufficient for that end is legitimate focus for the ongoing debate of a democratic society. And the formal commitment by the state to do as much as possible of what is necessary, for which the U.S. Catholic bishops have called, is clearly consistent with the understanding of democracy outlined earlier in this volume.[12]

It should perhaps be emphasized that the form in which such economic rights are provided can at the same time be structured against abuse by those who seek the rights but not the responsibilities of citizenship. If sufficient income is necessary for community participation, then community participation can be made a condition of sufficient income. Whether welfare benefits should be accompanied by work requirements is a legitimate debate. There is something to be said for the provision of a dependable economic "floor" upon which everyone can stand, regardless of her or his own contribution to the society, especially if the state of the economy is such that the specifically economic contributions of people who are dependent upon this "floor" are not crucial to the common good. On the other hand, everybody needs to be an active participant by making *some* contribution to society, and for some otherwise demoralized people a definite work requirement can be a blessing in disguise. One could at least argue the importance of guaranteed job opportunity, with government functioning as employer of last re-

---

[12]In earlier works I have emphasized the criterion of community participation for governmental welfare policies and full employment programs (see J. Philip Wogaman, *Guaranteed Annual Income: The Moral Issues* [Nashville: Abingdon Press, 1968], and idem, *Economics and Ethics: A Christian Inquiry* [Philadelphia: Fortress Press, 1986]). This has implications for our understanding of poverty. Many people think of poverty simply as physical deprivation—when we do not have enough food, clothing, and shelter to provide for our basic physical needs. But poverty also has a relational dimension when we are deprived of enough economic goods to be able to function as regular members of the community. It is possible to be poor in either the physical or the relational sense or in both at the same time. But both are obviously important to Christians.

sort. These, again, are questions worthy of considerable debate. But the general principle of recognizing economic rights in a democratic constitutional order is to be supported. In a modern industrial society, basic income support and employment opportunity appear to be fundamental to everything else—the first to assure adequate life support, the second to be sure that all members of society have a definite role to play in making their own contributions.

The provision of a welfare "safety net" by government is, therefore, more than simple compassion for the needy. In a deeper sense, it is a safety net for all of us, for the community as a whole. A society containing impoverished, insecure, frustrated people is itself unhealthy. The distress of some lowers the moral tone of the community for all. All of us are diminished by the needless suffering of others; and if we do not experience the suffering of others as our own, it may be because we have allowed ourselves to become insensitive and superficial. The distress of some may even create peril for the rest. Angry, frustrated people sometimes do very irresponsible things, and even when they do not, their situation contributes to social pathologies of all kinds.[13]

In light of this, the American Welfare Reform Act of 1996 was, it seems to me, morally ambiguous. On the one hand, the Aid to Families with Dependent Children program was thoroughly unsatisfactory. It had kept far too many people in a pattern of dependency—in some cases stretching to a second or third generation—but at income levels incapable of lifting them out of poverty. There were differences among the states; some few were relatively liberal, while others were cruelly ungenerous. These differentials put too much pressure on the more generous states. There was little incentive for recipients to venture into the job market for themselves, unless they could anticipate immediate wages matching their welfare benefits—plus provide for child care and transportation. One did not have to be a libertarian to see problems in the system.

On the other hand, the formal commitment by the federal government to provide a safety net for the poor was broken. The work

---

[13]In a study conducted for the Joint Economic Committee of the U.S. Congress, M. Harvey Brenner discovered that each percentage increase in the official unemployment rate correlated with definite percentage increases in social pathologies: that is, 4.3 percent increases in new admissions to mental hospitals, 4.1 percent increases in the suicide rate, 4 percent increases in the prison population, and 5.7 percent increases in homicide (see *Estimating the Social Cost of National Economic Policy* [Washington, D.C.: U.S. Congress, Joint Economic Committee, 1976]).

requirements (mitigated, to be sure, for those utterly incapable of working) combined with a lifetime limit upon welfare benefits but not with a guarantee of work availability meant that, in principle, an individual or family could become absolutely destitute. As I write, empirical study of the results is not sufficient to make final judgments (that would be beyond the purview of this book in any case). It does appear that numbers of people have gained psychologically, socially, and economically from the pressure to be on their own. Fortunately, the reform experiment came in the midst of the longest economic boom in recent American history, and the "trickle-down" effect doubtless played a role in increasing job availability and wage levels. Nevertheless, it is disquieting that political leaders have measured the results mostly in terms of the reduction of welfare rolls and expenditures and not in terms of the reduction of poverty and hunger. Tens of millions of people continue to lack the economic basis for real participation in American society. My concern, to repeat the point, is with the responsibility of the whole society to assure the opportunity for all to be full participants.

THE MAINTENANCE
OF ECONOMIC STABILITY

From the outset, capitalism has been vulnerable to periodic economic crises—the alternating times of prosperity and recession in the business cycle. Marx made much of this in the nineteenth century, believing that the economic crises would continue to arrive at ten-year intervals, worsening with each cycle until finally the system would collapse. If he did not prove to be much of a prophet about the final demise of capitalism, it is not because there have been no subsequent economic crises. It is rather because government has managed to mitigate their severity. Marx observed the relationship between such crises and the glut of products on the market for which demand had slackened. With the public unable or unwilling to buy the goods being produced, factories had to curtail production and workers had to be laid off. This, in turn, meant that workers had less money with which to buy the available goods, thus further contributing to economic recession in a vicious circle. Marx's somewhat intricate account of this in relation to "surplus value" need not detain us here. The point is that he did correctly observe that economic crisis occurs when there is not sufficient purchasing power available to absorb the goods being produced. One of the reasons that his predictions of the collapse of the system have not yet come to pass is that governments have found ways to counteract the lack of demand, either by monetary measures increasing the available purchasing power of the public or by such fiscal measures as increases in public spending or lowering of taxes. The Great Depression of the 1930s, probably the worst in capitalist history, finally came to an end in World War II, when full employment was ensured by government military procurement programs and the drafting of millions of persons into military service. The war was not created to end the depression, but it still demonstrated on a spectacular scale the effects of governmental fiscal policies in ending economic depressions.

Economic libertarians have contended, on the other hand, that business recessions are healthy and should be allowed to run their course. In their view, recessions signal a need to redirect economic resources away from forms of production that are inefficient or that no longer meet the felt needs of the buying public. Enterprises unable to adjust to changing needs should be allowed to fail, so their assets and employees can be put to work in more useful ways. Moreover, according to the libertarians, one need not fear long-lasting periods of recession in a free economy. There can be no permanent glut on the market. Every market will "clear" at *some* price. If there are too many automobiles for public demand to absorb, this only means that the prices must be lowered until all of the automobiles are sold. Some car makers will doubtless go out of business, but then their assets can be utilized by more efficient enterprises. So government, to the libertarians, should keep its hands off.

But whatever partial truth this laissez faire viewpoint might contain, the history of economic hard times over the past two centuries of the capitalist era does not support the thesis that things can simply be left to straighten themselves out. The prevailing wisdom of laissez-faire capitalism left ordinary people vulnerable to inordinate suffering. Governments would not have taken on the task of maintaining economic stability if there had been no need. A legitimate question may remain whether, in the long run, stability can be had on predominantly capitalist terms or whether greater degrees of socialism may be required. But the time is past when most people, including most economists, would be willing to entrust economic stability to the automatic workings of the market alone. In the Western European and North American countries, politicians are often voted in or out of office on the basis of current economic performance. Sometimes the specific economic circumstances are truly beyond the control of politicians. But the fact that their political fortunes are so largely dependent upon the economic well-being of the people at least means that it is widely believed that politics *does* affect the cycles of prosperity and recession. In this, the public reacts on the basis of a good deal of actual historical memory.

THE REGULATION OF COMMERCE

Classical laissez-faire capitalist theory relied heavily upon competition. Enterprises are made more efficient because they must compete with other enterprises in the same market. They must keep their costs as low as possible and the quality of their goods and services as high as possible in order to present the consumer with a better product at a lower price than their competitors. Enterprises persistently failing in such competition go bankrupt in the long run.

But this depends upon the actual existence of competition. Around the turn of the century, it became apparent in the United States that it is possible for powerful companies to act "in restraint of trade." They could form alliances with other major companies to set prices and allocate shares of the market. They could combine into "trusts," creating monopolies in given markets or forcing suppliers, freight carriers, and retailers to give them special advantages. They could muscle-out potential competitors by underpricing them long enough to make them go bankrupt, then raising prices again. Responding to the growing problem of monopolies, a number of antitrust laws (beginning with the Sherman Anti-Trust Act of 1890) were enacted to help preserve real competition. While enforced with greater or lesser degrees of enthusiasm through the years, the principle has been well established that it is proper for government to regulate commerce in this way.[14]

Even today such regulation is not accepted by everyone. George Gilder argues, for instance, that "without the aid of government, protecting patents or otherwise excluding competitors, . . . monopoly positions tend to be short-lived." This is because even the most complete monopoly must live in fear of *potential* competitors.

> The monopoly positions . . . are not at all unlimited, because they are always held—unless government intercedes to enforce them—under the threat of potential competitors and

---

[14]See Paul Samuelson, *Economics,* 9th ed. (New York: McGraw-Hill, 1973), chap. 26, for a historical and technical account of governmental antitrust policy.

substitutes at home or abroad. To the question of how many companies an industry needs in order to be competitive, economist Arthur Laffer answers: one. It will compete against the threat of future rivals. Its monopoly can be maintained only as long as the price is kept low enough to exclude others.[15]

Monopoly can, in his judgment, be a good thing: "The more dynamic and inventive an economy, the more monopolies it will engender.... A rapidly developing system will be full of monopolies as new industries repeatedly crop up and have a lucrative run before the competition can emerge and catch up, benefiting from the advantages of imitation." Sometimes even that period of monopoly, when a new industry is having a "lucrative run," can be beneficial: "Every now and then a company like IBM or Polaroid will get such a lead and exploit it so efficiently that it retains dominance for decades, to the great benefit of the country."[16] Gilder doubtless would apply the same optimism to the nation's experience with Microsoft, despite evidence that by the end of the 1990s that corporation had used its market position with some essential software products in such a way as to (some would say, ruthlessly) inhibit sales of even superior software products of rival companies.

There is no doubt some truth in views like Gilder's. But we are being asked to accept, almost as a canon of faith, that a free market will *always* be competitive even in the presence of large-scale monopoly. Is that not a rather large leap of faith? What are we to make of the kind of small-scale monopoly represented by the company town, where all land, housing, community facilities, and employment opportunities are controlled by a single company, and where the "company store" symbolizes the de facto absence of competition? Presumably people can always choose to live and work elsewhere, but, practically speaking, that was not the experience of thousands of people in the textile mill towns of the Piedmont region nor of mine workers in Western mining towns. What would it mean for a single monopoly to control utilities or vital communications or other necessities? Would the mere threat of potential competition be enough to hold corporate greed in check?

John Kenneth Galbraith's stress on the importance of countervailing power in economic life retains its point.[17] Galbraith under-

---

[15]George Gilder, *Wealth and Poverty* (New York: Basic Books, 1981), 38.

[16]Ibid.

[17]John Kenneth Galbraith, *American Capitalism: The Concept of Countervailing Power* (Boston: Houghton Mifflin, 1952).

stood something of the subtlety of competitive forces in a free economy, including forms of competition that may counter the power of
an absolute monopoly—such as the countervailing power of organized suppliers or retailers. But he also understood the importance
of governmental regulation in which the whole public becomes,
through the activity of regulatory agencies, a countervailing power.
Most such agencies initially came into being in response to widely
felt need. Of course, this does not mean that all regulation is wise
nor that regulatory agencies themselves invariably serve the public interest. It does mean that regulation and regulatory agencies
are an inevitable feature of democratic societies. The people are en-
titled, in the final analysis, to control the main directions of economic life.

CONSUMER PROTECTION

Similar things must be said about consumer protection. The principle of caveat emptor is time-honored and, no doubt, to some extent
unavoidable in a market economy. Consumers cannot always be protected from their own folly, and the art of selling—from time immemorial—has always involved emphasis on the strong and not the
weak points of the object being sold. Market forces themselves offer
some protection over time. Businesses selling shoddy or dangerous
products are likely to acquire a bad reputation; firms with a better
reputation may find it easier to keep their customers over the long
haul. The great, almost worldwide popularity of such fast-food
chains as McDonald's probably owes much to public confidence in
the standardized quality, or at least safety, of the food—as well as
its low cost. Such enterprises must be very careful not to allow quality to drop too low, even in remote places, lest their overall reputa-
tions suffer.

But is such protection enough? A vast amount of economic activity is conducted by enterprises of small size and short duration. And
even though it may be in the long-run interest of great corporations
to provide dependable products, it may be in the *short-run* interest
of key individuals in such corporations to cut corners for immediate
rewards. Even were this not so, the competitive market will often
reward the corporations that cut costs by cutting corners. That point
was made by Elmer W. Johnson, a General Motors Corporation official, in the following comments on the effects of market competition on business ethics:

While GM management can exercise a considerable degree of discretion in attending to its responsibilities in areas involving important social interests, this autonomy is not without limits. The competitive market system very promptly penalizes and ultimately bankrupts the firm that would go very far in promoting social goals at the expense of private profit. Thus, when there are important social interests that the market fails to protect, even with the application of long-term enlightened corporate self-interest, management may have an obligation to support efficient government intervention or to cooperate with church and other groups to advance particular social reforms. . . . Management should then utilize its expertise and judgment in suggesting the best means for removing or overcoming competitive impediments to corporate social responsibility.[18]

A strong case can be made for governmental regulation to ensure product safety. Then every enterprise faces the same ground rules and none are rewarded for cutting corners with public health and safety. Those who live in parts of the world where standards of public health and safety are not high—or have traveled in such areas extensively—know what it means to have to face decisions about food, water, medicines, and even housing with great personal care.

While living in a Central American country some years ago, I recall watching with fascination the construction of a three-story apartment house. It was built of poured concrete, but with very little use of reinforcing steel. That fact, of course, could not be detected after the construction was finished. Indeed, the completed building was quite attractive and was obviously intended for well-to-do tenants. Would they think to check out the quality of the construction? Would they perish in the next earthquake in that earthquake-prone country? (As a matter of fact, thousands of people did perish in Managua, Nicaragua, and Mexico City earthquakes, in some cases because of the construction of buildings they were occupying.) No country can be made totally safe. And even normally safe food products or water supplies occasionally present unforeseen problems, as in the Tylenol poisoning incident in the United States. Such things cannot be entirely prevented. But would it be wise to dismantle the regulatory apparatus in countries with building codes, pure food

---

[18]Elmer W. Johnson, "How Corporations Balance Economic and Social Concerns," *Business and Society Review* 54 (Summer 1985): 13.

and drug laws, and other protections upon which the consuming public has come to depend?

In an informed and provocative discussion of consumer protection, Milton and Rose Friedman essentially called for the abolition of most consumer protection agencies.[19] They based their judgment partly on a selection of incidents where regulations had the opposite effects from those intended and partly on their conviction that an environment of free and informed choice is best for regulating all economic matters. They therefore opposed food and drug regulation, governmental certification of health-care practitioners, and public inspection of the safety of such products as toys and children's clothing. Even their quite libertarian approach would be open to governmental involvement at a key point, however—the possibility of lawsuits to recover damages from faulty or dangerous products. People who are injured can always sue, or if they die their families can sue. Presumably the fear of such suits is as great a restraint upon corporate misbehavior as actual regulation would be.

But I am not so sure. Regulation places the disinterested public presence in the picture *before* and not after the damage is done. Who of us is eager to risk death, comforted by the prospect that our families can sue the company that did us in? And who would want to argue that large-scale lawsuits are more efficient in their use of resources than preventive regulation?

ENVIRONMENTAL PROTECTION

Similar points can also be made about environmental protection. Elaborate theoretical schemes can be concocted to show that the free market can be used to assess environmental costs, with devices to ensure that those who pollute the atmosphere are fairly charged for these costs.[20] It may be an indication of the widely recognized success of the ecology movement that even people such as the Friedmans, who generally oppose governmental regulation, accept the importance of *some* governmental role in discouraging environmental pollution. Their ideas about charging fees for industrial pollution as a way of ascertaining true costs may be worth exploring. But the

---

[19]Milton Friedman and Rose Friedman, *Free to Choose: A Personal Statement* (New York: Harcourt Brace Jovanovich, 1980), chap. 7.

[20]See ibid.

important point is that it is in the public interest to protect the environment and that one way or another government must be a central actor in defining the problem and implementing its solution.

Governmental action is no doubt even more important than the Friedmans suppose. In their discussion of the relative claims of governmental regulation and reliance on market mechanisms, these writers assert that

> the imperfect market may, after all, do as well or better than the imperfect government. . . . If we look not at rhetoric but at reality, the air is in general far cleaner and the water safer today than one hundred years ago. The air is cleaner and the water safer in the advanced countries of the world today than in the backward countries. Industrialization has raised new problems, but it has also provided the means to solve prior problems.[21]

There is some truth in the claim. But while industrialization may have provided the means to solve the problems it has created, it does not solve those problems automatically. If the air is cleaner and the water safer in the "advanced countries" today than one hundred years ago, it is largely because of vigorous governmental action. Left alone, polluting industries have no incentive other than simple good will to control their pollution. To the contrary, if control is costly they have an incentive to do nothing until required to do something. Even as early as the 1960s and 1970s it was becoming more and more apparent that automobile emissions were a major factor in global atmospheric pollution. Automobile manufacturers had no incentive to install emission control equipment on their products. The equipment is costly, increases fuel consumption, and decreases engine power. Similarly, buyers could hardly be expected to *choose* to buy, at higher prices, cars with such equipment. It took strong federal legislation in the United States to make auto emission equipment standard on all cars manufactured in or imported into this country. Along with stringent regulations governing the burning of high sulfur coal and other local and national regulations, such legislation has had much to do with improving the quality of air in the United States. Similar things could be said about the process of cleaning up the lakes and waterways in this and other countries.

Such actions have not happened automatically! It always takes

---

[21]Ibid., 208.

an aroused public and actions by courageous leaders to get things done. Some of the leaders, such as Ralph Nader, are sharply vilified by industrialists, but the results, years later, are what make it possible for people such as the Friedmans to speak of improvement.

A difficult dilemma remains. Developing nations often *are* the ones with the most severe environmental problems. Third World cities such as Bogotá, Lagos, Bangkok, and Mexico City are among the worst examples of atmospheric pollution in the world. In such places, the costs of environmental cleanup are just too great to be borne along with the costs of desperately needed industrial development. Should such countries insist upon environmental controls that match North America and Europe, only to watch their people starve?

The dilemma is not a purely local one. Neither air nor water stays in one place, nor can disease be limited to one place in our highly interdependent world. Bearing this fact in mind, it may increasingly be a matter of sheer self-interest for the more industrialized countries to help finance the environmental protection of poorer ones.

In any event, the role of government is crucial. Environmental protection simply will not happen if left to chance or to market forces alone.

DIRECT PROVISION
OF GOODS AND SERVICES

The foregoing suggests a number of points where the state is involved in economic activity. A brief discussion of this kind contains, of course, only the tip of the iceberg. The regulative and protective roles of modern government are complex and crucial to the well-being of people. We can expect that role to expand in years to come as economic life becomes ever more highly developed and, worldwide, more interdependent.

A serious debate has raged, almost from the beginning of the Industrial Revolution, over the proper role of government in the *direct* provision of goods and services. Libertarians have spoken their absolute No to this, while socialists of various kinds have asserted that government should finally own the means of production. Those who believe in a mixed economy argue, as the term suggests, for a mixture of private and public roles. Virtually all of the industrialized countries have mixed economies, though the particular mix of public and private varies from country to country. I can think of none that has no role at all for the public sector in the direct provision of goods and services.

Almost everywhere roads, parks, postal services, education, and harbors are maintained by government, though sometimes with co-existing private counterparts. Waste disposal is typically a public function, and frequently utilities such as gas, electricity, and water services are provided by governmental authorities. In many countries and localities, public transportation is maintained as a governmental responsibility; many countries—probably too many—have their own national airlines. A number of countries maintain health care services and some forms of insurance. Several assume primary responsibility for extractive industries, such as mining and the drilling of oil wells. Some governments participate in ownership of manufacturing industries, stopping short of total ownership or management. It is not unusual for public or quasi-public agencies to be involved in radio and television or even in the publication of newspapers.

The debate between the proponents of varying mixes of public and private economic activity will continue to rage for the foreseeable future—of that we can be sure.[22] We cannot enter fully into that here. But since this is a book on Christianity and politics, and since we have already noted the peculiar importance of democracy to a Christian perspective on political life, there is one question we must look at more closely: whether a predominance of capitalism or a predominance of socialism is necessary for democracy to work. In an earlier chapter, we observed that many of the neoconservatives consider capitalism necessary to democracy. Nowhere, they assert, do socialism and democracy coexist. While allowing that democratic socialism may be theoretically possible, the neoconservatives take the fact that it is not to be seen anywhere as warning that the union of political power with economic power may be fatal to democracy. But they overstate the point. The fact that a pure case of democratic socialism does not exist does not mean that there are no democratic countries with strongly socialistic elements (such as Sweden, the United Kingdom, Canada, France, and many more depending on how strongly the public sector must be emphasized to qualify as

---

[22]See Oliver F. Williams and John W. Houck, eds., *The Common Good and U.S. Capitalism* (Lanham, Md.: University Press of America, 1987), Walter Block, Geoffrey Brennan, and Kenneth Elzinga, eds., *Morality of the Market: Religious and Economic Perspectives* (Vancouver, B.C.: Fraser Institute, 1985), and J. Philip Wogaman, *The Great Economic Debate: An Ethical Analysis* (Philadelphia: Westminster Press, 1977), for essays exploring the ongoing debate among economic ideologies.

exhibiting "socialistic elements"). Is it not remarkable, in fact, that even publicly controlled radio and television can exist in countries such as the United Kingdom and Canada without compromising the integrity of democratic political life? There is already enough evidence of democratic control of combinations of economic and political power to make it too late to argue that this is not possible.

What about the opposite conclusion? Socialists have also argued that in the final analysis it is capitalism that is not consistent with democracy. Their side of the argument can be buttressed by the high costs of political campaigning in a democratic capitalist country, by the vulnerability of politicians to economic inducements offered by dominant commercial interests, by commercial control of the media of communication, and by the deep, interpenetrating relationships among public authorities, defense industries, and the military establishment in the "military-industrial complex." They argue that the constitutional forms of democracy do not reflect the substance of actual political power. Therefore, they conclude, it is *socialism* that is necessary to democracy.

But they, too, seem to overstate the case. Many of the concrete problems, such as the high cost of campaigning and free access to media, have been dealt with in some countries by specific reforms but without dismantling capitalism. And if capitalism were incompatible with democracy, it hardly seems possible that democratic political institutions could be used to hedge the power of major corporate interests. But that is exactly what has happened in many democracies with mixed economies. The auto industry has had to accept safety equipment and standards for emissions and fuel economy despite its vigorous opposition. Factory and mine owners have had to accept safeguards for worker health and safety and stringent standards for environmental protection. The whole business establishment has had to accept minimum-wage laws and regulations permitting, or even encouraging, unionization. In many countries, business leadership has had to accept the nationalization of certain industries or the participation of the state in the ownership or management of corporations. Would such measures have been possible if democratic governmental institutions were only a facade for moneyed interests? It could be argued that these measures are all reformist in character, and that they do not demonstrate the power of democratic government to effect *real* change. But such an argument assumes that the people *want* more sweeping changes. They may not. It can also be argued that some reforms, while stopping short of adopting out-and-out socialism, have indeed been quite fundamental. When President Franklin D. Roosevelt's reactionary opponents referred to him as a communist or a socialist they obviously exaggerated. But the vehemence of their attack left no doubt about their own perception that he was affecting the business system at its roots. How could that have been possible if he were merely a tool of the system?

Both socialists and capitalists can argue that their own preferred economic system would be more compatible with democracy than its alternatives. Such a debate is doubtless a useful one because it may encourage both capitalists and socialists to be more supportive of democracy than they have been. But in the final analysis we should face the truth that neither politics nor economics is simply reducible to the other. We have already seen that people are quite capable of making political decisions and acting politically on the basis of a whole range of possible human concerns, including but not limited to economic interests. It can also be argued that economic concerns of various kinds will appear and have to be dealt with regardless of the particular political order.

I am prepared to join Walter Muelder in saying that ultimate authority over the economic sphere must reside in the political order, particularly if the political order is democratic. On the evidence of recent years, I am also prepared to say that the market principle is also fundamentally important—certainly for sake of efficient and creative production and exchange but also to limit the future possibilities of totalitarian government. If the ultimate priority of the political over the economic is respected, we should be free to organize the economic life of the community in ways that best assure the fulfillment of those personal and communal values we find most fundamental. I suspect we shall continue to see different versions of the mixed economy in most countries for the foreseeable future.

ECONOMIC CHALLENGES
FOR THE TWENTY-FIRST CENTURY

As the world enters the twenty-first century, modern democratic governments are especially challenged at two points. While an adequate consideration of these points is well beyond the scope of this book, they are crucial enough at least to be noted.

The first, somewhat related to the previous section, is the high cost of electoral campaigning and the corruption of democracy that inevitably follows. A good democracy is always "one person, one vote," and on that score most modern democracies qualify. But what about the ability to *influence* those voters? For democracy to remain healthy, candidates and parties must be able to get their messages across. In local campaigns that can sometimes be done through low-cost forums, door-to-door canvassing, volunteer telephoning, and inexpensive mailings. But at the level of congressional or senatorial or gubernatorial elections—not to mention presidential elections—vast sums of money are required. As the statement by former senator Paul Simon (quoted earlier in this book) suggests, contributions buy access, and access spells disproportionate influence in the political process. The corruption may not involve the taking of bribes, but it is a corruption of the judgment of politicians and parties to become dependent upon centers of wealth. It seems to this observer that some form of public financing of electoral campaigns is the only way to avoid the corrupting influence of contributions and the time-consuming, demeaning requirements the quest for contributions place upon candidates and officeholders.

The other challenge lies in the sweeping changes in international economic activity. The world has become a very different place economically, and there is no going back. I greatly appreciate the moral sensitivities lying behind the effort by some to bring a halt to the growth in world trade, but it is like King Canute trying to hold back the sea! I am doubtful about M. Douglas Meeks's call for "a system of relatively self-sufficient markets in relatively small regions" as "an alternative to free trade."[23] An increase, not decrease, in trade is—it seems to me—precisely what is needed to level out the vast differences among the world's economies. That is happening already, very largely through the agency of large corporations capable of organizing production on a world scale in accordance with what economists call the "comparative advantage" of each region. In principle, that can be a very good thing, increasing the economic well-being of people everywhere and—among other things—lessening the pressures for migration from poor to rich countries.

In practice, it is not so simple. The regulatory protections typical of large industrialized countries such as those of North America, Europe, and East Asia are very imperfect when applied on a global scale. That includes protections against the marketing of harmful products (tobacco products, untested drugs, etc.) and ruinous envi-

---

[23]M. Douglas Meeks, "God's *Oikonomia* and the New World Economy," in Max L. Stackhouse, et al., *Christian Social Ethics in a Global Era* (Nashville: Abingdon Press, 1995), 121.

ronmental practices in countries without the power to resist. Perhaps even more it includes the exploitation of cheap labor with little prospect for the protection of labor unions and the enactment of laws defining minimum wages, benefits, and working conditions. In the long run, this may sort itself out, but there will also be vast suffering as a byproduct. An important task for caring people will be the exploration of more adequate systems of regulation, including improvements in regional free trade agreements such as NAFTA and in the World Trade Organization.

Part of the new economic reality for an America experiencing sustained high levels of prosperity is that American workers are competing more and more in a global labor market. The understandable tendency of American labor is often to resist further developments of free trade. On the whole I believe that is a mistake, partly because free trade has helped create millions of new jobs and partly because it neglects the needs of workers elsewhere in the world. Nevertheless, the labor movement in this and other countries faces a monumental challenge in the twenty-first century to forge more effective labor alliances worldwide and to be a political force seeking the enforcement of effective international standards. This is a very large subject; we ignore it at our peril.

15

Legislating Social Morality

> Morality cannot be legislated, but behavior can be regulated. Judicial decrees may not change the heart, but they can restrain the heartless. . . . The habits, if not the hearts of people, have been and are being altered everyday by legislative acts, judicial decisions and executive orders.
>
> —*Martin Luther King Jr. (1963)*[1]

This statement, written during the full flood of the civil rights movement, raises for us the question of what some have called "social engineering." Is it really possible for the state to determine patterns of social behavior? And if it is possible, is it proper?

King himself understood there are some limits, for he also wrote that the law cannot by itself change the inner attitudes of people. For interior change to occur, "something must touch the hearts and souls of men so that they will come together spiritually because it is natural and right." There is a "dark and demonic" side to human life that stands as a barrier to true social integration. And the "dark and demonic responses will be removed only as men are possessed by the invisible, inner law which etches on their hearts the conviction that all men are brothers and that love is mankind's most potent weapon for personal and social transformation."[2] The law, then, can regulate human *behavior,* but something more than law is required if *attitudes* are to be changed.

---

[1] Martin Luther King Jr., *A Testament of Hope: The Essential Writings of Martin Luther King, Jr.* (San Francisco: Harper & Row, 1986), 124.

[2] Ibid.

During the American civil rights struggle, King and other civil rights leaders worked on both fronts simultaneously. On the one hand, they sought to use the full power of the state to break down the institutions of racial segregation. On the other hand, they appealed to the conscience of the nation, seeking to change the fundamental attitudes of people. The first part of the project was vigorously rejected by those who felt that it is not the proper business of government to engage in regulating or trying to change social relationships. People holding such views—including numbers of church members and leaders—might agree that it is legitimate and desirable to try to change the way people think, but not by forcing them to behave in particular ways. King and his associates argued that the two approaches must go together. Later we shall discuss the particular issues posed by social discrimination. But first we must address the broader question: Is it really the proper business of the state to try to determine the pattern of social institutions and relationships?

THE THEOLOGICAL ISSUE

Clearly, Christians have theological views about those institutions and relationships. It truly matters how people relate to one another—how many pages of the Bible neglect to make *that* point? It also matters how institutions are structured, because social institutions deeply influence social relationships. Unjust, immoral institutions make it difficult for people to relate to one another in just and loving ways. On the other hand, institutions can embody justice and love.[3] Social institutions requiring persons of color to ride in the rear of the bus, use separate restroom facilities, and drink from different water fountains did not exactly *prohibit* loving human relationships between persons of different races in the American South of the "Jim Crow" era, but they made it very difficult. By the same token, institutions such as the family and school may not be able to *require* loving attitudes and behavior, but they can greatly facilitate them. Christians, as Christians, have every reason to want social

---

[3]Paul Ramsey made this point in his response to the "situation ethics" movement of the 1960s. Love (agape) is not simply present in a loving act. A "rule of practice" can also serve or embody love, so that those who act on the basis of the practice will normally express love whether or not they consciously intend to. See Ramsey, *Deeds and Rules in Christian Ethics* (New York: Charles Scribner's Sons, 1967), 133–42.

institutions that embody or at least encourage caring relationships and the fullest possible opportunity for all people to develop their creative potentialities as human beings. That is the kind of society Christians work and pray for.

Nor do Christians have general reasons for opposing an active role here by the state. The state is society acting as a whole. It cannot finally be neutral on the question of the shape and character of society itself. The state will tend to confirm or challenge the whole civilizational fabric. Those institutions it does not challenge or seek to modify will tend to be supported; those it wishes to change must be addressed by appropriate policies and actions. That in general is the situation.

But that does not mean that it is wise for the state to tamper with the whole fabric of social institutions, nor that it should be heavy-handed in confronting those it seeks to change. In exercising its role, the democratic state cannot avoid a dilemma: On the one hand, the basic character of society is a proper subject for the political dialogue and consequent decision and action. On the other hand, the people who are affected—like it or not—by the decisions of the state must have their freedom respected if it is truly a democratic state. We have already addressed this question in the different context of our discussion of democracy in chapter 11 and in the consideration of religious liberty in chapter 13. There it was apparent that a certain tension exists between the necessary respect for the transcendent freedom of every person and the necessary limitations implied by mutual acceptance of political outcomes that are arrived at democratically.

The rub is that people really are changed by what happens to their social institutions! That is why there is such a political struggle over them.

The dilemma is real. Actions fundamentally affecting social institutions and relationships do have the possibility of tampering with the transcendent freedom of persons which, as we have already seen, is an important part of the charter of the democratic political covenant. But democracy does not promise that its participants will not personally be affected by the democratic process and its outcomes; it does promise that they will remain free to express their views and to participate, along with others, in actual decision making. Both Christian theology and Christian history make clear that human beings can resist adopting un-Christian attitudes even when there is very great social or political pressure to do so.

The point must be registered because Christians have no reason to suppose they will always win in the political struggle to determine the character of basic social institutions and relationships. Even when they do "win" they sometimes wake up later to discover they were wrong, a point possibly illustrated by the U.S. experiment with prohibition. But the fallibility of Christian judgment and the possibility of political defeat should not inhibit Christian participation in this kind of political struggle. Political decisions do affect society, and those who care about social relationships and human well-being will not stand aloof.

DEFINING AND STRENGTHENING FAMILY LIFE

Those who think of social engineering as a recent and perverse invention should recall that the state has been involved in the definition and support of sexual relationships and family life as long as civil society has existed. Every society has customs governing such things, and most political communities have had legally enforceable regulations. Hebrew scripture contains stringent regulations governing relations between the sexes and between parents and children, with sanctions ranging to the ultimate penalty of death by stoning for those guilty of what were regarded as flagrant violations of approved patterns of relationship (see Deuteronomy 21–22 or Leviticus 18, 20). But while every society has had regulations governing sexual and familial relationships, the patterns and sanctions have of course varied widely. Ancient Israel accepted polygamy, as do a number of contemporary Arab and African states. Most contemporary societies do not. Most societies have made some provision for divorce, but not all. Premarital sexual intercourse is strictly forbidden in some societies but fully accepted in others. Education of the young is understood to be a parental responsibility in some societies, while in others the state exercises a virtual monopoly.

What kinds of social policies should be sought by Christians to govern sexual and familial patterns? Contrary to some stereotypes, Christian theology does not require a repressive attitude toward sex. Human sexuality is a powerful force, capable of both destructive effects and contributions to human fulfillment. But sex is a part of the created natural order of things, and it is a denial of the work of God the Creator to think of sex as intrinsically evil. The purpose of regulating this aspect of human life is not to keep it to the minimum! Indeed, the point of the state's involving itself at all is not so much the regulation of sexual activity for its own sake as it is the protection of persons and of the relationships upon which society depends.

Sex creates vulnerability. From time immemorial it has provided opportunity for the strong to exploit the weak, and it is the perennial responsibility of the just state to undergird the weak with the collective power of the whole community. Protection of women from threat of rape is a clear illustration of this responsibility, and is so regarded in most societies. Prostitution, which typically exploits the economic or psychological vulnerability of the persons involved, is usually either prohibited by law or tightly regulated. Sale of pornography is legally circumscribed in most societies, not just to preserve the morals of the community but to protect those who are exploited to provide the pornographic material. Insofar as such things involve what criminologists refer to as "victimless crimes," a case can be made for a more relaxed legal environment, although what appears to be "victimless" may not be when participants are dehumanized.

Societies vary widely in the extent of their regulation of such things. One can observe a kind of pendulum swing between more repressive and more libertarian policies as attitudes shift. We must expect that to continue. In recent years Western countries have experienced a reaction away from more tightly disciplined attitudes toward a more permissive cultural and legal environment. There is some evidence that the pendulum is in process of swinging back toward the more disciplined.[4] We can expect such pendulum swings to continue in the future as they have in the past. But the crucial issue for Christians will always be whether and how people are being hurt. When widespread social experimentation occurs, as in the great increases in premarital sexual activity and cohabitation before marriage, we can expect the movement to continue until it becomes clear that the experiments are dysfunctional. That was the reason for the failure of the communes of the 1970s, and since divorce is often dysfunctional for all concerned, I believe that the

---

[4]That certainly is the announced intention of right-wing evangelicals who have been preoccupied with issues of sexual morality in the last two decades of the twentieth century. Some of the rhetoric of these conservatives suggests they are still fighting battles that were largely "won" in the 1970s—an era of more widespread sexual experimentation. Still, there remains a brisk market in pornography, greater availability of pornography on the Internet, and (there is evidence to believe) more widespread practice of premarital sex. So the culture at the beginning of a new century is sending mixed signals, and it is hard to tell where the pendulum is.

presently high divorce rates will come down substantially in future years. We shall see.

The regulation of marital relationships is so universally practiced that one scarcely thinks of this as a political question at all. Yet the particular *forms* of regulation vary widely enough to reveal that this is also a matter of definite political policy. Here, too, the key questions have to do with the protections needed for personal well-being and social stability. For example, the issue of polygamy—long banned in most Western countries—carries erroneously the impression of sexual promiscuity attached to it. Actually, it has to do with whether women can receive equal respect in a society practicing polygamy. Such societies (which include long periods in the social history of ancient Israel) are generally male-dominated and women are expected to be submissive. A society committed to the equality of all persons could scarcely countenance social institutions in which women are intrinsically treated as inferior. Marriage is the most basic human relationship for most adults. Its stability matters for their own psychological security and well-being. The state, representing the whole community, can (and usually does) provide a broader undergirding for this stability. Wife and husband possess well-defined legal rights within the relationship. The state presumes the lifelong permanency of the marriage, and when marital relationships become troubled, the state's first objective is to try to save the marriage.

Divorce is permitted in most modern states, but it is rarely a casual process. Not infrequently, law calls for substantial cooling-off periods to protect both parties from impulsive decisions, and courts seek to provide counseling resources to try to save marriages. The bias, in other words, is definitely against divorce, although in most societies divorce is legally possible. That bias is also the Christian bias, so much so that a substantial body of Christian opinion (particularly in the Roman Catholic Church) opposes divorce altogether. To carry the bias that far is to neglect the reality of human suffering possible within a given marriage. People have found themselves locked into marriages with abusive spouses or with spouses who have lost every commitment to the marriage or with spouses who have simply deserted them. It seems less than compassionate to insist upon social policies making it utterly impossible for such people to dissolve the formal (it may be scarcely more than that) remaining marriage bond. Even in cases where neither spouse is abusive or disrespectful, it is questionable public policy to require spouses to maintain a marital union long after the will to do so is gone. But still, it is arguably good public policy to make divorce difficult, particularly when it is contested by one of the parties.

Most families at some stage include young children. Society has an enormous stake in how well children are nurtured and socialized. The state has particular responsibilities toward the young which we shall turn to next. But it should be noted here that children are particularly vulnerable in the breakup of family units. The bias of the state against divorce should be even greater in cases involving children, and in such cases the courts need to be particularly solicitous of the well-being of the children.

Such points, while obvious, remind us that the state is and must be deeply involved in the most basic social institution of all. Almost everybody, excluding only the most extreme libertarians, acknowledges such a role for the state. Beyond these minimal understandings, the role of the state with respect to the family can be highly controversial. What, for example, should the state's attitude be toward homosexuality or other nonmarital sexual relationships between consenting adults? For that matter, what should public policy be regarding committed unions of homosexual persons that are analogous to marriage? That has become an inflamed issue in many religious circles, with debates regarding legalization of such unions spilling into state and local politics. It is difficult to see why that should be so terribly controversial. If the key questions about sexual expression center on dependable interpersonal commitment that is mutually respectful and not promiscuous in character, it would seem that both church and state have an interest in promoting, not impeding, such unions. That would seem to be so particularly if (as many knowledgeable experts now believe) homosexual orientation is, at least for many people, neither chosen nor reversible. But even if same gender sexual relationships were regarded as sinful and not to be encouraged, stable unions would appear to be preferable to promiscuity. The issues are admittedly complex, but they illustrate very well the importance of the government's role in legislation on issues of social morality—and the difficulty of doing it well.

There are other issues that have consumed public attention in recent years. Should the state prohibit or regulate artificial forms of birth control, or should it operate public birth-control clinics? Should sexually active teenagers be provided with contraceptive aids, with or without the knowledge of their parents? Such questions often vex the modern community. Usually a plausible case can be made on either side of such issues, particularly if one accepts the assumptions of the protagonists. It would take us afield to venture into the debates on such issues here. It is interesting, though, that those who advocate the most regulative or repressive approach to such questions often do so out of a genuine concern for the well-being of family life and, perhaps, out of a fear that the acids of modernity are eating away at the familial foundations of contemporary civilization. Public policies based upon such free-floating anxieties can easily overshoot the mark. But the underlying belief that family life is important for persons and for a healthy civilization is surely well founded, and with it the notion that public policy should support and enhance family life wherever possible. In addition to the laws and policies directly governing marriage and family life, this has implications for some of the economic issues dealt with in the preceding chapter as well. Lack of income and job security and inadequate resources for basic familial needs have much to do with the erosion of family structure in contemporary society. (Of course, the reverse is also true: the erosion of family structure is an important cause of economic failure.)[5]

EDUCATING THE YOUNG

Next to the determination of basic family structure, the control of the education of young people may have more to do with the shaping of society than any other single thing. Is that a proper interest of the state? At one time it was generally believed that the state's responsibility for education should be limited to undergirding family life—it being assumed that education is primarily a parental re-

---

[5]George Gilder and Charles Murray, however, emphasize this point too much. In books widely heralded by economic conservatives and libertarians during the Reagan era, both authors sought to portray governmental welfare programs as the source of family disorganization while arguing that placing greater responsibility on the family would most effectively address the poverty problem. There is some truth in that. But neither author takes seriously enough the sheer financial inadequacy of federal income-maintenance programs, the disincentive to maintaining marital units built into the regulations of many state welfare programs (the "man in the house" rules), the work disincentive involved in not allowing welfare recipients to retain any earnings without losing welfare grants, and the unavailability of adequate employment at sufficient wage levels to provide for families. The real challenge is to make the programs more supportive of family life and productive citizenship. See G. Gilder, *Wealth and Poverty* (New York: Basic Books, 1981), and C. Murray, *Losing Ground: American Social Policy 1950–1980* (New York: Basic Books, 1984). I have addressed these issues more fully in *Economics and Ethics: A Christian Inquiry* (Philadelphia: Fortress Press, 1986).

sponsibility and not a concern of the state.[6] But it seems clear historically that universal education depends upon government. Prior to the middle of the nineteenth century, when the concept of universal free public education began to develop in North America, adequate education was largely limited to the offspring of wealthier parents.[7] Poor parents, themselves uneducated, simply lacked resources to secure a proper education for their children. Historically, churches also played a role here. But the churches of the postmedieval world themselves lacked sufficient resources to make education genuinely universal. If every child was to be educated, the state had to assume primary responsibility.

Profound issues lie just beneath the surface of this assumption of responsibility. Ultimately, to whom do the children belong? In the event of a conflict over the content of the educational experience, whose wishes should prevail? If parents have final responsibility, who is to protect the child from the cultural backwardness of those parents determined to ensure that the child not be exposed to the corruptions of modernity (some of which are not corruptions at all, except in the minds of the parents)? But, then, who is to say what is or is not culturally backward? And if the state is to have final responsibility, who is to protect the child from social standardization and the loss of his or her unique cultural heritage? And who is to determine what is desirable or undesirable standardization and what is valuable or useless in one's cultural heritage?

Some of these issues have played themselves out in the United States in the struggle over the education of Amish children. The Old Order Amish are tightly knit religious communities in rural areas of several states in the United States. Excellent and usually prosperous farmers, the Amish shun modern practices and technologies wherever possible. Amish areas are noted for the presence of horse-and-buggy transportation and the absence of radio and television

---

[6]Pope Pius XI stated this position classically in his encyclical *Divini Illius Magistri,* in which he observes that the family "holds directly from the Creator the mission and hence the right to educate the offspring, a right inalienable because inseparably joined to the strict obligation, a right anterior to any right whatever of civil society and of the State, and therefore inviolable on the part of any power on earth."

[7]While preceded by colonial common schools in many communities, the establishment of schools by the state to make education universally available for all children first appeared in the 1840s in Massachusetts, and by the end of the century was adopted as public policy in all states (along with the requirement of public school attendance prior to a specified age).

communication—and electricity, for that matter. They dress plainly, avoiding luxuries and the appearances of worldliness. They also seek, almost above all else, to determine the upbringing and education of their children. That has sometimes put them on a collision course with state authorities. In one 1965 incident in the state of Iowa, when Amish refused to send their children to the local public school, the question revolved around whether state-certified teachers could be secured for small Amish schools.[8] In another, finally resolved in the U.S. Supreme Court case *Wisconsin v. Yoder,*[9] the Amish refused to send their children to public schools beyond eighth grade (thereby defying the state law requiring school attendance up to age sixteen).

In such incidents, the claims of parents and the state are in stark conflict. In the Wisconsin case, the Amish claimed that for them to send their children to the public high school would "endanger their own salvation and that of their children."[10] The state authorities, on the other hand, were concerned about the rights of the children to be educated and equipped for life in the contemporary world. So the issue was joined: To whom, finally, do the children belong? Siding with the Amish parents in the Iowa case, Franklin Littell quoted from a 1951 statement by Pastor Lokies of Germany, who wrote, concerning children: "They don't belong to the state. They don't belong to the party. They belong to God, and under God to the family."[11]

Both Amish cases were resolved with some compromise, involving continued recognition of the state's responsibility to uphold specified educational standards, but with Amish parents having greater leeway in designation of teachers. But the question of *ultimate* responsibility for the education of children remains. Totalitarian societies do not hesitate to claim this ground for the state. Children are understood by them to be creatures of the state, to be socialized by the state for its (and their) own interests. But a democratic society has to wrestle more with the issue. On the one hand,

---

[8]Reports and commentary on this incident appear in *The Christian Century* 83 (February 23 and April 13, 1966).

[9]*Wisconsin v. Yoder,* 406 U.S. 227 (1971).

[10]Quoted in A. James Reichley, *Religion in American Public Life* (Washington, D.C.: Brookings Institution, 1985), 132.

[11]Quoted by Franklin H. Littell, "The State of Iowa vs. the Amish," *The Christian Century* 83, no. 8 (February 23, 1966): 235.

it must not undercut the nurturing base of family life and authentic cultural pluralism. On the other hand, it has a responsibility to protect the welfare of children and to prepare them for responsible citizenship. On the one hand, it must respect the transcendent character of each child's life ("they belong to God," as Pastor Lokies put it). But on the other hand, the state, too, has a role in preparing the child for a life of creative fulfillment.

The key question for Christians may well be whether Pastor Lokies is entirely accurate in saying that children belong "under God to the family." Most people would agree that that must be set aside in cases of child neglect or abuse, where the state must intervene and possibly even separate child from parents. But does not the state also have a responsibility to ensure that the education of children is not neglected? A democratic state cannot, by definition, be in the business of indoctrinating children for unthinking conformity to state decrees. But what of their preparation for the public dialogue and for responsible participation in the social and economic life of the community? Do children need to be made aware of the rich pluralism of society? Do they need to be exposed to existing bodies of knowledge about history and the physical world? Do they need to have opportunities for the development of their unique talents? And if the answer to such questions is in the affirmative (as I believe it should be), how is this to be reconciled with the claims of the family and unique cultural heritages?

Cultural pluralism is a precious asset to society at large, but contributions to cultural pluralism cannot be made by groups existing as totally isolated enclaves. A democratic society needs to provide a certain space for the existence of groups like the Amish, but it cannot absolutize that space. Seen in Christian perspective, the very fact that children belong to God means the democratic state cannot allow the claims of the family (or of a particular religious community) to be absolute. The democratic state is careful not to violate the integrity of the young. But it protects their long-run capacity to make their own judgments about their own cultural background, seen in light of other options. In other words, the democratic state not only refrains from making totalitarian claims over the lives of its children; it also prevents other groups in society from exerting totalitarian pressures upon the young.

To put the question in this way inevitably means that there must be a perpetual dialogue between state and parents and between state and the various cultural subgroups of society over the details of education. It is unthinkable in a democratic society that parents should have no influence on the education of their children. It is also unthinkable that they should absolutely determine the contents of that education, with no regard for educational standards tested by the whole community. Thus, for instance, parents have every right to review the textbooks their children are required to read and, where necessary, to seek changes. But on the other hand, educational authorities have the right to resist efforts to substitute cultural or religious bias for dependable scholarship.[12]

Both families and the state have important responsibility in the education of the young. Seen in Christian perspective, that responsibility is to help prepare the young for a life of responsible freedom. Where either family or state seek to foreclose such a future for the children by constricting their cultural horizons and not enlarging them, they should be resisted.

PREVENTION OF SOCIAL DISCRIMINATION

Social discrimination on the basis of race, ethnic background, or gender has a very long history. Prior to the twentieth century it existed as a little-questioned fact of life in many—perhaps most—societies. One reason why it was questioned so little is that such discrimination supplies its own justification. When groups are treated as inferior, their members provide evidence of inferiority: Deprived of adequate education, they will not be the educational equals of more favored groups; deprived of adequate income, they will dress shabbily or live in hovels; deprived of adequate medical care, they will appear to be physically inferior; deprived of self-esteem, they will appear subservient. Thus, black slaves and subsequent generations of segregated black people in America gave every appearance of social and intellectual inferiority. Thus, European Gypsy populations suffered unequal treatment and gave evidence to support the treatment. Thus, women in many cultures through history have

---

[12]Disputes over "creation science" erupted in several American states (notably Arkansas and Louisiana) in the 1970s and 1980s based upon parental objections to the teaching of evolution in public school science classes. Efforts were made in both states to require parallel teaching of creation science based on alleged evidence supporting the account of creation in the book of Genesis. The efforts were more successful in state legislatures than in the courts, which on review concluded that the teaching of science must be more rigorously accountable to scientific method than creation science could possibly be. One suspects that the last thing the proponents of creation science really wanted was rigorous application of scientific method.

314

been treated as unequal to men and, deprived of education and opportunity, were in many cases unable to keep up with men.

Sweeping social revolutions changed all this in the twentieth century. Part of the revolution has been scientific. The alleged inferiority of various racial and ethnic groups and women simply could not stand up before the contrary evidences accumulated by social scientists.[13] It has become increasingly difficult to justify discrimination on the basis of the superficial appearances of marginalized groups. Part of the revolution has come about through the increased contacts of the world's people in a century of increased trade, travel, and communication; part through the increased opportunities afforded by economic and technical development; part through the political and civil rights revolutions that have changed the civil status of more than a billion of the world's people.

The sweeping intellectual and political changes pose in a new way the question of the responsibility of the democratic state to protect people from social discrimination. It may not be premature to say that a near consensus that discrimination is wrong now exists among Christians. But the question can still be raised whether people can be forced by the state to behave in nondiscriminatory ways. The Christian objective for society is not just the absence of discrimination, but the fulfillment of genuine social integration. Christians seek a society of love, mutual support, and caring, in which the well-being and human fulfillment of each is the goal and celebration of all. The question is whether that can be achieved by the state or whether it depends upon the prior transformation (the moral conversion) of individuals.

We noted Martin Luther King Jr.'s comments on this at the beginning of the chapter. His distinction between "desegregation" and "integration" is to the point. The one represents the establishment of minimum standards of behavior to which all are expected to conform. The other represents positive caring and mutual interaction in what he elsewhere calls the "beloved community." King was well aware that the "beloved community" depends upon personal attitudes; he had no illusions that the needed changes of attitude can simply be legislated. In this he was doubtless right. He was also

---

[13]See especially Ashley Montagu, *Race and IQ* (New York and London: Oxford University Press, 1975), for definitive analysis of the spurious claims of racial and ethnic inequality. See also Arthur L. Caplan, *The Sociobiology Debate* (New York and San Francisco: Harper & Row, 1978).

doubtless right in insisting that whether or not personal attitudes ever change, all people have a right in a democratic society to be free of the overt injuries of social discrimination.

But more can be said about the relationship between the law and attitudes. One of the striking revelations of the civil rights changes in the United States from the 1950s on is that the attitudes of people often *follow* required behavioral changes. Desegregation of the armed forces, schools, public accommodations, and public transportation—while not exactly ushering in the beloved community—have led people to accept one another in new ways. It is easier to regard other persons as inferior if patterns of behavior are predicated upon their inferiority. But one tends to regard with respect those whom one is required to treat with respect. The law, therefore, has a teaching as well as a regulative function in social relations.

But how far can it go?

In principle, a democratic state appears fully justified in insisting upon the equal standing of all people before the law and in encouraging or even requiring nondiscrimination in those social and economic institutions that affect the ability of people to function normally and equally in the life of the community. But what about purely private institutions and associations? As a general principle, it could be argued that any institutions or associations receiving recognition or benefits from the state can and should be required to refrain from racial or ethnic discrimination, and that discrimination on the basis of gender should be required to bear a burden of proof to show that injury is not suffered by those excluded. Families which through the institution of marriage receive legal recognition can be excepted from this. But private schools and recreation clubs, which sprang up in the American South in an effort to avoid desegregation, are not good exceptions. The private schools, by being segregated, teach segregation. And recreation clubs, established in lieu of community-wide recreational facilities, are concretely divisive.

THE DILEMMA OF AFFIRMATIVE ACTION

In recent years the debate has moved beyond the prohibition of discrimination to the question of affirmative action. The question here is whether the state has a responsibility to require policies directly increasing the inclusiveness of institutions. Employers can be encouraged to seek out qualified women or members of racial or ethnic minority groups to overcome the effects of previous discrimination. Universities might give a special edge to such persons. Public schools might restructure enrollment patterns so as to achieve greater inclusiveness (the busing instituted in a number of American cities, sometimes under court order). The idea behind affirmative action is that it is not enough simply to terminate previous policies of discrimination since the negative effects of such policies will linger for many years. In order to achieve a real end to those effects, positive efforts must be undertaken.

The debate over affirmative action in the United States and Canada has been particularly complex and heated.[14] It has exposed a major dilemma facing any society attempting to rid itself of a legacy of discrimination. On the one hand, the effects of discrimination do linger on. Those effects include educational deprivation; lack of experience in many social roles; exclusion from the informal networks of friendship (the "old school ties") responsible for hiring, promotion, and leadership selection; and, above all, the low self-esteem perpetuated by years of being treated as unworthy. Elimination of overt discrimination makes it possible for outstanding members of a minority group to gain new opportunities, but it may leave most of the rest unaffected. The problem is particularly difficult in the case of competitive opportunities where minority group members are only given a chance to compete without discrimination against people who have never suffered discrimination. It can be very difficult to catch up if one must compete against those who have never suffered educational or experiential deprivation. That is one side of the picture.

The other is that affirmative action may itself deny opportunities to deserving individuals for no other reason than that they are not members of a minority group. This side of the dilemma was represented poignantly by the *Bakke* case, decided by the U.S. Supreme Court in 1978.[15] The case involved an applicant for admission to the medical school at the University of California at Davis. By all accounts, Allan Bakke was fully qualified for admission, with every promise of becoming a fine physician. He was denied admission, however, in order to make room in the incoming class for black candidates. The latter, though also fully qualified for admission, ranked lower than Bakke on the admission examination. So the

---

[14]See C. Eric Lincoln, *Race, Religion and the Continuing American Dilemma* (New York: Hill & Wang, 1984), for an excellent review of the affirmative action issue.

[15]Ibid., 206–21. Justice Blackmun, whose support for affirmative action went further than that of the Supreme Court as a whole, commented that "in order to get beyond racism we must take account of race. There is no other way. And in order to treat some persons equally, we must treat them differently" (p. 215).

university's affirmative action policy in effect denied Bakke an opportunity solely because of his *not* being a member of the minority group on whose behalf the policy existed. There were other complicating factors,[16] and the Supreme Court found a way both to allow Bakke's admission to the medical school and to reaffirm the concept of affirmative action (which it has also reaffirmed in subsequent decisions in other contexts). But, excluding the complicating factors, the *Bakke* case illustrates the dilemma of affirmative action: One cannot use this means of overcoming past discrimination without employing a different new form of discrimination against individuals who are in no way responsible for the past.

One way out of the dilemma is to define the problem solely as one of inclusiveness, thereby disregarding any moral claim a Bakke might have for equality of treatment. The difficulty with this is that everybody's equality before the law would be subordinated to their racial, ethnic, or gender status; this status would become the point of everybody's primary identity. Another way out of the dilemma is to disregard group status and past history altogether, within a new understanding of the state's obligation to be and to enforce equality of persons as individuals. The difficulty with this is that real equality will not be meaningful until the human effects of prior histories of discrimination have been erased.

Perhaps it is better to acknowledge that this is a real dilemma; that is, that both horns of the dilemma represent authentic moral claims. The history of discrimination against racial and ethnic minority groups and women is real and creates a moral claim upon the community for a rectification of the effects of that history. On the other hand, those who are not members of such groups still have a moral claim upon the community for equality of treatment. Both claims are valid in and of themselves.

A Christian communitarian perspective can help more than abstract moralism in resolving this dilemma. The real objective is a community in which all are accepted and valued regardless of gender, race, or ethnic considerations and where each person has the greatest possible encouragement and support in developing creative potentialities. Given the depth of the realities of past discrimination in many countries, not least the United States, policies and pro-

---

[16]One of the complicating factors was the fact that the dean of the medical school had long enjoyed the privilege of admitting a given number of applicants at his own discretion so long as they met basic minimal standards. Several of these admitted students, who were also white, had scores on the admission examination that were also below Bakke's!

grams need to move directly toward inclusion of the previously excluded. In the case of black people in the United States, for instance, there needs to be a substantial and visible *presence* where previously there has been little or none. That presence will be an encouragement to others, an improvement to the self-esteem of others, a visible sign to all that a new day has in fact arrived. To do this, affirmative action must sometimes contain a bias toward inclusion of those previously excluded—always with the understanding that it does not advance the cause of inclusiveness to place people in positions they are not even potentially capable of filling. Seen in Christian perspective, such affirmative action policies are really in *everybody's* interest, for all people gain from the inclusiveness of the community just as all people are injured by the oppression of any.

At the same time, it is best not to enshrine special privileges for minority groups or women in law or judicial precedent as though affirmative action were permanent public policy. In the *long* run, it is one's status as an individual in the wider community that confers one's rights within the community, not one's identity as part of a racial or ethnic group or as a woman or man. Affirmative action policies, while necessary for a transitional period, should be framed so as to disappear when they become unnecessary in overcoming the lingering effects of past discrimination. This may mean that laws and judicial rulings will have a certain element of openness and ambiguity about them during the time of transition.

AT THE FRONTIERS OF LIFE

Some of the most vexing problems facing modern politicians have resulted from new twentieth-century biological and demographic realities. The two are related. Demographically, the world has experienced a population explosion utterly without precedent in human history.[17] There are today at least four times as many people

---

[17]The "explosiveness" of twentieth century population growth is summarized by Lester R. Brown: "It took two million years for man's numbers to reach one billion [in the year 1830]. The second billion came in one hundred years [1930]. Successive billions came even faster. At the present rate of increase, the sixth billion will require less than a decade." At the time of publication of Brown's book in 1974, world population had reached nearly four billion. He predicted world population would reach five billion in 1986—which it did, like clockwork. World population grew from one-and-a-half to five billion since the beginning of the twentieth century. See Brown, *In the Human Interest: A Strategy to Stabilize World Population* (New York: W. W. Norton & Co., 1974), 20–27. At the end of the twentieth century, world population was estimated to be about six billion.

on earth as there were one hundred years ago, and it takes scarcely fifteen years to add a further billion to their number. This is related to biology through the enormous advances in medical science and food production that have alleviated disease and famine, greatly increasing average life expectancies. Meanwhile, medical science has greatly increased our understanding of human reproduction, while also making it possible to prolong physical existence beyond brain death.

Such developments pose new questions for the state. Should overall population size be subject to political debate and public policy decisions? During the Great Depression, when reproduction rates dropped, political leaders in some European countries became alarmed and adopted measures (such as family grants for children) designed to stimulate population growth. More recently, numbers of Third World countries and China have adopted measures of varying strictness designed to inhibit runaway population growth rates. Such policies suggest that there is an optimum population size, varying doubtless with geography, culture, and economic circumstance, and that it is a proper business of the state to define this and to try to achieve it. Against this, it is argued by many that reproductive decisions are strictly the business of individual families and that, in any case, population size will stabilize naturally where the basic needs and aspirations of people are met.[18]

This is not an easy subject to address theologically because there is so little biblical or historical precedent. Nevertheless, it is clear that population size, density, and growth rates can affect the well-being of a society as this is understood theologically. When population size and growth rates place too great a strain upon food supplies and other economic necessities, while also straining educational facilities, the fulfillment of human beings in communal life is threat-

---

[18]The debate over population stabilization enlivened both UN World Conferences on Population (Bucharest, 1974, and Mexico City, 1984). At the Bucharest Conference (which I attended), the U.S. delegation led the attempt to arouse the world to the imminent dangers of runaway population growth, especially in the Third World. The Chinese and Vatican delegations, seeking to counter this "neo-Malthusianism," were among those contending that population stabilization will occur without special measures when social justice has been achieved. By 1984 the Chinese and American positions had each essentially reversed, with the Chinese taking the more alarmist position and the Americans, now under the influence of the socially conservative Reagan administration, playing down the importance of a population problem. During the Clinton administration, U.S. policy shifted back.

ened whether or not their lives are endangered. The plight of Third World countries in the last quarter of the twentieth century is complex and subject to variable interpretation. But it is entirely plausible that rapid population growth rates in Asia, Africa, and Latin America have made it more difficult for the people of these regions and their communities.

As I have noted elsewhere, theology is not committed to the notion that the optimum number of people is the maximum number.[19] We live on a finite world because God has created it that way! The world could not possibly contain all the people who would have to be accommodated in the long run at present rates of growth. We can conclude, therefore, that there must be some stabilization point in population size—which inevitably means some limitation upon the number of lives brought into the world.

None of us knows exactly what that is. But is there sound reason for leaving that question entirely to the sum of the decisions reached by individual couples or for trusting that optimum population size will follow inevitably as a consequence of the attainment of social justice in general? Laissez-faire population policies may in the long run be as unhelpful as laissez-faire economics. It may be better for the democratic society to subject population size to public debate along with other matters of great consequence for the community's well-being. This does not imply use of draconian measures to guarantee limits. Instead, there is every reason for treating reproductive decision making with great sensitivity, even with reverence. But while prospective parents are the ones most immediately affected by such decisions, the rest of society is also affected and can, through the democratic state, play a legitimate role in setting some policy framework.

Politicians have also been vexed by problems at the frontiers of life—the question of when life begins, on which the debates over abortion so often center and the question of when life ends, on which debates over euthanasia and organ transplants often center. Some of these debates have been deeply acrimonious—particularly those dealing with abortion—and it is beyond our means to resolve them here beyond acknowledging that these are also legitimate matters

---

[19]See J. Philip Wogaman, "The Contribution of Ethics," in *The Population Crisis and Moral Responsibility,* ed. J. Philip Wogaman (Washington, D.C.: Public Affairs Press, 1973), 5–15.

for debate in a democratic society. The most important theological contribution to the debate may well be clarification of the criteria defining *human* life. That is relevant at both ends of the life spectrum. In the case of abortion, the issue is joined at that point in the development of prenatal life when one can say "This is or was a human being." Similarly, in the case of euthanasia or organ transplantation, the issue is also joined when one can say "We must not withdraw medical support or terminate this life because its authentic humanness is still present." Both kinds of questions entail many other considerations, but the definitional one is particularly important.

On that, Christians cannot be satisfied with a purely biological definition of human life. Nor can Christians be satisfied with a definition that depends upon whether or not a particular being is socialized or loved. But Christians do understand that our humanity inheres in our subjectivity, our capacity to experience reality. God's covenantal love for us is of our interior self, not of our physical organism. At the frontiers of life, therefore, much is to be said for definitions that recognize the importance of brain development or brain death. When there is not yet enough brain development to sustain even the rudiments of personal experience, it cannot yet be said that human life as such has begun; when brain death has occurred, it cannot be said that a human life is still present.

To what extent should Christians impose their definitions of the frontiers of life upon the political order? That is a pertinent question indeed in an era of acrimonious disagreement among Christians![20] Given the character and depth of the disagreements, it may be well for the state to show great sensitivity and restraint in requiring conformity to religious conceptions that are not generally shared. Still, the experience of recent decades in a number of countries indicates clearly enough that the frontier questions of life will be, and probably should be, subject to the political dialogue.

THE CHRISTIAN IMPERATIVE

So it is clear that the state cannot avoid legislating social morality. It is involved in that now as it has always been. The real questions center on what the people of a society want their society to be,

---

[20]See Frederick S. Jaffe, Barbara L. Lindheim, and Philip R. Lee, *Abortion Politics: Private Morality and Public Policy* (New York: McGraw-Hill, 1981).

and why they want it to be that and not something different, and how they propose to make it and keep it what they want it to be. A democratic state affords fullest opportunity for all the people to enter into this dialogue and to share in the power of actual decision. Christians, while affirming the right and responsibility of the state to deal with social questions and while affirming the democratic process, must make their own contributions to that process.

16

The State and Criminal Justice

> The end goal of the whole system of criminal justice
> ought to be *social restoration*—in a double sense. It
> should be the restoration of the social order to whole-
> ness from the disruption of which crime is both a symp-
> tom and an aggravation. It should also be an effort to
> restore each offender to an integral place in the society.
> —*L. Harold DeWolf (1975)*[1]

> A just society is one where everyone gets what he de-
> serves, and the wicked deserve to be punished—they
> deserve "many sorrows," as the Psalmist says—and the
> righteous deserve to be joyous. Punishment serves both
> these ends: it makes the criminal unhappy and it
> makes the law-abiding person happy. It rewards the
> law-abiding by satisfying the anger he feels at the sight
> of crime.
> —*Walter Berns (1979)*[2]

A perennial issue in all statecraft—indeed, perhaps the first issue
of all—is what is to be done about people who defy the public will.
That question has lurked behind most of the preceding chapters

---

[1] L. Harold DeWolf, *Crime and Justice in America: A Paradox of Conscience* (San Francisco: Harper & Row, 1975), 170.

[2] Walter Berns, *For Capital Punishment: Crime and the Morality of the Death Penalty*
(New York: Basic Books, 1979), 147.

of this book. Sometimes, as in the discussion of pacifism and anarchism, it has been necessary to discuss it more directly. But almost everything we have said thus far assumes, one way or another, that when the state acts it must also have the ability to *compel*. But what does that mean? Does a Christian perspective contribute anything to the resolution of the question?

The general problem facing Christians is how to do negative things without undercutting the positive purposes of human society. It is, in a way, the problem of how to do unloving things lovingly— or what Paul Tillich, following Luther, called the "strange work of love."[3] Tillich's statement of this is that "love must destroy what is against love, but not him who is the bearer of that which is against love."[4] This formulation affirms the positive intent behind every Christian approach to dealing with antisocial behavior, but it also introduces the basic dilemma. For how, in face of the depth of human sin and the realities of crime, is one to destroy the sin but not the sinner, or the crime but not the criminal? And does the specifically Christian organization of the problem around *love* really add anything to our understanding of what is to be done?

CONFLICTING THEORIES OF CRIMINAL JUSTICE

Deferring that question for the moment, we should note that there are a number of competing theories of criminal justice. Most of them have been around long enough to suggest that they represent perennial options and that our problem may be how to do justice to the legitimate claims of each without detracting from the similarly legitimate claims of the others. L. Harold DeWolf's listing of seven theories is a particularly useful one, and I shall follow it here.[5]

The first of these theories, *legal positivism*, holds that it is the simple obligation of the state to ensure obedience to law and the application of the legally prescribed penalties, without respect to any underlying ethical norms or theories of justice. The second, *vindication of the law*, holds that it is the purpose of prosecuting

---

[3]Paul Tillich, *Love, Power, and Justice* (New York and London: Oxford University Press, 1954), 113.

[4]Ibid., 114.

[5]DeWolf, *Crime and Justice in America*, 47–67.

and punishing offenders to ensure that the will of the community is taken seriously and that it has a chance to form the conscience of the members of the community and to guide their conduct. The third, *education in approved values,* holds that the function of law and the criminal justice system is to mold citizens in accordance with the approved values of the community. These first three theories are not necessarily inconsistent with one another, depending upon what is emphasized in each. The third one presupposes the values which society seeks to implement through the state. The second one is intent that they be taken seriously. The first one insists that the criminal justice system be based upon the law as enacted. But taken alone, each of the three neglects points raised by the others.

The fourth theory, *retribution,* is possibly the oldest one of all. That is the familiar "eye for an eye" theme, although in a good deal of recorded history it has been more usual for the punishment to be much more severe than the crime (as in capital punishment for shooting one of the king's deer). The fifth theory is *deterrence,* not to punish the deed that has already been done so much as to prevent its being done again by the same criminal or another. The sixth theory, *incapacitation,* is simply to make it impossible for *this* miscreant to do it again, either by executing or incarcerating or even physically disabling the criminal. The seventh theory is *rehabilitation,* the notion being that the real purpose of criminal justice is to change the attitudes and behavior of the criminal so he or she will not *want* to commit antisocial acts again.

Deterrence and incapacitation have a certain obvious point to them if it is important to prevent antisocial behavior from occurring. The term "deterrence" is negative, but its underlying point is that people should have strong incentives not to behave in antisocial ways. So long as there exists any inclination on anybody's part to do antisocial things which appears to be a perennial problem—it would seem important to have such incentives. That is so, although most incentives, even the positive rewards offered for good behavior, may violate the integrity of persons by leading them to act for the sake of something other than the goodness of the act itself. For the persistent offenders, some form of disablement may truly be necessary to prevent greater harm to others and to the social fabric. More can be said about these theories, of course, but they have an obvious contribution to make to our thinking if we agree that antisocial behavior cannot otherwise be prevented.

RETRIBUTION VERSUS REHABILITATION

The most sharply conflicting theories are those stressing retribution or rehabilitation. The first advocates punishment for the sake of balancing the scales of justice. The second is more concerned about the reform of the offender.

Since many Christians consider the case for rehabilitation to be overwhelmingly stronger than the case for retribution, we should perhaps linger over the latter and not dismiss it too easily. Walter Berns appeals to a version of the doctrine of retribution in his defense of capital punishment. His approach is not, however, limited to the question of capital punishment alone. The principle of retribution serves two important functions in his thinking. First, it provides a legitimate avenue for the expression of anger at the damage to the social fabric represented by crime. Social anger, in his view, can be a very positive thing. It can be an expression of our *caring* about injustice. Noting that Martin Luther King Jr. "embodied a people's quest for justice," Berns remarks that in King's civil rights movement "the servility and fear of the past had been replaced by pride and anger, and the treatment that had formerly been accepted as a matter of course or as if it were deserved was now seen for what it was, unjust and unacceptable." Thus, while King "preached love," the movement "depended on anger as well as love." The anger, in fact, was an expression of solidarity, of "a profound caring for others."[6] A retributive theory of criminal justice takes the importance of this anger directly into account. It gives people a way to express this legitimate anger in ways that are disciplined by law. Without legal retribution people would often feel impelled to express that anger in unrestrained ways—as in mob violence or private acts of vengeance, both of which can overshoot the limits of due process of law.

But what about the criminals against whom the retribution is aimed? Can one defend the morality of making actual people the objects of anger? Berns thinks so. The second important function of retribution as he understands it is that it "acknowledges the humanity of its objects: it holds them accountable for what they do." By holding criminals accountable as responsible persons "it pays

---

[6]Berns, *For Capital Punishment,* 154.

them that respect which is due them as men."[7] Berns's criticism of rehabilitative theories of criminal justice is that they take a psychologically patronizing view of criminals—that is, a view that treats them as *objects* and not as responsible human beings who are capable of choosing and accepting the consequences of their choices. By treating criminals as pathological or "sick," we mark them off as less than human. Anger toward malefactors thus expresses a certain regard or respect for them. Ultimately, Berns considers his view a support of the death penalty (a subject to which we shall return), but it also has implications for the use of indeterminate sentencing or for the extent to which psychiatry properly belongs in the courtroom. Berns's viewpoint has important historical antecedents in such philosophers as Immanuel Kant and Georg Wilhelm Friedrich Hegel and in the contract tradition of political theory. According to the latter, even the death penalty is understood to be an affirmation of the humanity of the condemned. All of us, by participating in the benefits of the political compact (above all, accepting its protection), affirm our willingness to accept the just penalty of law should we ourselves prove to be the lawbreakers. You have a right to expect me to fulfill the terms of our mutually advantageous covenant, if I have the right to expect you to fulfill your part of the covenant. And if I do not fulfill those terms, you have a right to be angry and to expect that the consequences of my infraction be enforced. But if I am treated as having been *incapable* of fulfilling the terms of our contract, my humanity is itself under question.

Berns duly notes the importance of the attachment of a certain solemnity, a certain measure of ceremony to the processes of judgment and execution of the law. Thus do we mark off the fulfillment of the course of justified social anger and its surpassing importance for social well-being. This is a serious position. It certainly does call into question the sentimentality that is sometimes expressed under the heading of "rehabilitation." But can rehabilitation be so readily dismissed as the principal goal of criminal justice?

Excluding sentimentality and paternalism, we are still faced with the fundamental moral question: Who *is* this one who has violated the

---

[7]Ibid. Emil Brunner makes a similar point when he emphasizes "the criminal's own sense of the need for expiation" (*The Divine Imperative* [Philadelphia: Westminster Press, 1947], 475). Brunner, whose views are developed with much greater theological depth than Berns's, acknowledges that the community also needs expiation for its collective role in making the criminal what she or he is.

criminal law, doing injury to others and to the community as a whole? Who is he or she to us? Is this person an alien being now, having lost all claim upon our regard—now an enemy of society, and therefore our enemy? The question is not clearly addressed by Berns, though by implication our "anger" is not only justified but an expression of our rejection of the offender as well. By fulfilling the retributive condition—the punishment designed to fit the crime—the offender can, perhaps, be readmitted to the society of moral beings. (In that sense alone Berns's own view could be understood as rehabilitative. An offender is rehabilitated by being punished; at best, of course, this is a posthumous prospect for those who are executed.) But the thrust of Berns's argument is not toward rehabilitation but toward the vindication of the law and the community's own moral sensibilities.

What I find missing in Berns from a theological standpoint is clarity in recognizing that the offender continues to be our sister or brother, one for whom Christ died, one who remains, even in the depth of evil, the object of God's gracious love. Is there not a remaining fundamental moral kinship between the offender and ourselves that is more than sentimental—a kinship based upon the objective truth that God does profoundly love each one of us, thereby constituting us a moral family? How can we resolve the issues of criminal justice retributively if our theological entry point is God's grace, taken to be prior to God's judgment?

These are weighty questions, however rhetorical they may sound. They do depend upon a theological orientation, and those who do not share this or a like theological orientation may simply have to say that this is not their ultimate starting point. But for those who *do* share the viewpoint, what difference does it make?

It may help all of us to visualize the implications by imagining that some person of our own biological family, one whom we love very dearly, has just been convicted of committing a very serious criminal offense and that we cannot doubt that this loved one actually did the deed. Would that make a difference in our viewpoint, at least for this instance? It is amazing how much criminal justice reformism has been generated by people of high social standing and intellectual attainment who have run afoul of the law and gone to prison! And the motivation to seek changes has often been present in their families as well. (In the United States, one thinks particularly of the dozens of high-ranking governmental officials who served prison terms in the wake of the Watergate scandals of the early 1970s. Such people, typified by Charles Colson, counsel to the president, have sought to change public attitudes toward criminals and to improve conditions in prisons.)[8] It all does seem to look different when one's own loved ones are involved. Would it be possible for Berns to generate the same depth of anger toward a loved one who had violated the law—and if so, would the relationship not seriously affect the character of the anger? Would it not be easier to see that chain of circumstances leading to the crime, to understand how terribly ambiguous the mixture between social-psychological forces and our own free will can be?

In reality, as well as in literature, people *have* responded with deep anger toward their own loved ones, even to the point of disowning them altogether. In literature the point is illustrated by an Afrikaner character in Alan Paton's *Too Late the Phalarope*[9] who utterly disowns his own son upon the latter's conviction of the crime of interracial adultery in apartheid-era South Africa. Of course, Paton's character was illustrating the utterly moralistic, graceless theology frequently exhibited by Afrikaners on racial or sexual matters. Those who are willing to apply a vindictive retributive theory of criminal justice even to their own loved ones may be consistent. But is that a morally attractive model of human relationship?

The point I am leading toward is that a Christian understands that we have the same moral relationship with *everybody* that we do with our own blood relations. There is no person in the courtroom dock or prison cell or execution chamber who is not a sister or brother! The moral reality is that they belong to us and we to them. We may be very angry with them, as we surely can be with loved ones. But our anger is in the presence of a deeper relationship, and it had better not obscure that relationship. We cannot but wish that somehow that offender, who is our brother or sister, should get his or her life straightened out. Morally we cannot "write them off."

Still, that may not mean we endorse all that goes under the heading of rehabilitation. In his own discussion of this theory of criminal justice, DeWolf notes serious problems with each of the six subtypes

---

[8]See Charles W. Colson, *Born Again* (Old Tappan, N.J.: Fleming H. Revell, 1976), and idem, "Towards an Understanding of Imprisonment and Rehabilitation," in *Crime and the Responsible Community,* ed. John Stott and Nicholas Miller (Grand Rapids: Wm. B. Eerdmans; London: Hodder & Stoughton, 1980). The turnabout in attitude by many of the former Nixon administration officials is particularly remarkable in light of the typically moralistic attitude toward criminals displayed by many of them prior to their own fall from grace.

[9]Alan Paton, *Too Late the Phalarope* (New York: Charles Scribner's Sons, 1953).

of rehabilitation he has surveyed—therapeutic treatment, education, behavior modification, religious conversion, moral awakening, and social readaptation.[10] Views clustered under these headings can fail to come to terms with the depths of real human nature or they may sentimentally neglect real practical problems. Each offers insight. None is sufficient to effect the real transformation of the offender that is sought by rehabilitation. In some cases, such as therapeutic treatment and behavior modification, the psychological models employed may, finally, be disrespectful of moral freedom and the dignity possessed by criminal offenders. Ironically, some approaches to rehabilitation that come from that quarter—such as the use of indeterminate sentences—can wind up imposing lengthier sentences or entailing a disregard for civil liberties. It is also true that a rehabilitation model can neglect the interests and well-being of the victims of crime and the interests of the community at large while focusing primary attention upon the rehabilitation of the offender. Nevertheless, the rehabilitation of offenders as positive members of the community must still have priority among all who consider them to be sisters and brothers.

PROTECTION AND RESTORATION
OF THE COMMUNITY

No single model of criminal justice is likely to prove satisfactory, given the complexity of the problem. But there is much to be said for an approach that seeks to protect the community from antisocial behavior and to restore the community as much as possible after such behavior has occurred. That is admittedly a large order. Protection of the community means that crime must be deterred realistically. It also means that conditions alienating people from society—such as poverty, unemployment, and social discrimination—have to be overcome. Restoration of the community means that after a crime has occurred, the primary focus is upon healing. DeWolf's concept of "social restoration" is suggestive. He makes the point that this does not mean "that we are merely to return the society or the offender's relation to it to its former state." Instead, "in most instances the *restoration* must be a renewal or reconstruction genuinely creative of relationships not previously existing."[11] DeWolf notes that

---

[10]DeWolf, *Crime and Justice in America,* 60–65.
[11]Ibid., 170.

this is the philosophy at work in a good family when children must be disciplined and, suggestively, that a good deal of traditional African culture follows this model.

The approach has implications for punishment. It does not rule out incarceration, both as a deterrent to crime and as a place for reconstructing the criminal. But it does suggest that prisons must stop being de facto schools for crime! They need to be better schools for the acquisition of skills really needed to cope with the world outside to which the criminal will in most cases eventually return. Prison sentences should not be so excessive that the prisoner's hope is lost in clouds of bitterness and his or her perspective further warped by institutionalization. While discipline must be maintained within the prison setting, prisoners should be treated with respect as human beings. Conjugal visits should be permitted for married prisoners, along with other measures to mitigate the unavoidable family disruptions. If such reforms appear to be coddling lawbreakers overmuch, let it be remembered that they are still a part of the moral community and that, in any case, society has a very great practical stake in their being brought into a positive relationship to society.

Restoration also has implications for the victims of crime, often totally neglected by the criminal justice system in the United States. Where possible, the system should require restitution or compensation by the offender, as provided for in the laws of a number of European countries. In the many cases where, practically speaking, the offender is unable to make restitution, provision should be made by the public for help to the victims of crime (who, after all, were not sufficiently protected by the state).

RESTORATION AND RETRIBUTION

Does a community restoration model of criminal justice rule out retribution altogether? It does indeed, insofar as retribution is based upon rejection of the offender as a person and insofar as the balancing of the scales of justice is understood to satisfy some abstract conception of right. The criminal offense does not abolish the deeper relationship we all have with one another through God; crime does not make the criminal an alien being, however much the offense may have arisen out of the criminal's own sense of alienation. And insofar as retribution is predicated on the self-righteousness of the innocent, the theological response must be that none of us are so innocent, all of us stand in need of the grace of God.

Nevertheless, there may still be a sense in which the theory of retribution has a contribution to make to our understanding of the restoration of community. To discover this, we must reflect more deeply on the sources of that deep anger to which Berns has referred. In part, no doubt, it is the simple response of injured people to the objective fact of their injury. At the psychological level, it is a perfectly understandable reaction to the loss of property (say, through robbery or vandalism), physical injury, or loss of the life of a loved one. And yet there may be a dimension to this anger that is not encompassed by the loss alone. We may be very angry when such losses come from purely natural causes—our house burns down because of a lightning strike, we are injured when we slip and fall down the stairs, a loved one is killed in an accident that can be blamed on no one. But while such things make us angry, the anger is directed at circumstance alone. It is an expression of frustration, of disappointment, of grief. The anger at being injured deliberately by others is deeper. It is not simply the expression of our sense of injury; more important, it is our response to the fact that we have not been respected as persons by somebody else. Somebody has rejected us or treated us as a thing. So our anger is not only a reflection of the injury itself; it is also a reflection of our being rejected. We are responding to being dehumanized by others. Our anger is a defense of our humanity. Those writers who encourage disprivileged women and minority groups to respond frankly with rage understand that this is a natural reaction to dehumanization and that when it is not expressed freely it is bottled up in the form of self-hatred.[12] Being victimized by crime entails the same psychological dynamics.

Retribution by the community may not restore any of the objective things that have been lost; but it can be a reaffirmation of our humanity by the community. By punishing the one who has injured us, the community is saying that injury to us *matters*. If the community were to ignore that injury or be preoccupied only with the rehabilitation of the offender, we might feel that we were not greatly valued. I believe that that, at bottom, is why people can respond so vindictively to crime and insist upon stiff penalties for criminals—sometimes out of all proportion to the crimes themselves. That is why it really seems to matter to people (judges, juries, the public at

---

[12]See William H. Grier and Price M. Cobbs, *Black Rage* (New York: Basic Books, 1968), for one analysis of this psychological problem.

large) whether a criminal shows remorse. For contrition is a recognition, however belated it may be, that the one whom one has injured is, after all, a fellow human being with a claim upon one's respect. When such contrition is not forthcoming there is all the more inclination to pour on the punishment so it will really affect the attitude of this one who has wronged others. Notice how important it has appeared in the trials of celebrated Nazi war criminals—such as Adolf Eichmann or Klaus Barbie—for their motives to be probed and for them to be almost compelled to acknowledge the enormity of their deeds. (The careful psychological examinations of Eichmann prior to his trial in Jerusalem were not merely for the sake of contributing to scientific knowledge. It had more to do with an intense probing by a whole injured people into the character of this dehumanization. The execution of Eichmann seemed to them to be wholly necessary to vindicate their humanity.)

The community, acting through the state, must respond to the fact of criminal injury with actions reaffirming the humanity of those who have been injured. Any theory of rehabilitation or restoration absolutely must include this element or it will not be healing. And it must indeed capture the full attention of the criminal with society's strong reaction against the offense and injury. Remorse is not an attitude that can be forced upon another human being, but it is part of the business of the criminal justice system to assert its own recognition of the humanity of those who have been injured.

One of the most creative imaginable efforts to reconcile these conflicting values was the Truth and Reconciliation Commission in South Africa, authorized by President Nelson Mandela and chaired by Archbishop Desmond Tutu, both of whom have exemplified extraordinary gifts of sensitivity. The Commission's existence was predicated on the nation's need to find a way to deal with the vast injustices and injuries inflicted by the previous white-controlled apartheid regime. It did not insist upon punishment but upon full disclosure. The perpetrators of atrocities could be granted amnesty for their evil deeds *provided that* they would step forward and recount the full details of what they had done. They need not even express remorse, but they had to tell the truth. That permitted full knowledge of the whole truth to become a part of the shared collective memory of a reconstituted South Africa. It also exposed, once and for all, the ugliness and hypocrisies of the racist regime (which had always paraded its self-righteousness so ostentatiously). A way forward became possible because the unacceptable past had become so thoroughly revealed. Not many societies in the history of humankind have been so creative in dealing with evil of such dimensions.

Nevertheless, the problem with leaving criminal law on the level of remorse—as theories of retribution generally do—is that it overlooks the dehumanization of the criminal which, itself, generally precedes the crime. If the offense is born out of a deep self-hatred, as often it is, how is vindictive punishment supposed to change that? Is it not merely another contribution to a vicious cycle of self-hatred and alienation, from which further crimes and further dehumanization must issue?

Restoration must address the dehumanization existing at all levels. While efforts are made, as they should be, to bring this offender into mature participation in the life of the community, they must be done in such a way that this injured person is also reaffirmed as a valued participant.

We cannot spell out here a whole program for criminal justice reform. But it is clear that most societies accepting this orientation to criminal justice would likely have to make substantial changes, both in the way offenders are handled and in the way injured citizens are reassured and compensated.

THE QUESTION OF CAPITAL PUNISHMENT

We must, however, attend to the special question of capital punishment. Issues of retribution, rehabilitation, restoration, deterrence, and incapacitation are illuminated in a special way when tested against the ultimate question of whether the state should ever take the lives of offenders. Berns, whose retributive theory of criminal justice is addressed to exactly this question, obviously accepts the sometime moral necessity of the state's use of capital punishment. Most believers in rehabilitation reject capital punishment, on the reasonable ground that the offender would hardly be rehabilitated. Those who are interested in incapacitating dangerous criminals may find capital punishment an attractive option, for the one executed, at least, will not commit further crimes—although many murderers are one-time offenders. Much of the debate over capital punishment has been prompted by deterrence theory, with views swinging back and forth on the basis of evidence that capital punishment does or does not deter people from committing capital crimes. We shall return to the question of deterrence below.

Everything that has been written here about restoration of community and the affirmation of the humanity of both offenders and victims of crime would seem to argue against, not for, capital punishment. To be sure, the taking of the offender's life does announce society's absolute rejection of the crime committed. In the case of murder, it is society's reaffirmation of the value of the life of the one who had been murdered—a presumed enhancement of the memory of that person in the community and especially to her or his loved ones. In such a case it is also a statement to other members of society that their lives are similarly valued by the community as a whole. But, curiously enough, the state's taking the life of the offender also places a qualification against the value it places on the lives of its citizens, as if to say, If you do this foul deed, we shall reject you—*totally*. That qualification diminishes the sense that one is fully accepted, in one's person, by society.

Let us put this in theological terms. The importance of the priority of grace to "works of the law" in the writings of Saint Paul is that one does not have to *earn* the gift of salvation. God's love is utterly dependable, absolutely steadfast. We are affirmed, we are valued at the center of our being even though, as sinners, we do not deserve this love. To say that we must first earn the love of God puts us, not God, in control of God's love. And we, being insecure at the center of our being, could not be released from the necessities of self-centeredness. Deep self-esteem has its grounding in the affirmation of one's self by God and by others. And a recognition that we are dependent upon God's grace, despite our failings, saves us from self-righteousness. As Paul writes, "Since all have sinned and fall short of the glory of God, they are justified by his grace as a gift. . . . Then what becomes of our boasting? It is excluded" (Rom. 3:23–24, 27). Of course, the state is not God. The state does not "justify" us, by faith or otherwise. But the state does represent the community, and the key question here is how the community is to support or undermine each citizen's sense of being valued. Obviously the state must protect its citizens, and that entails the maintenance of a criminal justice system. But on the ultimate question whether the state should employ capital punishment as a means of affirming the value of the lives of its citizens, is it not more likely that the means detracts from the desired end? Is it not a better affirmation of the value of life for the state to preserve the life of even a murderer? Might it not have been a more eloquent statement of the enormity of the evil of the Nazi Holocaust for the Israelis to have refrained from taking the life of even the hated Eichmann? That is not to stand in judgment against Israel in its trial and condemnation of the Nazi war criminal, for God knows that the Jewish people had ample provocation. It is only a question of how best to affirm the surpassing value of each human being and, in this instance, the enormity of the crime of genocide.

But are such theological judgments practical enough about the realities of crime? Indeed, Saint Paul himself promises nothing about the inevitable goodwill of erstwhile criminals when confronted by the grace of God. Elsewhere in Romans Paul even notes that the ruler "is God's servant for your good," and that the governing authority "does not bear the sword in vain; he is the servant of God to execute his wrath on the wrongdoer" (Rom. 13:3–4). What if it takes lethal force and, ultimately, capital punishment to deter and control crime?

If so, there is a strong case to be made for it, always bearing in mind that the rule of proportion must govern (that is, that capital punishment is not used to deter or control crimes of lesser magnitude than capital punishment itself). The presumption should be against use of capital punishment. There should be clear evidence of its being needed to deter murder before it is allowed. If the evidence is not there, or if serious doubt remains, the decision should be against, not for, capital punishment.

In fact, the evidence does not appear to be there.[13] Comparisons between similar jurisdictions, some utilizing capital punishment and some not, suggest that whether or not capital punishment is used has little or no deterrent effect. Capital punishment can, indeed, have exactly the opposite of the intended effect where murderers have suicidal tendencies. What *does* seem to deter crime, murders included, is the perception that detection and punishment are highly probable—a point that Jeremy Bentham made long ago in his tract on "Principles of Penal Law":

> The profit of a crime is commonly more certain than its punishment; or, what amounts to the same thing, appears so to the offender. It is generally more immediate: the temptation to offend is present; the punishment is at a distance. Hence there are two circumstances which

---

[13]Useful summaries of studies of the deterrent effect of capital punishment are contained in Hugo A. Bedau, ed., *The Death Penalty in America,* 3d ed. (New York and Oxford: Oxford University Press, 1982), see especially part 4, "Deterrence: Problems, Doctrines, and Evidence," 95–185.

> weaken the effect of punishment, its *uncertainty* and its
> *distance.* . . . It is therefore true, that the more the cer-
> tainty of punishment can be augmented, the more it
> may be diminished in amount.[14]

The point is reiterated, almost as a truism, by modern criminology.
It is not that severe penalties should not go with severe crimes, but
that the ultimate penalty appears to add nothing—in quality of deterrence—to the penalty of imprisonment if it is virtually certain
that one will not be able to evade the latter.[15]

This alone should be enough to cause the state under any but the
most unusual circumstances to forego the death penalty. But to this
lack of evidence in support of the death penalty as deterrence should
be added the point that, in the United States at least, the death
penalty has been applied in a most uneven, discriminatory way. In
America, black people are much more likely than white people to be
executed, particularly if their crimes were directed against white
people, and poor people are much more likely than the affluent.
Prejudice, while arguably diminishing, is yet real. Class position is
also affected by prejudice, which also determines the quality of legal defense an accused person can afford.[16] These points contribute
to the conclusion that capital punishment, except in highly unusual
circumstances, should not be employed as a form of deterrence.

THE PROFESSIONAL ROLE
OF THE POLICE

From a moral standpoint, society has no social role of greater difficulty than that of the professional police. In an earlier chapter, we
noted John Howard Yoder's conclusion (or near conclusion) that it is
not a possible role for Christians. I disagree with that. Any role that

---

[14]Jeremy Bentham, "Principles of Penal Law," reprinted in *Ethical Choice: A Case Study Approach,* ed. Robert N. Beck and John B. Orr (New York: Free Press, 1970), 339.

[15]Apparently capital punishment does not even serve as an effective deterrent to murder in a prison setting, where inmates have comparatively little more to lose. For a summary of evidence on this, see Wendy Phillips Wolfson, "The Deterrent Effect of the Death
Penalty upon Prison Murder," in Bedau, *Death Penalty in America,* 159–73.

[16]See Marvin E. Wolfgang and Marc Riedel, "Racial Discrimination, Rape, and the
Death Penalty," and William J. Bowers and Glenn L. Pierce, "Racial Discrimination and
Criminal Homicide under Post-*Furman* Capital Statutes," in Bedau, *Death Penalty in
America,* 194–205 and 206–24, respectively.

is necessary for the well-being of society is also a possible vocation for Christians. But police work surely is difficult. It entails frequent contact with alienated, antisocial people in the context of their antisocial behavior. It exposes one constantly to the seamy side of community life and to considerable physical danger. It is difficult in such a role to avoid becoming calloused and cynical, while retaining a sensitivity to human beings and commitment to the public good. But that is what police officers are called to. Because they are called upon to enforce public laws, police officers are a major point of contact between the community's will and the conflicting will of individuals. Their manner of enforcing the law contributes to or detracts from the moral quality of the community. Good professional police respect the law, holding themselves accountable to it and enforcing it in an evenhanded way. While police in even the most peaceful communities are sometimes required to use physical force, their professional standards call for the least use of force consistent with fulfillment of their responsibilities.[17]

Well-trained police forces are highly disciplined at this point. They are carefully instructed first to communicate rationally before even threatening use of force; then to warn an offender that they will use force if necessary; then, if necessary, to use the least amount of force consistent with gaining the cooperation of the offender. Police cannot be expected to forego deadly force in every conceivable instance, but that should always be a last resort, to be used only when an offender is likely to endanger the lives of others. There is much to be said, even, for police normally not to bear firearms but to rely instead upon the authority of their position and lesser weapons (such as the truncheon or tear gas). British police have operated successfully within that discipline for decades, and it would be difficult to argue, on the basis of relative crime statistics, that that is less successful than the usual American practice of police bearing firearms prominently displayed (a point that is admittedly

---

[17]In the United States, police standards on use of physical force vary with the local jurisdiction, subject to some standards imposed by the federal court system. Professional standards are suggested in such writings as Robert J. Friedrich, "Police Use of Force: Individuals, Situations, and Organizations," *The Annals* 452 (November 1980): 82–97; and William A. Geller, "Deadly Force: What We Know," in *Thinking about Police: Contemporary Readings,* ed. Carl B. Klockars (New York: McGraw-Hill, 1983), 313–31. The American Bar Association's Model Penal Code, Sec. 307(2)(b), suggests several criteria to restrain police use of deadly force. See Joseph J. Senna and Larry J. Siegel, *Introduction to Criminal Justice,* 3d ed. (St. Paul: West Publishing, 1984), 196.

complicated by the fact that American lawbreakers are often also armed to the teeth).

Again, use of force—even deadly force—is occasionally necessary. But the presumption should be against it in any particular instance, and the police should strive in whatever way possible to inculcate respect for law and commitment to live as law-abiding citizens. That depends partly on a public perception that the police do not think of themselves primarily as persons engaged in physically violent activities.

THE RIGHTS OF THE ACCUSED

It remains to be observed that not everybody accused of crime is guilty. Many countries presume the innocence of the accused until the latter is proved guilty beyond reasonable doubt. That presumption of innocence is more than a procedural nicety. It is an expression of the community's faith in the integrity of its members; indeed, it is a logical consequence of the doctrine of popular sovereignty. It is also a practical necessity for communal living, for life could quickly become intolerable where people could be placed in legal jeopardy merely on the basis of malicious accusation.

The Bill of Rights in the United States (along with similar constitutional protections in other countries) provides a series of protections against arbitrary arrest or injury of citizens by the state, many of them an extension of the presumption of innocence. Sometimes, inflamed by the application of procedural protections to persons popularly believed to be guilty, public opinion may question whether the rights of the community are being subordinated to the rights of the criminal. But legal rights enjoyed by the accused are actually *among* the rights of the community. They are a protection for every member of the community against arbitrary or malicious arrest or prosecution.

THE POSITIVE BASIS
OF CRIMINAL JUSTICE

Society obviously cannot dispense with police power and a criminal justice system. We should be prepared for that fact by the theological recognition of the pervasiveness and perversity of sin, humanity's ever-present tendency toward self-centeredness. Nevertheless, the need to protect the social fabric and the rights of persons against human aggressiveness should not lead to a basically negative view of society nor to the enshrining of vindictiveness and self-righteousness in law. The fundamental objective should be positive. It is based upon a norm of healthy community life and the integrity and public-spiritedness of citizens. Where these are endangered, it is the proper office of the criminal justice system to preserve, protect, and restore. At stake in this, from a theological standpoint, is whether God's good intentions for human well-being can be preserved concretely in a world that is constantly threatened by human sin.

17

Nation-States in
a Global Community

> We are thus driven to the conclusion that the shape and
> structure of political life in the modern world and the
> influence exercised by public authority in all the na-
> tions of the world are unequal to the task of promoting
> the common good of all peoples.
>
> *—Pope John XXIII (1963)*[1]

To understand these words from *Pacem in Terris,* we must remember that they come out of a tradition that emphasizes solving political problems at the most immediate, personal level possible.
According to the doctrine of subsidiarity, which lies behind Pope
John XXIII's comments, it is wrong to withdraw power and authority from individuals and lower-level institutions in order to give
them to higher-level institutions.[2] Thus, the British government
should not do what London or Edinburgh can do, and the governments of London or Edinburgh should not do what nongovernmental organizations or families or individuals can do. Economic life,
family life, education, religion, and so on, should not be politicized
unless absolutely necessary; if they are, it should be at the most immediate level possible.

With that point of view in the background, we sit up and take

---

[1]Pope John XXIII, *Pacem in Terris,* para. 135, in *Proclaiming Justice and Peace: Documents from John XXIII to John Paul II,* ed. Michael Walsh and Brian Davies (Mystic,
Conn.: Twenty-Third Publications, 1984 [1963]), 68–69.

[2]The doctrine of subsidiarity is classically stated in Pope Pius XI's encyclical, *Quadragesimo Anno,* para. 79.

notice when a pope declares that there are problems that can *only* be solved at the global level.

And is it not so? Most of what has been written thus far in this book presupposes that the political order is an expression of a given society. We have, in fact, defined the state as society acting as a whole. In chapter 2, where this and other definitions were offered, the point was made that no state has *complete* sovereignty. No society can act as a whole without confronting serious limitations, especially as it encounters other societies. But even that way of putting it is hopelessly abstract. For what is *a* society in this shrinking global community of ours? Are Canada and the United States *different* societies? France, Italy, and Germany? Poland and the Czech Republic? Costa Rica and Panama?

Typical writings on international relations[3] are based on the nation-state as a more or less discrete unit, with its own sovereignty, its own national interest, and representing its own society strongly or weakly, wisely or foolishly as it confronts other nation-states. Obviously there is truth in the portrait. But that must not be allowed to obscure the historical fact that the nation-state system is itself a fairly late development in world history. Historically, the term "state" could legitimately be attached to vastly different forms of society, ranging from tribal units and city-states and feudal fiefdoms to great empires. The modern nation-state emerged only in the late medieval world and has been around in its present form for, at most, four or five centuries. The portrait also must not be allowed to obscure the degree to which societies, in meaningful cultural and economic terms, cross national boundaries and even span the globe.

But Pope John XXIII's point, to which we shall return below, is that the world lacks meaningful political organization at the world level. If we already have a global society of sorts, it is a society without a state. It is a society that cannot yet act as a whole.

Meaningful political action remains at the national level, where sovereignty, such as it is, continues to have some reality. How are we to speak of nation-states in the global community from a Christian perspective?

---

[3]For example, Hans J. Morgenthau's classic, *Politics among Nations,* 3d ed. (New York: Alfred A. Knopf, 1960).

THE NATIONAL INTEREST
AS A MORAL CONCEPT

Writers in the tradition of Hans Morgenthau and Reinhold Niebuhr define "national interest" as a central concept for ethical analysis.[4] The term, in that tradition, is not without moral and intellectual power. It is by no means to be equated with crude nationalism or a fundamentally selfish outlook on the world. It recognizes the reality of the nation as political power center, addressing the nation in terms of its deepest, most enlightened interest. It does not ask the nation (or those who control its destinies) to be altruistic. Leaders are responsible to their societies, and the people of those societies cannot be expected to renounce their own existence as a society or even their fundamental interests as a society. As Ernest Lefever put this point, "each nation can be said to have a national purpose, a reason for its existence, which is based upon the central values held by the majority of its people. The government is morally bound to honor these basic values."[5]

But some interests are more central than others, some more enlightened than others. Some are truly vital—without them a society's basic existence or identity is threatened. The task of the Christian moralist as seen in this tradition is to interpret the interests of society in terms congruent with Christian faith. For instance, most of what has been written in this book can be interpreted, more or less, as defining what is central to the true, ultimate, or enlightened interest of a nation-state and the society it represents. Niebuhr writes that

> the "national interest" accurately describes the dominant motive of autonomous nation-states. But all nations are involved in a web of interests and loyalties. Their problem, therefore, is to choose between their own immediate, perhaps too narrowly conceived, interests and the common interests of their alliance, or more ultimately of their civilization, in which, of course, their "national interest" is also involved.[6]

---

[4]See Ernest Lefever, *Ethics and United States Foreign Policy* (New York: Meridian Books, 1957), which was written during the period when Niebuhr's and Morgenthau's "realist" position was most influential. But see also Morgenthau's *In Defense of the National Interest* (New York: Alfred A. Knopf, 1951) and *Politics among Nations* as well as Reinhold Niebuhr's *The Structure of Nations and Empires* (New York: Charles Scribner's Sons, 1959).

[5]Lefever, *Ethics and United States Foreign Policy,* 12.

[6]Niebuhr, *Structure of Nations and Empires,* 277.

What are we to make of the concept of national interest, seen in Christian perspective?

There is a sense in which the concept may indeed be unavoidable. Those Christians who are engaged in the political dialogue and the political struggle within any nation are bound to have to address the national interest, just as the Hebrew prophets spoke of what was truly (and not just apparently) necessary to the well-being of Israel. Prophetic Christians joined other high-minded people during the German Third Reich to warn that Hitler's policies would ultimately destroy the nation. In the United States during the Vietnam War period many Christians argued that the war would prove ruinous to the true national interest of the country. Similar debates have occurred in many countries when morally sensitive people have sought to question their government's foreign policies on moral grounds. Such a debate turns on how well the basic character of a society is expressed in the values by which political leaders guide its destinies and on how enlightened is their translation of the values into policies.

But the frame of reference set by the term "national interest" is not finally inclusive enough to fit the Christian perspective. For one thing, it is bound to a particular era, the era of the nation-state. But disregarding that, it is not universal enough to express the moral realities of a universal faith. God is God of every people (and some one hundred billion additional galaxies thrown in for good measure). Our moral relationship is with *all* other people, not just with those of our own land. Granted, global society is not yet complete. But is it not the mission of Christians to make it so? It may not be the vocation of Christians to encourage cultural and social uniformity upon this whole vast world, but it surely is a part of that vocation to establish and deepen ties of mutuality and human fellow-feeling that know no national frontiers. It is not my mission as an American Christian to hasten the day when all people speak English; it surely is a part of my vocation to work toward a world society in which people who speak Chinese or Spanish or Russian or Swahili or any of the hundreds of other languages are mutually supportive and cooperative in a larger, inclusive society.

Such things can, of course, still be said to belong to the enlightened national interest of every nation. But something subtle happens to our minds as we set the frame of reference. If the debate is always centered upon what is best for the nation, there may be space for an enlightened perspective—along with the inevitably unenlightened ones. But the term remains limited and ambiguous, suggesting to some that the retention of a particular nation in its particular form has the status of high moral principle, suggesting to others that the economic interests of the nation are the main value to be sought in international politics, suggesting to still others that the nation's cultural heritage is what needs to be protected. Such interpretations of the national interest may all be valid in context. But what is the deeper moral context? The root of the matter, as seen theologically, is that our objective is *global* interest—and even more, that our interest has a *cosmic* dimension. A moral conception of international politics that does not begin with the centrality and universality of God can hardly claim to be Christian. When the national interest is taken to be the basic category for ethical analysis, the interest of anything other than that of the nation must be evaluated on the basis of its contribution to the nation. Those who are enlightened in their conception of the national interest will be very concerned about the well-being of others; they will understand that the national interest cannot be divorced from the good of all. If they are theologically inclined, they will remember that the well-being of the nation requires that it be in conformity to the purposes of God. But the national interest remains the moral criterion. Ultimately, for the Christian, it cannot be. Moral reality is deeper than the nation.

Still, we have little choice but to continue to function at that level. In doing so, we remain committed to an enlightened conception of national interest. But that is to be grounded in our deeper commitment to God.

THE SPECIAL PROBLEM OF WAR

We have already examined the problem of the state's use of violence, concluding that this ultimate recourse cannot be precluded by Christian theology. Nevertheless, war remains the most direct challenge to Christian thinking about international relations in a global community.

What *evil* war spawns! In addition to the wholesale death and destruction, sorrow and suffering, war gives rise to such arrogance and self-righteousness, such rupturing of the bonds of fellow humanity. It is not even very practical, seen from a Christian theological perspective. Social conflicts resolved by the ultima ratio of war can claim no rational or moral basis for the solution achieved—only that the stronger prevailed. Sometimes Christians have ventured into militaristic crusades of one sort or another, convinced that God was on their side. But the main witness of Christian tradition has been deeply suspicious of war in face of its obvious evils.

That is not just true of the pacifists. From the earliest Christian beginnings, pacifist views have been expressed with great conviction within the church. But the general opposition to war has been shared by the far more numerous body of Christians supporting the just war approach. While sharing the pacifist abhorrence of war, the latter are convinced that war must sometimes be pursued in order to restrain injustice in this fallen world. But they are still deeply opposed to war.

The general opposition to war of the just war tradition must be emphasized anew because the term itself implies the goodness or justice of war. But the point of the tradition is rather to stress that any particular war must be required to face the moral burden of proof. Unless a particular war could be shown to be (1) a response to unjust aggression, (2) a last resort, after all other measures short of war have been found wanting, (3) declared by legitimate political authority, (4) proportionately less damaging in its own consequences than the injustices suffered by not going to war, and (5) winnable, it was not to be undertaken. That is, each of these conditions had to be met before a Christian could consider a particular war justified. (Hence, the terminology "*justified* war" is probably more faithful to the intent of the tradition than the term "just war," since the question always posed in the tradition is whether or not a war could be justified, always as a *last* resort in accordance with the standards.) In addition, Christians actually engaged in war must, in accordance with this tradition, do so with right intention—that is, without hatred, always open to reconciliation with the adversary. Moreover, Christians could not use illegitimate means, such as the intentional harming of innocents (who might, however, be hurt as an unintended secondary effect of the prosecution of war against the aggressor).

How well does this just war tradition hold up as a perspective of Christians on the recurring problem of war?

No question, the tradition has been abused! Often enough, just war doctrine has been used to excuse conflicts that were unnecessary and disproportionately evil in their consequences. And once a war has been justified on the basis of the just war criteria—however loosely applied—it has often been prosecuted without further restraint. Both of the great world wars were undertaken with a certain amount of self-righteousness, supplied in part by selective reading of just war doctrine, and once begun, both became the arena for unrestrained violence. The Vietnam War, perhaps the first to which non-Catholic as well as Catholic Christians applied just war criteria, was justified by some despite the unleashing of unprecedented firepower and the utter devastation of a land and its population.

At the same time, just war doctrine has provided a new basis for selective conscientious objection to particular wars (an interpretation not yet widely accepted by the courts in the United States or most other countries) and even for direct opposition to particular wars. Again, Vietnam may be the best recent illustration, for a substantial number of American Christians declared their opposition to that conflict on explicitly just war grounds. Such use of just war doctrine is a good reminder that when a set of moral principles is wrongly applied to a particular conflict, that is neither inevitable nor a basis for rejecting the principles. The classical ethical principle still applies, *abusus non tollit usam*—the fact that a principle can be abused does not disqualify it from proper use. Pacifists, of course, are not receptive to just war doctrine, having made a commitment to oppose *all* war.

But even apart from pacifists, there have been further Christian questions raised about it. Thus, Alan Geyer, while not a pacifist and while not disputing the placing of the burden of proof against any particular war, has questioned whether the just war tradition goes far enough in emphasizing positive peacemaking. One could argue that the point about war as a last resort at least implies that more positive and peaceful modes of conflict resolution should always be tried first. Still, Geyer's point is well taken. Peacemaking is more than deciding when things are desperate enough to justify war. The positive dimension needs to be emphasized more by Christians who are genuinely appalled by the evil of war. As Geyer puts it,

> traditional differences among Christians in matters of war and peace have actually been defined in terms of their varied orientations toward war alone. Their distinctive and positive orientations toward the imperatives of peacemaking have been underdeveloped if not altogether neglected. Peace is not the same subject as war.[7]

---

[7]Alan Geyer, *The Idea of Disarmament! Rethinking the Unthinkable* (Elgin, Ill.: Brethren Press, 1982), 192.

By the same token, of course, war is not the same subject as peace, and decisions about war—when and how to engage in it—are properly referred to some version of just war theory.

There are also those who argue that most social violence in our time is not international in character and therefore that the just war tradition, focused mainly upon conflicts among nation-states, has become less relevant. But social violence need not be international to be classified as war. Civil wars and revolutions are surely wars. No doubt there is a problem of definition lurking here: At what point on the scale of social violence, from the gang wars in some cities to the all-out warfare of major nation-states, does one define it as a real war?

This question of definition is interesting, but it may be irrelevant to the moral issue. The just war criteria really can be taken to apply to *any* decision for or against use of social violence. The criteria, suitably phrased, certainly are relevant to the police problems discussed in the preceding chapter. They are also quite applicable to revolutionary situations, a point that has been registered by both Roger Shinn and Jose Miguez Bonino.[8] To apply just war criteria to revolution one does need to modify the point about the declaration of war by legitimate authority, substituting for that the clear prospect that the revolution will succeed in creating, possibly for the first time, a genuinely legitimate political authority.

There are also those who wonder whether the awesome destructiveness of nuclear war now makes the just war tradition obsolete. Does the fact that nuclear war is so utterly disproportionate to any conceivable moral purpose mean that in the era of nuclear war the just war tradition has become irrelevant? That question may be based on a misunderstanding of the just war tradition as a method of evaluating the morality of war. If nuclear war is in fact disproportionate to any moral purpose, a point I will examine below, then that does not demonstrate the irrelevance of the just war tradition so much as its continued applicability in this new era. That new fact, if it is a fact, merely shows that nuclear war fails to pass the moral test. That is, it is not the criteria of the just war that are shown to be irrelevant, but it is nuclear war that is shown (by those very cri-

---

[8]See Roger L. Shinn, "Liberation, Reconciliation and Just Revolution," *The Ecumenical Review* 30 (1978): 324, and Jose Miguez Bonino, *Toward a Christian Political Ethics,* (Philadelphia: Fortress Press, 1983), 108–9. See also Jose Miguez Bonino, "Violence and Liberation," *Christianity and Crisis* 32, no. 12 (July 10, 1972): 169–72.

teria) to be problematic. As a matter of fact, those nonpacifists who oppose all nuclear war almost certainly have some version of the just war theory in mind. But they point to an extraordinary new circumstance in history: the possibility that humanity might destroy itself in one great nuclear catastrophe.

Then, too, even in the nuclear age, by far the majority of armed conflicts have not involved even the threat of nuclear war, much less its reality. Revolutions, ethnic conflicts, armed conflicts between or among a small number of nations, international interventions and "police actions," and large-scale civil insurrections, in addition to bloody and/or long-lasting wars such as the Korean conflict, Vietnam, the Gulf War, Kosovo—these have pockmarked the nuclear age with vivid reminders that conventional weaponry continues to predominate. In some respects, the era of greatest nuclear threat, approximately 1950 to 1990, was a time when the nuclear stalemate between the U.S. and the USSR made the world "safe" for a lot of vicious little wars. Each and every one of these small, medium, and large military conflicts demonstrated in one way or another the continued relevance of just war criteria (or something like them). I cannot think of a single exception. We may not agree in our assessment of which of these many military conflicts pass the test, for the histories we bring and our appraisal of facts will vary. But the method remains useful.

THE NUCLEAR DILEMMA

When the first edition of this book was published (1988), the perilous nuclear confrontation between the U.S. and the USSR was about to end. At the time, we did not know how soon that would be. In a few short years, the Soviet Union itself had disintegrated, and the Russian military establishment—long perceived to be on a par with that of the United States—was reduced to but a fraction of its former power. (That fact was strangely demonstrated in the weakness of Soviet weaponry in the hands of Iraq during the Gulf War of 1991.) In subsequent years, mutual reductions of nuclear capability between Russia and the U.S. have occurred, and as I write, more are in prospect. So the world can breathe a collective sigh of relief.

But this must not lead to complacency. Vast nuclear weaponry remains in parts of the former Soviet Union and in the United States, even a small fraction of which is capable of inflicting awful destruction. If any major nuclear power should fall into the hands of an irresponsible government, its use or sale to other countries (to help with economic problems) is always a possibility. Moreover, the number of countries possessing nuclear capabilities continues to grow. Of late, both India and Pakistan have acquired some capability, and neither has shown much restraint in brandishing this sword as a chilling threat in the longstanding and bitter dispute over Kashmir.

The heart of the problem is that once such scientific discoveries and technologies have been mastered, they cannot be reversed. The genie cannot be put back in the bottle. We can be certain that more and more countries will acquire the ability to construct nuclear weapons, although every effort to prevent their spread is surely justified. Adding to the problem, the capability of nations to develop ever more efficient, smaller, less detectable nuclear weaponry is also in prospect. Humankind has been incredibly fortunate in that only twice, at Hiroshima and Nagasaki in 1945, have nuclear bombs been used. That fact owes much to the leadership and restraint of a succession of world leaders in the countries possessing such weapons. We cannot simply count on such gifts of statecraft.

So the prospect of nuclear war must continue to concern Christians and all other people of goodwill in the world. How are we to sort this out?

We begin by noting that the twentieth century has been bloody enough anyway. This century, which began with such optimism about peace and prosperity among nations and the progressive movement of all toward the perfecting of civilization, has proved instead to be the century of total war. Two great world wars, even apart from the use of atomic bombs toward the end of the second, were vast and unrestrained. The perennial problem of war has acquired new meaning in the new levels of unspeakable violence. Even so, the military effort to put an end to the genocidal nightmare and aggression of Naziism has been understood by many Christians to have been justified in relation to just war doctrine, particularly in view of the more enlightened policy of the allied victors toward the vanquished nations. And some of these Christians *were* capable of remaining disciplined by just war restraints. But the nuclear age now poses a terrible dilemma. Given the destructiveness of nuclear weapons, how could a Christian possibly countenance their use? But given the fact that potential adversaries also have nuclear weapons, how could a Christian advocate nuclear disarmament?

The dilemma cannot be escaped by claiming that the weapons are not really so different ("you are just as dead if killed by a bow and arrow"). No knowledgeable person disputes that the power now exists to wipe out whole civilizations—if not the whole of humanity—in a single night. The future of humanity as such creates a difference of kind, not simply one of degree, when compared with the destructiveness of previous weapons. Nor can the dilemma be escaped by combining a limited strategy with this unlimited power—as by the doctrine of "counterforce," which proposes to limit the weaponry to use against the warmaking power of a nation's adversaries.[9] The forces of the adversary can exist anywhere, including within centers of population. And it seems sanguine to think it possible to limit the sphere of destructiveness to levels commensurate with the just war test of proportionality. Nor does there seem to be any realistic prospect of resolving the dilemma technologically—for example, by the creation of the perfect defensive weapons making the world invulnerable to nuclear attack, the chimerical goal of former president Ronald Reagan's Strategic Defense Initiative (dubbed "star wars" at the time).

Nor can the dilemma be resolved easily by the nuclear pacifist position with its commitment to unilateral disarmament, for that could create a seriously unstable world, tempting nuclear powers with fewer scruples to use their power to intimidate others. I am impressed by the force of Geyer's arguments against a doctrine of nuclear deterrence;[10] at the very least they indicate the profound inadequacy of official thinking on the subject in the United States. But there seems little doubt that the possession of nuclear power by any nation has an inhibiting effect upon aggressive behavior by others. And, as Geyer himself comments, "those who are most aggressive tend to overreach themselves unless they are confronted with some kind of powerful resistance."[11]

The dilemma was illustrated in 1986 by a pastoral letter on the nuclear crisis by the (predominantly American) bishops of the United Methodist Church.[12] This document was hailed by some as

---

[9]Paul Ramsey, whose writings on just war theory have helped revitalize that tradition for the nuclear age, has placed great emphasis on counterforce doctrine as an application of just war thinking to the nuclear dilemma. By that, he specifically urges the exclusion of centers of population from targeting or attack—unless the adversary harbors its military capabilities in such centers (see Ramsey, *War and the Christian Conscience: How Shall Modern War Be Conducted Justly?* [Durham, N.C.: Duke University Press, 1961]). In the nuclear age that "unless" is a very important qualification.

[10]Geyer, *Idea of Disarmament,* 27–59. See also David Hollenbach, S.J., *Nuclear Ethics: A Christian Moral Argument* (New York: Paulist Press, 1983), 63–88.

[11]Geyer, *Idea of Disarmament,* 58–59.

[12]United Methodist Council of Bishops, *In Defense of Creation: The Nuclear Crisis and a Just Peace* (Nashville: Graded Press, 1986).

moving beyond a similar statement by U.S. Roman Catholic bishops in that, unlike the Catholics, the Methodists had firmly renounced deterrence. But had they? They did mount a persuasive case against deterrence doctrine, concluding that "deterrence must no longer receive the churches' blessing, even as a temporary warrant for the maintenance of nuclear weapons."[13] But the bishops immediately made clear that they were not calling for unilateral nuclear disarmament by the United States:

> The interim possession of such weapons for a strictly limited time requires a different justification—*an ethic of reciprocity* as nuclear-weapon states act together in agreed stages to reduce and ultimately to eliminate their nuclear arms. Such an ethic is shaped by an acceptance of mutual vulnerability, a vision of common security, and the escalation of mutual trust rather than mutual terror. . . . We believe that neither the US nor any other nuclear power can extricate itself unilaterally from all nuclear perils.[14]

A critic of the bishops' statement might well ask, Why keep the weapons at all if they cannot morally be used? While renouncing deterrence have the bishops not countenanced its continued use, ad interim, while nations negotiate mutual deescalation of the forces of terror? Does it make sense to keep the weapons at all unless it is to make somebody else believe a nation has them ready for use? Is that not a form of deterrence? Are the bishops being consistent?

Perhaps not. But if not, it may be that their inconsistency is an instance of what David Hollenbach calls "the right kind of inconsistency."[15] Noting that "one dimensional solutions to the dilemma are not only wrong but impossible," Hollenbach observes that our task "is not that of eliminating unreason from our world, but of containing it, keeping it from getting the upper hand, and reducing it."[16] On the one hand, the bishops clearly marked the utter unacceptability of nuclear war, its utter inconsistency with a Christian understanding of God's purposes for the world. On the other hand, the bishops acknowledged that extricating ourselves from the demonic possibility of nuclear war cannot be accomplished by one clear

---

[13]Ibid., 48.
[14]Ibid.
[15]Hollenbach, *Nuclear Ethics,* 81.
[16]Ibid.

stroke; it will require creative patience, goodwill, and a certain amount of political shrewdness.

I believe that is so. Several points may help guide us through the perilous interim between the present nuclear arms race and a time when the world will be relatively free of this threat. First, all countries should renounce first use of nuclear weapons. Second, the United States, as the world's dominant nuclear power, can demonstrate its own restraint by not inviting spiraling nuclear arms races with potential adversaries. Third, disarmament treaties should be sought, even in the full knowledge that total disarmament in such a world is hardly a realistic prospect for many years, if ever. The sheer number of nuclear weapons on hand[17] is part of the threat. Great reductions in the numbers, if this can be verified and monitored, would make the world relatively much more secure. Moreover, progress in disarmament can be a contribution toward the creation of more adequate forms of international conflict resolution.

But we must not harbor the illusion that a permanent "solution" will be found. The ineradicable fact of nuclear weaponry will require perpetual vigilance.

OTHER WEAPONRY, OTHER PROBLEMS

Nuclear threats and conventional wars and revolutions are not the only challenges confronting humankind as we enter a new millennium. In terms of weaponry, there is cause for alarm in the development of new chemical and biological weapons. These can be less detectable, and can carry threats far beyond the borders of intended targets. In principle, chemical and biological weapons are also, like nuclear bombs, highly indiscriminate. What moral justification can there possibly be for research and development of such forms of indiscriminate killing? I know none, though much can possibly be said about the need for research on methods of *countering* such lethal threats.

In the 1990s the world has had to confront vicious new waves of genocide and (as the chilling euphemism names it) "ethnic

---

[17]Estimates of current stockpiles of such weapons indicate a total of fifty thousand nuclear warheads—most with explosive capacities greatly exceeding the bombs that destroyed Hiroshima and Nagasaki.

cleansing." Some of this, like the Nazi Holocaust against Jews, has been based upon sheer ethnic animosity. Some has represented the accumulation of generations, even centuries, of resentments and the seizing of opportunities to settle scores once and for all. The Balkans (where the term "ethnic cleansing" originated), Northern Ireland, Israel/Palestine, Rwanda and Burundi—each has presented the world with variations on the theme of old conflicts, bitter resentments, unforgiving attitudes, and unwillingness to compromise or reconcile with perceived enemies of longstanding.

What responsibility do other countries (and the international community as a whole) have to intervene in what often are real atrocities within the borders of sovereign states? Active intervention by the U.S. and other powers in Kuwait (a response to international aggression by Iraq in 1990) was prelude to interventions in such locales as Somalia, Haiti, and the Balkans by the U.S. and allies, and in Liberia, Congo (former Zaire), and Sierra Leone by regional military coalitions. None of these interventions has been without its critics. Where genocide or "ethnic cleansing" and terrorism had occurred, the critics had to carry the special burden of massive numbers of deaths and atrocities resulting from inaction. To Christians, the principle of national sovereignty could hardly constitute a theological shield against any international intervention. A national government making war upon its own people cannot, without hypocrisy, invoke that principle anyway!

Still, even though the problem is hardly novel in human history, the recognition of collective responsibility is—and we have not come far enough along to have this thought through very well. I believe the criteria of the just war tradition are relevant, but they must be developed with greater creativity. All of which points us toward the larger question: How can humankind develop institutions of global scale to cope with problems faced at that level?

TOWARD WORLD GOVERNMENT

The essence of the problem is how to develop peaceful, civil systems of conflict resolution at the global level along with methods of policing that in fact draw down the actual uses of violence. In an intriguing discussion published during the height of the Cold War, Walter Millis and James Real wrote of the increasing obsolescence of the "war system" as the final means of resolving the otherwise unresolvable political conflicts among nations.[18] The system worked reasonably well in the nineteenth century, when certain restraints were observed and many present-day military technologies had yet to be developed. The latter have proved to be increasingly unusable or irrelevant to the resolution of actual political conflict. Millis and Real may have overstated the point, in light of subsequent history. But it is instructive to note how irrelevant massive American military power proved to be in the Vietnam conflict, and similar points could be made about Soviet power in Afghanistan. The military hardware can inflict vast suffering, to be sure. But can it really resolve the conflicts?

Faced with the argument that nuclear power at least preserved the admittedly uneasy peace between the U.S. and the USSR, one could reply that it also (and at the same time) made the world safe for dozens of other vicious little wars. As we have noted, the post-World War II era—the era of the Cold War—was terribly bloody. It also was a time of enormous conflict, with issues of economics, human rights, race relations, and even religion proving to be intractable. It was exactly the kind of impotence at the international level of which Pope John XXIII spoke in his call for a more effective international regime in *Pacem in Terris*. But is this, too, a chimera?

Thoughtful political observers, even in the realist tradition associated with Niebuhr and Morgenthau, join the late pope in acknowledging the point. For instance, Morgenthau commented remarkably in 1960 in the preface to the third edition of his classic work, *Politics among Nations:* "I am still being told that I believe in the prominence of the international system based upon the nation-state, although the obsolescence of the nation-state and the need to merge it into supranational organizations of a functional nature was already one of the main points of the First Edition of 1948." And Niebuhr, in one of his more nationalistic books, wrote of "the one remaining hope . . . that the recognition by both sides of being involved in the common fate of the nuclear dilemma may create the first strands of community which could be enlarged by the various forms of mutuality."[19] But both writers warned of the impossibility of creating a world government at the present time in light of the vast ideological, cultural, and economic differences dividing humanity, stressing particularly the conflict between the Soviet bloc and the West.

The real question is whether there is enough recognition of

---

[18]Walter Millis and James Real, *The Abolition of War* (New York and London: Macmillan Co., 1963). See also Walter Millis, *An End to Arms* (New York: Atheneum, 1965).

[19]Niebuhr, *Structure of Nations and Empires,* 266.

mutual interest to form the basis of a world-level "covenant" for conflict resolution. Presumably that depends upon a recognition of mutual need by the various nations. The differences are not necessarily unbridgeable, but they are very great (and I am understating and simplifying them here). Cold War hostilities have thankfully abated. But new tensions involve militant forms of religion and the growing militarization of numbers of small countries. The Third World countries pose little threat, but unless they are incorporated politically and economically into the rest of the world they are potentially a source of deepening instability. In particular, it is in the plainest interest of the industrialized and prosperous countries of the world to hasten the economic development of the "have-nots." In the long run, the overcoming of poverty and insecurity in all parts of the world is basic to the peace and security of all.

The United Nations was, from the outset, an expression of Western liberal political thought. Born out of the political crisis of World War II, it was designed to create political alternatives to global conflict. In that, it was also based on a commitment by the victorious allies not to repeat the mistakes of the post-World War I period, with the weakly supported League of Nations. But the Western democracies did not keep faith with their own vision, at least not adequately. They had an immense opportunity to draw the new Third World nations into this vision in the 1950s and 1960s, just as these nations were emerging from their colonial pasts. Indeed, at first most of these countries looked to the United Nations for their primary recognition, proudly symbolizing their new nationhood by adding their new flags to those already flying at the UN headquarters in New York. Many thoughtful leaders in the new nations were, at least initially, committed to Western democratic political values, although all were struggling with enormous economic and political problems and beset by the usual temptations of personal aggrandizement. We shall never know, but I think it possible that during those years the Western democracies might have enlisted these new countries in the broadening and deepening of a truly global political covenant, based primarily upon democratic traditions. To some extent this did in fact occur in the 1950s and early 1960s. But through time, the United States and other Western democracies increasingly subordinated the broader global vision to a narrower conception of national interest. The UN has been seen increasingly as a debating society by some or, at best, as a convenient location for conducting some forms of diplomacy while scoring occasional propaganda points.

But while some historic opportunities can be lost forever, history also can generate new ones. Even through this period, UN-related agencies have forged a positive record in dealing with economic, social, and health-related problems facing the world community. It may be that this kind of activity is the real opportunity in the present era for laying the foundations for a new world order. It is too late to enlist the energies of new nationhood for the foundation of a new internationalism; that generation is now past. But as the world community addresses common problems of health, illiteracy, hunger, population stabilization, environmental pollution and resource depletion, and economic development and trade relationships, new possibilities will come into being as well. In some respects the world truly is already one community.

Yet it is a community without deep habits and secure institutions for mutual problem-solving at the global level. Visionary political leadership will catch every opportunity to strengthen such habits and institutions, while knowing that this will have to be the work of more than one generation of leaders. Some UN involvements in peacekeeping and (to a modest degree) actual intervention have been promising.

In a pamphlet published forty years ago, Paul Nitze made the point that policy makers rarely have the opportunity to do everything they would like to do. The range of their options may indeed be very limited. But decisions made well today in face of severely limited alternatives may contribute to a much wider set of alternatives tomorrow.[20] Even the most enlightened world leaders today do not have the alternative of creating a world government in the manner of the U.S. Constitutional Convention of 1787. The problems and cultural divisions are too great, the ideological differences too vast, the forces of nationalism too overwhelming and divisive. But where problems *can* be addressed internationally, wise leadership will seize the opportunities. As leaders acquire greater experience in mutual problem-solving, the precedents can be created for further ventures founded on greater mutual understanding and trust.

Perhaps there is need today to reverse the traditional principle of subsidiarity at the international level (at least to some extent) by saying that any problems that *can* be solved at that level *ought* to be. For what the world most needs today is problem-solving experience as a global community.

---

[20]Paul Nitze, *The Recovery of Ethics* (New York: Church Peace Union, 1960).

Epilogue

God Active within
and beyond History

> The difference between believers and unbelievers is not
> defined by church membership, or even, in the last
> analysis, by baptism. The difference is defined by imag-
> inative and behavioral sensitivity to what God is doing
> in the world to make and to keep human life human, to
> achieve the maturity of men, that is, the new humanity.
> —*Paul L. Lehmann (1963)*[1]

There are, as we have seen, many different Christian perspectives
on politics. There are the divergent, even bitterly contradictory perspectives of different Christian thinkers and movements. There are
the different angles of vision afforded by the many theological entry
points offered by Christian tradition. There are the unique perspec
tives we find helpful in dealing with the different concrete issues of
public policy.

Every Christian perspective must somehow come to terms with
the notion that the world of politics is a place of encounter between
humanity and God. That notion, by itself, can give rise to insufferable arrogance among Christians who are too confident that they
alone are sure interpreters of the will of God. If God is *God,* then
none of us had better be too self-confident about that nor too self-
righteous about our own capacity to be what God intends us to be.
As we have seen, the contemporary world offers many illustrations
of exactly such arrogance, though not all of them are Christian in
background.

But if it is arrogant to claim to know all about God's will for

---

[1]Paul L. Lehmann, *Ethics in a Christian Context* (New York: Harper & Row, 1963),
117.

politics, it may be equally so to try to maintain one's moral purity by avoiding politics altogether. Everybody who participates at all in the social world is inescapably involved in politics, for politics draws upon all of us whether we like it or not. Nor is it possible to divorce our political selves from our religious selves, leaving God safely in a theological ghetto while we busy ourselves with affairs of state. For again, if God is *God* then we surely are in encounter with God at every moment in every aspect of our being.

The Lehmann quotation with which this epilogue began suggests a different way to see this. It is to understand that God is at work everywhere (making and keeping "human life human"). Christians have no corner on that God, nor for that matter does humanity in this world have a corner on God, for God is at the same time the source and sustainer of all that is. Yet Christians are convinced that Jesus Christ is the decisive clue, the deepest disclosure, of how God is at work within and beyond human history.

Through Jesus Christ, Christians are given to understand that *God loves everybody* and that when human life is structured on that insight the deeper possibilities begin to open up. That insight is not, as some suppose, mere naivete, for that insight is also the ground of the deepest human confrontation with the tragedy of sin, with political ramifications we have already explored. But in Jesus Christ we confront the ultimate political issue: Either human will and political power will be devoted to the good of all or it must serve selfish personal and group interests. The drama of Christ is the contest of the power of God's love over against the power of human evil to resist it, and the resurrection faith asserts the final victory of that love over that evil.

Where is there credible evidence of that victory in the political life of this world?

Perhaps one should not ask such hard questions, particularly not during a century as bloody and mean-spirited as this one! And yet, as we have seen again and again in this book, there really are possibilities and it really does make a difference whether one acts politically on the basis of the better possibilities rather than acquiescing in the face of evil. It is possible for people to construct social and political institutions that liberate human potentialities and respect human rights. It is possible to confront and severely limit the "principalities and powers of this present world darkness," as Saint Paul referred to the forces that are arrayed against love.

Still, the Christian faith does not invest everything in the historical struggle. God is at work in history, and ultimately humanity is bound to encounter God there. But God is also beyond history, beyond its beginning as well as its ending. Ultimately it is the faith that God's love for us transcends all the good or evil that can happen to us in this world that makes it possible for us to be persons of courage and creativity in the midst of this struggle. That attitude, that perspective, is far removed from Christian otherworldliness; otherworldliness is seen in that perspective to be an attempt to escape not just the world but also the God who is at work in the world. But by the same token, that attitude recognizes that the drama of this world is a part of the larger cosmic drama. Most of all it recognizes that it is possible to trust the outcome of the cosmic drama because its author has already said yes to us in love.

As I conclude the revised edition of this book, we are in the last months of 1999, the end of a whole millennium of human history. How active Christians have been throughout that thousand years in attempting to shape history in the light of their faith. What wonderful things they have done, in response to their faith. What dreadful mistakes they have made, in ignorance or in the abandonment of their faith. But now it is time to let go of that past and to look toward the future. I am conscious that this book will be published and read after the turn of the century, in the new millennium. What should our spirit be as we face a whole new era of human history?

Alfred Tennyson's poem *In Memoriam* includes several verses that record thoughts on a New Year's Eve, part of which include these lines:

> Ring out, wild bells, to the wild sky,
>   The flying cloud, the frosty light.
>   The year is dying in the night;
> Ring out, wild bells, and let him die.
> . . . .
> Ring out a slowly dying cause,
>   And ancient forms of party strife;
>   Ring in the nobler modes of life,
> With sweeter manners, purer laws.
> . . . .
> Ring out false pride in place and blood,
>   The civic slander and the spite;
>   Ring in the love of truth and right,
> Ring in the common love of good.

Could we not join Tennyson with our own list of things to be "rung out" or "rung in"?

I prefer to think now of the new. And my prayer is that Christians, in concert with people of goodwill of all faiths and nations, will not shy away from the political arena—that they will use it in forging a whole new era of global community with peace and justice. As we move into this new millennium, the pace of global economic life and communication has quickened noticeably. We have splendid opportunities to seize the new technologies and use them in service to the common good. My fear is that if we do not do so, the very pace of change will work toward catastrophe. But my greater hope is that we have learned important lessons from the past and that we are prepared now to do better.

INDEX